Fifth Editi

"ORDER UNDER LAW"

Readings in Criminal Justice

Robert G. Culbertson
University of Wisconsin-Platteville

Ralph A. Weisheit
Illinois State University

WAVELAND
PRESS, INC.

Prospect Heights, Illinois

For information about this book, write or call:
    Waveland Press, Inc.
    P.O. Box 400
    Prospect Heights, Illinois 60070
    (847) 634-0081

Contents

Section III Confrontation and Compromise: The Courts   159

Section IV Change without Progress: Corrections   277

Preface

By the 1990s the number of people in American prisons was at its highest level ever, and the rate at which people were imprisoned was higher than that for any other industrialized country. This high imprisonment rate reflects not only a willingness to use imprisonment as a punishment, but a general approach in which social problems are seen as crime problems to be dealt with by police, the courts, and corrections. Domestic violence, for example, is now a high priority for many police departments and prosecutors, but was largely seen as a private issue, not the law's business, just a few decades ago.

Although the public seems to demand simple solutions, there is nothing simple about the crime problem. The complexity of criminal justice issues is well illustrated by the fact that, while crime went down during the early 1990s, the fear of crime remained high and the public continued its demand that something be done about the "growing" problem. Further, some crime problems are discovered while others seem to have vanished from the public consciousness. For example, the issue of missing children was front page news during the 1980s, but is seldom given much attention as a general problem in the 1990s.

High public concern about crime is one factor that explains the current fascination with the study of criminal justice. Another factor is the fact that the criminal justice system plays an important role in our lives. Rare is the individual who has never had contact with or has never witnessed the operation of the police. A smaller number of us have had occasion to view the courts and the corrections components of the system.

Criminal justice also generates widespread and intense interest due to the significance of the issues involved. When one studies criminal justice, he or she must come to grips with some of the most emotional and complex questions confronting our society. Do we have two standards of justice, one for the wealthy and another for the poor? Does our criminal justice system discriminate against minorities? What is the proper goal of punishment? Have moral and ethical issues been ignored in the "people changing" techniques used in rehabilitation? Is it proper for the state to take a life? One could continue to cite questions such as these—questions that reflect individual and collective value conflict.

Another explanation for our interest in criminal justice can be linked to the fact that much remains to be done. Police organizations are too often out of touch with the communities they serve and there are still too many news accounts of misbehavior by the police. The courts still face enormous caseloads and continue to wrestle with striking a balance between fairness and efficiency. The correctional system continues to function in an environment of confusion because of years of neglect, a lack of consensus regarding the goals for this component, and a staggering increase in the number of offenders who must be processed. Ironically, the importance of these reforms has been recognized at precisely the time when federal, state, and local budgets are already strained.

The issues and controversies in the field of criminal justice have been closely scrutinized over the past thirty years and the result is a massive body of literature. In this publication we have attempted to focus on some of the major issues which have emerged from this literature. We have assembled a group of articles which illustrate some of the complexities of criminal justice, and do so in a way that is accessible to the general reader. Our primary interest, however, has been to provide a set of readings for the student commencing his or her study in criminal justice.

This fifth edition is necessary because of developments in knowledge about criminal justice. Further, while many problems persist, the issues on which our society has focused have shifted over time. The six new articles (and two which have been updated) reflect a heightened awareness of issues related to victims, career criminals, illegal drugs, police practices, an overloaded court system, and current dilemmas facing prisons.

It is hoped that readers will find this collection to be both enjoyable and illuminating. In order to profit fully from the following selections, the reader should keep in mind the phrase which serves as our title—"Order Under Law." This phrase, coined by Jerome Skolnick in his landmark publication, *Justice Without Trial*, does much to explain the conflicts and controversies found in the criminal justice system. We demand that our police apprehend suspects, that our courts convict the accused, and that our correctional system, in some way, punish the convicted. We demand order. The tasks involved in insuring order would be relatively straightforward were it not for our simultaneous demand that the police, courts and correctional agencies operate within the constraints placed upon them by law. In other words, we want order, but we also want fairness and justice.

Robert G. Culbertson
Ralph A. Weisheit

Section 1

Crime: An American Institution

America has a long history of concern about crime and crime control. In recent decades, crime control has become a political issue. Richard Nixon made crime control a key part of his 1968 presidential campaign. Although crime is often a local problem, the issue has continued to dominate national politics through the 1990s. And, while the general issue of crime has remained, the focus of the public and of politicians jumps from one particular crime concern to another. Missing children, illegal drugs, youthful violence, sex crime, and domestic violence are just a few of the issues vying for center stage in the war on crime. Further, changes in our society have led to the emergence of new forms of crime. Improved anti-theft devices in automobiles have led to carjacking, in which anti-theft devices can be circumvented by simply taking a car that is already running. The development of computers and advanced communications has given rise to crimes involving "electronic theft," new approaches to distributing child pornography, and to offenses involving the sabotage of information systems. Sometimes our legislators have a difficult time keeping up with the dizzying array of new forms that crime can take.

Americans are not only concerned about crime. Many seem to feel the justice system itself is nearing collapse. Stories of police corruption and brutality are commonplace. The courts seem increasingly removed from justice, handing down sentences that are either too harsh or too lenient. Our corrections systems seem to do little to correct offenders. To complicate matters, our efforts to fix the system sometimes only seem to make matters worse. If scientific research and modern management methods have improved the operation of our justice system, the public has been slow to get the message.

Politicians have been quick to respond to public demands that something be done about the crime problem, and about the rise of new crimes. However, public fears and political responses often forget several basic facts. First, crime statistics, upon which crime rates are based, have never been very accurate. Published crime rates may or may not reflect the actual amount of crime at any particular time. Rather, these published rates reflect police activity and are strongly influenced by changes in enforcement activity. Second, it is often forgotten that American society has always been plagued by criminal activity of one kind or another. Youth gangs roamed the streets of our major cities in the early 1800s, and by mid-century, New York's Central Park was dominated by young thugs during hours of darkness. Lynchings were a common feature in our society during the late 1800s and continued into the 1900s as racial strife permeated America. During the 1920s and 1930s criminals became heroes as John Dillinger and others pursued the American dream of wealth and affluence at a time when our economic system had failed. The "crime plague" that has concerned Americans since the 1960s is not, therefore, a departure from a pattern of lawfulness, but reflects a historical pattern of lawlessness in the United States.

This first section reflects many of the concerns facing criminal justice today—the plight of victims, the problem of career offenders, the conflict between efficiency and fairness, and a concern with the rise of "new" offender groups. Crime is a complicated issue. If the solutions to crime were simple we would have found them long ago. The materials in this section help illustrate the complexities of dealing with the crime problem and set the stage for the remaining sections, each of which addresses a different aspect of the criminal justice system.

In the first article, "Crime Victims," Andrew Karmen notes that in early America victims played a leading role in resolving criminal matters. Over time the government took on most aspects of law enforcement and the administration of justice. In recent years there has been a growing awareness of victims and an effort to give victims a larger role in the resolution of criminal cases. Objectively understanding the problems facing victims and developing useful responses is complicated by the difficulty of determining who is a victim and by the rise of businesses and social movements that have an interest in promoting the cause of particular victim groups.

Controlling crime with limited resources has led to a focus on efficiency. This, in turn, has drawn attention to those few offenders who commit many crimes over a period of many years, the so-called "career criminals." In his article, "Choosing Crime," Kenneth Tunnell uses interviews with repeat offenders to demonstrate that normal assumptions about using the law to stop crime may not fit these offenders. In general, they do not fear being caught, they expect the punishment to be light, and they find prison a relatively nonthreatening experience.

In the third article in this section, "Two Models of the Criminal Process," Herbert Packer addresses value conflicts in criminal justice. Packer's analysis of the Crime Control Model and the Due Process Model illustrates the philosophical differences between these models. On the one hand, we want persons who commit crimes to be apprehended, prosecuted, convicted and punished. We want these activities carried out effectively, efficiently and expediently. We want crime control. On the other hand, we have strong commitments to the Bill of Rights, and we insist that criminal justice officials act within constitutional limits set by the courts which reinforce due process. We are both intense and emotional about these rights and their protection.

Because of these ideological differences, we have little consensus about what should be the goals for the criminal justice system. As a result, agencies often work from conflicting perspectives, the criminal justice system is seen as generally ineffective, and the public servants who run criminal justice agencies are criticized because they cannot solve the crime problem.

Among the crime issues of great concern to the public are the use and sale of illegal drugs and the re-emergence of street gangs. In the final article in this section, "Slinging Dope," Scott Decker and Barrik Van Winkle shed light on the issue of drug dealing by street gangs. Their findings suggest that gang members are heavily involved in street-level drug dealing, but such dealing is not highly structured and is not highly coordinated by gang leaders. Among other things, their study suggests that gang activity is not primarily the result of a desire by young people to participate in the drug market.

Crime Victims

Andrew Karmen

Victims and Offenders

The word *victim* can be traced back to ancient cultures and the earliest languages. Its roots lie in the notion of sacrifice. In the original meaning of the term, a victim was a person or an animal put to death during a ceremony in order to appease some supernatural power or deity. Over the centuries, the word has picked up additional meanings. Currently, in everyday usage, the term refers to all those who experience injury, loss, or hardship due to any cause. People commonly speak of accident victims, cancer victims, flood victims, and victims of discrimination and similar injustices. Crime victims are individuals or groups that suffer because of illegal activities. Direct, or primary, victims experience the criminal act and its consequences firsthand. Indirect, or secondary, victims (such as family members) also suffer emotionally or financially but are not immediately involved or injured. Survivors are the relatives of people killed by murderers.

Victimology, the scientific study of crime victims, focuses on the physical, emotional, and financial harm people suffer at the hands of criminals. Victimologists study the victim-offender relationship, the public's reaction to the victim's plight, the criminal justice system's handling of victims, and victims' attempts to recover from their negative experiences. Victimization is an asymmetrical relationship that is parasitical, abusive, destructive, and unfair. Criminals force their victims to play roles (almost as if following a script) that mimic the dynamics between predator and prey, winner and loser, even master and slave, if only temporarily, while the crime is in progress.

The Need for Objectivity

The importance of reserving judgments, refraining from jumping to conclusions, and resisting the urge to take sides might not be self-evident at first. An angry gut reaction might be to ask,"What decent person could possibly side with criminals against their law-abiding, totally innocent victims? What is wrong with championing the interests of people who have been hurt by unjust and illegal actions?"

There are several good answers to these crucial questions.

First of all, victimization arises from conflicts between people with opposing interests. The initial clash occurs between victims and offenders, of course. But victims may also become embroiled in disputes and find themselves at odds with persons and groups besides the perpetrators: journalists reporting about their cases; police officers and detectives investigating their complaints; prosecutors representing them, as well as defense attorneys working on behalf of those they accuse; lawyers handling their lawsuits in civil court; juries and judges deciding how to resolve their cases; probation, parole, and corrections officers supervising convicts who harmed them; governmental agencies and legislative bodies shaping their legal rights;

social movements ostensibly rallying to their side or openly opposing their wishes; businesses seeking to sell them security products and services; and other law-abiding people. Impartiality aids the observer in understanding the reasons for this friction and in finding solutions to these antagonistic relations.

Consider the charges leveled by some victims that the officers who responded to their calls for help showed disrespect or insensitivity. Shouldn't victimologists approach the controversy from a neutral stance, rather than from a provictim or propolice orientation?

Second, impartiality is called for when injured parties turn out to be offenders themselves. What could it possibly mean to be faithfully "provictim" in those rather common cases in which criminals victimize other criminals? To put it bluntly, predators prey upon each other, as well as upon innocent, law-abiding members of the general public. When rival factions of organized crime families engage in a "mob war" and a gangster is "hit" or "rubbed out," the dead man in this case is not an unsuspecting target of random violence. Similarly, when a turf battle erupts between drug dealers and one attacks the other, the loser aspired to be the victor. When youth gangs feud with each other by carrying out "drive-by" shootings, the young gang members who get gunned down are casualties of their own brand of retaliatory street justice. In shoot-outs between the police and heavily armed bank robbers, the dead crooks are not "murder victims" but rather "justifiable homicides." Researchers (see Singer, 1981; Fattah, 1990) have noted that people routinely engaged in lawbreaking are more likely to be harmed than their law-abiding counterparts and that a considerable proportion of the people who get robbed, assaulted, or killed were engaged in illegal activities at the time. Hustlers, con men, smugglers, high-stakes gamblers, and others living life in the fast lane on the fringe of the underworld often are hurt because they find themselves in volatile situations and in the company of persons known to be dangerous.

To further complicate matters, consider the possibility of a "cycle of violence" over time, in which a victim transforms into a victimizer (see Fagan, Piper, and Cheng, 1987). For example, a group of picked-on children may band together to beat up a bully; a physically abused child may grow up to parent his sons in the same punitive way he was raised; or a battered wife may launch a vengeful surprise attack against her brutal husband. In one study that tracked the fortunes and fates of about 900 abused children over a follow-up period of from fifteen to twenty years, researchers estimated that being victimized increased their odds of future delinquency and criminality by 40 percent (Widom, 1992).

Even more confusing are the situations of certain groups of people who continuously switch roles as they lead their twisted daily lives. For instance, desperate heroin addicts are repeatedly victims of consumer fraud (dealers constantly cheat them by selling heavily adulterated packets of this forbidden substance), but then the addicts routinely go out and commit property crimes to raise the cash that pays for their habits (see Kelly, 1983). Of course, it is possible for lawbreakers to be genuine victims deserving of protection and redress through the courts. For example, prostitutes who illicitly trade sexual favors for money are frequently beaten by sadistic "Johns" and are robbed of their earnings by exploitive "pimps" (see Boyer and James, 1983). Suspects (who may, in fact, be guilty) all too often become victims of police brutality when they are unlawfully beaten by the arresting officers who use far more force than the law allows to subdue and take them into custody, or who apply force to extract a confession. Convicts become victims when they are assaulted, gang-raped, or robbed by other, more vicious, inmates with whom they are locked up.

The third and final answer to the question "Why shouldn't victimologists be openly and squarely provictim?" is that on occasion this allegiance provides no real guidance. Some situations are not so simple and clear-cut. There is a constant stream of cases coming to public attention over which observers may have honest and legitimate disagreements over who should be labeled the victim and who should be designated the offender. These real-life situations dramatize the necessity for impartiality in analyzing and untangling convoluted relationships in order to make a rational argument, as well as a reasonable legal determination, that one person or the other should be arrested, prosecuted, and punished. Unlike the dramatic examples in which obvious wrongdoers harm clearly innocent, law-abiding citizens, these more complicated incidents reflect clashes between two people who are both victims, or both offenders, or victims and offenders (to some degree) simultaneously. Consider the following news accounts, which, though admittedly atypical, illustrate just how difficult it can be to try to establish exactly who did the wrong thing and who acted appropriately:

> Two brothers, eighteen and twenty-one, barge in upon their wealthy parents as they are watching television in their mansion and slay them with fifteen shotgun blasts. For months, the police search for the murderers until the brothers concede they did it. Putting them on trial for first-degree murder (which carries the death penalty), the prosecution contends that the sons killed their parents in order to get their hands on their $14 million inheritance (they quickly spent $700,000 on luxury cars, condos, and fashionable clothing). But the brothers contend they acted in self-defense, believing that their parents were about to

attack them. The two college students give tearful, haunting, emotionally compelling testimony that denigrates their dead parents with vivid (but uncorroborated) descriptions of how their father sexually molested and emotionally abused them as boys. When the jurors become deadlocked over whether to find them guilty of murder or only the lesser charge of voluntary manslaughter, the judge declares a mistrial and the prosecution vows to retry the case. (Berns, 1994; Mydans, 1994)

An ex-marine who works as a bouncer in a bar wakes up and discovers to his horror that his wife has sliced off his penis with a kitchen knife. She drives off and tosses his "extremity" into a weed-filled lot and a friend rushes him to a hospital to have it reattached. Arrested for "malicious wounding," she tells the police that her mutilation of his body followed his attack on her earlier that evening when, in a drunken stupor, he awakened her and forced himself upon her. Arrested and put on trial for marital sexual abuse, he is acquitted by a jury that does not believe her testimony about a history of beatings, involuntary rough sex, and other humiliations. But when she is put on trial (ironically, by the same prosecutor) for the bloody bedroom assault, many people rally to her side. To her supporters, she is seen as undermining the debilitating stereotype of female passivity with a single stroke; she literally disarmed him and threw the symbol of male sexual dominance out the window. To her detractors, she is a master at manipulation, publicly playing the role of sobbing, sympathetic victim to divert attention from her act of rage against a sleeping husband who lost sexual interest in her. Facing up to twenty years in prison, she declines to negotiate a guilty plea and demands her day in court. The jury accepts her defense that she was a traumatized battered wife, deeply depressed, beset by flashbacks, and susceptible to "irresistible impulses" because of years of cruelty and abuse, and finds her not guilty by reason of temporary insanity. After forty-five days of observation in a mental hospital, she is released, the couple divorces, and then they both cash in on all the international media coverage, sensationalism, titillation, voyeurism, and sexual politics. (Margolick, 1994; Sachs, 1994)

A man riding a subway train is approached by two teenagers who ask him for $5 while two of their friends look on. Fearing that he is about to be robbed and injured as in a previous incident, the man rises from his seat, draws an unlicensed revolver, and empties it of the bullets he hollowed out for greater impact, shooting two of the teens in the chest, one in the side, and the fourth youth twice, once in the back at close range. Dubbed the "Subway Vigilante" by reporters, he is widely hailed as a hero who stood up and fought back, striking a symbolic blow on behalf of all victims against all criminals. Others, however, including some high officials, depict him as a trigger-happy gunman who overreacted to stereotypes and mowed down four unarmed teenagers, two of them fleeing, before they made their intentions clear. He is arrested, indicted, and tried for attempted murder, assault, and reckless endangerment. His lawyer puts on a prosecutorial defense, arguing that the four wounded victims are really injured criminals, and that the accused is actually an intended victim who justifiably resorted to deadly force to protect himself. The jury convicts him only of possessing an unlicensed handgun. The judge sentences him to a jail term followed by probation, community service, psychiatric observation, and a fine (Fletcher, 1988).The young man who was shot twice ends up in a wheelchair, paralyzed from the waist down. He sues the man who shot him for millions of dollars.

In each of the above cases, the persons officially designated as the victims by the police and prosecutors—the slain parents, the slashed husband, the wounded teenagers—could be considered deserving victims, and, indeed, they were viewed by substantial segments of the public and of the juries just that way, as wrongdoers who got what was coming to them. The individuals who got in trouble with the law—the brothers, the wife, the subway rider—denied that they were criminals and insisted that they were victims: abused children, a battered woman, or an innocent commuter about to be robbed. When opinion differs sharply over who is the genuine victim and who is the actual victimizer, any simple provictim or anticriminal allegiance loses its meaning. The confusion inherent in the unrealistically simplistic labels of "offender" and "victim" underscores the need for objectivity when trying to sort out who is responsible for what happened.

The Decline of Crime Victims

Legal historians report that there was a time centuries ago when victims played a leading role in the resolution of criminal matters. To discourage retaliation and endless feuding, simple societies around the world established direct repayment schemes that enabled victims and their families to receive money or valuables from the persons who wronged them to compensate them for the pain, suffering, and losses. This type of victim-oriented justice process prevailed when social relations were based on family ties, personal obligations, strong emotions, and sacred traditions and when people lived in small villages and engaged in farming. But the victim's role diminished as industrialization and urbanization brought about social relations that were voluntary, secular, impersonal, rationalized, and contractual. Victims lost control over the process of determining the fate of the individuals who harmed them. The government dominated judicial proceedings and extracted fines from criminals and/or physically punished or executed them. The seriousness of the wounds and losses inflicted by the offender was of importance only insofar as it determined the charges and penalties upon conviction. Restoring victims to the condition they were in before the crimes occurred was no longer the main concern. In fact, the recovery of damages became a separate matter to be handled in another arena (civil court) according to different rules (tort law), after criminal proceedings were concluded (Schafer, 1968).

In the history of the United States, this same rise and fall can be observed. Over the course of several hundred years, victims went from central figures to passive spectators relegated to the sidelines. In colonial America, police forces and public prosecutors had not yet been established. Victims conducted their own investigations, paid for warrants to have sheriffs make arrests, and hired private attorneys to indict and prosecute their alleged attackers. Convicts were forced to repay victims up to three times as much as they damaged or stole. Victims were key decision makers within and direct beneficiaries of the criminal justice process. But after the Revolutionary War and the adoption of the Constitution and Bill of Rights, crimes were considered hostile acts directed against the authority of the state, as the representative of the people. Addressing the suffering of victims was deemed to be less important than dealing with the symbolic threat posed by lawbreakers to the social order. Public prosecutors, as representatives of the government and of society, took over the powers and responsibilities formerly assumed by victims. Federal, state, and district attorneys were granted the authority to decide whether or not to press charges against defendants and what sanctions to ask judges to invoke against convicts. The goals of deterring crime through punishment, protecting society by incapacitating dangerous persons, and rehabilitating deviants through treatment began to overshadow the demands of victims that they be restored to financial, emotional, and physical health.

Over the next two centuries, the government increasingly assumed the obligation of providing detainees and inmates with food, housing, medical care, recreational opportunities, schooling, job training, psychological counseling, and legal representation while leaving victims to fend for themselves. As victims lost control over their cases, their role was limited to two contributions: initiating investigations by complaining to the police, and testifying for the prosecution as just another piece of evidence in the state's presentation of damning facts against the accused. When plea bargaining replaced trials as the means of resolving the overwhelming majority of cases, most victims lost their last opportunity to actively participate in the process by telling their stories on the witness stand. Victims became so routinely overlooked in criminal justice proceedings that they were rarely asked what actions the prosecution should take; often were never even informed of the outcomes of "their" cases. Thoroughly marginalized, victims often sensed that they had been harmed twice, the second time by a system ostensibly set up to help them but in reality more intent on satisfying the needs of its constituent agencies and officials (McDonald, 1977; Davis, Kunreuther, and Connick, 1984).

Renewed Interest

The rediscovery of the plight of crime victims was initiated in the late 1950s and early 1960s by a small number of self-help advocates, social scientists, crusading journalists, enlightened criminal justice officials, and responsive lawmakers. They started to make the public aware of what they defined as problematic: systematic neglect of victim issues. Through writings, meetings, and events such as petition drives and demonstrations, these activists communicated to a wider audience their message that victims were forgotten persons who needed to be rediscovered. Discussion and debate emerged in the late 1960s and intensified throughout the 1970s and 1980s over why the situation existed and what could be done about it. Various groups with their own distinct agendas formed coalitions and mobilized to campaign for changes. As a result, criminal justice policies are being reformed and new laws favorable to victims are being passed.

The News Media: Portraying the Victim's Plight

The news media—newspapers, magazines, and radio and television stations—deserve a great deal of credit for contributing to the rediscovery of victims. Featuring accounts of crimes as front-page items or as lead stories in broadcasts is a long-standing journalistic tradition. Today, everyone is familiar with America's crime problem—not because of firsthand experience but because of secondhand accounts relayed through the news media. In the past, the offender received the lion's share of attention. But now details about the injured party are routinely included to inject some "human interest." Drawing upon an inexhaustible source—a steady flow of new cases emanating from a crime-ridden society—the news media are saturated with stories about deception, loss, brutality, death, and tragic irony. Administered this daily dose of horror stories, members of the general public might well be expected to be experts about how, when, and where illegal acts are committed and what it is like to be victimized. But if the media's historical preoccupation with violence and mayhem spreads misinformation and perpetuates false stereotypes, the public may harbor illusions.

At its best, crime reporting can explain the plight of victims in precise detail: how they are harmed, what losses they incur, what emotions they feel, how they are handled by the legal system, and what helps or hinders their recovery. By remaining faithful to the facts, journalists can enable their audiences to transcend their own limited experiences with criminals and to see emergencies, tragedies, triumphs, and dangers through the victims' eyes. Skillful reporting can convey a sharp picture of the consequences of lawlessness, from the raw emotion and drama of the situation to the institutional responses that make up the criminal justice process. Accurate information and well-grounded, insightful interpretations allow nonvictims to better understand and empathize with the actions and reactions of victims.

But often the news media's coverage can be misleading instead of enlightening, a source of fallacies and myths instead of the truth. First of all, almost by definition, the items considered newsworthy must be attention grabbers; that is, some aspect of the act, the perpetrator, or the target must be unusual, unexpected, strange, perverse, or shocking. What is typical, commonplace, or predictable is just not news. As a result, as soon as some pattern of victimization becomes "routine" and well known, it loses its "shelf life." The media's roving eye has a notoriously short attention span. For example, victims of drive-by shootings who are caught in the cross fire between rival gang members might be the subject of lead stories for a week or so. Then this topic will disappear from the news, and a spate of incidents in which motorists get shot on congested highways might seize center stage. After that, a series of mysterious deaths among hospital patients might be featured. These events could then be superseded by coverage of a rash of poisonings due to product tampering. Then stories might dwell on the slayings of taxi drivers by robbers, or on holdups of elderly women by teenage boys, or on murders of children by abusive parents, or on attacks on teachers by angry students. The procession of grisly, depressing, and infuriating tidbits never ceases, although eventually the subjects begin to be repeated. Such "pack journalism" can create the impression that a particular kind of crime is on the rise, when actually it is temporarily the focus of a number of competing reporters who generate variations of each other's stories until the topic is exhausted. The rediscovery of a group of victims by one news department can inspire imitators to search for additional newsworthy stories on the same theme. As editors scour the press releases of police departments for still more cases of this type, a "crime wave" can be created.

Superficiality of coverage characterizes much crime reporting. Space and time limitations (meeting deadlines) dictate that items be short and quick, making fast-paced news more entertaining but less informative. Complex issues must be oversimplified, caricatured, reduced to clichés, edited out, or simply ignored. As a result, the intricacies of the victim-offender relationship, and the complicated reactions of victims to crimes, are rarely examined in any depth. For example, in covering rapes, reporters tend to portray the victims as either "virgins" (good, pure, innocent, unsuspecting) or as "vamps" (evil, seductive, wanton). A woman is likely to be pictured as a vamp if she knew her assailant, if no weapon was used to intimidate her, if she belongs to the same racial or ethnic group and social class as the aggressor, if she is young and considered "pretty," and if she does not fit the traditional image of a housewife and mother preoccupied with her family. Greater interest is shown toward the plight of white women than minority women, especially if the offenders are not white. Rapes are more likely to be written off as isolated, bizarre, and exceptional events than to be attributed to deeply rooted and long-standing social problems involving gender roles, power relationships, race and class tensions, child-rearing practices, and misogynist themes pervading popular culture. In their moralistic narratives, reporters keep old myths alive, sympathizing with virgins ravished by depraved monsters while blaming vamps for arousing the lust of regular guys (Benedict, 1992).

Sensationalism is another problem. For a case to receive exaggerated importance and undue attention, some aspect of the victim-offender relationship must stand out. Historically, the heinous crimes that have received the most coverage have one or more of these elements in common: a child or woman as the victim or the defendant; a high-class or well-known victim or defendant; intimations of promiscuous behavior by the victim or defendant; and some doubts about the guilt of the accused (Stephens, 1988). Editors and journalists sift through an overwhelming number of real-life tragedies that come to their attention (largely through their contacts with the local police department) and select out the cases they anticipate will shock people out of their complacency or arouse the public's social conscience. The stories that are featured strike a responsive chord in their audiences because the incidents symbolize some significant theme—for example, that anyone can be chosen at random to be brutally attacked (simply for being at the wrong place at the wrong time); that bystanders may not come to a victim's aid, especially in anonymous, big-city settings; or that complete strangers cannot be trusted (Roberts, 1989).

Another bias that colors media coverage is a tendency to accentuate the negative. Bad news sells better than good news. However, dwelling on defeat, destruction, and tragedy breeds cynicism, pessimism, even a sense of despair. The public is led to believe that victims suffer endless misery, that extreme reactions are typical responses, that crime is spiraling out of control, and that nothing positive can be done or is being tested to counteract the damage inflicted by offenders.

The kind of coverage that can be called "scandal-mongering," "pandering," "yellow journalism," and "tabloidism" occurs primarily because the news media that employ the journalists are commercial enterprises. Newspapers, magazines, radio stations, and television networks are profit-oriented businesses. Shocking stories attract readers, listeners, and viewers. Blaring headlines, gripping accounts, colorful phrasing, memorable quotes, and other forms of media "hype" build the huge audiences that permit media firms to charge sponsors high rates for advertising. But other factors are operating as well, such as considerations of personal gain (getting an "inside story" and "scooping" the competition, for example) and organizational imperatives (meeting inflexible deadlines and space limitations). Producers, editors, and reporters seeking to play up the human-interest angle have rediscovered the victims' plight because they have found that crime stories attract large crowds if they are spiced up with a heavy dose of sex, gore, and raw emotions. As a result, readers and viewers are increasingly confronted with tasteless images of slain policemen and their grieving widows, missing children and their distraught parents, wounded teenage gang members and their vengeful friends, and surveillance camera footage of fleeing robbers leaving behind shopkeepers lying in pools of blood. Overzealous journalists are frequently criticized for maintaining deathwatch vigils at victims' homes or for shoving microphones in the faces of bereaved, dazed, or hysterical persons. When reporters turn a personal tragedy into a media event, and thus into a public spectacle, the victim's right to privacy is invaded. The injured party receives unwanted publicity and exposure and experiences a loss of control as others comment on, interpret, draw lessons from, and impose judgments on the case.

And yet, it can be argued that this media reaction is a necessary evil. Criminal acts not only harm particular victims but also threaten society as a whole. The public has a right and a need to know about

the emergence of dangerous conditions and threatening developments. The news media have a right to carry crime stories, perhaps
even a duty to probe into, disclose fully, and disseminate widely all
relevant details regarding significant violations of the law. Reporters
and news editors have a constitutional right arising from the First
Amendment's guarantee of a free press to present the facts to the
public without interference from the government. The problem is
that the public's right to know about news and the media's right to
report it clash with the victim's right to privacy.

Questions of fairness and ethics concerning how members of the
media portray the plight of victims and survivors are being
addressed by editors, journalists, and victims' advocates and organizations in confrontations, in court, and at conferences. Several rem-
edies have been proposed to curb the abusive treatment of victims by
insensitive journalists. One approach would be to enact new laws to
protect victims from needless public exposure, such as the unnecessary disclosure of their names and addresses. An alternative
approach would be to rely on the self-restraint of journalists and
their editors. The fact that most news accounts of rapes no longer
reveal the victims' names is an example of this approach in action. A
third remedy would be for the media to adopt a code of professional
ethics. Journalists who abide by the code would "read victims their
rights" at the outset of interviews, just as police officers read suspects their Miranda rights when taking them into custody (see Thomason and Babbilli, 1987; Karmen, 1989).Victimologists could play
an important role by studying how frequently and how seriously
news reporters offend the subjects of their stories, and by monitoring
how successfully the different reform strategies prevent abuses or
minimize harm.

Businesses: Selling Products and Services to Victims

Some businesses have discovered in victims an untapped market
for goods and services. After suffering through an unpleasant experience, many victims become willing, even eager consumers, searching
for products that will protect them from any further harm. Potential
victims—essentially everyone else—constitute a far larger market, if
they can be convinced that the personal security industry can reduce
the odds of their becoming a statistic.

But the attention paid to the victim's plight by businesses may
turn out, like media coverage, to be a mixed blessing. Along with the
development of this new market for anti-theft devices and protective
services comes the possibility of commercial exploitation. Profiteers
can engage in false advertising and fear mongering to cash in on the

crime problem and capitalize on the legitimate concerns and needs of vulnerable and sometimes panicky customers.

As industries producing security products and services for personal, automobile, and home use experience dramatic growth, private efforts based on these commercial services and products (such as guards, guns, bullet-proof clothing, and alarms) to deter and reduce crime are becoming increasingly important. Individuals and small groups equipped with the latest in technological gadgetry are enlisted as troops in the "war on crime" as responsibility shifts away from the corporate and governmental sources of the problem and away from collective, societal solutions.

Social Movements: Taking Up the Victims' Cause

Aside from having been harmed by criminals, victims as a group may have very little in common. They differ in age, gender, race, class, political orientation, and in many other important ways. However, sustained efforts are being made to organize them into self-help groups and to recruit these groups into a larger social movement. This victims' movement is now a broad alliance of activists, support groups, and advocacy organizations that lobbies for increased rights and expanded services, demonstrates at trials, educates the public, trains criminal justice professionals and care givers, sets up research institutes and information clearinghouses, designs and evaluates experiments, and holds conferences to share ideas and experiences. The guiding principle holding this diverse coalition together is that victims who otherwise would feel powerless, guilty, and enraged can regain a sense of control over their lives through practical assistance, mutual support, and involvement in the criminal justice process (Friedman, 1985).

The emergence, growth, and development of the victims' movement have been influenced by other social movements. The most important contributions have been made by the law-and-order movement, the women's movement, and the civil rights movement.

The conservative, hard-line, law-and-order movement was the first to proclaim that victims deserve better treatment and formal rights. Alarmed by an upsurge in street crime during the late 1960s, law-and-order advocates argued that the average American should be more worried about becoming a victim than about being falsely accused, mistakenly convicted, and unjustly punished (Hook, 1972).The rediscovered victim was portrayed as a solitary figure who lacked rights (but deserved them), in sharp contrast to the presumably guilty person who seemed well protected by loopholes and technicalities that undermined the government's efforts to arrest, detain, convict, incapacitate, and punish. The scales of justice were said to be unfairly tilted in favor of the bad guys and to the disadvantage of innocent, law-abiding citizens and their allies on the police force and in the prosecutor's office. In the victim-oriented justice system that law-and-order advocates envisioned, punishment would be swift and sure. Permissiveness (unwarranted leniency) and the coddling of criminals would be ended; more offenders would be locked up for longer periods of time; and fewer would be granted bail, probation, or parole. Opponents of these hard-line policies were branded as "procriminal" and "antivictim" (see Carrington, 1975).

Activists in the women's movement helped to launch both the antirape and the antibattering movements. The antirape movement originated when radical feminists set up the first rape crisis centers in Berkeley, California, and Washington, DC, in 1972. The centers were not only places of aid and comfort; they were also rallying sites for outreach efforts, consciousness raising, and political organizing (see Rose, 1977; Largen, 1981; and Schechter, 1982). Some antirape activists went on to protest street harassment, uniting behind the slogan "Take back the night" (see Lederer, 1980), while others helped to organize the battered women's movement and set up the first "safe house," or refuge, in St. Paul, Minnesota, in 1974. The movement to shelter battered women paralleled the provictim, antirape movement in a number of ways. Both were initiated for the most part by former victims. Both viewed the victims' plight as an outgrowth of societal and institutional problems rather than personal troubles and individual weaknesses. Both sought to empower women by confronting established male authority, challenging existing procedures, providing peer support and advocacy, and devising alternative places to go for assistance. The overall analysis that originally guided the women's movement was that male-versus-female offenses (such as rape, wife beating, sexual harassment in the streets and at work, and incest) pose a threat to all women and slow down progress toward equality and liberation. The gravest dangers are faced by women who are socially disadvantaged because of economic insecurity, racial discrimination, and separation or divorce. The men at the helm of the criminal justice system have demonstrated that they cannot be counted on to effectively protect or assist victimized girls and women.

The civil rights movement (a loose coalition composed of organizations representing the interests of a wide range of racial and ethnic minority groups) campaigns for equality and fair treatment in the face of deeply entrenched discriminatory practices. Earlier in this century, the major problem was racist violence, which took the form of thousands of lynchings of minority males by vicious mobs. These murders usually went unsolved and unpunished. At present, the movement's major concern centers upon hate-motivated *bias crimes*. These acts range from vandalism and harassment (such as cross burnings) to physical violence (such as beatings, bombings, and assassinations). Civil rights groups have been instrumental in setting up antibias task forces and human rights commissions and in establishing specialized police squads and prosecutorial teams to deter or solve these divisive and inflammatory crimes that otherwise would polarize communities along racial and ethnic lines (see Levin and McDevitt, 1993).

Civil rights groups argue that a discriminatory double standard still infects the operations of the criminal justice system. They maintain that crimes by perpetrators from minority groups against victims drawn from the white majority are taken very seriously (thoroughly investigated, solved, vigorously prosecuted), whereas crimes by whites against minorities, and by minorities against minorities, are routinely assigned a lower priority (unless the offenders were obviously motivated by bias and the incidents are likely to cause interracial conflict). "Black-on-black crime" was rediscovered during the 1970s, when representatives of minority communities pointed out that blacks were victimized more often than whites in nearly every category of serious street crime; that fear levels were higher in minority ghettos than in more affluent neighborhoods; that intraracial victimization was undermining the solidarity needed for political progress; and that the problem of street crime and arson was destroying housing, driving away jobs, and closing down services (see *Ebony*, 1979). Activists in the civil rights movement also point out that members of minority groups face greater risks of becoming victims of official misconduct, in the form of police brutality (or even worse, the unjustified use of deadly force), false accusations, frame-ups, and other miscarriages of justice.

Other social movements, besides those concerned with law and order, women's equality, and civil rights, have contributed to the public's awareness of the victims' plight. Most notable among the social movements that have rallied to the defense of specific kinds of street crime victims, starting in the 1960s and 1970s, are those that champion the causes of civil liberties, children's rights, senior citizens' rights, homosexual rights, and self-help.

The civil liberties movement's main focus is to preserve constitutional safeguards and due-process guarantees that protect the rights of suspects, defendants, and prisoners from abuses of governmental power by criminal justice officials. However, civil liberties organizations have won court victories that have benefited victims of street crime in two ways: by furthering police professionalism and by extending the doctrine of "equal protection under the law." In professionalized police departments, officers must meet higher educational and training requirements and must abide by more stringent written regulations. As a result, victims are more likely to receive prompt responses, effective service, and sensitive (nonracist, nonsexist) treatment. If they don't, channels now exist through which they can redress their grievances. The extension of equal-protection guarantees, as ordered by the courts, improves the chances that people whose calls for help were largely ignored in the past will no longer have to fend for themselves and will gain access to police and prosecutorial assistance (Walker, 1982; Stark and Goldstein, 1985).

Members of the children's rights movement campaign against the physical abuse, sexual abuse, and neglect of children. Their successes include more effective parenting programs; stricter reporting requirements; improved procedures for arrest, prosecution, and conviction; greater sensitivity to the needs of victimized children as complaining witnesses; and enhanced protection and prevention services.

Activists in the senior citizens' movement are concerned about the abuse of older persons by care givers as well as street crimes. As a result of their campaigns, in some jurisdictions special police squads have been formed to protect older persons from younger persons; stiffer penalties apply when victims are over sixty; and extra benefits and forms of assistance are available to victims of "elder abuse" who are mistreated financially, emotionally, and physically (see Smith and Freinkel, 1988).

The gay rights movement originally called attention to the vulnerability of homosexuals and lesbians to blackmail, to exploitation by organized crime syndicates that ran some of the bars and clubs, and to police harassment of those who needed police protection (see Maghan and Sagarin, 1983). Currently, the movement's antiviolence task forces point out that "gay-bashing" street attacks against suspected homosexuals and lesbians have escalated since the outbreak of the AIDS epidemic; nevertheless, they contend, such acts, motivated by the offenders' hatred for the victim's presumed sexual orientation, are not consistently classified and prosecuted as serious bias crimes. Although the killers of gay men and women tend to use "excessive violence" ("overkill" in the form of sadistic beatings and/or multiple stab or gunshot wounds), the police solve these murders less often than other homicides, according to a nationwide survey of about 150 cases in 30 states during 1992–1994 (Dunlap, 1994).

Groups that are part of the "self-help movement" can be given credit for making some substantial contributions toward alleviating needless suffering. These groups unite the participatory spirit of the grass roots protest movements of the 1960s and the self-improvement ideals of the human-potential movement of the 1970s. Self-help groups tend to be impatient with and distrustful of large, distant bureaucracies and detached professional care givers. Their simple organizing principle is to bring together individuals who share the same problems. The groups provide mutual assistance and dependable support networks. Their underlying assumption is that the most effective aid and insights come from people who have directly experienced and overcome similar hardships themselves. By accepting the role of helper and caring for others, victims facilitate their own recoveries. They empower themselves to cope with the distressing situations that arise in everyday life, and they engage in political activism to spare others such anguish in the future (Gartner and Riessman, 1980).

The social movements that have stimulated the growth of the victims' movement, and the self-help groups that form its base, need to be studied more closely by victimologists. The demographic characteristics of their membership and backers, their alliances, and their rivalries must be analyzed objectively, and their effectiveness as advocates for their constituents assessed. Public opinion polls indicate that the goals of the victims' movement are endorsed by large majorities of respondents. Females, older persons, better-educated people, and former victims with firsthand experience are the most supportive of the movement's legislative initiatives (Smith, 1985; Smith, Sloan, and Ward, 1990).

The Continuing Process of Rediscovery

There is no end in sight to the process of rediscovering victims. All kinds of "new" victims are being constantly rediscovered—that is, there is a steady stream of fresh revelations reminding the public about neglected groups with unmet needs, compelling stories to tell, and legitimate demands for assistance and support. Some groups of victims whose plight is beginning to be examined scientifically include:

- People whose attackers cannot be arrested and prosecuted because they are members of foreign delegations that have been granted diplomatic immunity (Ferrigno, 1987; Trescott, 1987).

- Recipients of crank phone calls, laced with threats or obscenities, from "heavy-breathers" and bored teenagers (Savitz, 1986).

- Unsuspecting consumers who lose money, time, and their reputations because of credit card scams in which thieves purchase goods and then falsely bill their victims' charge accounts (Berreby, 1988; Hinds, 1988).

- Illegal aliens who feel they cannot come forward and ask the police for help without revealing that they lack the proper documents and run the risk of being deported.

- Children who are sexually molested by religious ministers they respected and their parents trusted (Berry, 1992; Woodward et al., 1993).

- Students assaulted, robbed, even fatally shot by fellow students or by intruders in school buildings and yards. (More than 3 million crimes of all kinds are committed each year in or near the nation's 85,000 public schools. But these figures are probably undercounts, since principals tend to cover up incidents to make it appear that the intermediate and high schools they preside over are more orderly. Nearly 25 percent of all students and 10 percent of their teachers report they have been victims of violence on or near school property. Whereas, in the recent past, teachers complained about students talking out of turn, chewing gum, making noise, or running through the halls, now the top disciplinary concerns include sexual harassment, robbery, fights, and the smuggling of guns into school buildings (Bastian and Taylor, 1991; Associated Press, 1993d; Toby, 1983; and Dillon, 1994).

- Homeless persons robbed and assaulted on the streets and in shelters (Holloway, 1995).

- Hotel guests who suffer thefts and assaults at the hands of intruders when security measures are lax (Prestia, 1993).

- Tourists who blunder into dangerous situations avoided by street-wise locals (Rohter, 1993) and are easy prey because they let their guard down (Boyle, 1994).

- Delivery-truck drivers, who may wear bulletproof vests and illegally carry weapons to protect themselves against robbers and hijackers (Sexton, 1994).

- Good Samaritans who try to break up a crime in progress and rescue the intended victim but are injured or killed themselves (McFadden, 1993).

- Innocent bystanders wounded or killed by stray bullets intended for others, often when caught in the cross fire between rival street gangs or drug dealers fighting over turf. (For example, in New York City prior to 1984, there were fewer than 10 reports in newspapers of such shootings per year; by 1988, there were 54 [Sherman, Steele, Laufersweiler, Hoffer, and Julian, 1989]. Then the police department began to track these incidents; after peaking in 1991 at 535, the number of bystanders hit by bullets meant for other targets dropped to 342 in 1992, 335 in 1993, and about 170 during the first six months of 1994 [Onishi, 1994].)

- People deceived and then held up by robbers impersonating plainclothes detectives. (In New York City during 1993, 1,300 complaints were received about impostors flashing false credentials and then committing crimes; about 400 were holdups by fake cops [Sanchez, 1994]. The problem was deemed serious enough to merit the formation of a special detective squad, the first of its kind in the nation, to investigate these complaints [Holloway, 1994].)

- Motorists and pedestrians slammed into by fugitives seeking to avoid arrest, or by squad cars, during high-speed chases. (An estimated 500,000 police pursuits result in almost 300 accidental civilian deaths per year ["Justice by the numbers," 1993]. In some states, the police department can be sued if bystanders are injured or killed because of Hollywood-style hot-pursuit crashes [Gray, 1993].)

- Unsuspecting persons grabbed as hostages by desperate criminals seeking to escape by using the captive as a bargaining chip or a human shield (Wolff, 1993a).

- Individuals injured or killed by explosives. (According to the Treasury Department's Bureau of Alcohol, Tobacco, and Firearms, approximately 2,500 bombs and incendiary devices claimed 45 lives, injured nearly 470 people, and caused $22.6 billion in damage during 1992 [Clark, 1994].)

- Workers murdered on the job. (Cabdrivers, who must take complete strangers to remote destinations where these passengers might rob or even kill them, have the most dangerous of all jobs [Wolff, 1993b]. About 15 of every 100,000 are slain each year ["Justice by the numbers," 1993]).

- Unrelated individuals whose lives are snuffed out by vicious and demented serial killers. (Some unknown proportion of the over 5,000 unsolved murders per year are the work of an estimated 350 serial killers still on the prowl, who claim an average of about ten lives each over a period of years [Holmes and DeBurger, 1988; Hickey, 1991].)

- Suspects subjected to police brutality (unjustifiably beaten and shot by officers) and prisoners assaulted by guards or gang-raped and murdered by other inmates (see Lockwood, 1980; and Silberman, 1995).

Victimology complements criminology by drawing attention to "that other party" and thereby corrects the tendency within criminology to fix all attention on the offender. But if victimologists are to contribute significantly to the understanding of the crime problem, they must transcend any inclination to confine their analyses to the interaction between the victim and the offender. An approach that is preoccupied with doling out the proper mix of exoneration and blame to just two people is shortsighted because the influences of social forces and conditions are eliminated from consideration. Given the limited choices of either victim blaming or victim defending, policymakers concerned about crime prevention can attempt to control either would-be offenders or potential victims. But adopting a system-blaming perspective opens up many more promising strategies to reform the social institutions that generate both offenders and victims.

References

Associated Press. 1993a. "Boy recants rape account, freeing suspect." *New York Times*, May 28, p. B6.

———. 1993b. "A disabled child is seen more likely to be abused." *New York Times*, October 7, p. A21.

———. 1993c. "High murder rate for women on job." *New York Times*, October 3, p. A29.

———. 1993d. "Survey finds school violence hits 1 in 4 students." *New York Times*, December 17, p. A37.

Bastian, L., and Taylor, B. 1991. School crime: A National Crime Victimization Survey Report. Washington, DC: U.S. Department of Justice.

Benedict, H. 1992. *Virgin or vamp: How the press covers sex crimes*. New York: Oxford University Press.

Berns, W. 1994. "Getting away with murder." *Commentary* 97(4) (April): 25–29.

Berreby, D. 1988. "The ordeal of the credit fraud victim." *New York Times*, September 4, Sec. 3, p. 4.

Berry, J. 1992. *Lead us not into temptation*. New York: Doubleday.

Boyer, D., and James, J. 1983. "Prostitutes as victims." In D. MacNamara and A. Karmen (Eds.), *Deviants: Victims or victimizers?* (pp. 109–46). Newbury Park, CA: Sage.

Boyle, P. 1994. "Travel industry launches drive to protect tourists." *New York AAA Motorist*, April, pp. 1, 18.

Carrington, F. 1975. *The victims*. New Rochelle, NY: Arlington House.

Clark, J. 1994. "Crime in the 90's: It's a blast." *Law Enforcement News*, March 15, pp. 1, 7.

Davis, R., Kunreuther, F., and Connick, E. 1984. "Expanding the victim's role in the criminal court dispositional process: The results of an experiment." *Journal of Criminal Law and Criminology* 75(2): 491–505.

Dillon, S. 1994. "Report finds more violence in the schools." *New York Times*, July 7, pp. B1, B7.

Dunlap, D. 1994. "Survey details gay slayings around U.S." *New York Times*, December 21, p. D21.

Ebony Magazine. 1979. *Black on black crime* (Special issue, August).

Fagan, J., Piper, E., and Cheng, Y. 1987. "Contributions of victimization to delinquency in inner cities." *Journal of Criminal Law and Criminology* 78(3): 586–611.

Fattah, E. 1990. "Victims and victimology: The facts and the rhetoric." *International Review of Victimology* 1(1): 43–66.

Ferrigno, R. 1987. "How foreign diplomats get away with crime." *New York Newsday*, October 2, p. 81.

Fletcher, G. 1988. *A crime of self-defense: Bernhard Goetz and the law on trial*. Chicago: University of Chicago Press.

Friedman, L. 1985. "The crime victim movement at its first decade." *Public Administration Review* 45 (November): 790–94.

Gartner, A., and Riessman, F. 1980. "Lots of helping hands." *New York Times*, February 19, p. A22.

Gray, J. 1993. "New Jersey court says victims of car chases cannot sue police." *New York Times*, July 29, pp. B1, B6.

Hickey, E. 1991. *Serial murderers and their victims*. Pacific Grove, CA: Brooks/Cole.

Hinds, M. 1988. "The new fashioned way to steal money: Fake credit." *New York Times*, December 31, p. A28.

Holloway, L. 1994. "Impersonators bearing badges of dishonor." *New York Times*, November 12, pp. B1, B28.

———. 1995. "Despite the bitter cold, many homeless resist the shelters." *New York Times*, February 8, p. B3.

Holmes, R., and DeBurger, J. 1988. *Serial murder*. Newbury Park, CA: Sage.

Hook, S. 1972. "The rights of the victims: Thoughts on crime and compassion." *Encounter*, April, pp. 29–35.

"Justice by the numbers." 1993. *Law Enforcement News*, December 31, p. 27.

Karmen, A. 1989. "Crime victims and the news media: Questions of fairness and ethics." In J. Sullivan and J. Victor (Eds.), *Annual editions: Criminal justice 1988–1989* (pp. 51–57). Guilford, CT: Dushkin Publishing Group.

Kelly, R. 1983. "Addicts and alcoholics as victims." In D. MacNamara and A. Karmen (Eds.), *Deviants: Victims or victimizers?* (pp. 49–76). Newbury Park, CA: Sage.

Largen, M. 1981. "Grassroots centers and national task forces: A herstory of the anti-rape movement." *Aegis* 32 (Autumn): 46–52.

Lederer, L. 1980. *Take back the night*. New York: Morrow.

Levin, J., and McDevitt, J. 1993. *Hate crimes: The rising tide of bigotry and bloodshed.* New York: Plenum.

Lockwood, D. 1980. *Prison sexual violence.* New York: Elsevier.

Maghan, J., and Sagarin, E. 1983. "Homosexuals as victimizers and victims." In D. MacNamara and A. Karmen (Eds.), *Deviants: Victims or victimizers?* (pp. 147–62). Newbury Park, CA: Sage.

Margolick, D. 1994. "Does Mrs. Bobbitt count as another battered wife?" *New York Times,* January 16, p. E5.

McDonald, W. 1977. "The role of the victim in America." In R. Barnett and J. Hagel III (Eds.), *Assessing the criminal: Restitution, retribution, and the legal process* (pp. 295–307). Cambridge, MA: Ballinger.

McFadden, R. 1993. "A stranger is stabbed saving a life." *New York Times,* May 14, p. B3.

Mydans, S. 1994. "The other Menendez trial, too, ends with the jury deadlocked." *New York Times,* January 29, pp. A1, A8.

Onishi, N. 1994. "Stray gunfire kills man in Bronx." *New York Times,* May 26, p. B3.

Prestia, K. 1993. *Chocolates for the pillows—Nightmares for the guests.* Silver Spring, MD: Bartleby Press.

Roberts, S. 1989. "When crimes become symbols." *New York Times,* March 7, Sec. 4, pp. 1, 28.

Rohter, L. 1993. "Fearful of tourism decline, Florida offers assurances on safety." *New York Times,* September 16, p. A14.

Rose, V. 1977. "Rape as a social problem: A by-product of the feminist movement." *Social Problems* 25 (October): 75–89.

Sachs, A. 1994. "Now for the movie." *Time,* January 31, p. 99.

Sanchez, R. 1994. "Fake cops' crime wave." *Long Island Newsday,* January 28, p. 31.

Savitz, L. 1986. "Obscene phone calls." In T. Hartnagel and R. Silverman (Eds.), *Critique and explanation: Essays in honor of Gwynne Nettles* (pp. 149–58). New Brunswick, NJ: Transaction Books.

Schafer, S. 1968. *The victim and his criminal.* New York: Random House.

Schechter, S. 1982. *Women and male violence.* Boston: South End Press.

Sexton, J. 1994. "Brooklyn drivers fear reckless young guns." *New York Times,* December 3, pp. A1, A26.

Sherman, L., Steele, L., Laufersweiler, D., Hoffer, N., and Julian, S. 1989. "Stray bullets and 'mushrooms': Random shootings of bystanders in four cities, 1977–1988," *Journal of Quantitative Criminology* 5:297–316.

Silberman, M. 1995. *A world of violence: Corrections in America.* Belmont, CA: Wadsworth.

Singer, S. 1981. "Homogeneous victim-offender populations: A review and some research implications." *Journal of Criminal Law and Criminology* 72(2): 779–88.

Smith, B. 1985. "Trends in the victims' rights movement and implications for future research." *Victimology* 10(1–4): 34–43.

Smith, B., Sloan, J., and Ward, R. 1990. "Public support for the victim's rights movement: Results of a statewide survey." *Crime and Delinquency* 36(4): 488–502.

Smith, S., and Freinkel, S. 1988. *Adjusting the balance: Federal policy and victim services.* New York: Greenwood Press.

Stark, J., and Goldstein, H. 1985. *The rights of crime victims: An American Civil Liberties Union handbook.* New York: Bantam Books.

Thomason, T., and Babbilli, A. 1987. *Crime victims and the news media.* Fort Worth: Texas Christian University Department of Journalism.

Toby, J. 1983. "Violence in school." In M. Tonry and N. Morris (Eds.), *Crime and justice: An annual review of research* (Volume 4) (pp. 1–47). Chicago: University of Chicago Press.

Trescott, P. 1987. *Diplomatic crimes.* Washington, DC: Acropolis Books.

Walker, S. 1982. "What have civil liberties ever done for crime victims? Plenty!" *ACJS Today (Academy of Criminal Justice Sciences),* October, pp. 4–5.

Widom, C. 1992. "The cycle of violence." *NIJ Research in Brief* (October). Washington, DC: U.S. Department of Justice.

Wolff, C. 1993a. "Former police officer stabbed while intervening in an attack." *New York Times,* May 19, p. B3.

———. 1993b. "Hostages mean hard lessons for police." *New York Times,* February 7, p. A37.

Woodward, K., Friday, C., Quade, V., and Sparkman, R. 1993. "The sins of the fathers . . ." *Newsweek,* July 12, p. 57.

2

Choosing Crime
Close Your Eyes and Take Your Chances

Kenneth D. Tunnell

Previous research on property crimes shows that a small group of repetitive offenders is responsible for a substantial percentage of index crimes (Blumstein 1986). One study found that 25 percent of a sample of 624 California inmates were "career criminals" who committed 60 percent of armed robberies and burglaries (Peterson, Braiker, and Polich 1980). A more recent study of recidivists informs us that at least "80 percent of the men and women held in local jails in 1983 had a prior criminal conviction. About two-thirds had served time before in a jail or prison, and about a third had served a prior sentence at least twice" (Beck and Shipley 1987, p. 1).

From *Justice Quarterly*, Vol. 7 No. 4, December 1990, © 1990 Academy of Criminal Justice Sciences. Reprinted by permission.

This group of chronic offenders is labeled a "problem population" because during their "careers" in crime they are responsible for the majority of thefts, burglaries, armed robberies, and forgeries. Still, little is known about the *nature* and the *incidence* of their offending and the way in which they incorporate the threat of punishment into their decisions to commit crimes. Researchers and policy makers have not determined "whether those individuals who habitually make criminal decisions think in different ways from other people" (Clarke and Cornish 1985, p. 161). Despite calls for greater understanding of this population, little is known about what makes them tick (e.g., Clarke and Cornish 1985; Feeney 1986; Glassner and Carpenter 1985; Paternoster 1987).

Previous research on crime neglected to examine criminals' explanations and elaborations of their perceptions of the risks and rewards from crime commission, how they make decisions to engage in crime, and how they conceptualize the threat of sanction. This weakness remains despite the recognized need for studies that employ personal and qualitative measures of deterrent effects and of the offender's perspective (e.g., Clarke and Cornish 1985; Glassner and Carpenter 1985; Jacob 1979; Jensen, Erickson, and Gibbs 1978; Paternoster, Saltzman, Waldo, and Chiricos 1982; Piliavin, Thornton, Gardner, and Matsueda 1986; Tuck and Riley 1986).

Attempts have been made to learn the offender's perspective, but these attempts have suffered from certain limitations. Previous studies of individual criminals engaged in decision-making about crime focused only on *target selection* for various crimes rather than on the decision to commit a crime—a decision that precedes both target selection and the criminal act (e.g., Akerstrom 1985; Bennett and Wright 1984a, 1984b; Maguire 1980; Moe and Bennett 1982; Rengert and Wasilchick 1985). These studies ignore the individual's assessment of behavioral options, namely to commit or not to commit a crime. Doubtless these decisions are interrelated, but they involve different assessments of different decision-making problems.

In light of the recent research on target selection and the calls or further inquiry, I designed this research, in which the central objective was to learn how repetitive criminals make decisions about committing typical property crimes and how they incorporate the various sanction threats into their assessment of various behavioral options. As a way of situating this study within a broader theoretical explanation and of relying on previous research, I used deterrence and decision-making theories for theoretical and empirical guidance. This study is not a test of these theories; rather, it incorporates some of the theoretical suppositions into the types of questions posed to the individual respondents. As a result, the findings from this study have implications for these theories and for public policy.

The social science community has developed a greater understanding of minor illegality and of the decision-making processes among individuals facing risky legitimate decisions than among repetitive property criminals (e.g., Grasmick 1985; Grasmick and Milligan 1976; Jensen and Stitt 1982). In recent years, deterrence theorists have emphasized the importance of the psychological processes of individual criminals' decision making, which includes their perceptions of the risks and rewards of crime commission (e.g., Brown 1981; Carroll 1982; Cornish and Clarke 1987; Feeney 1986; Jacob 1979). This shift in focus has resulted in the development and use of perceptual deterrence theory—a rational-choice model of criminal decision making. It highlights the importance of the actor's assessment of the potential costs and benefits of various choices of behavior.

Perceptual deterrence and decision-making theories inform us that individuals, before acting, think about the potential positive and negative consequences of their actions (e.g., Cook 1980; Cornish and Clarke 1987). The decision whether to engage in a particular act is a product of the individual's rational calculation of the expected benefits and risks associated with that act. The logic of the theories, then, informs us that if the action is believed to produce greater positive than negative results, the actor is more than likely to proceed. In such a case it can be said that the rewards are believed to outweigh the risks. On the other hand, if the actor believes that the act will produce greater negative than positive consequences, he or she is more than likely not to engage in the act. In this case, the risks are believed to outweigh the benefits. Individual behavior is considered the product of *rational* deliberation about the expected risks and benefits of a particular course of action, compared to those of alternative courses of action (e.g., Brown and Reynolds 1973; Carroll 1978; Clarke and Cornish 1985).

Perceptual deterrence and decision-making theories emphasize the actor's ability to relate action to consequence, which is of the utmost importance in understanding how "risky" decision problems are resolved (e.g., Paternoster, et al. 1983; Rettig and Rawson 1963; Rim 1984; Sullivan 1973; Tversky and Kahneman 1981). Relating action to consequence is a result of the actor's *perceptions* of the likely outcome of actions, which propel him or her to act in one way or another.

Research Methods

The objective of this study was to obtain an insider's description of decision making among this overlooked and very important problem population (Petersilia, Greenwood, and Lavin 1978; Peterson et al. 1980)—repetitive property criminals—and to determine how they incorporate sanction threats into their criminal calculus.

To this end, I selected a sample of 60 "ordinary" repetitive male property offenders incarcerated in a state prison system, in cooperation with the state's Department of Corrections and Board of Parole (see Table 2.1 for demographics). I used this particular sample of offenders to learn how they decide to commit a crime and how the possibility of legal punishment is processed cognitively and socially in a problem population. Certainly repetitive property criminals are undeterred by the threat of legal and extralegal sanctions. They may not represent the average street criminal and certainly do not represent the average citizen, but they belong to a population that society would like most to see deterred (see Table 2.2 for numbers of self-reported crimes).

Table 2.1
Demographics of the Sample (N=60)

	Mean
Age	34
Years of Education	10
Age at First Arrest	11
Racial composition: 38 white, 22 black	

I used three criteria in the sample selection. First, each respondent must have been serving at least his second prison incarceration for felony property crimes. Second, one of these incarcerations must have been for either burglary or armed robbery. Because these offenses represent the most "serious" types of index property crimes, it was important to select a sample of criminals who had histories of committing such crimes frequently. Third, each respondent had to be at least 25 years of age. I used this minimum age to eliminate younger participants from the sample for two reasons. First, this research depended on individual self-reflection of the kind that often eludes young adults. In addition, because sample members were required to be serving at least their second incarceration, they would have had opportunities to commit many more crimes than individuals below age 25.

The sample was limited to males because they represent ordinary property offenders more fully. Research shows that males account for the great majority of all serious property crimes and that females traditionally have not been involved actively in such crimes as burglary and armed robbery (Mann 1984; Morris 1987).

I contacted each of the 60 by letter, told him of the research, and said that I would visit him soon in prison. After agreeing to participate in the project, each respondent was interviewed in a private conference room that had been arranged by prison officials. Each participant and I had complete privacy; on those rare occasions when a prison official entered the room, we ceased our conversation immediately. This privacy further assured the participants of confidentiality. Each interview lasted from one to three hours. Much of the interview focused on one specific crime, the events leading up to that crime, the individual's description of his thoughts and conversations during the actual decision, and his thoughts of arrest and confinement. The crime itself and the target were only of peripheral interest. I asked each respondent to recall the most recent and most typical crime he had committed and could remember clearly. At that point we reconstructed in temporal order all events that occurred both before and during the crime. The emphasis, however, was on the individual's *decision* to commit the crime.

Because this research was informed by decision-making and deterrence theories, I gave attention to variables indicative of decision-making processes, namely the individual's knowledge and perceptions of the likely positive and negative consequences of his actions, the alternatives he considered in resolving the decision problem, and the neutralization technique (if applicable) that facilitated his decision to participate in the risky decision or event. The interviews were audiotaped and later were transcribed. Then I subjected the interview transcripts to qualitative analysis whereby I sought out patterns and constructed typologies from the in-depth descriptions.

The interviews produced 60 detailed descriptions of how the offenders reached the decision to commit a crime. In other words, they yielded a retrospective description of the offenders' *criminal calculus*. I accomplished this by asking the participants to describe specifically 1) the most recent and most typical crime they had committed, 2) the context within which they reached the decision to commit the crime, and 3) their method of assessing the perceived risks and rewards of committing the crime. These three lines of inquiry produced the nucleus of the data for this study.

Table 2.2
Total Number of Self-Reported Crimes by Type and Number of Offenders

Crime Type	Number of Offenders	Total Number Committed*
Armed robbery	29	1,080
Strong-armed robbery	17	907
Residential burglary	43[a]	5,011
Business burglary	43[b]	2,441
Auto theft	37	3,400
Shoplifting	40	4,040
Dealing stolen goods	43	13,946
Forgery	24	6,441
Grand theft	41	7,581
Petty theft	38	3,879
Total number of crimes committed		48,626

* These figures represent self-report data. The participants were asked whether they
had committed each of these crimes. If the answer was affirmative, they were
asked how many they had committed as a juvenile, as a young adult, and as an
adult. I also asked them about the frequency with which they had committed each
of the self-reported crimes. The only possible validity check was to compare the
types of crimes they reported committing with their official arrest and incarceration
records. If they reported committing several burglaries, I expected to find some
indication of burglary among their official arrest records. Again, such a method of
data collection presents problems.
[a] Nine of the 43 reported that they had committed no business burglaries.
[b] Eight of the 43 reported that they had committed no residential burglaries.

Findings and Theoretical Implications

Until this point in their lives, these offenders certainly had been
undeterred by the threat of legal sanction. Only after having served at
least two prison sentences and after suffering serious extralegal consequences did the majority claim that they would desist from committing property crimes. What aspect of the nature of their decision
making and of their perceptions of legal punishment explains why
the deterrent effect was lacking until now?

Three themes were most common in explaining the absence of
deterrent effects on these respondents' actions. First, they believed
that they would not be caught for their crimes (the most active criminals, high-rate offenders, knew from personal experience that the

probability was low). Second, they believed that if they were caught, they would be imprisoned for a relatively short time. Third, they considered prison to be a nonthreatening environment. Each of these themes is explicated below; they suggest that the most active property offenders operate beyond the reach of the law and of policies designed to deter criminal behavior.

Getting Caught: Fat Chance

All 60 respondents reported that they (and nearly every thief they knew) simply do not think about the possible legal consequences of their criminal actions before committing crimes. This is especially true for criminals of grave concern to deterrence-minded policy makers—those who commit crimes at a very high rate. Rather than thinking of the possible negative consequences of their actions, those offenders reported thinking primarily of the anticipated positive consequences.

Deterrence and decision-making theories inform us that "risk" ideally is conceptualized and evaluated before acting. Again, however, contrary to decision-making theories, those few participants who conceptualized the possible negative consequences of their actions when deciding to commit a crime reported that they did not evaluate them. They managed to put thoughts of negative consequences out of their minds to complete the crime. Their fear was neutralized as they turned away from signs of danger. This finding suggests that the use of fear to influence behavior through punitive policies for repeat property criminals may be misplaced and may lack empirical support.

Even more important, the respondents reported that they rarely thought of the prison environment or their incarceration. Fifty-two reported that they simply believed they would not be caught and refused to think beyond that point. One 29-year-old rural burglar, who fancied himself an outlaw in the fashion of John Dillinger, reported the following during our conversation:

> Come on, now. You're not saying you didn't think about getting caught, are you?

> I never really thought about getting caught until, pow, you're in jail, you're in juvenile or something. That's when you go to think about it.

An inner-city hustler reported similar thoughts.

> So how much do you think you feared getting caught?

> I didn't. I never did think about it really. Not to a point that it would make me undecided or anything like that. I knowed I wasn't supposed

to get caught. I just figured every time I wouldn't get caught. I never thought that I would get caught for nothing that I did.

During the crime, thinking of risks was distracting and interfered with performing well. I asked a 33-year-old burglar who specialized in stealing kitchen appliances from newly built apartment complexes about his thoughts of risks before committing a crime.

As you did burglaries, what came first—the crime or thinking about getting caught for the crime?

The crime comes first because it's enough to worry about doing the actual crime itself without worrying about what's going to happen if you get caught.

Even those who knew the possible consequences of their actions functioned with the belief that they would not be apprehended or suffer. The following conversation with a 29-year-old armed robber illustrates how he made the decision to commit a crime even though he was aware of the potential negative consequences.

So, it sounds like as you were approaching an armed robbery you thought about going to prison.

Yeah.

And you said you also knew that your mama knew what you were into, and you said that bothered you.

Yeah.

And you also just now said you were worried about getting killed or killing somebody. So knowing all those things . . . how did you manage to go ahead and do the armed robberies?

I was doing it just to get money. I didn't really . . . think about all the trouble . . . I'd end up in or anything.

Nearly all offenders claimed to have thought rarely of the potential legal consequences of criminality. Table 2.3 illustrates not only that thoughts of legal consequences were considered rarely, but that such thoughts changed with age (see, e.g., Shover 1985).

The decision-making process appears *not* to be a matter of rational evaluation or calculation of the benefits and risks that these criminals perceive as possible. Rather, they consider only the benefits; risks 1) are thought about only rarely or 2) are considered minimally but are put out of their minds. Risk was a distraction to those individuals. The decision was a matter of how to commit the crime. It was predicated on the anticipated benefits, *not* on the calculated expected outcome of the benefits versus the risks. The offenders put the possible negative consequences out of their minds; such percep-

Table 2.3

Those Who Reported Not Worrying about Arrest and Incarceration by Percentage and Age Category

Response	Juvenile[a]	Young Adult[b]	Adult[c]
Never or occasionally worried about arrest	60	56.7	21.7
Never or occasionally worried about going to jail	66.7	60	28.3
Chances of arrest[d]	61.7	51.7	21.7
Chances of incarceration[d]	60	50	18.3

[a] Younger than age 18
[b] Ages 18 through 26
[c] Age 27 and older
[d] Responses are based on an eight-point Likert scale: 1 represents the belief that they had no chance of being arrested or incarcerated, and 8 represents a certain chance. The respondents were asked to state their perceptions of their chances for the three age periods. These figures represent cumulative percentages for numbers 1 through 4 on the eight-point scale.

tions of consequences distracted them from the act itself. A few reported that they could not commit a crime if negative thoughts lingered in their minds. If they were unable to rid themselves of these perceptions, they would not go through with the act. Thus in this sample, risk does not appear in the calculus of typical crimes. When perception of risk surfaces, it is evaluated (e.g., the individual asks whether it is instinctive or real) and acted upon. Typically the offender casts it aside and considers it a nuisance.

Because this sample of repetitive property offenders believed that they would not be apprehended or punished for their crimes, they were undeterred.

Getting Caught: No Time

Many of the offenders had unrealistic or erroneous perceptions of the severity of the punishment for their crimes. Each participant reported that he knew his actions were illegal, and therefore did his best to avoid capture. Yet, a surprising number (N=32) did not know the severity of the punishment for their offenses before their arrest. Most learned the "going rate" *after* arrest (Walker 1985).

The respondents' perceptions of the severity of legal sanction were unrealistic. Therefore risk carried less weight than ideally it should have carried. One armed robber (the same as mentioned above) thought that his first conviction would yield a probationary sentence rather than a lengthy prison term. He never considered his chances of going to prison for a long time.

> So, before you learned the penalty for armed robbery, did you know that you could go to the penitentiary for it?

> I hadn't never got caught for robbery or nothing. I thought I'd go to jail and they'd put me on probation or something the first two times. So I really didn't pay too much attention to the penalty because I knew if I got caught that first time I might spend a few days in jail and I knew that my first time . . . I could get probation since it was my first offense. After my first conviction, five years for robbery, I really found out the penalty.

The offenders typically believed that the prison sentence for their actions would be less than the actual prescriptive punishment. I posed the following question to an inner-city offender who typically committed both armed robbery and strong-armed robbery.

> Did you have knowledge of the potential penalty for doing [strong-armed robbery]?

> In the state of ———, absolutely not. This Class X crime penalty that's supposed to be a deterrent . . . I wasn't aware of any Class X. I wasn't aware of any penalties whatsoever.

The rationality of the respondents' decisions is debatable because they could not have considered realistically the possible outcomes of their actions. They were predisposed to calculate erroneously because they assessed the degree of punishment unrealistically.

I asked a participant who "specialized" in burglary about his worries of incarceration as a juvenile.

> Did you know you could get some time as a juvenile for burglary?

> Everybody told me, said, "Hey, all they're going to do is give you probation."

These offenders resolved problems about criminal decisions with less than full knowledge of the real possible outcomes of various decisions and actions.

Going to Prison: No Threat

Before their first incarceration, when considering a prison environment, these men thought of the same types of threats as nearly every other individual (e.g., physical and verbal abuse, threats of sexual assault, no contact with the outside world). During their first incarceration, however, they reached the conclusion that the state's punishment for committing property crimes was not as severe as they had feared. The worst punishment that the state could impose on them could be endured relatively easily; from that time on they viewed it as no great threat. The following dialogue with a 28-year-old burglar with a tenth-grade education illustrates how he came to define prison as a fairly insignificant threat and also to believe that it contributed to his manhood.

> Prison must not be much of a threat to you.
>
> It's not. Prison wasn't what I thought it was.
>
> What do you mean by that?
>
> When I went in . . . well, at that point in time it was kind of an awful thing to go to prison. That's what I had always heard, but when I got there and then found out the "Well hell, look who is here". . . "I didn't know he was here or they was here". . . And then I seen that I'm a man just like they are and I can make it, and I went and come back so quick.

These individuals learned the ins and outs of the correctional system (e.g., sentence reduction for "good and honor time"). They could rationalize their sentences more easily by knowing that actually they would not serve the full term. While committing crimes after they had learned the system, they calculated another prison sentence as a fairly insignificant threat. I held the following conversation with a 42-year-old who had committed dozens of residential burglaries and who also had served six prison sentences.

> When I asked you how much time you did, you said "Nothing, 18 months." Did that not seem like much time to you?
>
> I always thought it wasn't nothing because I went and did it and come on back here. But it really wasn't eighteen months, it was thirteen months and something. See they give me eighteen months . . . they give me so much off for good behavior. Just like this time I'm doing now. To you fifteen years would be a lot of time because you don't quite understand it, but after you get into the system here then they give you so many points for this and so many points for that . . . and when you get through looking at that you really don't have to stay as long as you might think.

Incarceration was no threat to many of these individuals (N=36), who calculated it as a less than serious negative consequence. Even those few who did consider the potential for legal punishment and those who had encountered it previously perceived it as not a great threat.

While serving their first prison sentence, these offenders acquired a typical education about prison lifestyles and learned for the first time about prison sentences. For most of them this knowledge was new. Afterward some offenders desisted from crime for a while. They attributed this decision to 1) their new knowledge of legal punishment and the threat it imposed and 2) extralegal factors in their lives (e.g., new family commitments, abstinence from drugs and alcohol, legitimate employment). During this period, some claimed to have considered and pursued legitimate alternatives to crime for the first time since they began to commit crimes frequently. They also reported going through phases of desistance which were not related to the threat of legal sanction. Rather, these phases were related to periods when conditions in their lives were positive and rewarding.

According to these findings, the most significant argument against deterrence theory and deterrence-guided policy is that the majority who desisted temporarily did so for reasons other than the threat of legal sanction. These findings give some support to "temporary deterrence," since the offenders desisted for a while because of the threat of legal punishment. Recent research suggests that desistance "is not necessarily permanent and may simply be part of a continuing process of lulls in the offending of persistent criminals" (Clarke and Cornish 1985, p. 173). Thus these respondents could be labeled cyclical or temporary desisters.

Those who did *not* desist for a time and who continued to commit crimes after their first incarceration changed their decision making in one of two ways. Some thought about the possibility of legal sanction much more than in the past. This thinking often led, at best, to a minimal increase in planning a crime. Others claimed that they simply chose not to think about the legal consequences of their actions. Such a choice was one of several neutralization techniques used by the participants to enable them to commit a crime even in the face of real consequences.

While committing crimes, most of the respondents (N=51) considered themselves immune from arrest and incarceration, although they believed that every habitual criminal eventually would be arrested. In their "profession" they internalized and exhibited what Tom Wolfe (1979) referred to among test pilots as the "right stuff." Their belief in their own immunity disallowed adequate consideration of the likelihood of legal consequences.

Although these participants had served several cumulative years in prison, few had served many years in a single prison term. Now, however, because of their habitual criminal involvement and their histories of repetitive incarcerations, they were faced with the threat of reincarceration as habitual criminals if they should be convicted of further property crimes. (States with "habitual criminal" statutes mandate that habitual criminal convictions result in a lifetime prison sentence.) Fifty-five percent of the sample (N=33) reported that they had been threatened with trial as habitual criminals. The respondents also said that they believed their chances of rearrest were greater now than at any point in their lives, and that their arrest on new criminal charges certainly would result in another prison sentence. This finding is similar to those of previous research efforts with chronic offenders (e.g., Petersilia et al. 1978; Shover 1985).

The participants also reported that they believed any future prison sentence would be long—given their age, too long for them at this point in their lives. (Table 2.3 illustrates the dynamics of their perceptions of the chance of arrest and imprisonment in relation to aging and the realities of long prison sentences.) All of those previously threatened with the "bitch" claimed that the severity of punishment posed too great a risk to justify continued commission of property crimes. This very severe penalty may act as a deterrent to these repetitive property offenders, who already have served several years in prison, who now perceive the threat of being tried as habitual criminals as real and consequential, and who realize that age is creeping up on them.

Even so, these responses may not indicate a deterrent effect. Prisoners, when talking of their plans for life after release from prison, construct such events rather questionably. They actually may believe that they will go straight until they are released and encounter the tribulations of being a two-time losing ex-con (e.g., stigma, reduced job marketability, loss of family trust). Again, when predicting their post-release behavior, they may be unable to separate the researcher from other members of "legitimate society" with whom they have had contact during their imprisonment, even if they can do so at other times. In other words, they may convey to researchers the same assertions that they make to prison counselors, parole board members, prison administrators, prospective employers, and family members—assertions that their life of crime is finished and that they are willing and eager to make a contribution to society. They may be telling us what they believe we want to hear, or they actually may be deterred by this severe punishment at this point in their lives; such a punishment would rob them of the remainder of their quickly passing years (see, e.g., Shover 1985). Although only 33 of these respondents have been threatened with this possibility, all now are potentially eligible for habitual criminal status and punishment—the most severe penalty the state can levy on property offenders.

Conclusion

For this sample of very active repeat offenders, deterrence theory and policy lack an adequate explanation. This sample represents a criminal population that commits a disproportionate number of street crimes, and does so with little concern for the law, arrest, or imprisonment. The implementation of harsher penalties may be adequate to deter those populations who either do not commit crime or do so infrequently, but it appears to be dubious when applied to frequent offenders. They view themselves as immune from criminal sanction, and hence are undeterred. They tend to believe that they simply will not be apprehended for their criminal actions; if they are caught, they will be imprisoned for a very short amount of time. Those who actually consider the possibilities of brief imprisonment view prison as a nonthreatening environment.

Further research using larger samples of active criminals would inform us further about perceptions of legal punishment and would allow generalizations to be made to other populations of offenders. Better yet, a participant observational research design (which may be impossible) using a sample of active property criminals would contribute invaluable insight on decision making in this problem population. Such research would allow data to be collected at the moment when decisions are made rather than retrospectively.

References

Akerstrom, Malin. 1985. *Crooks and Squares*. New Brunswick, NJ: Transaction.

Beck, Allen J. and Bernard E. Shipley. 1987. "Recidivism of Young Parolees." *Criminal Justice Archive and Information Network*.

Bennett, Trevor and Richard Wright. 1984a. "What the Burglar Saw. " *New Society*, 2:162–63.

———. 1984b. *Burglars on Burglary*. Hampshire, England: Gower.

Berk, Richard A. and Joseph M. Adams. 1970. "Establishing Rapport with Deviant Groups." *Social Problems*, 18:102–18.

Blumstein, Alfred. 1986. *Criminal Careers and Career Criminals*. Washington, DC: National Academy Press.

Borcherding, K. and R. E. Schaefer. 1982. "Aiding Decision-Making and Information Processing." In Martin Irle (ed.), *Studies in Decision-Making*. Berlin: Walter de Gruyter, pp. 627–73.

Brown, Ivan D. 1981. "The Traffic Offense as a Rational Decision." In Sally Lloyd-Bostock (ed.), *Psychology in Legal Contexts*. London: Macmillan, pp. 203–22.

Brown, William and Morgan Reynolds. 1973. "Crime and Punishment Risk Implications." *Journal of Economic Theory*, 6:508–14.

Carroll, John S. 1978. "A Psychological Approach to Deterrence: The Evaluation of Crime Opportunities." *Journal of Personality and Social Psychology*, 36:1512–20.

———. 1982. "Committing a Crime: The Offender's Decision." In Vladimir J. Konecni and Ebbe B. Ebbesen (eds.), *The Criminal Justice System: A Social-Psychological Analysis*. San Francisco: Freeman, pp. 49–67.

Clarke, Ronald V. and Derek B. Cornish. 1985. "Modeling Offenders' Decisions: A Framework for Research and Policy." In Michael Tonry and Norval Morris (eds.), *Crime and Justice: An Annual Review of Research*, Volume 6. Chicago: University of Chicago Press, pp. 147–85.

Cook, Philip J. 1980. "Research in Criminal Deterrence: Laying the Groundwork for the Second Decade." In Norval Morris and Michael Tonry (eds.), *An Annual Review of Research*. Chicago: University of Chicago Press, pp. 211–68.

Cornish, Derek B. and Ronald V. Clarke. 1987. "Understanding Crime Displacement: An Application of Rational Choice Theory." *Criminology*, 25: 933–47.

Feeney, Floyd. 1986. "Robbers as Decision-Makers." In Derek B. Cornish and Ronald V. Clarke (eds.), *The Reasoning Criminal*. New York: Springer-Verlag, pp. 53–71.

Glassner, Barry and Cheryl Carpenter. 1985. *The Feasibility of an Ethnographic Study of Adult Property Offenders*. Washington, DC: U.S. Department of Justice.

Grasmick, Harold G. 1985. "The Application of a Generalized Theory of Deterrence to Income Tax Evasion." Paper presented to the Law and Society Conference.

Grasmick, Harold G. and Herman Milligan. 1976. "Deterrence Theory Approach to Socioeconomic/Demographic Correlates of Crime." *Social Science Quarterly*, 57:608–17.

Jacob, Herbert. 1979. "Rationality and Criminality." *Social Science Quarterly*, 59:584–85.

Jensen, Gary F., Maynard L. Erickson and Jack P. Gibbs. 1978. "Perceived Risk of Punishment and Self-Reported Delinquency." *Social Forces*, 57: 57–78.

Jensen, Gary and B. Grant Stitt. 1982. "Words and Misdeeds: Hypothetical Choices Versus Past Behavior as Measures of Deviance." In John Hagan (ed.), *Deterrence Reconsidered*. Beverly Hills: Sage, pp. 33–54.

Maguire, Mike. 1980. "Burglary as Occupation." *Home Office Research Bulletin*, 10:6–9.

Maguire, Mike and Trevor Bennett. 1982. *Burglary in a Dwelling*. London: Heinemann.

Mann, Coramae. 1984. *Female Crime and Delinquency*. Birmingham: University of Alabama Press.

Morris, Allison. 1987. *Women, Crime, and Criminal Justice*. Oxford: Basil Blackwell.

Paternoster, Raymond. 1987. "The Deterrent Effect of the Perceived Certainty and Severity of Punishment: A Review of the Evidence and Issues." *Justice Quarterly*, 4:173–17.

Paternoster, Raymond, L. E. Saltzman, G. P. Waldo and T. G. Chiricos. 1982. "Causal Ordering in Deterrence Research." In John Hagan (ed.), *Deterrence Reconsidered*. Beverly Hills: Sage, pp. 55–70.

———. 1983. "Perceived Risk and Social Control: Do Sanctions Really Deter?" *Law and Society Review*, 17:457–79.

Petersilia, Joan, Peter W. Greenwood and Marvin Lavin. 1978. *Criminal Careers of Habitual Felons*. Washington, DC: National Institute of Law Enforcement and Criminal Justice.

Peterson, Mark A., H. B. Braiker and Suzanne M. Polich. 1980. *Doing Crime: A Survey of California Prison Inmates*. Santa Monica: Rand.

Piliavin, Irving, C. Thornton, R. Gartner and R. L. Matsueda. 1986. "Crime, Deterrence and Rational Choice. " *American Sociological Review*, 51: 101–19.

Rengert, George and John Wasilchick. 1985. *Suburban Burglary*. Springfield, IL: Charles C Thomas.

Rettig, S. and H. E. Rawson. 1963. "The Risk Hypothesis in Predictive Judgments of Unethical Behavior." *Journal of Abnormal and Social Psychology*, 66:243–48.

Rim, Yeshayahu. 1964. "Social Attitudes and Risk Taking." *Human Relations*, 17:259–65.

Shover, Neal. 1985. *Aging Criminals*. Beverly Hills: Sage.

Sullivan, Richard F. 1973. "The Economics of Crime: An Introduction to the Literature." *Crime and Delinquency*, 19:138–49.

Sykes, Gresham M. and David Matza. 1957. "Techniques of Neutralization: A Theory of Delinquency." *American Sociological Review*, 22:664–70.

Tuck, Mary and David Riley. 1986. "The Theory of Reasoned Action: A Decision Theory of Crime." In Derek B. Cornish and Ronald V. Clarke (eds.), *The Reasoning Criminal*. New York: Springer-Verlag, pp. 156–69.

Tversky, Amos and Daniel Kahneman. 1981. "The Framing of Decisions and the Psychology of Choice." *Science*, 211:453–58.

Walker, Samuel. 1985. *Sense and Nonsense about Crime: A Policy Guide*. Monterey, CA: Brooks/Cole.

Wolfe, Tom. 1979. *The Right Stuff*. New York: Farrar, Strauss, and Giroux.

3

Two Models of the Criminal Process

Herbert L. Packer

People who commit crimes appear to share the prevalent impression that punishment is an unpleasantness that is best avoided. They ordinarily take care to avoid being caught. If arrested, they ordinarily deny their guilt and otherwise try not to cooperate with the police. If brought to trial, they do whatever their resources permit to resist being convicted. And even after they have been convicted and sent to prison, their efforts to secure their freedom do not cease. It is a struggle from start to finish. This struggle is often referred to as the criminal process, a compendious term that stands for all the complexes of activity that operate to bring the substantive law of crime to bear (or to keep it from coming to bear) on persons who are suspected of having committed crimes. It can be described, but only partially and inadequately, by referring to the rules of law that govern the appre-

Reprinted from *The Limits of the Criminal Sanction*, by Herbert L. Packer with the permission of the publishers, Stanford University Press. © 1969 by Herbert L. Packer.

hension, screening, and trial of persons suspected of crime. It consists at least as importantly of patterns of official activity that correspond only in the roughest kind of way to the prescriptions of procedural rules.

At the same time, and perhaps in part as a result of this new accretion of knowledge, some of our lawmaking institutions—particularly the Supreme Court of the United States—have begun to add measurably to the prescriptions of law that are meant to govern the operation of the criminal process. This accretion has become, in the last few years, exponential in extent and velocity. We are faced with an interesting paradox: the more we learn about the Is of the criminal process, the more we are instructed about its Ought and the greater the gulf between Is and Ought appears to become. We learn that very few people get adequate legal representation in the criminal process; we are simultaneously told that the Constitution requires people to be afforded adequate legal representation in the criminal process. We learn that coercion is often used to extract confessions from suspected criminals; we are then told that convictions based on coerced confessions may not be permitted to stand. We discover that the police often use methods in gathering evidence that violate the norms of privacy protected by the Fourth Amendment; we are told that evidence obtained in this way must be excluded from the criminal trial. But these prescriptions about how the process ought to operate do not automatically become part of the patterns of official behavior in the criminal process. Is and Ought share an increasingly uneasy coexistence. Doubts are stirred about the kind of criminal process we want to have. . . .

Two models of the criminal process will let us perceive the normative antinomy at the heart of the criminal law. These models are not labeled Is and Ought, nor are they to be taken in that sense. Rather, they represent an attempt to abstract two separate value systems that compete for priority in the operation of the criminal process. Neither is presented as either corresponding to reality or representing the ideal to the exclusion of the other. The two models merely afford a convenient way to talk about the operation of a process whose day-to-day functioning involves a constant series of minute adjustments between the competing demands of two value systems and whose normative future likewise involves a series of resolutions of the tensions between competing claims.

I call these two models the Due Process Model and the Crime Control Model. There is a risk in an enterprise of this sort that is latent in any attempt to polarize. It is, simply, that values are too various to be pinned down to yes-or-no answers. The models are distortions of reality. And, since they are normative in character, there is a danger of seeing one or the other as Good or Bad. The reader will have his preferences, as I do, but we should not be so rigid as to demand consistently polarized answers to the range of questions posed in the criminal process. The weighty questions of public policy that inhere in any attempt to discern where on the spectrum of normative choice the "right" answer lies are beyond the scope of the present inquiry. The attempt here is primarily to clarify the terms of discussion by isolating the assumptions that underlie competing policy claims and examining the conclusions that those claims, if fully accepted, would lead to.

Values Underlying the Models

Each of the two models we are about to examine is an attempt to give operational content to a complex of values underlying the criminal law. As I have suggested earlier, it is possible to identify two competing systems of values, the tension between which accounts for the intense activity now observable in the development of the criminal process. The actors in this development—lawmakers, judges, police, prosecutors, defense lawyers—do not often pause to articulate the values that underlie the positions that they take on any given issue. Indeed, it would be a gross oversimplification to ascribe a coherent and consistent set of values to any of these actors. Each of the two competing schemes of values we will be developing in this section contains components that are demonstrably present some of the time in some of the actors' preferences regarding the criminal process. No one person has ever identified himself as holding all of the values that underlie these two models. The models are polarities, and so are the schemes of value that underlie them. A person who subscribed to all of the values underlying one model to the exclusion of all of the values underlying the other would be rightly viewed as a fanatic. The values are presented here as an aid to analysis, not as a program for action. . . .

Crime Control Values

The value system that underlies the Crime Control Model is based on the proposition that the repression of criminal conduct is by far the most important function to be performed by the criminal process. The failure of law enforcement to bring criminal conduct under tight control is viewed as leading to the breakdown of public order and thence to the disappearance of an important condition of human freedom. If the laws go unenforced—which is to say, if it is perceived that there is a high percentage of failure to apprehend and convict in the criminal process—a general disregard for legal controls tends to develop. The law-abiding citizen then becomes the victim of all sorts of unjustifiable invasions of his interests. His security of person and property is sharply diminished, and, therefore, so is his liberty to function as a member of society. The claim ultimately is that the criminal process is a positive guarantor of social freedom. In order to achieve this high purpose, the Crime Control Model requires that primary attention be paid to the efficiency with which the criminal process operates to screen suspects, determine guilt, and secure appropriate dispositions of persons convicted of crime.

The model, in order to operate successfully, must produce a high rate of apprehension and conviction, and must do so in a context where the magnitudes being dealt with are very large and the resources for dealing with them are very limited. There must then be a premium on speed and finality. Speed, in turn, depends on informality and on uniformity; finality depends on minimizing the occasions for challenge. The process must not be cluttered up with ceremonious rituals that do not advance the progress of a case. Facts can be established more quickly through interrogation in a police station than through the formal process of examination and cross-examination in a court. It follows that extra-judicial processes should be preferred to judicial processes, informal operations to formal ones. But informality is not enough; there must also be uniformity. Routine, stereotyped procedures are essential if large numbers are being handled. The model that will operate successfully on these presuppositions must be an administrative, almost a managerial, model. The image that comes to mind is an assembly-line conveyor belt down which moves an endless stream of cases, never stopping, carrying the cases to workers who stand at fixed stations and who perform on each case as it comes by the same small but essential operation that brings it one step closer to being a finished product, or, to exchange the metaphor for the reality, a closed file. The criminal process, in this model, is seen as a screening process in which each successive stage—pre-arrest investigation, arrest, post-arrest investigation, preparation for trial, trial or entry of plea, conviction, disposition—involves a series of routinized operations whose success is gauged primarily by their tendency to pass the case along to a successful conclusion.

What is a successful conclusion? One that throws off at an early stage those cases in which it appears unlikely that the person apprehended is an offender and then secures, as expeditiously as possible, the conviction of the rest, with a minimum of occasions for challenge, let alone post-audit. By the application of administrative expertness, primarily that of the police and prosecutors, an early determination of probable innocence or guilt emerges. Those who are probably innocent are screened out. Those who are probably guilty are passed quickly through the remaining stages of the process. The key to the operation of the model regarding those who are not screened out is what I shall call a presumption of guilt. The concept requires some explanation, since it may appear startling to assert that what appears to be the precise converse of our generally accepted ideology of a presumption of innocence can be an essential element of a model that does correspond in some respects to the actual operation of the criminal process.

The presumption of guilt is what makes it possible for the system to deal efficiently with large numbers, as the Crime Control Model demands. The supposition is that the screening processes operated by police and prosecutors are reliable indicators of probable guilt. Once a man has been arrested and investigated without being found to be probably innocent, or, to put it differently, once a determination has been made that there is enough evidence of guilt to permit holding him for further action, then all subsequent activity directed toward him is based on the view that he is probably guilty. The precise point at which this occurs will vary from case to case; in many cases it will occur as soon as the suspect is arrested, or even before, if the evidence of probable guilt that has come to the attention of the authorities is sufficiently strong. But in any case the presumption of guilt will begin to operate well before the "suspect" becomes a "defendant."

The presumption of guilt is not, of course, a thing. Nor is it even a rule of law in the usual sense. It simply is the consequence of a complex of attitudes, a mood. If there is confidence in the reliability of informal administrative fact-finding activities that take place in the early stages of the criminal process, the remaining stages of the process can be relatively perfunctory without any loss in operating efficiency. The presumption of guilt, as it operates in the Crime Control Model, is the operational expression of that confidence.

It would be a mistake to think of the presumption of guilt as the opposite of the presumption of innocence that we are so used to thinking of as the polestar of the criminal process and that, as we shall see, occupies an important position in the Due Process Model. The presumption of innocence is not its opposite; it is irrelevant to the presumption of guilt; the two concepts are different rather than opposite ideas. The difference can perhaps be epitomized by an example. A murderer, for reasons best known to himself, chooses to shoot his victim in plain view of a large number of people. When the police arrive, he hands them his gun and says, "I did it and I'm glad." His account of what happened is corroborated by several eyewitnesses. He is placed under arrest and led off to jail. Under these circumstances, which may seem extreme but which in fact characterize with rough accuracy the evidentiary situation in a large proportion of criminal cases, it would be plainly absurd to maintain that more probably than not the suspect did not commit the killing. But that is not what the presumption of innocence means. It means that until there has been an adjudication of guilt by an authority legally competent to make such an adjudication, the suspect is to be treated, for reasons that have nothing whatever to do with the probable outcome of the case, as if his guilt is an open question.

The presumption of innocence is a direction to officials about how they are to proceed, not a prediction of outcome. The presumption of guilt, however, is purely and simply a prediction of outcome. The presumption of innocence is, then, a direction to the authorities to ignore the presumption of guilt in their treatment of the suspect. It tells them, in effect, to close their eyes to what will frequently seem to be factual probabilities. The reasons why it tells them this are among the animating presuppositions of the Due Process Model.

In this model, as I have suggested, the center of gravity for the process lies in the early, administrative fact-finding stages. The complementary proposition is that the subsequent stages are relatively unimportant and should be truncated as much as possible. This, too, produces tensions with presently dominant ideology. The pure Crime Control Model has very little use for many conspicuous features of the adjudicative process, and in real life works out a number of ingenious compromises with them. Even in the pure model, however, there have to be devices for dealing with the suspect after the preliminary screening process has resulted in a determination of probable guilt. The focal device, as we shall see, is the plea of guilty; through its use, adjudicative fact-finding is reduced to a minimum. It might be said of the Crime Control Model that, when reduced to its barest essentials and operating at its most successful pitch, it offers two possibilities: an administrative fact-finding process leading (1) to exoneration of the suspect or (2) to the entry of a plea of guilty.

Due Process Values

If the Crime Control Model resembles an assembly line, the Due Process Model looks very much like an obstacle course. Each of its successive stages is designed to present formidable impediments to carrying the accused any further along in the process. Its ideology is not the converse of that underlying the Crime Control Model. It does not rest on the idea that it is not socially desirable to repress crime, although critics of its application have been known to claim so. Its ideology is composed of a complex of ideas, some of them based on judgments about the efficacy of crime control devices, others having to do with quite different considerations. The ideology of due process is far more deeply impressed on the formal structure of the law than is the ideology of crime control; yet an accurate tracing of the strands that make it up is strangely difficult. What follows is only an attempt at an approximation.

The Due Process Model encounters its rival on the Crime Control Model's own ground in respect to the reliability of fact-finding processes. The Crime Control Model, as we have suggested, places heavy reliance on the ability of investigative and prosecutorial officers, acting in an informal setting in which their distinctive skills are given full sway, to elicit and reconstruct a tolerably accurate account of what actually took place in an alleged criminal event. The Due Process Model rejects this premise and substitutes for it a view of informal, nonadjudicative fact-finding that stresses the possibility of error. People are notoriously poor observers of disturbing events—the more emotion-arousing the context, the greater the possibility that recollection will be incorrect; confessions and admissions by persons in police custody may be induced by physical or psychological coercion so that the police end up hearing what the suspect thinks they want to hear rather than the truth; witnesses may be animated by a bias or interest that no one would trouble to discover except one specially charged with protecting the interests of the accused (as the police are not). Considerations of this kind all lead to a rejection of informal fact-finding processes as definitive of factual guilt and to an insistence on formal, adjudicative, adversary fact-finding processes in which the factual case against the accused is publicly heard by an impartial tribunal and is evaluated only after the accused has had a full opportunity to discredit the case against him. Even then, the distrust of fact-finding processes that animates the Due Process Model is not dissipated. The possibilities of human error being what they are, further scrutiny is necessary, or at least must be available, in case facts have been overlooked or suppressed in the heat of battle. How far this subsequent scrutiny must be available is a hotly controverted issue today. In the pure Due Process Model the answer would be: at least as long as there is an allegation of factual error that has not received an adjudicative hearing in a fact-finding context. The demand for finality is thus very low in the Due Process Model.

This strand of due process ideology is not enough to sustain the model. If all that were at issue between the two models was a series of questions about the reliability of fact-finding processes, we would have but one model of the criminal process, the nature of whose constituent elements would pose questions of fact not of value. Even if the discussion is confined, for the moment, to the question of reliability, it is apparent that more is at stake than simply an evaluation of what kinds of fact-finding processes, alone or in combination, are likely to produce the most nearly reliable results. The stumbling block is this: how much reliability is compatible with efficiency? Granted that informal fact-finding will make some mistakes that can be remedied if backed up by adjudicative fact-finding, the desirability of providing this backup is not affirmed or negated by factual demonstrations or predictions that the increase in reliability will be x per cent or x plus n per cent. It still remains to ask how much weight is to be given to the competing demands of reliability (a high degree of probability in each case that factual guilt has been accurately determined) and efficiency (expeditious handling of the large numbers of cases that the process ingests). The Crime Control Model is more optimistic about the improbability of error in a significant number of cases; but it is also, though only in part therefore, more tolerant about the amount of error that it will put up with. The Due Process Model insists on the prevention and elimination of mistakes to the extent possible; the Crime Control Model accepts the probability of mistakes up to the level at which they interfere with the goal of repressing crime, either because too many guilty people are escaping or, more subtly, because general awareness of the unreliability of the process leads to a decrease in the deterrent efficacy of the criminal law. In this view, reliability and efficiency are not polar opposites but rather complementary characteristics. The system is reliable *because* efficient; reliability becomes a matter of independent concern only when it becomes so attenuated as to impair efficiency. All of this the Due Process Model rejects. If efficiency demands shortcuts around reliability, then absolute efficiency must be rejected. The aim of the process is at least as much to protect the factually innocent as it is to convict the factually guilty. It is a little like quality control in industrial technology: tolerable deviation from standard varies with the importance of conformity to standard in the destined uses of the product. The Due Process Model resembles a factory that has to devote a substantial part of its input to quality control. This necessarily cuts down on quantitative output.

The combination of stigma and loss of liberty that is embodied in the end result of the criminal process is viewed as being the heaviest deprivation that government can inflict on the individual. Furthermore, the processes that culminate in these highly afflictive sanctions are seen as in themselves coercive, restricting, and demeaning. Power is always subject to abuse—sometimes subtle, other times, as in the criminal process, open and ugly. Precisely because of its potency in subjecting the individual to the coercive power of the state, the criminal process must, in this model, be subjected to controls that prevent it from operating with maximal efficiency. According to this ideology, maximal efficiency means maximal tyranny. And, although no one would assert that minimal efficiency means minimal tyranny, the proponents of the Due Process Model would accept with considerable equanimity a substantial diminution in the efficiency with which the criminal process operates in the interest of preventing official oppression of the individual.

The most modest-seeming but potentially far-reaching mechanism by which the Due Process Model implements these anti-authoritarian values is the doctrine of legal guilt. According to this doctrine, a person is not to be held guilty of crime merely on a showing that in all probability, based upon reliable evidence, he did factually what he is said to have done. Instead, he is to be held guilty if and only if these factual determinations are made in procedurally regular fashion and by authorities acting within competences duly allocated to them. Furthermore, he is not to be held guilty, even though the factual determination is or might be adverse to him, if various rules designed to protect him and to safeguard the integrity of the process are not given effect: the tribunal that convicts him must have the power to deal with his kind of case ("jurisdiction") and must be geographically appropriate ("venue"); too long a time must not have elapsed since the offense was committed ("statute of limitations"); he must not have been previously convicted or acquitted of the same or a substantially similar offense ("double jeopardy"); he must not fall within a category of persons, such as children or the insane, who are legally immune to conviction ("criminal responsibility"); and so on. None of these requirements has anything to do with the factual question of whether the person did or did not engage in the conduct that is charged as the offense against him; yet favorable answers to any of them will mean that he is legally innocent. Wherever the competence to make adequate factual determinations lies, it is apparent that only a tribunal that is aware of these guilt-defeating doctrines and is willing to apply them can be viewed as competent to make determinations of legal guilt. The police and the prosecutors are ruled out by lack of competence, in the first instance, and by lack of assurance of willingness, in the second. Only an impartial tribunal can be trusted to make determinations of legal as opposed to factual guilt.

Beyond the question of predictability this model posits a functional reason for observing the presumption of innocence: by forcing the state to prove its case against the accused in an adjudicative context, the presumption of innocence serves to force into play all the qualifying and disabling doctrines that limit the use of the criminal sanction against the individual, thereby enhancing his opportunity to secure a favorable outcome. In this sense, the presumption of innocence may be seen to operate as a kind of self-fulfilling prophecy. By opening up a procedural situation that permits the successful assertion of defenses having nothing to do with factual guilt, it vindicates the proposition that the factually guilty may nonetheless be legally innocent and should therefore be given a chance to qualify for that kind of treatment.

The possibility of legal innocence is expanded enormously when the criminal process is viewed as the appropriate forum for correcting its own abuses. This notion may well account for a greater amount of the distance between the two models than any other. In theory the Crime Control Model can tolerate rules that forbid illegal arrests, unreasonable searches, coercive interrogations, and the like. What it cannot tolerate is the vindication of those rules in the criminal process itself through the exclusion of evidence illegally obtained or through the reversal of convictions in cases where the criminal process has breached the rules laid down for its observance. And the Due Process Model, although it may in the first instance be addressed to the maintenance of reliable fact-finding techniques, comes eventually to incorporate prophylactic and deterrent rules that result in the release of the factually guilty even in cases in which blotting out the illegality would still leave an adjudicative fact-finder convinced of the accused person's guilt. Only by penalizing errant police and prosecutors within the criminal process itself can adequate pressure be maintained, so the argument runs, to induce conformity with the Due Process Model.

Another strand in the complex of attitudes underlying the Due Process Model is the idea—itself a shorthand statement for a complex of attitudes—of equality. This notion has only recently emerged as an explicit basis for pressing the demands of the Due Process Model, but it appears to represent, at least in its potential, a most powerful norm for influencing official conduct. Stated most starkly, the ideal of equality holds that "there can be no equal justice where the kind of trial a man gets depends on the amount of money he has."[1] The factual predicate underlying this assertion is that there are gross inequalities in the financial means of criminal defendants as a class, that in an adversary system of criminal justice an effective defense is largely a function of the resources that can be mustered on behalf of the accused, and that the very large proportion of criminal defendants who are, operationally speaking, "indigent" will thus be denied an effective defense. This factual premise has been strongly reinforced by recent studies that in turn have been both a cause and an effect of an increasing emphasis upon norms for the criminal process based on the premise.

The norms derived from the premise do not take the form of an insistence upon governmental responsibility to provide literally equal opportunities for all criminal defendants to challenge the process. Rather, they take as their point of departure the notion that the criminal process, initiated as it is by government and containing as it does the likelihood of severe deprivations at the hands of government, imposes some kind of public obligation to ensure that financial inability does not destroy the capacity of an accused to assert what may be meritorious challenges to the processes being invoked against him. At its most gross, the norm of equality would act to prevent situations in which financial inability forms an absolute barrier to the assertion of a right that is in theory generally available, as where there is a right to appeal that is, however, effectively conditional upon the filing of a trial transcript obtained at the defendant's expense. Beyond this, it may provide the basis for a claim whenever the system theoretically makes some kind of challenge available to an accused who has the means to press it. If, for example, a defendant who is adequately represented has the opportunity to prevent the case against him from coming to the trial stage by forcing the state to its proof in a preliminary hearing, the norm of equality may be invoked to assert that the same kind of opportunity must be available to others as well. In a sense the system as it functions for the small minority whose resources permit them to exploit all its defensive possibilities provides a benchmark by which its functioning in all other cases is to be tested: not, perhaps, to guarantee literal identity but rather to provide a measure of whether the process as a whole is recognizably of the same general order. The demands made by a norm of this kind are likely by their very nature to be quite sweeping. Although the norm's imperatives may be initially limited to determining whether in a particular case the accused was injured or prejudiced by his relative inability to make an appropriate challenge, the norm of equality very quickly moves to another level on which the demand is that the process in general be adapted to minimize discriminations rather than that a mere series of post hoc determinations of discrimination be made or makeable.

There is a final strand of thought in the Due Process Model that is often ignored but that needs to be candidly faced if thought on the subject is not to be obscured. This is a mood of skepticism about the morality and utility of the criminal sanction, taken either as a whole or in some of its applications. The subject is a large and complicated one, comprehending as it does much of the intellectual history of our times. It is properly the subject of another essay altogether. To put the matter briefly, one cannot improve upon the statement by Professor Paul Bator:

> In summary we are told that the criminal law's notion of just condemnation and punishment is a cruel hypocrisy visited by a smug society on the psychologically and economically crippled; that its premise of a morally autonomous will with at least some measure of choice whether to comply with the values expressed in a penal code is unscientific and outmoded; that its reliance on punishment as an educational and deterrent agent is misplaced, particularly in the case of the very members of society most likely to engage in criminal conduct; and that its failure to provide for individualized and humane rehabilitation of offenders is inhuman and wasteful.[2]

This skepticism, which may be fairly said to be widespread among the most influential and articulate contemporary leaders of informed opinion, leads to an attitude toward the processes of the criminal law that, to quote Mr. Bator again, engenders "a peculiar receptivity toward claims of injustice which arise within the traditional structure of the system itself; fundamental disagreement and unease about the very bases of the criminal law has, inevitably, created acute pressure at least to expand and liberalize those of its processes and doctrines which serve to make more tentative its judgments or limit its power." In short, doubts about the ends for which power is being exercised create pressure to limit the discretion with which that power is exercised.

There are two kinds of problems that need to be dealt with in any model of the criminal process. One is what the rules shall be. The other is how the rules shall be implemented. The second is at least as important as the first. The distinctive difference between the two models is not only in the rules of conduct that they lay down but also in the sanctions that are to be invoked when a claim is presented that the rules have been breached and, no less importantly, in the timing that is permitted or required for the invocation of those sanctions.

As I have already suggested, the Due Process Model locates at least some of the sanctions for breach of the operative rules in the criminal process itself. The relation between these two aspects of the process—the rules and the sanctions for their breach—is a purely formal one unless there is some mechanism for bringing them into play with each other. The hinge between them in the Due Process Model is the availability of legal counsel. This has a double aspect. Many of the rules that the model requires are couched in terms of the availability of counsel to do various things at various stages of the process—this is the conventionally recognized aspect; beyond it, there is a pervasive assumption that counsel is necessary in order to invoke sanctions for breach of any of the rules. The more freely available these sanctions are, the more important is the role of counsel in seeing to it that the sanctions are appropriately invoked. If the process is seen as a series of occasions for checking its own operation, the role of counsel is a much more nearly central one than is the case in a process that is seen as primarily concerned with expeditious determination of factual guilt. And if equality of operation is a governing norm, the availability of counsel to some is seen as requiring it for all. Of all the controverted aspects of the criminal process, the right to counsel, including the role of government in its provision, is the most dependent on what one's model of the process looks like, and the least susceptible of resolution unless one has confronted the antinomies of the two models.

I do not mean to suggest that questions about the right to counsel disappear if one adopts a model of the process that conforms more or less closely to the Crime Control Model, but only that such questions become absolutely central if one's model moves very far down the spectrum of possibilities toward the pure Due Process Model. The reason for this centrality is to be found in the assumption underlying both models that the process is an adversary one in which the initiative in invoking relevant rules rests primarily on the parties concerned, the state, and the accused. One could construct models that placed central responsibility on adjudicative agents such as committing magistrates and trial judges. And there are, as we shall see, marginal but nonetheless important adjustments in the role of the adjudicative agents that enter into the models with which we are concerned. For present purposes it is enough to say that these adjustments are marginal, that the animating presuppositions that underlie both models in the context of the American criminal system relegate the adjudicative agents to a relatively passive role, and therefore place central importance on the role of counsel.

What assumptions do we make about the sources of authority to shape the real-world operations of the criminal process? Recognizing that our models are only models, what agencies of government have the power to pick and choose between their competing demands? Once again, the limiting features of the American context come into play. Ours is not a system of legislative supremacy. The distinctively American institution of judicial review exercises a limiting and ultimately a shaping influence on the criminal process. Because the Crime Control Model is basically an affirmative model, emphasizing at every turn the existence and exercise of official power, its validating authority is ultimately legislative (although proximately administrative). Because the Due Process Model is basically a negative model, asserting limits on the nature of official power and on the modes of its exercise, its validating authority is judicial and requires an appeal to supra-legislative law, to the law of the Constitution. To the extent that tensions between the two models are resolved by deference to the Due Process Model, the authoritative force at work is the judicial power, working in the distinctively judicial mode of invoking the sanction of nullity. That is at once the strength and the weakness of the Due Process Model: its strength because in our system the appeal to the Constitution provides the last and the overriding word; its weakness because saying no in specific cases is an exercise in futility unless there is a general willingness on the part of the officials who operate the process to apply negative prescriptions across the board. It is no accident that statements reinforcing the Due Process Model come from the courts, while at the same time facts denying it are established by the police and prosecutors.

Notes

[1] Griffin vs. Illinois, 351 U.S. 12, 19 (1956).

[2] *Finality in Criminal Law and Federal Habeas Corpus for State Prisoners*, 76 Harvard Law Review 441, 442 (1963).

4

"Slinging Dope"
The Role of Gangs and
Gang Members in Drug Sales

Scott H. Decker
Barrik Van Winkle

Concern about street gangs has grown in the last decade. Objects of this concern include the spread of gangs into cities with little previous gang activity, their role in violence, and their involvement in property crime. Perhaps no other topic, however, has received as much attention as the role of gangs in drug sales. Because street gangs and "crack" cocaine emerged at about the same time in many cities, a number of observers have drawn a causal link between the two. Such concerns reflect the view of federal and local law enforcement that these activities are well organized and have national connections (National Institute of Justice 1993). This view has received considerable support in the literature. An alternative position suggests that gangs are involved more casually in the sale of drugs.

From *Justice Quarterly*, Vol. 11 No. 4, December 1994. © 1994 Academy of Criminal Justice Sciences. Reprinted by permission.

To control drug sales effectively, gangs must possess several characteristics. First, an organizational structure must be present. This hierarchy must have leaders, roles, and rules. Second, group goals must be shared widely among members. Third, allegiance to the larger organization must be stronger than to any subgroups within it. Finally, the gang must possess the means to control and discipline its members so as to produce compliance with group goals.

This view of gangs as formal-rational organizations is inconsistent, with descriptions of gangs from the 1970s (Klein 1971; Moore 1978; Short and Strodtbeck 1974). In commenting about the level of organization and status of goals within gangs, Short observed:

> Individual gangs, such as the Vice Lords and the Stones, sometimes have given the appearance of moving from largely expressive to more instrumental goals; but the extent to which such changes are in fact real is far from clear (1974:426).

Have gangs in fact changed in the last generation? Recent evidence has emerged to support the notion that—at least in regard to drug sales—gangs operate as formal-rational organizations.

In this paper we examine three sets of questions regarding the nature of gang involvement in drug sales: the extent of involvement, the level of organization, and gang members' motives in selling drugs. A number of studies have addressed this matter, but our work provides a new perspective on the issue because it is based on the results of interview data collected from 99 active gang members during a three-year field study of gangs in St. Louis.

Review of Literature

The two positions in the debate about gang involvement in drug sales are represented most clearly by Skolnick et al. (1988), Skolnick (1990), and Sanchez-Jankowski (1991), on the one hand, and by Klein, Maxson, and Cunningham (1991) and Klein and Maxson (1994), on the other. Skolnick and colleagues describe gangs as formal-rational organizations with a leadership structure, roles, rules, and control over members; Klein and colleagues describe gangs as loosely confederated groups generally lacking persistent forms of cohesion or organization. The extent and nature of gang involvement in drug sales are derived from these views of organizational structure.

On the basis of interviews with 39 inmates in state correctional facilities and 42 police and correctional officials, Skolnick et al. (1988) and Skolnick (1990) argue that many gangs are organized solely for the purpose of selling drugs. They find that gangs' involvement in drug distribution is well organized and provides the primary motivation for membership, and that many gangs in California effectively control the drug markets in their territory. These authors distinguish between "entrepreneurial gangs and what they refer to as "cultural gangs," or territorially based neighborhood gangs. Cultural gangs are involved only casually in street drug sales: these gangs use violence to maintain their identity in the neighborhood, primarily against rival gangs for expressive purposes.

The entrepreneurial gangs, found mostly in northern California and among black gangs in Los Angeles, have a much stronger commitment to street drug sales. In fact, this involvement is their reason for existing, and the motivation for individuals to join the gang. Skolnick et al. argue that many of these gangs are "organized solely for the purpose of distributing drugs" (1988:4). The gang offers many rational advantages to individuals interested in selling drugs, including protection, a controlled territory in which to sell, rules that proscribe turning in a fellow gang member, and a wealth of market information. Members of these gangs perceive membership to be permanent, and see themselves as "organized criminals." These findings are consistent with the view of gangs as formal-rational organizations.

Sanchez-Jankowski (1991) depicts gangs as well-organized groups with strongly held group goals. In a study based on 10 years of field work with 37 gangs representing six different ethnic groups in three cities, he describes gangs as highly structured organizations. Although they are composed of "defiant individualists" (1991:23), Sanchez-Jankowski describes gangs as highly rational organizations with formal leadership structures, roles, codes of conduct, and specific duties. In keeping with this description, he argues that gangs have collective economic goals and that members contribute time and effort toward these goals. These efforts result in the creation of capital to pursue both legal and illegal commodities. Drug sales play a primary role in such pursuits, and consequently are well organized and effectively managed. This effective management is evident in the collective use of the profits from drug sales for gang purposes.

Support for the Sanchez-Jankowski and Skolnick view is found in Taylor's (1990, 1991) fieldwork with Detroit gangs. Taylor identified three types of gangs: 1) scavenger, 2) territorial, and 3) corporate. The corporate gangs were well organized, with effective leaders and widely shared group goals. They had evolved from less well-organized structures into what Taylor called the "big leagues" (1990:99) of drug distribution. Members of these gangs operated drug sales like a business.[1] According to Taylor, the key to understanding the evolution of gangs from relatively disorganized neighborhood groups to their highly structured state was the level of organization they had attained. Effective drug distribution requires strong leadership, commitment to organizational goals, and powerful rewards. Taylor found that corporate gangs possessed all of these attributes.

Mieczkowski (1986) studied the heroin distribution network of Young Boys Incorporated (YBI), a black gang in Detroit. Using the results of a field study of 15 gang members, Mieczkowski characterized heroin street sales as a rational enterprise conducted by a highly organized gang. The sales were coordinated by a leader, who enforced a system of discipline based on rules generally accepted by all members of the gang. Individuals were recruited specifically to sell heroin, held clear-cut roles in the distribution network, and operated within a "bureaucratic" structure. Similarly, Padilla characterized drug sales by Puerto Rican gangs in Chicago as an "ethnic enterprise" (1992:3). On the basis of the results of a year-long ethnography, he found that the viability of the gangs he studied depended on their ability to make money. Padilla discovered specific criminal roles in the gang, the most prestigious of which was street dealing. Large capital was not accumulated, however, and gang members generally used the profits from drug sales to support individual commodity needs.

The image of gangs as well-organized groups sharing common goals in the sale of drugs contrasts sharply with the findings of Klein et al. (1991) and Reiner (1992). These authors argue that gangs lack the organizational structure and the commitment to common goals to be successful in drug sales. In an extensive report, Reiner (then District Attorney of Los Angeles County) notes that gangs fail to control drug sales effectively in Los Angeles because of their disorganized and loosely confederated structure:

> In truth, traditional street gangs are not well suited for drug distribution or any other businesslike activity. They are weakly organized, prone to unnecessary and unproductive violence, and full of brash, conspicuous, untrustworthy individuals who draw unwanted police attention. For all these reasons, big drug operators—those who turn to drug dealing as a serious career—typically deemphasize gang activity or leave altogether (Reiner 1992:97).

Klein et al. (1991) used police arrest records from five Los Angeles-area police stations to examine the differences between crack sales involving gang members and nongang members. They were interested in several specific hypotheses, particularly that crack increased the control of drug markets by gangs, and that increases in violence were linked to gang members' disproportionate involvement in crack sales. They found no support for either of these contentions, and emphasized that each was based on a conception of the nature of gang organizational structure and social processes which disagreed with the sociological literature on gangs. Central to their concerns were the consistent lack of an effective organizational structure within gangs, the absence of permanent membership or roles, and the lack of shared goals. Gang crack sales were more likely than non-gang transactions to occur on the street, to involve firearms, to include younger suspects, and to disproportionately involve black suspects. Most of these differences were small, however. Klein et al. (1991) concluded by noting that gang membership added little which was distinctive to street drug sales; although the problems associated with gangs and with drug sales intersected, they were not a single problem (1991:635).

One of the dilemmas in using data either from inmates or from police files is that they have undergone a considerable filtering process. In an attempt to meet this criticism, a number of researchers have interviewed gang members directly. In 1984 and 1985, Fagan (1989) interviewed 151 gang members through a snowball sampling procedure in high-crime neighborhoods in Los Angeles, Chicago, and San Diego. In general, gang members reported lower levels of drug sales than nongang members, especially in comparison with their levels of participation in other forms of crime. These findings support the contention that selling drugs is not the primary motivation for joining the gang, nor is it the primary outlet for gang activities. On the basis of the nature of their activities, Fagan offered four topologies of gangs. For two of the types, social gangs and serious delinquents, drug sales were not a primary activity. Taken together, these gangs accounted for nearly two-thirds of the individuals interviewed. For party gangs and emerging organizations, however, drug sales were a major focus of activity. Party gangs, despite their involvement in drug sales, lacked structure, rules, and roles, elements considered essential for the control of drug markets and found among serious delinquents and emerging organizations. Fagan concluded by noting that gang life, regardless of type, is characterized by "informal social processes" and provides an opportunity to "hang out" more than a formal structure within which to make money.

Sheley, Shang, and Wright (1993) analyzed the results of a survey completed by 381 self-identified male gang member prison inmates in California, Illinois, Louisiana, and New Jersey and 835 male gang members in six juvenile facilities in those states. They developed typologies of gangs based on their level of organization, and identified three types: 1) quasi-gangs, 2) unstructured gangs, and 3) structured gangs. In keeping with the results of Fagan (1989) and Klein et al. (1991), Sheley et al. argued that informal group processes dominate gang activities, including involvement in drug sales. Indeed, they found no difference among the gang types in gang members' or gangs' involvement in drug sales.

Hagedorn (1988), who interviewed 47 gang members from 19 of Milwaukee's largest gangs, characterized gangs as dynamic, evolving associations of adolescents and men. In general, he observed, gangs lacked formal roles and effective organizational structures for achieving consensus among members regarding goals or techniques for achieving those goals. Hustling (including street drug sales) was seldom well organized because gangs lacked the structure to control their members effectively. Only about one-half of the members sold drugs, and the proceeds of such sales provided only modest income. In updating that research, Hagedorn (1994) obtained similar results. The gang leaders he had interviewed in the 1980s remained involved in the sale of drugs, and still did so in a fashion consistent with their earlier involvement.

In a study of urban drug sales and the effect of the underground economy on licit work, Fagan (1992) examined the drug market in two distressed New York neighborhoods. Using chain referral sampling techniques, he recruited 1,003 subjects from a variety of sources in an attempt to create a sample broadly representative of drug arrestees. Most drug sales were relatively disorganized: groups of individuals involved in street drug sales (primarily crack cocaine) had little structure and operated informally.

The money earned from drug sales was used for short-term concerns, was given to family members, or was spent on items of food, clothing, or gifts for women. Fagan concluded by noting that drug sales had become institutionalized, but few of his findings support the argument that drug selling has become a formal role for specific individuals.

Drug-selling organizations evidently are haphazard, ad hoc groups that may represent a decentralized distribution system more accurately than a coherent, formal, or lasting organization. Even when such groups or crews do form, they are likely to be temporary (Williams 1989) or to have shifting at the lower ranks (Fagan 1992:116).

Because only a relatively small percentage of the general population engages in criminal acts and because the admission of criminal involvement in response to survey questions creates concerns about validity, field studies have been used more frequently than surveys to study gang members. One exception, however, is the work of

Esbensen and Huizinga (1993). Using data from the Denver Youth Survey, a longitudinal study of families and youths, these authors obtained data on the involvement of gang and nongang members in a number of illegal activities. By aggregating four years of data, they achieved acceptable sample sizes for self-reported gang members. In general, gang members (both male and female) could be distinguished from nongang members by the increased prevalence and incidence of their criminal behaviors. Gang members had significantly higher prevalence scores for drug sales than nongang members (.29 to .03), whereas nongang members had higher "individual offending rates" (30.5 to 22.8) for their involvement in drug sales. These results suggest that more gang members sell drugs than do their nongang counterparts, but that gang involvement in street drug sales does not increase the frequency of sales. Also, Esbensen and Huizinga characterized gangs as informal organizations lacking structure. Indeed, the definitions of a gang varied considerably across members of the sample. Finally, most gang members reported that membership in their gang was of relatively short duration, typically about a year.

Despite the diversity of methods employed, this second group of studies provides a rather consistent picture of the role of gangs and gang members in drug sales. Their conclusions are unlike those of Sanchez-Jankowski, Skolnick, Mieczkowski, Padilla, and Taylor, who argue that gangs bring a high level of organization to drug sales. Yet despite the evidence to the contrary, many public officials, especially those in law enforcement (NIJ 1993), continue to express the belief that gang involvement in drug sales more closely resembles the model presented by Sanchez-Janowski.

In an effort to address this issue more directly, we examine the nature of gang involvement in street drug sales, using the results of a three-year field study of gang members. Certainly it is useful to examine police records, and valuable to learn from gang members in institutions such as prisons and schools. Our procedure, however, offers insight into the lives of active gang members, a perspective underrepresented in the current debate about the role of gangs and gang members in drug sales.

Research Questions

The literature review suggests several areas to examine in attempting to determine the nature of gangs' involvement in drug sales. These can be organized around three primary questions. First, we wish to learn how extensively gang members are involved in drug sales. Much of the research reviewed above suggests that gang members are involved substantially. Thus our first goal is to document the extent of that involvement by exploring three specific questions. If street gangs exist primarily to generate profits from drug sales, this purpose should be reflected in the process by which individuals come to join the gang and in the expectations for membership in the gang. This can be determined by asking a variety of questions, including the following:

Was the decision to join the gang motivated by a desire to participate in drug sales?

Is each gang member expected to sell a certain quantity of drugs?

Do all members of the gang engage in drug sales?

Our second concern is to provide a description of the organization of drug sales by gang members. An effective organizational structure would be necessary to sustain continuous, successful sales and distribution of profits. Gangs with a vertical organization or hierarchy would be more likely to conduct effective drug sales than horizontally organized or balkanized gangs. Evidence of such a structure could be observed in a variety of mechanisms, as reflected in these questions:

Are specific roles involved in the sale of drugs?

Do gangs have leaders? If so, do they assume that role on the basis of their expertise in drug sales?

How is the supply of drugs generated?

Do gangs control street drug sales effectively?

Finally, we wish to examine the extent to which common goals exist within the gang. Organizations with common goals held strongly by their members should be able to organize drug sales. Specifically, we are interested in knowing whether the profits from drug sales are spent for group or for individual purposes.

Does the gang have goals shared by most members?

Is the money generated from drug sales used primarily for gang purposes?

Is the money generated from drug sales used primarily by individuals for their own purposes?

Data and Methods

Data for this study come from a three-year field study of gangs conducted in St. Louis from October 1990 through September 1993. We chose to use field techniques, contacting gang members directly in the community and conducting interviews at a neutral site.[2] In this way we sought to learn about drug sales (and other matters) in the words and terms that gang members themselves used to describe them.

Our working definition of a gang is an age-graded peer group that exhibits permanence, engages in criminal activity, and has symbolic representations of membership. This definition is broad enough to include a wide assortment of potential gangs and gang members, ranging from the least organized streetcorner groups to highly organized drug gangs. Contacts were made with active gang members by a street ethnographer who verified membership and observed gang activity in neighborhoods. The ethnographer, an exoffender himself, had built a reputation as "solid" on the street, both through work in the community and in previous research (Wright and Decker 1994). Using snowball sampling procedures (Biernacki and Waldorf 1981; Wright, et al., 1992), we made initial field contacts with gang members and built the sample to include more subjects. As is the case with most field studies, the pace of our study was erratic: some months were characterized by frequent interviews, while in others we held no interviews as we attempted to extend our chain of respondents to new gangs and new locations in the city.

Individuals who met our criteria, acknowledged membership, and agreed to an interview were included in our sample. Membership was verified by information from previous subjects, by our own observations, or both. A number of contacts—often as many as eight to 10—were necessary to generate a single interview. We used a semistructured questionnaire to guide our interviews; it was based on a number of unstructured interviews conducted before the beginning of the study. Interviews lasted approximately two hours, and requested information about several domains of gang membership and activity. We sought information about joining the gang, the nature of gang organization, illegal activities, legal activities, links to other gangs, ties to traditional institutions, and the bond between gang members and their families. In addition to the interviews, we made a number of observations of gang activities and individual gang members. We were able to observe the entire gang only on relatively few occasions; most often, subgroups of four to 10 members were observed. To supplement the semistructured interviews, we talked frequently with these groups. Such observations and conversations occurred regularly, at least four times per week during the course of our study.

One concern throughout our study was the dynamic nature of the gang situation in St. Louis. According to accounts by police and social service agencies, as well as our own observations, gangs in that city began to expand in size and increase in number in the mid-1980s. When our study "hit the field" two years later, we were constantly aware of the need to understand how the gang situation changed as the study proceeded. We used several procedures for this purpose. First, our questionnaire included items asking each gang member to describe how his gang specifically and the gang scene in St. Louis generally had changed over the last year. Second, we compared the responses of gang members from the early part of our fieldwork to those we interviewed later. Finally, we were able to recontact several of the early members of our sample at a later stage in the study. If gangs are evolving organizations, our findings may reflect their status in an early stage. Where we observed changes, they are noted in the findings.

Gangs in St. Louis generally have a strong orientation to their neighborhood, but also claim affiliation to a larger gang that extends well beyond neighborhood boundaries. The bond between gang members and their local subgroup was generally stronger than to the larger gang. In all, we interviewed 99 currently active gang members representing 29 different gangs. Sixteen of these gangs were affiliated with the Crip name, and represented 67 of our 99 respondents. The remainder (13 gangs that included 32 members) were affiliated with the Bloods. Members of our sample came from six different "constellations" of these gangs (four within the Crip designation and two groups of Bloods); we use the term *constellation* to refer to the larger gang, which may be composed of many subgroups. Thus, for example, the "Genevieve Thrush Posse" is affiliated with the Rolling Sixties, a larger gang of Crips. Our sample is quite diverse, representing the views of a number of different gangs and gang members.

Respondents ranged in age from 13 to 29, with an average age of 17. Most were black (96%) and male (93%). On average, the gang members we interviewed had been active members for three years. Most respondents reported that their gang existed before they joined; the average age of gangs in our sample was six years. The average number of gang members involved in the larger gang was 213; subgroups ranged from six to 10 members. Members of our sample had extensive involvement in criminality: more than 70 percent reported committing a property crime and 90 percent reported participating in violence. Thus, it is not surprising that our subjects also had extensive experience with the criminal justice system: 80 percent reported an arrest.

Our work is consistent with other research (Hagedorn 1988, 1991; Moore 1978, 1991; Padilla 1992; Vigil 1988) that seeks to understand gang members' perspective by recruiting them directly on the streets of their neighborhoods without filtering by official agencies. Three features, however, distinguish our work from many other studies. First, we used no criminal justice contacts in gaining access to the members of our sample. We felt strongly that employing criminal justice channels (e.g., police, courts, probation) to contact gang members would lead us to a very different kind of gang member than we could find in the field. Second, we depended on the gang members themselves to tell their story. Although we used an interview instrument, we wanted to be sure that their concerns and insights informed our study. Third, because this was a field study of gangs, we did not conduct the study in the offices of a social service or youth agency. All of our participants were contacted initially in the neighborhoods where they lived and engaged in their gang activities. Throughout we were able to maintain our commitment to all of these features of our study.

Findings

One of the most difficult issues in studying gangs is distinguishing between the activities of individual gang members and those of the gang (Short 1985). Short distinguishes between large aggregations (such as gangs), smaller aggregations of individuals (such as gang subgroups), and individuals. Our results show that these distinctions are important, and that gang membership is not a "master status" in the sense that it controls an individual gang member's behavior. Rather, individual gang members often act on their own or in subgroups outside the gang; this distinction applies to members' noncriminal and criminal activities, including drug sales. Accordingly, it is possible for an individual gang member to sell drugs outside the structure or influence of his gang or subgroup. At the other extreme, gangs may effectively control drug sales by subgroups and individuals. Determining the extent of control is the primary focus of this paper.

Almost all members of our sample (95%) reported having sold drugs at some time in their lives. This finding makes our sample similar to that reported by Fagan (1992). The primary drug sold by the gang members was crack cocaine; little marijuana or heroin was sold. As other investigators have reported, crack cocaine has virtually driven other drugs off the market. Despite the ready availability of crack, few gang members reported using the drug, but used marijuana regularly.

Nature of Involvement

We are concerned first with establishing the extent of gang members' involvement in drug sales. Greater involvement would be consistent with the position of those who argue that drug sales are an integral part of gang activities. The data addressing this issue are presented in Table 4.1.

Table 4.1
Nature of Involvement in the Gang

	Frequency	Percentage
Why did you join the gang?		
Individual Interest	17	17%
Relative	14	14%
Friend	14	14%
Protection	14	14%
Grew Up in Gang	14	14%
Other	9	9%
Status	8	8%
Material Gain	6	6%
Curiosity	1	1%
Refused to Answer	2	2%
Did you join the gang for an opportunity to sell drugs?		
Yes	15	16%
No	77	84%
Is each gang member expected to sell a certain amount of drugs?		
Yes	18	21%
No	68	79%
How many gang members are involved in drug sales?		
All	24	27%
Most	38	43%
Half	5	6%
Fewer Than Half	19	22%
None	2	2%

We first examine the reasons our respondents gave as most important for joining their gang. The responses with the largest frequencies—individual interest, relatives or friends in the gang, protection, or growing up in the gang—do not reflect the monetary benefits of gang membership.[3] Rather, all of these reasons are consistent with a view of the gang as a neighborhood-based friendship group composed of members who know each other, which develops in response to the threat of gangs in rival neighborhoods. Only six members of the sample stated that the desire for material gain was the most important reason for joining the gang, far fewer than for the other categories. Even if we acknowledge that the decision to join a gang may be motivated by many reasons, it is still significant that monetary gain—specifically through drug selling—was seldom chosen by members of our sample. Only 15 of our respondents told us that this was an important reason; the great majority did not acknowledge drug sales as an important reason to join the gang. For most gang members, drug sales were simply part of a larger overall set of activities pursued with other gang members.

Interviewer: What kind of things do members of your gang do together? Legal and illegal things.

004: Go to dances, go to parties, sell drugs together, beat up people together, rob people together, stuff life that.[4]

Indeed, a number of the individuals in our sample acknowledged that it was generally unnecessary to belong to a gang to be involved in drug sales. Two gang members stated that their brothers were involved in selling drugs, but found it unnecessary to belong to a gang.

Int: Is your younger brother in the gang?

001: He say he don't wanna be in no gang. He say he just wanna sell drugs.

Int: Were any of your brothers in the gang before you were?

002: Naw. My brother was always dope dealer, just he didn't really like gangs . . . he just, he sell dope and stuff like that, I mean he party wit us, into shootin and all that . . . but he didn't really, really run wit a gang, he was his own self.

If drug sales are an integral part of gang life, it is likely that all members will be expected to participate. We addressed this issue directly by asking individuals whether their gang expected members to make a certain amount of drug sales. In agreement with the evidence reviewed above, most gang members stated that their gang did not require members to sell a specified amount of drugs. Indeed, only about one in five said that this was the case in their gang. The informal character of street drug sales within gangs is illustrated by the following quotes, which support the distribution of responses presented in Table 4.1.

Int: So you guys don't sell drugs as a group; you don't require people to sell drugs?

003: No. We do it ourselves. If we short on money and wanna make some money, we just go in the lane and talk to this guy . . . and get anything we want.

Int: Is each gang member expected to sell drugs?

043: No. We can't force a person, they do what they want to do.

These responses make it clear that gangs did not generally require their members to sell drugs, a situation that varied little throughout the three years of our study. Most subjects told us that at least half of the members of their gang sold drugs. These findings suggest that drug sales by gang members are common, but that the gang does not play a central role. "Making money" or "selling drugs," however, was cited by nearly half of our subjects as good reasons for belonging to their gang. Once they joined, they viewed participation in drug sales as more important than before they joined.

The distinction between drug sales as a reason to join the gang and drug sales as a gang activity is important; it points to the role of group process within the gang. Few members joined the gang or were recruited specifically to sell drugs. Once in the gang, however, they regarded the opportunities to make money and engage in collective activities with other gang members as positive features of membership. Our results support the view that although gang membership facilitates drug sales, it does little to attract new members.

In sum, few gang members joined their gang for an opportunity to sell drugs; instead they chose to affiliate themselves with the gang for more expressive reasons pertaining to prior associations in the neighborhood. Though three-quarters of the respondents told us that half or more of the members were involved in selling drugs, it was not required as a condition of membership. Also, we found no evidence that new members were recruited because of their entrepreneurial skills.

Organization of Drug Sales

A second set of questions seeks to determine how gangs organize drug sales (see Table 4.2). To examine this, we explore the roles in selling drugs. The majority of respondents (58%) could not identify any specific roles in drug sales played by members of the gang. This finding did not change during the course of our study. Among those who did identify a role, however, the modal category was "seller," hardly evidence of a highly structured or rational organization. The most significant finding in Table 4.2 is the lack of role specification in drug sales.

Int: What kinds of different jobs do they do? Watchers?

005: No, everybody just out to make their money. They run out there like idiots instead of having a plan. They run out there try to be fools.

Table 4.2
Organization of Drug Sales

	Frequency	Percentage
What are the roles in selling drugs?		
Seller	27	27%
Lookout	11	11%
Runner	4	4%
None Identified	57	58%
Are there leaders in the gang?		
Yes	49	51%
No	48	49%
Are the main suppliers of drugs leaders in the gang?		
Yes	33	33%
No	43	43%
Don't Know	23	23%
Does selling drugs in the gang increase a member's influence?		
Yes	50	59%
No	35	41%

Our respondents were so unfamiliar with specific roles that several of them mistook our questions about jobs to mean legitimate employment.

Int: Do people who sell them have different jobs? Do they organize it as a group?

011: They have jobs. Most of them have McDonald's or something like that.

Int: I mean when they sell drugs. You said mostly when they sell drugs, they sell by themselves?

011: Yeah, they ain't selling in no group, they selling like first come first serve. If one person don't have no drugs, they will send them on to the next person. They really got their own customers (Lisa).

Others thought we meant specific areas rather than specific jobs.

Int: Did you guys divide up the jobs in selling drugs?

018: Yeah, we divide up the sets. You can be over here and I can be over there.

Int: But everybody sells drugs themselves?

018: Yeah.

Int: What are the different jobs involved in selling drugs? Do you have lookouts, or is it every man for himself, or what?

033: You go look out. Everybody standing on the corner. Most of the time nobody don't have no dope on them. They lay it down, it be all the way across the street up by somebody's front door. It never be around where we stand at. I cut a hole like this, I cut a hole right here and put some little rocks in there. They never suspect that (Smith and Wesson).

Int: Do you guys divide up the jobs when you sell it?

057: No, when you sell dope, you sell dope. Somebody might front you some so you can sell some more.

Several respondents, however, told us that different jobs were involved in selling drugs, though none of them required special training, were held by a single individual, or were of any permanence. In sum, the different jobs reflect the disorganized, informal nature of gang members' involvement in drug sales.

Int: What are the different jobs in selling drugs?

019: Records, salesmen, muscles, same as a legal business.

Int: What are the different jobs in selling drugs?

040: Distribution, street hustlers, and the rock up man and the PP, pistol packer (Knowledge).

Int: What are the different jobs in selling drugs? Do you guys have lookouts?

058: Yeah, we got some people hold it, some people sell, some people get the money (Roach).

These responses demonstrate two important findings about roles in drug sales. First, few respondents could identify well-defined roles in the sale of drugs by members of their gang. Second, the responses to questions about roles were quite diverse; often they elicited answers unrelated to roles, such as a discussion of the importance of turf or jobs in the legitimate economy. In sum, these responses support the contention that drug sales by gang members lack formal roles and are not well organized.

The gang members we interviewed were divided evenly as to whether there were leaders in their gang. Half of the sample stated that their gang lacked leaders, suggesting that the level of organization and leadership in their gang was not very high. Without a leader, it would be difficult for gangs to coordinate drug sales effectively. Further evidence of the "disorganized" nature of gang involvement in drug sales is found in responses to questions about the main suppliers of drugs. The modal response was that the leaders in the gang did not provide drugs.

> Int: The guy who supplies you with the drugs, is he a leader in the group?
>
> 028: No, he ain't even a Crip, he ain't nothing. He just sells dope (Killa 4 Ren).

About one-third of the respondents said that the leaders provided drugs, but about one-quarter told us that they didn't know where the gang got its drugs. Even when large suppliers had apparent gang connections, these connections become less organized or less "formal-rational" on closer inspection. One gang, for example, obtained its drug supply from a "California drug seller" who happened to be the uncle of a gang member.

> Int: Where are you guys getting that stuff [large supplies of cocaine that is rocked up into crack] from?
>
> 012: From California.
>
> Int: So you got hooked up with some gang for drugs?
>
> 012: Well like this dude uncle, he sell dope in California. He drive up there and get some and drive back.

A majority of gang members told us that selling drugs increased a member's influence in the gang. That influence, however, was most often due to the availability of money for immediate gratification (parties, alcohol, or women), not to the status of drug sales or the ability to produce revenue for the gang.

Gangs do not completely control street drug sales in their own neighborhoods. The presence of local, nongang drug sellers was mentioned quite often; this competition was tolerated as long as it was not direct. Seventy-one subjects said there were drug houses in their neighborhood, though these were seldom operated by gangs. Gang members in general had little to do with drug house proprietors and customers. Competition for customers exists; it was acknowledged by half of the respondents. It was not always intense, however, and sometimes it existed between members of the same gang, especially when a gang member tried to entice customers away from another seller or to cut in front of fellow members. Nevertheless, serious and violent conflicts arise from competition over drug sales turf. Forty-three subjects said that fights occurred over drug customer turf, usually precipitated by rival gang members' incursions onto neighborhood turf.

Common Goals

The final set of questions concerns the extent to which common goals exist among gang members (see Table 4.3). We explore this issue by examining the activities gang members pursue most often together, as well as the uses for the profits from drug sales. The modal gang activity was "hanging out," reported by 39 percent of our respondents. Fighting was the next most frequent activity, reported by just over one gang member in five. Drug sales accounted for the third largest category, though only 12 percent of the sample members gave this response. The remainder included a wide range of activities typical of adolescent males. Clearly, most gang members were involved in noncriminal activities characteristic of young males for whom street culture is a focal concern.

A crucial aspect of any organized entrepreneurial activity is what happens to the profits. If street gangs organize and control drug sales, it is reasonable to assume that some fraction of their profits are reinvested into the gang. Such profits may be used to purchase more drugs ("recop," as it is called) or to buy commodities needed by the gang, such as guns, houses, cars, or legitimate business fronts. Nearly half of our respondents indicated that some of the profits from drug sales went to the gang, but in most cases these gang activities were parties; a few subjects mentioned purchases of weapons.

Most gang members told us that they used the money from drug sales for personal reasons. Nearly two-thirds stated that they used the profits to buy clothes. Only four reported that they used the profits to purchase more drugs.

Int: How did you spend the money that you made selling drugs?

038: Clothes, gold tooth in my mouth, buying my kids stuff.

Int: What were you doing with the money?

015: Going crazy buying Nintendos and toys and VCRs and clothes.

Table 4.3
Common Goals among Gang Members

	Frequency	Percentage
What activites do you do the most with gang members?		
Hang Out	35	39%
Fights	19	21%
Sell Drugs	11	12%
Drink Beer	8	9%
Sports	6	7%
Dances	4	4%
Cruising	2	2%
Look for Women	2	2%
Do Drugs	2	2%
Parties	1	1%
Do any of the profits from drug sales go to the gang?		
Yes	47	58%
No	34	42%
How do you spend the money you make from selling drugs?		
Buy Clothes	45	65%
Spend on My Kids	3	4%
Buy a Car	4	6%
Spend on Women	1	1%
Give Some to Family	2	3%
Give to Other Members' Family	1	1%
Save at Home	7	10%
Save in Bank	1	1%
Buy More Drugs	4	6%
Buy Furniture	1	1%

"Shortdog," a gang member very active in drug sales, was pressed to tell how he used the considerable money he made from drug sales. Despite our prompts, he maintained that clothes were the primary outlet for his profits.

Int: How do you spend the money you make selling drugs?

067: I got me two golds [teeth] and I got me some clothes.

Int: Do you buy guns?

067: No. Clothes.

Int: Do you guys ever pool any of the money that you make selling drugs for the whole gang, for the whole set?

067: No ($hortdog).

Conclusions

Using a sample of 99 active gang members recruited through field-based snowball sampling methods, we examined the role of gang members in drug sales. We asked three sets of questions to determine the nature of gang involvement in drug sales: 1) the extent to which gang membership revolved around drug sales, 2) the organization of drug sales within the gang, and 3) the existence of a common goal within the gang. Our results unequivocally support the conclusion that the involvement of gangs in drug sales does not affect recruitment, lacks organization, and fails to produce commitment to a central goal.

Skolnick et al. (1988:3) and others suggest that the instrumental benefits of drug sales act as a powerful magnet, attracting potential members to the gang and leading to well-coordinated drug sales. Our results, however, suggest that the reasons for joining are more expressive, reflecting the group process of neighborhood networks and friendships. Consequently, the extent of involvement, the level of organization, and the use of profits from drug sales remain consistent with the view of Klein et al. (1991) and Fagan (1989), namely that gangs' involvement in street drug sales reflects their loose organizational structure.

The common theme that unites these findings points to the group processes involved in gang membership and the strength of the ties that bind members to their gangs. In general, the gangs we studied were loosely confederated associations of young men and women united through shared expressive concerns about protection of turf, reputation, and threats to their own safety or that of other gang members. Commitments to instrumental concerns were expressed only with regard to pursuits of more immediate gratification such as obtaining money for clothes or parties.

This view of gang structure and activity is consistent with findings from a number of different cities, for different ethnic groups, and based on different research strategies (Hagedorn 1988; Klein 1971; Klein and Maxson 1994; Miller 1958; Moore 1978, Sanders 1994; Short and Strodtbeck 1974, Vigil 1988). Indeed, as others have suggested (Klein et al. 1991; Reiner 1992), the gang is unsuited for the tasks of building consensus among its members and organizing their activities, characteristics essential for a business operation. To a great extent, this is the case because most gang members are focused on short-term needs, to the virtual exclusion of long-term concerns. Because gangs in St. Louis lacked effective organizational structures and collective goals, they were unable to control drug sales among their members. These shortcomings also would prevent gangs from effectively organizing other profit-making ventures such as burglary, robbery, or auto theft.

The differences between Skolnick's results and ours may be due to the nature of the two samples. Our data come from a city where gangs have reemerged in the last 10 years; in contrast, gangs in California, the source of Skolnick's data, have been active since the turn of the century. Further, his respondents were drawn from four California state correctional institutions. On the one hand, it may be that the more seriously criminally involved gang members go to prison, and Skolnick's results thus may reflect the involvement of a more serious group of gang members. It is also possible that prison gangs are more highly organized than street gangs. On the other hand, interviews conducted in prison may result in outcomes that would not occur on the street. As Moore (1990:172) noted, distortions are inevitable when interviews are conducted in prisons. Cromwell, Olson, and Avery (1991) argue that offenders in prison often present "rational reconstructions" of past events, and that interviews conducted outside the social context in which they occur (the street) assume a rational character. Hagedorn (1991) makes this point more strongly, stating that the perspectives of imprisoned gang members provide more information about prison gangs than about neighborhood gangs.

One key to understanding street drug sales lies in understanding the market. The urban drug market is primarily a crack market; its customers are not involved in the organized networks that characterize the distribution of other drugs. Crack users generally lead disorganized lives, and their need for the drug is powerful. Often it results in "crack runs," periods of intense use. Users' desire for the drug creates demand for a market that provides easy, open access for its customers. As MacCoun and Reuter (1992) demonstrated, street-level drug dealing is a sporadic occupation, used to supplement other sources of income. Such markets are more likely to be served by the loosely organized gang members (among others) engaged only episodically in selling drugs than by members of well-organized, persistent groups.

References

Biernacki, P. and D. Waldorf (1981) "Snowball Sampling: Problems and Techniques of Chain Referral Sampling." *Sociological Methods and Research* 10:141–63.

Cromwell, P., J. Olson, and D. Avery (1991) *Breaking and Entering*. Beverly Hills: Sage.

Esbensen, F. and D. Huizinga (1993) "Gangs, Drugs and Delinquency in a Survey of Urban Youth." *Criminology* 31:565–90.

Fagan, J. (1989) "The Social Organization of Drug Use and Drug Dealing among Urban Gangs." *Criminology* 27:633–69.

———. (1992) "Drug Selling and Licit Income in Distressed Neighborhoods: The Economic Lives of Street-Level Drug Users and Dealers." In A. Harrell and G. Peterson (eds.), *Drugs, Crime and Social Isolation*, pp. 99–146. Washington, DC: Urban Institute Press.

Hagedorn, J. (1988) *People and Folks*. Chicago: Lake View Press.

———. (1991) "Back in the Field Again: Gang Research in the Nineties." In R. Huff (ed.), *Gangs in America*, pp. 240–59. Newbury Park, CA: Sage.

———. (1994) "Homeboys, Dope Fiends, Legits, and New Jacks." *Criminology* 32:197–220.

Klein, M. (1971) *Street Gangs and Street Workers*. Englewood Cliffs, NJ: Prentice-Hall.

Klein, M. and C. Maxson (1994) "Gangs and Cocaine Trafficking." In D. MacKenzie and C. Uchida (eds.), *Drugs and Crime: Evaluating Public Policy Initiatives*, pp. 42–58. Thousand Oaks, CA: Sage.

Klein, M., C. Maxson, and L. Cunningham (1991) "Crack, Street Gangs, and Violence." *Criminology* 29:623–50.

MacCoun, R. and P. Reuter (1992) "Are the Wages of Sin $30 an Hour?: Economic Aspects of Street-Level Drug Dealing." *Crime and Delinquency* 38:477–91.

Mieczkowski, T. (1986) "Geeking Up and Throwing Down: Heroin Street Life in Detroit." *Criminology* 24:645–66.

Miller, W. (1958) "Lower Class Culture as a Generating Milieu of Gang Delinquency." *Journal of Social Issues* 14:5–19.

Moore, J. (1978) *Homeboys: Gangs, Drugs and Prison in the Barrios of Los Angeles*. Philadelphia: Temple University Press.

———. (1990) "Gangs, Drugs and Violence." In M. De La Rosa, E. Lambert, and B. Gropper (eds.), *Drugs and Violence: Causes, Correlates and Consequences*, pp. 160–76. Washington, DC: National Institute on Drug Abuse.

———. (1991) *Going Down to the Barrio: Homeboys and Homegirls in Change*. Philadelphia: Temple University Press.

National Institute of Justice (1993) *NIJ Program Plan*. Washington, DC: U.S. Department of Justice.

Padilla, F. (1992) *The Gang as an American Enterprise*. New Brunswick: Rutgers University Press.

Reiner, I. (1992) *Gangs, Crime and Violence in Los Angeles*. County of Los Angeles: Office of the District Attorney.

Sanchez-Jankowski, M. (1991) *Islands in the Street*. Berkeley: University of California Press.

Sanders, W. (1994) *Gang Bangs and Drive-Bys: Grounded Culture and Juvenile Gang Violence*. New York: Aldine.

Sheeley, J., J. Shang, and J. Wright (1993) "Gang Organization, Routine Criminal Activity, and Gang Members' Criminal Behavior." Report to the National Institute of Justice and the Office of Juvenile Justice and Delinquency Prevention, City.

Short, J. (1974) "Collective Behavior, Crime and Delinquency." In D. Glaser (ed.), *Handbook of Criminology*, pp. 403–49. New York: Rand McNally.

———. (1985) "The Level of Explanation Problem." In R. Meier (ed.), *Theoretical Methods in Criminology*, pp. 51–72. Beverly Hills: Sage.

Short, J. and F. Strodtbeck (1974) *Group Process and Gang Delinquency*. Chicago: University of Chicago Press.

Skolnick, J. (1990) "The Social Structure of Street Drug Dealing." *American Journal of Police* 9:1–41.

Skolnick, J., T. Correl, E. Navarro, and R. Robb (1988) "The Social Structure of Street Drug Dealing." *BCS Forum*. Sacramento Office of the Attorney General, State of California.

Taylor, C. (1990) *Dangerous Society*. East Lansing: Michigan State University Press.

———. (1991) "Gang Imperialism." In R. Huff (ed.), *Gangs in America*, pp. 103–15. Newbury Park, CA: Sage.

Vigil, J. (1988) *Barrio Gangs*. Austin: University of Texas Press.

Williams, Terry (1989) *The Cocaine Kids: The Inside Story of a Teenage Drug Ring*. Reading, MA: Addison-Wesley.

Wright, R. and S. Decker (1994) *Burglars on the Job: Streetlife and Residential Burglary*. Boston: Northeastern University Press.

Wright, R., S. Decker, A. Redfern, and D. Smith (1992) "A Snowball's Chance in Hell: Doing Field Research with Active Offenders." *Journal of Research in Crime and Delinquency* 29:148–61.

Notes

[1] Indeed, Taylor uses the analogy of Fortune 500 companies in discussing how drug sales are organized by corporate gangs.

[2] Each gang member was transported to and from the interview site by the street ethnographer. This occasion offered the opportunity to speak informally about gang and nongang matters. It also provided an opportunity to discuss the nature of the interview, both before and after it was administered. Many of the most interesting insights gained from the study came from this part of the research process.

[3] Subjects were presented with a list of reasons why some people might want to join a gang, and were instructed to choose as many as applied to their decision.

[4] Subjects are identified by an interview number and by their gang name, when it was provided.

Section II

Justice and Injustice in the Streets: The Police

The role of the police in American society is one of the least understood aspects of the criminal justice system. Philosophical conflicts in the field of criminal justice are personified in the police officer. Handcuffed, according to crime control groups; riotous and corrupt, according to due process groups, the police officer finds that the role he or she must play in the criminal justice system is wrought with conflicting expectations.

There are a variety of issues which contribute to the conflict and confusion in law enforcement. While most would agree that the police mission is to achieve "order under law," it is not always easy to apply this abstract concept to street situations. The officer does not have a lawyer by his or her side when making the decision to arrest a suspect who may have been involved in a crime. The officer may feel that probable cause exists for an arrest. However, in the days following the arrest, made perhaps in a crowded tavern after a fight in which the officer was injured, the decision will be subjected to intense scrutiny.

There are a variety of situations in which the legal basis for a decision to arrest is not always clear. In these situations the officer exercises considerable discretion. The authority to search, to arrest, and to use deadly force constitutes enormous responsibility for the officer. The police officer is the "gatekeeper" of the criminal justice system. The police officer who sees the victim before the blood has been washed away must act while legal issues are unclear and must temper the use of force in the face of extreme provocation. The decision as to whether the person will become an arrest statistic is ultimately left to the officer.

Study of the police role was ignored for many years. There are a number of factors that contribute to neglect of study in this area. First, much police behavior has low visibility. That is, the police officer is generally unsupervised in many areas of decision making and the behavior is, therefore, difficult to study. Second, many persons believe that the prosecutor and the courts make the major decisions affecting the accused. Third, when a sensational crime occurs, the focus is quite naturally on the offender, often ignoring those responsible for initial decisions regarding the offender. Fourth, police departments in many metropolitan centers have been intensely political. This has contributed to the hesitation of police administrators to open their organization for systematic study. It has also fostered an image of police as less than professional, and perhaps not worthy of study.

The 1990s saw a renewed interest in studying the police. Some of this interest was the product of changes in the way police viewed their role. Police came to play an increasingly active part in crime prevention through such things as community policing and through such school-based programs as Drug Abuse Resistance Education (D.A.R.E.). Perhaps even more attention was focused on police because of misbehavior of police following a series of sensational cases, including the beating of Rodney King by Police in Los Angeles, allegations of racism and sloppy police work against some officers involved in the O.J. Simpson murder trial, and drug-related corruption by police in a number of departments, including New York and Philadelphia. The articles in this section address several key issues regarding police in modern America, including several of those mentioned above.

In "Observations on the Making of Policemen," John Van Maanen has presented an analysis of the processes involved in becoming a police officer. It is important to understand the expectations the police system has of the recruit and the socialization processes which bring about the realization of those expectations. Van Maanen has provided a clear picture of both the expectations and the socialization process.

In "Community Policing in Small Town and Rural America," Ralph Weisheit, Edward Wells, and David Falcone use the rural police setting to illustrate key issues in community policing. They argue that what has been touted as a new approach to urban policing has been in place for some time in rural communities. What has been called community policing may, in fact, simply be an effort to put into a formal bureaucratic structure the kinds of activities that rural police have done informally for years. Rural police do a better job of clearing crime by making an arrest, and the wall that seems to separate urban police and urban citizens is less pronounced in rural areas. It is ironic that while many have been unhappy with the way urban police go about their work, we have almost always turned to urban examples when looking for ways to make the police more effective and more responsive to the public. Perhaps it is time to consider alternative models.

Some crimes, such as drug use, gambling, and prostitution, have no complaining victim and few witnesses who will cooperate with the police. Investigating these types of crime requires the police to take a more active stance, often using undercover techniques and confidential informants. In "Vice Isn't Nice," Mark Pogrebin and Eric Poole examine the consequences of working undercover, using interviews with forty undercover officers. The undercover officer must maintain two separate identities—one in which he or she pretends to be part of a criminal lifestyle, and the other in which the officer is part of the "legal" world of policing. Keeping these identities separate can be difficult, particularly since the longer an officer stays undercover the longer they are separated from friends, relatives and others in the conventional world. Departments need to carefully monitor undercover officers, and officers who go undercover need to be particularly sensitive to changes in their own perspective on the world.

Finally, in "Reflections on Police Corruption," James W. Birch examines one of the consequences of police work for some officers—corruption. Birch, a former Philadelphia police officer, provides a graphic account of his feelings of deep bitterness and disappointment in his fellow officers and their behavior. At the same time, Birch has also provided important insights on a number of factors that contribute to potentials for corruption and the extent to which the routine often borders on the corrupt.

5

Observations on the Making of Policemen

John Van Maanen

In recent years the so-called "police problem" has become one of the more institutionalized topics of routine conversation in this society. Whether one views the police as friend or foe, virtually everyone has a set of "cop stories" to relate to willing listeners. Although most stories dramatize personal encounters and are situation-specific, there is a common thread running through these frequently heard accounts. In such stories the police are almost always depicted as a homogeneous occupational grouping somehow quite different from most other men.

Occupational stereotyping is, of course, not unknown. Professors, taxicab drivers, used-car salesmen, corporate executives all have mythological counterparts in the popular culture. Yet, what is of interest here is the recognition by the police themselves of the implied differences.

Reproduced by permission of the Society for Applied Anthropology from *Human Organization* 32(4):407–18, 1973.

Policemen generally view themselves as performing society's dirty work. As such, a gap is created between the police and the public. Today's patrolman feels cut off from the mainstream culture and unfairly stigmatized. In short, when the policeman dons his uniform, he enters a distinct subculture governed by norms and values designed to manage the strain created by an outsider role in the community.[1]

To classify the police as outsiders helps us to focus on several important things: the distinctive social definitions used by persons belonging to such marginal subcultures (e.g., "everybody hates a cop"); the outsider's methods for managing the tension created by his social position (e.g., "always protect brother officers"); and the explicit delineation of the everyday standards of conduct followed by the outsider (e.g., "lay low and avoid trouble"). Furthermore, such a perspective forces a researcher to delve deeply into the subculture in order to see clearly through the eyes of the studied.

Context

While observation of the police in naturally occurring situations is difficult, lengthy, and often threatening, it is imperative. Unfortunately, most research to date relies almost exclusively upon interview-questionnaire data (e.g., Bayley and Mendelsohn 1969; Wilson 1968), official statistics (e.g., Webster 1970; President's Commission on Law Enforcement and the Administration of Justice 1967), or broad-ranging attitude surveys (e.g., Sterling 1972; McNamara 1967). The very few sustained observational studies have been concerned with specific aspects of police behavioral patterns (e.g., Skolnick 1966—vice activities; Reiss 1971—police-citizen contacts; Bittner 1967, Cicourel 1967—police encounters with "skid row alcoholics" and juveniles, respectively). This is not to say these diverse investigations are without merit. Indeed, without such studies we would not have even begun to see beneath the occupational shield. Yet, the paucity of in-depth police-related research—especially from the outsider perspective—represents a serious gap in our knowledge of a critical social establishment.[2]

In particular the process of becoming a police officer has been neglected.[3] What little data we presently have related to the police socialization process come from either the work devoted to certain hypothesized dimensions of the police personality (e.g., dogmatism, authoritarianism, cynicism, alienation, etc.) or cross-sectional snapshots of police attitudes toward their public audiences. Using a dramaturgic metaphor, these studies have concentrated upon the description of the actors, stage setting, and "on stage" performance of the police production. Little attention has been paid to the orientation of the performers to their particular role viewed from "backstage" perspective. Clearly, for any performance to materialize there must be casting sessions, rehearsals, directors, stagehands, and some form(s) of compensation provided the actors to insure their continued performance. Recognizing that to some degree organizational socialization occurs at all career stages, this paradigm focuses exclusively upon the individual recruit's entry into the organization. It is during the breaking-in period that the organization may be thought to be most persuasive, for the person has few guidelines to direct his behavior and has little, if any, organizationally based support for his "vulnerable selves" which may be the object of influence. Support for this position comes from a wide range of studies indicating that early organizational learning is a major determinant of one's later organizationally relevant beliefs, attitudes, and behaviors (Van Maanen 1972; Lortie 1968; Berlew and Hall 1966; Evan 1963; Hughes 1958; Dornbush 1955). Schein (1971) suggested perceptively that this process results in a "psychological contract" linking the goals of the individual to the constraints and purposes of the organization. In a sense, this psychological contract is actually a modus vivendi between the person and the organization representing the outcomes of the socialization process.

Method

The somewhat truncated analysis that follows was based upon the observation of novice policemen in situ. The study was conducted in Union City over a nine-month period.[4] Approximately three months of this time were spent as a fully participating member of one Union City Police Academy recruit class. Following the formal training phase of the initiation process, my fully participating role was modified. As a civilian, I spent five months (roughly eight to ten hours a day, six days a week) riding in patrol units operated by a recruit and his FTO (i.e., Field Training Officer charged with imputing "street sense" into the neophyte) as a back-seat observer.

From the outset, my role as researcher-qua-researcher was made explicit. To masquerade as a regular police recruit would not only have been problematic, but would have raised a number of ethical questions as well (particularly during the field training portion of the socialization sequence).[5]

The conversational data presented below are drawn primarily from naturally occurring encounters with persons in the police domain (e.g., recruits, veterans, administrators, wives, friends, reporters, court officials, etc.) While formal interviews were conducted with some, the bulk of the data contained here arose from far less structured situations.

Making of a Policeman: A Paradigm

For purposes here, the police recruit's initiation into the organizational setting shall be treated as if it occurred in four discrete stages. While these stages are only analytically distinct, they do serve as useful markers for describing the route traversed by the recruit. The sequence is related to the preentry, admittance, change, and continuance phases of the organizational socialization process and are labeled here as choice, introduction, encounter, and metamorphosis, respectively.

Preentry: Choice

What sort of young man is attracted to and selected for a police career? The literature notes that police work seems to attract local, family-oriented, working-class whites interested primarily in the security and salary aspects of the occupation. Importantly, the authoritarian syndrome which has popularly been ascribed to persons selecting police careers has not been supported by empirical study. The available research supports the contention that the police occupation is viewed by the recruits as simply one job of many and considered roughly along the same dimensions as any job choice.

While my research can add little to the above picture, several qualifications are in order which perhaps provide a greater understanding of the particular choice process. First, the security and salary aspects of the police job have probably been overrated. Through interviews and experience with Union City recruits, a rather pervasive meaningful work theme is apparent as a major factor in job choice. Virtually all recruits alluded to the opportunity afforded by a police career to perform in a role which was perceived as consequential or important to society. While such altruistic motives may be subject to social desirability considerations, or other biasing factors, it is my feeling that these high expectations of community service are an important element in the choice process.

Second, the out-of-doors and presumably adventurous qualities of police work (as reflected in the popular culture) were perceived by the recruits as among the more influential factors attracting them to the job. With few exceptions, the novice policemen had worked several jobs since completing high school and were particularly apt to stress the benefits of working a nonroutine job.

Third, the screening factor associated with police selection is a dominating aspect of the socialization process. From the filling out of the application blank at City Hall to the telephone call which informs a potential recruit of his acceptance into the department, the individual passes through a series of events which serve to impress an aspiring policeman with a sense of being accepted into an elite organization. Perhaps some men originally take the qualifying examination for patrolman lightly, but it is unlikely many men proceed through the entire screening process—often taking up to six months or more—without becoming committed seriously to a police career. As such, the various selection devices, if successfully surmounted, increase the person's self-esteem, as well as buttress his occupational choice. Thus, this anticipatory stage tends to strengthen the neophyte's evaluation of the police organization as an important place to work.

Finally, as in most organizations, the police department is depicted to individuals who have yet to take the oath of office in its most favorable light. A potential recruit is made to feel as if he were important and valued by the organization. Since virtually all recruitment occurs via generational or friendship networks involving police officers and prospective recruits, the individual receives personalized encouragement and support which helps sustain his interest during the arduous screening procedure. Such links begin to attach the would-be policeman to the organization long before he actually joins.

To summarize, most policemen have not chosen their career casually. They enter the department with a high degree of normative identification with what they perceive to be the goals and values of the organization. At least in Union City, the police department was able to attract and select men who entered the organization with a reservoir of positive attitudes toward hard work and a strong level of organizational support. What happens to the recruit when he is introduced to the occupation at the police academy is where attention is now directed.

Admittance: Introduction

The individual usually feels upon swearing allegiance to the department, city, state, and nation that "he's finally made it." However, the department instantaneously and somewhat rudely informs him that until he has served his probationary period he may be severed from the membership rolls at any time without warning, explanation, or appeal. It is perhaps ironic that in a period of a few minutes, a person's position vis-a-vis the organization can be altered so dramatically. Although some aspects of this phenomenon can be found in all organizations, in the paramilitary environment of the police world, the shift is particularly illuminating to the recruit.

For most urban police recruits, the first real contact with the police subculture occurs at the academy. Surrounded by forty to fifty contemporaries, the recruit is introduced to the harsh and often arbitrary discipline of the organization. Absolute obedience to departmental rules, rigorous physical training, dull lectures devoted to various technical aspects of the occupation, and a ritualistic concern for detail characterize the academy. Only the recruit's classmates aid his struggle to avoid punishments and provide him an outlet from the long days. A recruit soon learns that to be one minute late to a class, to utter a careless word in formation, or to be caught walking when he should be running may result in a "gig" or demerit costing a man an extra day of work or the time it may take to write a long essay on, say, "the importance of keeping a neat appearance."

Wearing a uniform which distinguishes the novices from "real" policemen, recruits are expected to demonstrate group cohesion in all aspects of academy life. The training staff actively promotes solidarity through the use of group rewards and punishments, identifying garments for each recruit class, inter-class competition, and cajoling the newcomers—at every conceivable opportunity—to show some unity. Predictably, such tactics work—partial evidence is suggested by the well-attended academy class reunions held year after year in the department. To most veteran officers, their police academy experiences resulted in a career-long identification. It is no exaggeration to state that the "in-the-same-boat" collective consciousness which arises when groups are processed serially through a harsh set of experiences was as refined in the Union City Police Department as in other institutions such as military academies, fraternities, or medical schools.[6]

The formal content of the training academy is almost exclusively weighted in favor of the more technical aspects of police work. A few outside speakers are invited to the academy (usually during the last few weeks of training), but the majority of class time is filled by departmental personnel describing the more mundane features of the occupation. To a large degree, the formal academy may be viewed as a didactic sort of instrumentally oriented ritual passage rite. As such, feigning attention to lectures on, for example, "the organization of The Administrative Services Bureau" or "state and local traffic codes" is a major task for the recruits.

However, the academy also provides the recruit with an opportunity to begin learning or, more properly, absorbing the tradition which typifies the department. The novices' overwhelming eagerness to hear what police work is really like results in literally hours upon hours of war stories (alternately called "sea stories" by a few officers) told at the discretion of the many instructors. One recruit, when asked about what he hoped to learn in the academy, responded as follows:

> I want them to tell me what police work is all about. I could care less about the outside speakers or the guys they bring out here from upstairs who haven't been on the street for the last twenty years. What I want is for somebody who's gonna level with us and really give the lowdown on how we're supposed to survive out there.

By observing and listening closely to police stories and style, the individual is exposed to a partial organizational history which details certain personalities, past events, places, and implied relationships which the recruit is expected eventually to learn, and it is largely through war stories that the department's history is conveyed. Throughout the academy, a recruit is exposed to particular instructors who relate caveats concerning the area's notorious criminals, sensational crimes, social-geographical peculiarities, and political structure. Certain charismatic departmental personalities are described in detail. Past events—notably the shooting of police officers—are recreated and informal analyses passed on. The following excerpt from a criminal law lecture illustrates some of these concerns.

> I suppose you guys have heard of Lucky Baldwin? If not, you sure will when you hit the street. Baldwin happens to be the biggest burglar still operating in this town. Every guy in this department from patrolman to chief would love to get him and make it stick. We've busted him about ten times so far, but he's got an asshole lawyer and money so he always beats the rap. . . . If I ever get a chance to pinch the SOB, I'll do it my way with my thirty-eight and spare the city the cost of a trial.

The correlates of this history are mutually held perspectives toward certain classes of persons, places, and things which are the objective reality of police work. Critically, when war stories are presented, discipline within the recruit class is relaxed. The rookies are allowed to share laughter and tension-relieving quips with the veteran officers. A general atmosphere of comraderie is maintained. The near lascivious enjoyment accompanying these informal respites from academy routine serves to establish congeniality and solidarity with the experienced officers in what is normally a rather harsh and uncomfortable environment. Clearly, this is the material of which memories are made.

Outside the classroom, the recruits spend endless hours discussing nuances and implications of war stories, and collective understandings begin to develop. Via such experiences, the meaning and emotional reality of police work starts to take shape for the individual. In a sense, by vicariously sharing the exploits of his predecessors, the newcomer gradually builds a common language and shared set of interests which will attach him to the organization until he too has police experience to relate.

Despite these important breaks in formality, the recruits' early perceptions of policing are overshadowed by the submissive and often degrading role they are expected to play in the academy. Long, monotonous hours of class time are required, a seemingly eternal set of examinations are administered, meaningless assignments consume valuable off-duty time, various mortifying events are institutionalized rituals of academy life (e.g., each week, a class "asshole" was selected and received a trophy depicting a gorilla dressed as a policeman), and relatively sharp punishments enacted for breaches of academy regulations. The multitude of academy rules make it highly unlikely that any recruit can complete the training course unscathed. The following training division report illustrates the arbitrary nature of the dreaded gigs issued during the academy phase.

> You were observed displaying unofficerlike conduct in an academy class. You openly yawned (without making any effort to minimize or conceal the fact), (this happened twice), you were observed looking out the window constantly, and spent time with your arms lying across your desk. You will report to Sergeant Smith in the communications division for an extra three hours of duty on August 15 (parentheses theirs).

The main result of such stress training is that the recruit soon learns it is his peer group rather than the "brass" which will support him and which he, in turn, must support. For example, the newcomers adopt covering tactics to shield the tardy colleague, develop cribbing techniques to pass exams, and become proficient at constructing consensual ad hoc explanations of a fellow-recruit's mistake. Furthermore, the long hours, new friends, and ordeal aspects of the recruit school serve to detach the newcomer from his old attitudes and acquaintances. In short, the academy impresses upon the recruit that he must now identify with a new group— his fellow officers. That this process is not complete, however, is illustrated by the experience of one recruit during this last week of training before his introduction to the street. This particular recruit told his classmates the following:

> Last night as I was driving home from the academy, I stopped to get some gas. . . . As soon as I shut off the engine some dude comes running up flapping his arms and yelling like crazy about being robbed. Here I am sitting in my car with my gun on and the ole buzzer (badge) staring him right in the face. . . . Wow! . . . I had no idea what to do; so I told him to call the cops and got the hell away from there. What gets me is that it didn't begin to hit me that I WAS A COP until I was about a mile away (emphasis mine).

To this researcher, the academy training period serves to prepare the recruits to alter their initially high but unrealistic occupational expectations. Through the methods described above, the novices begin to absorb the subcultural ethos and to think like policemen. As a fellow recruit stated at the end of the academy portion of training:

> There's sure more to this job than I first thought. They expect us to be dog catchers, lawyers, marriage counselors, boxers, firemen, doctors, baby-sitters, race-car drivers, and still catch a crook occasionally. There's no way we can do all that crap. They're nuts!

Finally, as in other highly regulated social systems, the initiate learns that the formal rules and regulations are applied inconsistently. What is sanctioned in one case with a gig is ignored in another case. To the recruits, academy rules become behavioral prescriptions which are to be coped with formally, but informally dismissed. The newcomer learns that when The Department notices his behavior, it is usually to administer a punishment, not a reward. The solution to this collective predicament is to stay low and avoid trouble.

Change: Encounter

Following the classroom training period, a newcomer is introduced to the complexities of the "street" through his Field Training Officer (hereafter referred to as the FTO). It is during this period of apprenticeshiplike socialization that the reality shock encompassing full recognition of being a policeman is likely to occur. Through the eyes of his experienced FTO, the recruit learns the ins and outs of the police role. Here he learns what kinds of behavior are appropriate and expected of a patrolman within his social setting. His other instructors in this phase are almost exclusively his fellow patrolmen working the same precinct and shift. While his sergeant may occasionally offer tips on how to handle himself on the street, the supervisor is more notable for his absence than for his presence. When the sergeant does seek out the recruit, it is probably to inquire as to how many hazardous traffic violations the "green pea" had written that week or to remind the recruit to keep his hat on while out of the patrol car. As a matter of formal policy in Union City, the department expected the FTO to handle all recruit uncertainties. This traditional feature of police work—patrolmen training patrolmen—insures continuity from class to class of police officers regardless of the content of the academy instruction. In large measure, the flow of influence from one generation to another accounts for the remarkable stability of the pattern of police behavior.

It was my observation that the recruit's reception into the Patrol Division was one of consideration and warm welcome. As near as interviewing and personal experience can attest, there was no hazing or rejection of the recruit by veteran officers. In all cases, the recruits were fully accepted into the ongoing police system with good-natured tolerance and much advice. If anyone in the department was likely to react negatively to the recruits during their first few weeks on patrol, it was the supervisor and not the online patrolmen. The fraternal-like regard shown the rookie by the experienced officers stands in stark contrast to the stern greeting he received at the police academy. The newcomer quickly is bombarded with "street wise" patrolmen assuring him that the police academy was simply an experience all officers endure and has little, if anything, to do with real police work. Consequently, the academy experiences for the recruits stand symbolically as their *rites de passage,* permitting them access to the occupation. That the experienced officers confirm their negative evaluation of the academy heightens the assumed similarities among the rookies and veterans and serves to facilitate the recruit's absorption into the division. As an FTO noted during my first night on patrol:

> I hope the academy didn't get to you. It's something we all have to go through. A bunch of bullshit as far as I can tell. . . . Since you got through it all right, you get to find out what it's like out here. You'll find out mighty fast that it ain't nothing like they tell you at the academy.

During the protracted hours spent on patrol with his FTO, the recruit is instructed as to the real nature of police work. To the neophyte, the first few weeks on patrol is an extremely trying period. The recruit is slightly fearful and woefully ill-prepared for both the routine and eccentricities of real police work. While he may know the criminal code and the rudimentaries of arrest, the fledgling patrolman is perplexed and certainly not at ease in their application. For example, a two-day veteran told the following story to several of his academy associates.

> We were down under the bridge where the fags hang out and spot this car that looked like nobody was in it. . . . Frank puts the spot on it and two heads pop up. He tells me to watch what he does and keep my mouth shut. So I follow him up to the car and just kind of stand around feeling pretty dumb. Frank gives 'em a blast of shit and tells the guy sitting behind the wheel he's under arrest. The punk gets out of the car snivelling and I go up to him and start putting the cuffs on. Frank says, "just take him back to the car and sit on him while I get the dope on his boyfriend here." So I kind of direct him back to the car and stick him in the backseat and I get in the front. . . . While Frank's filling out a FIR (Field Investigation Report) on the other guy, the little pansy in the backseat's carrying on about his wife and kids like you wouldn't believe. I'm starting to feel sorta sorry for arresting him. Anyway, Frank finishes filling out the FIR and tells the other guy to get going and if he ever sees him again he'll beat the holy shit out of him. Then he comes back to the car and does the same number on the other fag. After we drove away, I told Frank I thought we'd arrested somebody. He laughed his ass off and told me that's the way we do things out here.

To a recruit, the whole world seems new, and from his novel point of view it is. Like a visitor from a foreign land, the daily events are perplexing and present a myriad of operational difficulties. At first, the squawk of the police radio transmits only meaningless static; the streets appear to be a maze through which only an expert could maneuver; the use of report forms seems inconsistent and confusing; encounters with a hostile public leave him cold and apprehensive; and so on. Yet, next to him in the patrol unit is his partner, a veteran. Hence, the FTO is the answer to most of the breaking-in dilemmas. It is commonplace for the rookie to never make a move without first checking with his FTO. By watching, listening, and mimicking, the neophyte policeman learns how to deal with the objects of his occupation— the traffic violator, the hippie, the drunk, the brass, and the criminal justice complex itself. One veteran reflected on his early patrol experiences as follows:

> On this job, your first partner is everything. He tells you how to survive on the job . . . how to walk, how to stand, and how to speak and how to think and what to say and see.

Clearly, it is during the FTO phase of the recruit's career that he is most susceptible to attitude change. The newcomer is self-conscious and truly in need of guidelines. A whole folklore of tales, myths, and legends surrounding the department is communicated to the recruit by his fellow officers—conspicuously by his FTO.

Through these anecdotes—dealing largely with mistakes or "flubs" made by policemen—the recruit begins to adopt the perspectives of his more experienced colleagues. He becomes aware that nobody's perfect and, as if to reify his police academy experiences, he learns that to be protected from his own mistakes, he must protect others. One such yarn told to me by a two-year veteran illustrates this point.

> Grayson had this dolly he'd been balling for quite a while living over on the north side. Well, it seemed like a quiet night so we cruise out of our district and over to the girl's house. I baby-sit the radio while Grayson goes inside. Wouldn't you know it, we get an emergency call right away. . . . I start honking the horn trying to get the horny bastard out of there; he pays me no mind, but the neighbors get kind of irritated at some cop waking up the nine-to-fivers. Some asshole calls the station and pretty soon Sparky and Jim show up to find out what's happening. They're cool but their Sergeant ain't, so we fabricate this insane story 'bout Sparky's girlfriend living there and how he always toots the horn when passing. Me and Grayson beat it back to our district and show up about 45 minutes late on our call. Nobody ever found out what happened, but it sure was close.

Critical to the practical learning process is the neophyte's own developing repertoire of experiences. These events are normally interpreted to him by his FTO and other veteran officers. Thus, the reality shock of being "in on the action" is absorbed and defined by the recruit's fellow officers. As a somewhat typical example, one newcomer, at the prodding of his patrol partner, discovered that to explain police actions to a civilian invited disrespect. He explained:

> Keith was always telling me to be forceful, to not back down and to never try and explain the law or what we are doing to a civilian. I didn't really know what he was talking about until I tried to tell some kid why we have laws about speeding. Well, the more I tried to tell him about traffic safety, the angrier he got. I was lucky to just get his John Hancock on the citation. When I came back to the patrol car, Keith explains to me just where I'd gone wrong. You really can't talk to those people out there, they just won't listen to reason.

In general, the first month or so on the street is an exciting and rewarding period for the recruit. For his FTO, however, it is a period of appraisal. While the recruit is busy absorbing many novel experiences, his partner is evaluating the newcomer's reaction to certain situations. Aside from assisting the recruit with the routines of patrol work, the training officer's main concern is in how the recruit will handle the "hot" or, in the contemporary language of the recruits, the "heavy" call (i.e., the in-progress, or on-view, or help the officer situation which the experienced officer knows may result in trouble). The heavy call represents everything the policeman feels he is prepared for. In short, it calls for police work. Such calls are anticipated by the patrolmen with both pleasure and anxiety, and the recruit's performance on such calls is in a very real sense the measure of the man. A Union City Sergeant described the heavy call to me as follows:

> It's our main reason for being in business. Like when somebody starts busting up a place, or some asshole's got a gun, or some idiot tries to knock off a cop. Basically, it's the situation where you figure you may have to use the tools of your trade. Of course, some guys get a little shaky when these incidents come along, in fact, most of us do if we're honest. But, you know deep down that this is why you're a cop and not pushing pencils somewhere. You've got to be tough on this job and situations like these separate the men from the boys. I know I'd never trust my partner until I'd seen him in action on a hot one.

While such calls are relatively rare on a day-to-day basis, their occurrence signals a behavioral test for the recruit. To pass, he must have "balls." By placing himself in a vulnerable position and pluckily backing-up his FTO and/or other patrolmen, a recruit demonstrates his inclination to share the risks of police work. Through such events, a newcomer quickly makes a departmental reputation which will follow him for the remainder of his career.

At another level, testing the recruit's propensity to partake in the risks which accompany police work goes on continuously within the department. For example, several FTO's in Union City were departmental celebrities for their training techniques. One officer made it a ritual to have his recruit write parking citations in front of the local Black Panther Party headquarters. Another was prominent for requiring his recruit to "shake out" certain trouble bars in the rougher sections of town (i.e., check identifications, make cursory body searches, and possibly roust out customers, a la *The French Connection*). Less dramatic, but nonetheless as important, recruits are appraised as to their speed in getting out of the patrol car, their lack of hesitation when approaching a suspicious person, or their willingness to lead the way up a darkened stairwell. The required behaviors vary from event to event; however, contingent upon the ex post facto evaluation (e.g., Was a weapon involved? Did the officers have to fight the suspect? How many other patrolmen were on the spot?), a novice makes his departmental reputation. While some FTO's promote these climactic events, most wait quietly for such situations to occur. Certainly varying definitions of appropriate behavior in these situations exist from patrolman to patrolman, but the critical and common element is the recruit's demonstrated willingness to place himself in a precarious position while assisting a brother officer. In the police world, such behavior is demanded.

Although data on such instances are inherently difficult to collect, it appears that the behaviorally demonstrated commitment to one's fellow officers involved in such events is a particularly important stage in the socialization process. To the recruit, he has experienced a test and it provides him with the first of many shared experiences which he can relate to other officers. To the FTO, he has watched his man in a police work situation and now knows a great deal more about his occupational companion.

Aside from the backup test applied to all recruits, the other most powerful experience in a recruit's early days on patrol is his first arrest. Virtually all policemen can recall the individual, location, and situation surrounding their first arrest. One five-year veteran patrolman stated:

> The first arrest is really something. I guess that's because it's what we're supposedly out here for. . . . In my case, I'd been out for a couple of weeks but we hadn't done much. . . . I think we'd made some chippies, like stand-ups, or DWI's, but my partner never let me handle the arrest part. Then one night he tells me that if anything happens, I've got to handle it. Believe me, I'll never forget that first arrest, even if it was only a scumbag horn (wino) who had just fallen through a window. . . . I suppose I can remember my first three or four arrests, but after that they just start to blur together.[7]

It is such occurrences that determine the recruit's success in the department. To some extent, both the back-up test and the first arrest are beyond the direct control of the newcomer. The fact that they both take place at the discretion of the FTO underscores the orderliness of the socialization process. In effect, these climactic situations graphically demonstrate to the recruit his new status and role within the department. And after passing through this regulated sequence of events, he can say, "I am a cop!"

Continuance: Metamorphosis

This section is concerned broadly with what Becker et al. (1961) labeled the final perspective. As such, the interest is upon the characteristic response recruits eventually demonstrate regarding their occupational and organizational setting. Again, the focus is upon the perspectives the initiates come to hold for the backstage aspect of their careers.

As noted earlier, one of the major motivating factors behind the recruit's decision to become a policeman was the adventure or romance he felt would characterize the occupation. Yet, the young officer soon learns the work consists primarily of performing routine service and administrative tasks—the proverbial clerk in a patrol car. This finding seems well-established in the pertinent literature and my observations confirm these reports (e.g., Wilson 1968; Webster 1970; Reiss 1971). Indeed, a patrolman is predominantly an order taker—a reactive member of a service organization. For example, most officers remarked that they never realized the extent to which they would be "married to the radio" until they had worked the street for several months.

On the other hand, there is an unpredictable side of the occupation and this aspect cannot be overlooked. In fact, it is the unexpected elements of working patrol that provides self-esteem and stimulation for the officers. This unpredictable feature of patrol work has too often been understated or disregarded by students of police behavior. To classify the police task as bureaucratically routine and monotonous ignores the psychological omnipresence of the potential "good pinch." It is precisely the opportunity to exercise his perceived police role that gives meaning to the occupational identity of patrolmen. Operationally, this does not imply patrolmen are always alert and working hard to make the "good pinch." Rather, it simply suggests that the unexpected is one of the few aspects of the job that helps maintain the patrolman's self-image of performing a worthwhile, exciting, and dangerous task. To some degree, the anticipation of the "hot call" allows for the crystallization of his personal identity as a policeman. One Union City patrolman with ten years' experience commented succinctly on this feature. He noted:

> Most of the time being a cop is the dullest job in the world . . . what we do is pretty far away from the stuff you see on Dragnet or Adam 12. But, what I like about this job and I guess it's what keeps me going, is that you never know what's gonna happen out there. For instance, me and my partner will be working a Sunday first watch way out in the north end and expecting everything to be real peaceful and quiet like; then all of a sudden, hell breaks loose . . . Even on the quietest nights, something interesting usually happens.

Reiss noted perceptually the atypical routine enjoyed by patrolmen. After examining the police "straight eight"—the tour of duty—he stated:

> No tour of duty is typical except in the sense that the modal tour of duty does not involve the arrest of a person (Reiss 1971:19).

Still, one of the ironies of police work is that recruits were attracted to the organization by and large via the unrealistic expectation that the work would be adventurous and exciting. In the real world such activities are few and far between. Once a recruit has mastered the various technical and social skills of routine policing (e.g., "learning the district," developing a set of mutual understandings with his partner, knowing how and when to fill out the myriad of various report forms) there is little left to learn about his occupation which can be transferred by formal or informal instruction. As Westley (1951) pointed out, the recruit must then sit back and wait, absorb the subjective side of police work and let his experiences accumulate. The wife of one recruit noted this frustrating characteristic of police work. She said:

> It seems to me that being a policeman must be very discouraging. They spend all that time teaching the men to use the gun and the club and then they make them go out and do very uninteresting work.

It has been suggested that for a newcomer to any occupation, "coping with the emotional reality of the job" is the most difficult problem to resolve (Schein 1963). In police work, the coping behavior appears to consist of the "learning of complacency." Since the vast majority of time is spent in tasks other than real police work, there is little incentive for performance. In other words, the young patrolman discovers that the most satisfying solution to the labyrinth of hierarchy, the red tape and paperwork, the plethora of rules and regulations and the "dirty work" which characterize the occupation is to adopt the group norm stressing staying out of trouble. And the best way in which he can stay out of trouble is to minimize the set of activities he pursues. One Union City veteran patrolman explained:

> We are under constant pressure from the public to account for why we did or did not do this or that. It's almost as if the public feels it owns us. You become supersensitive to criticisms from the public, almost afraid to do anything. At the same time, the brass around here never gives a straightforward answer about procedures to anyone and that creates a lot of discontent. All communication comes down. But, try and ask a question and it gets stopped at the next level up. It gets to the point where you know that if you don't do anything at all, you won't get in trouble.

In a similar vein, another veteran officer put it somewhat more bluntly. He suggested caustically:

> The only way to survive on this job is to keep from breaking your ass . . . if you try too hard you're sure to get in trouble. Either some civic-minded creep is going to get outraged and you'll wind up with a complaint in your file; or the high and mighty in the department will come down on you for breaking some rule or something and you'll get your pay docked.

These quotations suggest that patrolman disenchantment has two edges. One, the police with the general public—which has been well-substantiated in the literature—and two, the disenchantment with the police system itself. In short, a recruit begins to realize (through proverb, example, and his own experience) it is his relationship with his fellow officers (particularly those working the same sector and shift—his squad) that protects his interests and allows him to continue on the job—without their support he would be lost.[8]

To summarize, the adjustment of a newcomer in police departments is one which follows the line of least resistance. By becoming similar in sentiment and behavior to his peers, the recruit avoids censure by the department, his supervisor and, most important, his brother officers. Furthermore, since the occupational rewards are to be found primarily in the unusual situation which calls for "real" police work, the logical situational solution is for the officers to organize their activities in such a way as to minimize the likelihood of being sanctioned by *any* of their audiences. The low visibility of the patrolman's role vis-a-vis the department allows for such a response. Thus, the pervasive adjustment is epitomized in the "Lie low, hang loose and don't expect too much" advice frequently heard within the Union City Police Department. This overall picture would indicate that the following tip given to me by a Union City veteran represents a very astute analysis of how to insure continuance in the police world. He suggested:

> There's only two things you gotta know around here. First, forget everything you've learned in the academy 'cause the street's where you'll learn to be a cop; and second, being first don't mean shit around here. Take it easy, that's our motto.

The above characterization of the recruit socialization process, while necessarily a drastic condensation of a much more complex and interdependent process, does delineate the more important aspects of becoming a policeman. Furthermore, this descriptive narrative hints that many of the recent attempts to alter or reform police behavior are likely to meet with frustration and failure.

A Coda For Reformers

Most police reformers view the behavior of individual patrolmen as a problem for the department or society, not vice versa. I have, in a small way, tried to correct this bias by describing the point of view of the entering recruit. This emphasizes the intelligibility of the newcomer's actions as he works out solutions to his unique problems. In short, we "looked up" at the nature of the network above the recruit rather than using the usual approach which, in the past, has "looked down" on the "outsider." Perhaps this approach indicates the dilemma in which our police are indeed trapped.

In a very real sense, this article suggests a limit upon the extent to which the police can be expected to solve their own problems. Regardless of how well-educated, well-equipped, or professional the patrolman may become, his normative position and task within society will remain unchanged. From this perspective, the characteristic response of police officers to their present situation is indeed both rational and functional. Clearly, the police subculture—like subcultures surrounding bricklayers, lawyers, or social workers—will probably exist in even the most reformed of departments. To change the police without changing the police role in society is as futile as the labors of Sisyphus.

The long-range goal should be a structural redefinition of the police task and a determination of ways in which the external control principle—so central to the rule of law—may be strengthened. Of course, ways must be found to make the policeman's lot somewhat more tolerable, both to him and to the general citizenry. Organizational change can aid this process by designing training programs which place less stress on the apprenticeship relationship. However, it is doubtful that without profound alterations in the definition and structural arrangement of the police task (and in the implied values such arrangements support), significant change is possible.

Thus, plans to increase the therapeutic and operational effectiveness of police institutions by "in-house" techniques must be judged in terms of what is being done now and what might be done—and, given the features of the police institution as described here, the difference is painfully small. The particular pattern of police practices is a response to the demands of the larger complex and, as such, reflects the values and norms prevalent throughout the society. The extent to which the police system undermines the rule of law; the extent to which the public is willing to alter the crime fighter image of police; the extent to which the police bureaucracy will allow change; and ultimately, the extent to which the police system as presently constructed can operate under strict public accounting—these are the major issues confronting the police, not the degree to which the individual policeman can be professionalized.[9]

Notes

[1]The use of the term "outsider" in the above context is not intended to invidiously portray the police. Rather, the term simply connotes the widespread conviction carried by the police themselves that they are, of necessity, somehow different, and set-off from the larger society. To most police observers, isolationism,

secrecy, strong in-group loyalties, sacred symbols, common language, and a sense of estrangement are almost axiomatic subcultural features underpinning a set of common understandings among police in general which govern their relations with one another as well as with civilians (Bayley and Mendelsohn, 1969; President's Commission, 1967; Skolnick, 1966). Such a perspective emphasizes the necessity to view the world from the eyes of the outsider—a perspective which ideally is empathetic but neither sympathetic or judgmental.

[2]If one takes seriously research findings regarding esoteric subcultures, social scientists interested in police behavior are limited in their choice of methodological strategy. If we are to gain insight into the so-called police problem, researchers must penetrate the official smoke screen sheltering virtually all departments and observe directly the social action in social situations which, in the last analysis, defines police work.

[3]One exception is Westley's (1951) insightful observational study of a midwestern police department. However, his research was devoted mainly to the description of the more salient sociological features of the police occupation and was concerned only peripherally with the learning process associated with the police role.

[4]Union City is a pseudonym for a sprawling metropolitan area populated by more than a million people. The police department employs well over 1,500 uniformed officers, provides a salary above the national average, and is organized in the classic pyramidal arrangement (see Van Maanen, 1972). Based on interviews with police personnel from a number of different departments and, most importantly, critical readings of my work by policemen from several departments, the sequence of events involved in recruit socialization appears to be remarkably similar from department to department. This structural correspondence among recruit training programs has been noted by others (see Ahern, 1972; Berkeley, 1969; Neiderhoffer, 1967).

[5]While it cannot be stated categorically that my presence had little effect upon the behavior of the subjects, I felt I was accepted completely as a regular group member in my particular police academy class and little or no behavior was (or, for that matter, could be) altered explicitly. Furthermore, the lengthy, personal, and involving nature of my academy experiences produced an invaluable carry-over effect when I moved to the street work portion of the study. The importance of continuous observation and full participation as an aid for minimizing distortions and behavior change on the part of social actors has been strikingly demonstrated by a number of social scientists (e.g., see Whyte, 1943; Becker, 1963; Dalton, 1964; and, most recently, Schatzman and Strauss, 1973).

[6]Significantly, a recruit is not even allowed to carry a loaded weapon during the classroom portion of his academy training. He must wait until graduation night before being permitted to load his weapon. To the recruit, such policies are demeaning. Yet, the policies "stigmatizing" the recruits-as-recruits (e.g., different uniforms, old and battered batons, allocation of special parking spaces, special scarfs, and name plates) were exceedingly effective methods of impressing upon recruits that they were members of a particular class and were not yet Union City Police Officers.

[7]By "chippies," the officer was referring to normal arrests encountered frequently by patrolmen. Usually, a chippie is a misdemeanor arrest for something like drunkenness. The chippie crimes the officer noted in the quotation, "stand-up" and "DWI's" refer to drunk-in-public and driving-while-intoxicated, respectively.

[8]In most ways, the patrolmen represent what Goffman (1959) calls a team. In Goffmanesque, a team is "a set of individuals whose intimate co-operation is required if a given projected definition of the situation is to be maintained" (1959:104). The situational definition to be sustained in the patrol setting is that "all-is-going-well-there-are-no-problems." The covert rule for patrolmen is to never draw attention to one's activities. An analysis I conducted on written weekly FTO progress reports illustrates this point convincingly. Of over 300 report forms, only one contained an even slightly negative evaluation. Uniformly, all forms were characterized by high praise for the recruit. The topics the FTO's chose to elaborate upon were typified by such concerns as the recruit's driving skill, the recruit's pleasing personality, the recruit's stable home life, and so on. The vast majority of reports contained no reference whatsoever to the types of activities engaged in by the recruits. The point is simply that in no case was an FTO Report filed which might result in departmental attention. It should be clear that such behavior does not pass unnoticed by the recruit. Indeed, he learns rapidly the importance and value of his team as well as the corresponding definition of the police situation.

[9]I have attempted to suggest in this article that the intelligibility of social events requires they be viewed in a context which extends both spatially and in time. Relatedly, social actors must be granted rationality for their behavior. Given the situational imperatives faced by patrolmen, is it any wonder our police recoil behind a blue curtain? Perhaps we have reached what R. D. Laing (1964) calls the "theoretical limit of institutions." According to Laing, this paradoxical position is characterized by a system which, when viewed as a collective, behaves irrationally, yet is populated by members whose everyday behavior is eminently rational.

References

Ahern, J. F. (1972) *Police in Trouble*. New York: Hawthorn Books.

Bayley, P. H., and H. Mendelsohn (1969) *Minorities and the Police*. New York: The Free Press.

Becker, H. S. (1963) *Outsiders: Studies in the Sociology of Deviance*. New York: The Free Press.

Becker, H. S., B. Greer, E. C. Hughes, and A. Strauss (1961) *Boys in White: Student Culture in Medical School*. Chicago: University of Chicago Press.

Berkeley, G. E. (1969) *The Democratic Policeman*. Boston: Beacon Press.

Berlew, D. E., and D. T. Hall (1966) The socialization of managers: Effects of expectations on performance. *Administrative Science Quarterly* 11: 207–23.

Bittner, E. (1967) The police on skid row. *American Sociological Review* 32:699–715.

Cicourel, A. V. (1967) *The Social Organization of Juvenile Justice*. New York: John Wiley and Sons.

Dalton, M. (1964) Preconceptions and methods in men who manage. In *Sociologists at Work*, P. Hammond, ed. New York: Doubleday.

Dornbush, S. M. (1955) The military academy as an assimilating institution. *Social Forces* 33:316–21.

Evan, W. M. (1963) Peer group interaction and organizational socialization: a study of employee turnover. *American Sociological Review* 28:436–40.

Goffman, E. (1959) *The Presentation of Self in Everyday Life*. New York: Doubleday.

Greer, B. (1964) First days in the field. In *Sociologists at Work*, P. Hammond, ed. New York: Doubleday.

Hughes, E. C. (1958) *Men and their Work*. Glencoe, IL: The Free Press.

Laing, R. D. (1964) The obvious. In *Dialectics of Liberation*, D. Cooper, ed. London: Institute of Phenomenological Studies.

Lortie, D. C. (1968) Shared ordeal and induction to work. In *Institutions and the Person*, H. S. Becker, B. Greer, D. Riesman, and R. T. Weiss, eds. Chicago: Aldine.

McNamara, J. (1967) Uncertainties in police work: the relevance of police recruits' background and training. In *The Police: Six Sociological Essays*, D. J. Bordura, ed. New York: John Wiley and Sons.

Neiderhoffer, A. (1967) *Behind the Shield*. New York: Doubleday.

President's Commission on Law Enforcement (1967) *Task Force Report: The Police*. Washington, DC: Government Printing Office.

Reiss, A. J. (1971) *The Police and the Public*. New Haven: Yale University Press.

Schatzman, L., and A. Strauss (1973) *Field Research: Strategies for a Natural Sociology*. Englewood Cliffs, NJ: Prentice-Hall.

Schein, E. H. (1963) Organizational socialization in the early career of industrial managers. Paper presented at the New England Psychological Association. Boston, Massachusetts.

———. (1971) Organizational socialization and the profession of management. *Industrial Management Review* 2:37–45.

Skolnick, J. (1966) *Justice Without Trial: Law Enforcement in a Democratic Society*. New York: John Wiley and Sons.

Sterling, J. W. (1972) *Changes in Role Concepts of Police Officers*. Washington, DC: International Association of Chiefs of Police.

Van Maanen, J. (1972) Pledging the police: a study of selected aspects of recruit socialization in a large, urban police department. Ph.D. Dissertation, University of California, Irvine.

———. (1976) Breaking-in: socialization to work. In *Handbook of Work, Organization, and Society*, R. Dubin, ed. Chicago: Rand-McNally.

Webster, J. A. (1970) Police task and time study. *Journal of Criminal Law, Criminology and Police Science* 61:94–100.

Westley, W. A. (1951) The police: a sociological study of law, custom and mortality. Ph.D. Dissertation, University of Chicago, Chicago, Illinois.

Whyte, W. F. (1943) *Street Corner Society*. Chicago: University of Chicago Press.

Wilson, J. Q. (1968) *Varieties of Police Behavior*. Cambridge: Harvard University Press.

6

Community Policing in Small Town and Rural America

Ralph A. Weisheit
L. Edward Wells
David N. Falcone

In recent years, American policing has seen the emergence of a new vocabulary and, some would argue, a new philosophy of policing. The *idea* of community policing has swept the country, although in practice the term has been defined in many ways, some of them seemingly contradictory. At the heart of community policing is the idea that police departments must be more responsive and connected to the communities they serve, that policing is properly a broad problem-solving enterprise that includes much more than reactive law enforcement, and that individual line officers on the street and in the community should have a major role in this process.

From *Crime & Delinquency*, Vol. 40 No. 4, October 1994, pp. 549–67 © 1994 Sage Publications, Inc. Reprinted by permission.

Community policing by no means represents an isolated development. Rather, it seems to have emerged as a correlate of various social trends and movements, particularly the victim's rights and civil rights movements, each of which has organized citizens to demand that police be more accountable to the public (Karmen 1990). Similarly, such grassroots organizations as Mothers Against Drunk Driving (MADD) have focused on monitoring criminal justice agencies and have demanded that they be more accountable to the public for their decisions. The interest in community policing among police administrators also parallels general management trends that have emerged in the business world. Total quality management (TQM), for example, concerns itself with reducing layers of bureaucracy, empowering line employees, and increasing responsiveness to customers (e.g., Walton 1986)—ideas that have figured prominently in discussions of community policing. Health care and medicine have shown parallel developments, particularly in the growing trend toward medicine as proactive wellness production, rather than simply reactive disease treatment. The result is an emphasis on holistic, coproductive, general practitioner, and family practice medicine, as contrasted with segmented, specialty-oriented medicine. Given the developments in policing's recent past, the greater organization of citizens, and management trends more generally, it would have been surprising if some form of community policing had *not* become a dominant philosophy among police administrators.

Although community policing clearly has roots in earlier police strategies, as an organizational philosophy, its boundaries, implications for specific programs, and the circumstances under which it might be effective are still being explored. This article examines the idea of community policing by considering the fit between police practices in rural areas and the philosophy of community policing as an urban phenomenon. We suggest that experiences in rural areas provide examples of successful community policing, but the comparison also raises questions about the simple applicability of these ideas to urban settings.

What is Community Policing?

Although a relatively new idea, the concept of community policing has already generated a sizable and rapidly growing body of literature (e.g., Brown 1989; Goldstein 1987; Greene and Mastrofski 1988; Moore 1992; Trojanowicz and Bucqueroux 1990; Wilson and

Kelling 1989). Although there is agreement on some broad dimensions of the concept, there is substantial variability in the types of program activities included under this conceptual umbrella and in the presumed central focus of the approach. Some discussions depict community policing as primarily a matter of reorganizing the nature of *police work*, from reactive law enforcement to proactive policing (in the classical sense of that term), order maintenance, and problem solving. At other times, the emphasis is on the implications of community policing for the *organizational structure* of police agencies as formal organizations. These discussions suggest that community policing is primarily a move from segmented, hierarchical, paramilitary bureaucracies that flatter, to more participatory and flexible organizations. Still other discussions of community policing stress the *community* half of the term and center on the idea that social order is most effectively a coproduction by police and the community, where police-citizen connections and cooperation are essential to doing the job effectively and properly.

The focus here is not on the organizational structure of police departments, although the rural setting does provide opportunities to study the issue of formal organization variability. Most rural municipal police departments are small and have simple organizational structures; however, it is possible for sheriff's departments to be rather large and organizationally complex while still serving a predominantly rural area. Rather than organizational structures, this study focuses on the relationship between the community and the police in rural areas and how this relationship affects police practices.

It is possible to extract three broad themes from the literature on community policing that are relevant to the relationship. The first has to do with the police being *accountable* to the community as well as to the formal police hierarchy. The second is that police will become more *connected* with and integrated into their communities, which means that police will interact with citizens on a personal level, will be familiar with community sentiments and concerns, and will work *with* the community to address those concerns. A third and final theme requires that police will be oriented to *solving general problems*, rather than only responding to specific crime incidents. The discussion that follows reflects each of these broad themes and how it plays out in rural areas. First, however, we will describe the existing literature that can also be used to build our arguments.

Existing Evidence

We begin with the simple observation that community policing looks and sounds a great deal like rural and small town policing, as it has been practiced for a long time. Although there have been no studies that directly examine the extent to which rural policing reflects many key elements of community policing, there are many scattered pieces of evidence with which one can make this case.

In his study of tasks regularly performed by police in 249 municipal agencies of differing sizes, Meagher (1985) found that small agencies were more concerned with crime prevention, medium-sized agencies showed the greatest concern for providing noncrime services, and large agencies focused on enforcing criminal laws and controlling crime through arrests. Similarly, Flanagan (1985) examined public opinion data about the police role. He found that the larger and more urban the community, the more citizens were likely to believe that police should limit their role to enforcing criminal laws. Conversely, people from smaller communities were more likely to want police to perform a wide variety of problem-solving and order-maintenance functions. Gibbons (1972) also saw evidence of this emphasis on order maintenance in his study of "crime in the hinterland." In the sheriff's department in rural Pine County (a pseudonym), Decker (1979) observed that

> the police were called upon and *expected* to render services for a wide variety of irregular occurrences, only a few of which were statutorily defined as law enforcement responsibilities. For example, the deputies complied with a request to inspect a boundary line between two farmers' property that was only accessible by tractor. In a related incident, the same mode of transportation was used to check on a foundered cow. Many instances required the symbolic presence of a sheriff's deputy to legitimate its occurrence in the citizen's eyes. (p.104)

In many rural areas, police *must* provide a wide range of services because other social services are either nonexistent or are more remote than the police. Marenin and Copus (1991) observed that in rural Alaska, where all types of social services are scarce, traditional law enforcement is a relatively small part of the service police are expected to perform: "Village policing is not normal policing, in the sense of law enforcement or crime control, but is much more of a social work kind of job" (p. 16), which includes fire fighting, emergency medical services, and rescue operations.

A number of researchers have observed that styles of policing are partly a reflection of the relationship between police and the community. Although police in many urban areas may be viewed as outsiders, in rural areas they are viewed as an integral part of the community (Decker 1979). In interviews with officers from one rural department and several urban departments, Kowalewski, Hall, Dolan, and Anderson (1984) found that whereas officers in rural and urban departments had many similar concerns, they differed in several interesting respects. Urban officers thought they were less respected and less supported by citizens, whereas police in rural communities felt more public support for being tough, particularly with juveniles. Dealing with juveniles is an important function for rural police because this is often a major concern for rural community members (Decker 1979).

Consistent with the greater informality of social interaction processes in rural areas, rural and urban officers believed they were given public respect for different reasons (Decker 1979). In urban areas, respect went to the position, the role, or the badge, and it was believed that a good way to improve public respect was through professionalizing the department. In contrast, respect was thought to be given to rural officers as *individuals*, who had to prove that respect was *personally* deserved. This was often done by establishing a reputation for toughness and fairness early in their career.

Given the nature of rural culture and of social interactions in rural areas, police-community relations probably will be very different in rural and urban departments. In rural areas, officers are likely to know the offenders, the victims, and their families, just as the officer and his family will be known by the community. Rural officers are also more likely to know and appreciate the history and culture of an area and to use that information in their work, something observed by Weisheit (1993) in his study of rural marijuana growers. Given the close social ties between police and the community, it should be expected that rural officers will use policing styles that are responsive to citizens in their area and that, in turn, local residents should be supportive of the police. In fact, a 1991 Gallup survey found measurable rural-urban differences in the support that citizens show for the local police. In urban areas, 54% of the citizens reported having a great deal of respect for the local police, contrasted to 61% of rural citizens. The differences were even more pronounced when asked about police brutality and the discretionary use of force by police. In the survey, 59% of urban residents thought that there was police brutality in their area, but only 20% of rural residents believed this to be the case ("Americans Say Police Brutality Frequent" 1991).

The same features of rural policing that compel officers to be more responsive to the public also mean that rural police may have relatively less discretion because their work is more visible to the public:

> A major explanation for the high degree of police discretion found in urban areas is the *low visibility* of police actions. In smaller communities the actions of police officers are known to most of the population thanks to the effectiveness and extensiveness of informal communication networks; there they are more highly visible. As a result, small town police enjoy less latitude in deviating from dominant community values. (Eisenstein 1982, p. 117)

Consistent with this idea, Crank (1990) found that organizational and community factors had a different impact on the adoption of a legalistic police style in rural and urban areas. In urban areas, characteristics of the police organization, such as the number of ranks or the ratio of administrators to sworn officers, were better predictors of police style than were characteristics of the community, such as percentage Black or level of economic distress. In rural areas, these relationships were reversed, with community factors being more important than organizational ones. As might be expected, Crank's data suggested that rural departments are more responsive to the local community, whereas urban departments may be more sensitive to the dynamics of the police organization. Or, as a publication of the International Association of Chiefs of Police (IACP) put it, "The urban officer answers to the police department. The rural or small town officer is held accountable for his actions by the community" (IACP 1990, p. 9).

In many ways, rural departments are positioned to be the very embodiment of community policing. According to the IACP document,

> Rural and small town police are closer to their community than are urban police. Rural and small town police are a part of the local culture and community, whereas urban police tend to form a subculture and move apart from the community. . . . Urban police tend to be efficient; rural police tend to be effective. (IACP, 1990, p. 8)

These scattered pieces of evidence suggest it would be fruitful to more fully examine the link between rural policing and community policing. They also suggest that rather than modifying rural departments to fit an urban definition of good policing, or of community policing, urban departments might well look to rural areas for insights into policing in general and community policing in particular.

The Study

The information presented here is drawn from a larger study of rural crime and rural policing funded by the National Institute of Justice. The larger study involves collecting and reviewing relevant literature, conducting a focus group with rural sheriffs, locating and cataloging data sets relevant to rural crime, and, finally, interviewing officials familiar with rural crime and rural policing. This article is based on information from interviews conducted to date. The larger study was not specifically designed to study community policing but to consider rural crime and rural policing issues more generally. In the course of reviewing the literature and in interviews with rural police, we were continuously presented with ideas that paralleled those raised in discussions of community policing in urban areas. Thus what follows explores one dimension of a larger study which is itself exploratory. The purpose is not to reach definite conclusions but to stimulate thinking and suggest patterns that merit further study.

Although over 100 people from a variety of perspectives have been interviewed thus far, this discussion is based on interviews with 46 rural sheriffs and with 28 police chiefs in small towns. Of these 74 interviews, 13 (18%) were face-to-face, and the remainder were by telephone. Although we wanted to include jurisdictions of varying sizes, the focus was on the most rural jurisdictions. Among interviewed municipal chiefs, their community ranged in size from 900 to 50,000 people, with an average of 7,500 persons. Departments ranged in size from 1 to 66 uniformed officers, with an average of 17 officers. The departments of the interviewed county sheriffs ranged in size from 1 to 182 uniformed officers, with an average of 23 officers. This figure is a very rough approximation because sheriff department size is difficult to compute due to sometimes high numbers of part-time employees, jail staff who are sometimes also sworn officers, and some counties having a large number of reserves. The county populations served by these sheriffs ranged from 2,100 to 712,000 people, with only 8 of the 46 sheriffs working in a county of more than 50,000.

As an exploratory study, locating subjects for interviews focused on identifying individuals from the widest possible range of social and physical environments, rather than on studying "average" rural settings. Indeed, the differences across rural areas are so substantial that speaking of averages is probably misleading and is certainly of limited use for policy. Rural Montana and rural Delaware, for example, probably are as dissimilar as they are similar. To capture as much of this range as possible, we selected police officers from across the country, attempting to include every state, while giving particular attention to the 18 states identified as predominantly rural by the federal General Accounting Office (1990).

Because we are engaged in an exploratory study, we felt it important to use largely unstructured interviews. Appreciating rural variation, and always keeping it in mind, we were still interested in identifying common themes. Thus we used the available literature and information gathered from a series of preliminary interviews to develop a list of question areas to be covered in the course of the interviews, but we also encouraged subjects to explore other areas they thought were important. Question areas included crime concerns, police-citizen interactions, police practices, and the working relationship between police and other criminal justice agencies. The length of interview ranged from 20 minutes to 2 hours but was typically about 40 minutes long.

Observations

There was general agreement among the interviewed rural police that their long-standing police practices fit well into what has been termed community policing. However, the concept of community policing is a broad one, encompassing a variety of ideas. Consequently, we focus here on more specific ways in which rural police practices seem to mirror the principles of community policing.

Community Connections

A key element of community policing is police-citizen familiarity and interaction. For example, having officers walk through neighborhoods and talk with people means that more citizens will know officers personally, and, at the same time, officers will come to know many individuals in a neighborhood. The bonds between rural police and the community are also strengthened by the practice of hiring local citizens in police agencies. Thus the officers not only know the community and share many of the values of its members, they are also members of that community and are often involved in community activities. As Decker (1979) noted:

> All members of the sheriff's department had biographies not uncommon to those of the community. The sheriff and his three deputies were all born and educated in the county. Prior to joining the force, every member was involved in an agricultural form of employment, the dominant form of employment for the county. There is evidence of integration into the community in other ways. Each member participates in an important community function; i.e., the softball team, Jaycees, Rotary, Elk's Club, etc. (p. 105)

Many urban departments have recently tried, with varying degrees of success, to induce individual officers to live in their work area, sometimes even providing financial incentives for them to do so. Living in the areas they patrol, however, has been a long-standing practice in rural and small town agencies that has occurred naturally and without special effort. Through increased citizen-police interactions, it is believed that citizens will be more likely to cooperate with the police, and police, in turn, will be more sensitive to the community.

Sheriffs and chiefs with whom we spoke frequently saw what they had been doing in rural areas as community policing and believed they were well ahead of urban areas in this regard. One sheriff's comments are typical:

> Yes, there's far more community policing taking place in rural agencies than urban. We have been doing community policing since time began, I believe. We have always stopped and talked with the ranchers, the businessmen. We have walked the streets, rattled doors, and checked on sick folks. We know the various workers in the community and what they do. We see the kid delivering papers at 6:00 A.M. and talk with him. We have always done that. We are much closer to the people. Consequently, your whole mode of operation changes. Our method of gathering information derives from our personal contact on a day-to-day or minute-to-minute basis. In an urban setting, you're out "developing informants." We do that too, but the vast majority of our information comes from regular folks on a regular basis. I'm a believer in scanners. That would cause cardiac arrest in a lot of agencies. We have gotten more help from folks that have heard us out on a chase and we have lost the guy. They call up and say, "He's two blocks away going down this street." Plus, it tells them we are on the job, what we're doing.

This illustration shows how a strong bond between police and the community in rural settings is helpful in enforcing the law. It is also true, however, that rural police themselves act differently when such a bond exists:

> You cannot call somebody an SOB on the street here because the next day you could be buying tires from him or going in to eat in his restaurant. You've got to know these people because you deal with them day

after day. I worked in Fort Worth, Texas. You get into a row with some guy down there—he's smart mouthing you, bad mouthing you. You can give it right back because you're not going to see that man again, except in court. After court, you'll never lay eyes on him again. Here, he's the cousin of the deputy who works the night shift.

Knowing their citizens well also allows rural officers greater latitude in disposing of cases informally:

The street officer sees ol' Joe on the street and waves to him. When Joe gets drunk and gets into a row, he can just grab him and stuff him into the car. If he doesn't need to go to jail, he can just take him home and turn him over to Martha. She's going to straighten him out.

In smaller communities, particularly with juveniles, which is most of the crime problem in small communities, in my experience, the parents were not some faceless, mythical creatures from the middle of nowhere. I could grab up little Johnny by the scruff of his neck or whatever and we would go talk to Mommy and Daddy, who also knew me. We could work things out a lot easier, without having to get involved in the formal justice system. . . . The small communities, at least where I worked, generally if we had to make an arrest, it was the exception rather than the norm. We almost looked at arrests as a last resort. Everything else either has not worked or will not work. If I had to make an arrest, it was almost as if I'd done something wrong further back down the line.

These close personal interactions also mean that citizens expect more of their police, both in the range of services offered and in the personal attention that will be paid to individual cases:

The city residents expect the man in blue to come by and be very perfunctory, a Joe Friday. We're expected to do the follow-up and a lot more caring. People expect caring from rural law enforcement. We're not there to just take the reports of crimes; we also scoot the kiddies across crosswalks. It's an obligation. We have to wave at everybody we pass by. We have to be more caring.

We've had a lot of examples. An officer might go to a domestic one night and he'll stop by the next night and see how things are going. It's not uncommon for an officer, a couple of juveniles have gotten into trouble, the next day he's got off to go get 'em and take them fishing. They try and get involved personally and make a difference.

In rural areas, police are highly visible members of the community, and it is not unusual for citizens to know individual officers by name. It also appears rather common for a citizen to consider a particular police officer *his* or *her* officer and to request him or her by name when problems arise. Although this also happens to some extent in urban areas, it appears to be far more common in rural communities.

These examples illustrate how close police-citizen interactions in rural areas shape the nature of police work in those areas. For the most part, the features of rural policing described above arise quite naturally and spontaneously and are not the result of formal policies or of specific community policing *programs*.

General Problem Solving

Another central characteristic of community policing is the focus on general problem solving, rather than more narrowly on reactive law enforcement. That is, officers not only respond to specific criminal incidents, but, more importantly, they recognize and respond to more general problems that set the stage for specific criminal acts. These problems are not limited to "crimes" and the solutions need not involve arrests.

> This lady just recently passed away. We've changed light bulbs for people. She called up, she's old, she's not very mobile, she's scared. The power went off, and now she's hearing things. Tell us the name, we know we're going to change a light bulb, talk to her for five or ten minutes and everything's fine. That is a service that fortunately we can still do—spend the time, especially on some of the older residents. Everything is OK, we're here. You call, we're going to be there.

When asked about the kinds of problems to which his department was expected to respond, one small-town chief responded:

> Everything, including the kitchen sink. I've had people in here to counsel families on their sex life because they think I'm the Almighty and can do that. I've had people come in who are having problems making ends meet, and we intercede for them in getting assistance, helping them file for welfare. We do a lot of service-oriented work. I consider it non law enforcement. Somebody needs a ride, like an elderly lady needs a ride to the doctor. We'll take her to the doctor or go get her groceries for her.

Because they are closer to the public they serve, and because they are often the only 24-hour service providers in rural areas, rural police receive calls for a wide range of services. If they respond to a wider variety of non-police problems than do urban police, it is not because they are required to do so by statute or because written departmental policies demand it. Rather, it is because they define police work differently, perhaps because the people they serve are neighbors and fellow community members, rather than nameless, faceless citizens. As such, it is not a conscious formal decision but a necessity arising from the social context.

Rural Versus Urban Policing

We found some of the most telling evidence that rural and urban policing styles are very different in the experiences of rural sheriffs and chiefs who had previously worked outside of rural areas or who hired officers with such experiences:

> Their [police and citizens'] kids go to the same school. You see them on the street. You see them in the grocery store. It isn't like a city. In fact, I've worked with several cities and their officers are cold. They treat the good people the same way they treat the bad people. They are callous.

> If you hire somebody from a larger agency who has been in a situation where they specialized, they tend to look at a "hay seed" operation and say things need to be done in a different way . . . We've had some real problems with them having personality conflicts with the public in general because they are used to dealing with people as faces and not as neighbors or friends or relatives.

> I'm willing to be shown that I'm wrong, but it's a lot harder being a sheriff of a small rural county than it is to be the sheriff of [a city] with a population of 250,000 because everybody in that [rural] county—they want to be able to pick up that phone, whether it be Saturday night at 2:00 in the morning and they have a problem. They want to be able to pick up that phone and call that sheriff. They don't want to talk to a deputy, or the dispatcher. They want the sheriff, "I have a problem." It may be dogs barking.

One officer who had worked in an urban department and then moved to a rural part of Alaska declared:

> If there's a bar fight and I get involved, and somebody comes toward me with the intent of attacking me, I've had several bar patrons jump on them and take them down and even put their hands behind their back so I can handcuff them. It's not like a bar in the lower 48. You still have to watch your back, but we're a part of the community here more than you are there. In an urban area, the police officer is not part of the community. Here, a police officer is a part of the community. We live here, we work here, our kids run around with their kids, date their kids, and go to basketball games. I encourage my officers, and I do it by example, to participate as much as possible in all community functions. . . . But we just don't have problems that we can't take the time to sit down and talk it over with them. In the lower 48, I never had time. At the end of my shift, I was handing call cards out for burglaries

in progress and rapes to the following shift. I had already worked 2 hours overtime and I couldn't get to all of them. But here, we have time to take care of the problems. I don't know if they would even use it [the time] if they had it in the lower 48.

Another chief who was asked if he thought rural police had to be more sensitive to the public than urban police responded:

Absolutely. I come from a bigger agency. In the bigger agencies, you lose that personal day-to-day touch with the actual citizenry, unless you're there for a specific reason. Here, we're very close to these people. There's not too many of us, so they all get to know you. They come in all the time with their problems, and not just law enforcement-related problems. Yes, we're extremely sensitive. It's a very close-knit operation.

These comments repeat many of the contrasts between rural and urban policing noted in earlier sections. Routine personal contact between the police and the policed changes the relationship between the two. And the fact that many rural officers live in the communities they police seems to further strengthen the ties between the two groups.

Effectiveness

Aside from being good public relations, it has also been argued that community policing is more effective. The idea that rural departments may be more effective is not consistent with stereotypes of rural police, and there may be some disagreement about what constitutes effective. One bit of evidence about the relative effectiveness of rural police comes from the *Uniform Crime Reports*, which report the percentage of crimes cleared by arrest by size of the community served. As Table 1 shows, agencies in rural counties have consistently higher clearance rates than departments in cities of 250,000 or more. This pattern holds for every index crime except rape, for which the clearance rates are essentially the same.

The gap in clearance rates between rural and urban areas shown in Table 1 is particularly marked for violent crimes. Some of the rural-urban differences might be attributable to differences in reporting and recording practices. Rural police might, for example, be less likely to write up a report on a larceny if there are no suspects. However, this cannot explain the very large rural-urban difference in clearance rates for homicides. Homicides will almost certainly be recorded regardless of whether there are suspects. It is also possible that the close social networks in rural areas make it easier to solve crimes. One police chief told us:

You've got a specific number of kids who are committing things and it's very easy after a crime to determine who did it here. The closeness of the community and the wide variety of MOs, when something happens they usually leave enough of a telltale sign that we know exactly who committed it. We only have one school that we have to listen to for rumors and things. We've got a lot of law-abiding kids that let us know what they are hearing. We solved almost every one of our crimes here. For every one of our thefts, burglaries, we know who has done it.

Table 6.1 Percentage of Index Crimes Cleared by Arrest, 1992

Crime Type	Cities 250,000+	Rural Counties
Violent	38.5	60.7
Murder	59.6	74.5
Rape	53.4	53.0
Robbery	21.4	38.1
Aggravated Assault	53.2	63.4
Property	14.3	18.4
Burglary	11.3	16.4
Larceny	16.9	18.3
Vehicle Theft	10.3	32.4
Arson	9.2	21.8
All Index Crimes	18.8	23.0

Source: Uniform Crime Reports 1992, Table 25, pp. 208–9.

A county sheriff echoed this view by noting:

For example, my secretary's husband owns the tire store. His tire store got burglarized. People know him and they know her, so they come and tell me "I know who did it." All we have to do is prove it. In some place like Fort Worth [Texas], that's not going to happen—ever. The people on the street don't know the cop; the cop doesn't know the person on the street. They don't intermix too much.

Finally, when one chief was asked if knowing people in the community made his job easier, he replied:

Yeah, I'll give you an example. I live on a road, and when I heard on the squawk box here of a burglary at a neighbor's house three doors down, I immediately called my neighbor across the street, because I knew the two girls were home at that time. I just asked them, "Did you see anything?" They said, "Yeah, I saw this person that was passing around." We picked them up and recovered the goods. Because we are small, my neighbors saw the car and recognized the person, the thief. It happens with some frequency because of the fact that people know each other.

The circumstantial evidence presented here suggests that rural police are more effective than urban police, and that effectiveness may be related to the close bonds among community members and between the community and the police. This was also suggested by Cordner (1989), who found that rural departments were more effective investigators, and this was in part due to the close social networks in those areas:

> Consider two small police departments, one located in a rural area and the other in a metropolitan area. Although the residential populations served by the two agencies may be the same size, the investigators in the rural departments have some natural advantages. They actually know, by name, by sight, and/or by reputation, a much greater proportion of the people in their jurisdiction and its surrounding area than the metropolitan agency investigators know of theirs. The witnesses that they deal with are much more likely to have recognized suspects they observed. Also, the rural investigator has only a few neighboring jurisdictions to keep in contact with, whereas the metropolitan investigator may have a dizzying array of other police departments in close proximity. (p. 153)

Factors in the rural environment that seem to make rural police more effective are those interpersonal networks that community policing tries to foster in urban areas. Thus a better understanding of how rural departments use these networks may have implications for community policing in urban areas.

Other Issues

Looking at policing in rural areas leads one to think about community policing in other ways, particularly to adopt a more elaborate conception of *the community* than is common in discussions of community policing. For example, community policing discussions often allude to the community in terms of lay citizens or nonpolice agencies that might be helpful to citizens. In the rural environment, however, the community in which the police officer works includes not only citizens but other criminal justice officials as well. As one sheriff describes it:

> I tell the guys, we are as much social workers as we are law enforcement officers—community policing. We are expected to work for solutions for these people—what brought them to our attention. When these cases are brought to court, myself, the state public defender, the chief deputy, the prosecutor, and the judge have all set [sic] around a table and discussed what actions we're going to do to this guy, what treatment program we can come up with to keep him from becoming a repeater. I think that's probably unusual, even in rural areas. We take

an interest. At court time, it's not unusual for the officer working the case, the prosecutor, and the public defender to go over here to the restaurant and get in the back corner where you have some privacy, and try to work out a solution to the case. What's best for him and what's best for the community?

It is easy to see how this informal approach can be a two-edged sword. In many cases it can render justice in the very best sense of the word. At the same time, however, it is less clear what happens to justice when the defendant is an outsider, such as a migrant worker, or an insider who is simply disliked, or when rural officers do not use good sense or sound judgment. Accordingly, it is easy to see why some critics are concerned that community policing can shift away from something that is *for* the good of the public to a technique for manipulating the public and doing things *to* it (see Bayley 1988). After all, the development of the formal, militarized style of modern urban police was itself a response to corruption and misbehavior by police, arising from informality that also meant a lack of control (Klockars 1988). Although our study was not designed to examine misconduct or corruption among rural police, such a study would provide insights into problems that arise when the police and the community are *too* close.

Policing in rural areas can also illustrate the idea of decentralizing police department activities. One municipal chief, who previously had been a police officer in a large city, suggested that as generalists, rural police do not simply involve themselves in a variety of nonpolice functions, but they also have to be generalists within policing:

> In a rural area, you do everything yourself. You do the fingerprinting, the pictures, the interviews, the crime scene, everything. In a big department in an urban area, you specialize. As a patrolman in an urban area, I would simply secure the scene of a crime. Once the detective arrived, it was theirs. The detective called in whoever they [sic] needed. Here, there's one officer on duty; he's the primary officer. If he calls for a backup and I come out, he is still the primary officer. The future of policing is where a complete, mature, well-rounded police officer can step into a situation and handle it, or call for the necessary elements to handle it. The day will come in this country . . . where all police officers, no matter where they are stationed, they're it. . . . There won't be chiefs and things like that. There might be supervisors, but they'll be stationed in one place where they can respond to many, many officers from many, many areas.

Rural police practices also raise questions about the nature of police accountability to the public and highlight the difference between *formal* and *informal* accountability. Formal accountability is more explicit but less direct, being concentrated through specific established channels of communication and authority within the organization. In contrast, informal accountability is diffused through multiple channels spread throughout the community, which are also more direct. For example, under formal accountability, the officer is accountable through the organization, and citizens make their complaints through formal channels. Their complaints are processed and eventually fed back to the officer. In contrast, informal accountability means that officers are more directly and immediately aware of citizen concerns and may hear about those concerns from a variety of people, both inside and outside the police organization, in a variety of social settings.

We have argued throughout that as a result of close social ties between police and community in rural settings and in the absence of organizational buffers in small rural departments, rural police are more accountable and responsive to local citizens than are urban police. Although this appears to be true of rural police as a group, rural sheriffs with whom we spoke were emphatic that, as *elected* officials, they were compelled to be much more sensitive to citizen concerns than were municipal chiefs. *If* their perceptions are accurate, and *if* accountability to the public is a worthwhile goal, then it is interesting to speculate what might happen if municipal departments shifted to a system in which chiefs were elected officials.

Discussion

We have argued that modern community policing draws heavily on ideas and practices that have long been traditions in rural areas, although this link is rarely made explicit. It is important to understand the rural dimensions that matter most. What makes the rural community unique in the examples given here is not simply low population density, but also relatively dense social networks. Even among rural areas there is variation in the density of these networks, and it is possible to police rural areas without having the kinds of experiences described here. State police, for example, may operate in rural areas but have relatively little connection to local social networks. As one sheriff observed about his own prior experience as a state trooper:

> I was in 11 stations in 25 years with the state police. I worked all over the place. You see a group of young state troopers come in, they work there for a very short period of time, they go out, they don't care about the individual population. They're statistically oriented—A, B, C—so they are out to make numbers. I think your [sheriffs'] deputies are

there for life. They develop a better relationship with the people, on the whole, where they are *their* cop.

Similarly, one may be an officer whose background and/or personality make it difficult for him or her to fit in with the local culture—and it is our experience that such officers have a particularly difficult time doing their work. Thus a rural area is not simply a physical place but a *social place* as well. This is something community policing advocates in urban areas recognize when they suggest that beats cover *natural* (i.e., social) neighborhood boundaries, rather than those created for bureaucratic expediency. Of course, the social characteristics of crime and policing in rural areas are shaped by the size of the population and the size of the department. We do not know the threshold size for either departments or communities, that is, the size at which they cease to be clearly *rural*. However, we did encounter a number of departments in which rapid population growth had transformed their rural conditions and eroded the police-community networks that once characterized their community:

> That is the one thing that I'm crying about. We are now responding to in excess of 3,000 calls for service in a year. We are losing some of that personal contact. [His city] and some of the urban areas are having to limit the types of calls they will respond to, such as whether they will do funeral escorts. It's a Catch 22; when you become incident driven, the community plays a less active role, and it's a downward spiral.

Although we have gone to great lengths to show themes common to community policing and rural policing, we would argue that community policing is *not* simply and invariably identical to rural policing. Rather, community policing is a formalized and rationalized version of small town policing—where the purpose is to introduce accountability and provide a measure of legal rationality to what, in rural areas, is a much more spontaneous and informal process. Thus community policing and rural policing are not identical. Community policing is small town policing set in a rational framework that attempts to formalize the spontaneous acts of good sense and good citizenship found in many rural officers into a *program* that can be taught and that can be monitored and evaluated. This observation suggests a fundamental paradox of community policing—in many ways it is the formalization of informal custom and the routinization of spontaneous events.

It is also true that rural policing is not homogenous across the country. One implication of this is that, to be effective, there can be no *one* program of community policing. Effective community policing must be tailored to the needs and wishes of each individual community, just as rural police tailor their activities to their local communities.

Further, what we have learned about community policing in rural departments suggests there are elements of the model that chiefs and line officers in urban departments might *not* find attractive or acceptable. For example, the closeness between citizens and police in rural areas may have many benefits for both groups, but it also comes at the expense of the privacy of rural chiefs and line officers. We have observed there are very few rural chiefs or rural sheriffs whose home telephone numbers are unlisted—and many reported that citizens were more than willing to call them at home at any hour, even regarding minor problems. In many communities, line officers could also expect to routinely be contacted at home on police business. One rural chief provided a particularly telling example, an example that is unlikely to be duplicated by any large urban chief:

> In a small town you lose your private life, too. It has taken a toll on my wife and our kids. Two years ago on Thanksgiving we had our family over and then we had a domestic that ended up on my front porch. The husband came over to tell me the problem and then she came over. . . . It was pretty embarrassing. I have since put a sign up on my porch that says this is not the police department, it is our home. Dial 911 if you have an emergency. It hasn't worked. The amount of calls that you get at your house, and . . . if you get an unlisted number, they will come by your house. I would rather have them call me.

This chief, and a number of others, also observed that when off duty they could not have a beer at the local bar without starting rumors in the community. In such cases it is not unusual for chiefs, sheriffs, and their officers go to nearby towns if they wish to have a quiet evening or if they wish to have a drink. How many urban chiefs and line officers are willing to "live" their jobs to this extent?

Another feature common to rural policing that may not be welcomed by urban officers is the high level of community involvement expected of rural officers. In most rural areas, officers live in the community in which they work. Beyond that, it is our impression that rural police are more involved in civic organizations than are urban police. In most rural communities this is voluntary. One sheriff was more explicit, expressing his philosophy this way:

> I tell them [deputies] before they are ever employed that I want my people involved in the community in some way. It may be a service club, a fraternal organization, your church—I don't care what it is. But I don't want you and your partner to just work together all day and drink together all night. When you deal with the rear end of society, and the majority of our work deals with those kinds of people, it's awful easy to build a negative, horrible attitude where everybody is a SOB or a jerk.

... Some kind of community activity, but in some way to deal with real people, just like themselves and see that they are not all criminals. If they'll do that, then they try to make their community a better place rather than just through law enforcement.

In summary, rural policing presents an *ideal type* example of community policing. A more extensive study of rural policing should allow us to determine which aspects of the rural police experience can be applied to urban models of community policing. At the same time it is important to determine if there are key elements of successful rural policing that will *never* fit the urban setting. By improving our understanding of these contrasting areas, the study of rural policing can also provide a better understanding of community policing's potential and its limitations.

References

"Americans Say Police Brutality Frequent." 1991. *The Gallup Poll Monthly* 306:53–56.

Bayley, David H. 1988. "Community Policing: A Report From a Devil's Advocate." Pp. 225–37 in *Community Policing: Rhetoric or Reality*, edited by J. R. Greene and S. D. Mastrofski. New York: Praeger.

Brown, Lee P. 1989. *Community Policing: A Practical Guide for Police Officials*. Washington, DC: National Institute of Justice.

Cordner, Gary W. 1989. "Police Agency Size and Investigative Effectiveness." *Journal of Criminal Justice* 17:145–55.

Crank, John P. 1990. "The Influence of Environmental and Organizational Factors on Police Style in Urban and Rural Environments." *Journal of Research in Crime and Delinquency* 27:166–89.

Decker, Scott. 1979. "The Rural County Sheriff: An Issue in Social Control." *Criminal Justice Review* 4:97–111.

Eisenstein, James. 1982. "Research on Rural Criminal Justice: A Summary." Pp. 105–43 in *Criminal Justice in Rural America*, edited by S. Cronk, J. Jankovic, and R. K. Green. Washington, DC: U.S. Department of Justice.

Flanagan, Timothy J. 1985. "Consumer Perspectives on Police Operational Strategy." *Journal of Police Science and Administration* 13:10–21.

General Accounting Office. 1990. *Rural Drug Abuse: Prevalence, Relation to Crime, and Programs*. Washington, DC: U.S. General Accounting Office.

Gibbons, Don C. 1972. "Crime in the Hinterland." *Criminology* 10:177–91.

Goldstein, Herman. 1987. "Toward Community-Oriented Policing: Potential, Basic Requirements, and Threshold Questions." *Crime & Delinquency* 33:6–30.

Greene, Jack R. and Stephen D. Mastrofski, eds. 1988. *Community Policing: Rhetoric or Reality*. New York: Praeger.

International Association of Chiefs of Police (IACP). 1990. *Managing the Small Law Enforcement Agency.* Dubuque, IA: Kendall/Hunt.

Karmen, Andrew. 1990. *Crime Victims: An Introduction to Victimology,* 2nd ed. Pacific Grove, CA: Brooks/Cole.

Klockars, Carl B. 1988. "The Rhetoric of Community Policing." Pp. 239–58 in *Community Policing: Rhetoric or Reality,* edited by J. R. Greene and S. D. Mastrofski. New York: Praeger.

Kowalewski, David, William Hall, John Dolan, and James Anderson. 1984. "Police Environments and Operational Codes: A Case Study of Rural Settings." *Journal of Police Science and Administration* 12:363–72.

Marenin, Otwin and Gary Copus. 1991. "Policing Rural Alaska: The Village Public Safety Officer (VPSO) Program." *American Journal of Police* 10:1–26.

Meagher, M. Steven. 1985. "Police Patrol Styles: How Pervasive is Community Variation?" *Journal of Police Science and Administration* 13:36–45.

Moore, Mark Harrison. 1992. "Problem-Solving and Community Policing." Pp. 99–158 in *Modern Policing,* edited by M. Tonry and N. Morris. Chicago: University of Chicago Press.

Trojanowicz, Robert and Bonnie Bucqueroux. 1990. *Community Policing: A Contemporary Perspective.* Cincinnati, OH: Anderson.

Walton, Mary. 1986. *The Deming Management Method.* New York: Perigee.

Weisheit, Ralph A. 1993. "Studying Drugs in Rural Areas: Notes from the Field." *Journal of Research in Crime and Delinquency* 30:213–32.

Wilson, James Q. and George L. Kelling. 1989. "Making Neighborhoods Safe." *Atlantic Monthly* 263:46–52.

7

Vice Isn't Nice
A Look at the Effects
of Working Undercover

Mark R. Pogrebin
Eric D. Poole

Undercover police operations have increased greatly since the 1970s (Marx, 1988). An extensive body of work has addressed a variety of issues involving covert police activities, such as deceptive tactics (Skolnick, 1982), criminal inducements and entrapment (Marx, 1988; Stitt and James, 1985), corruption (Pogrebin and Atkins, 1979), and moral dilemmas and ethical decisionmaking (Schoeman, 1986). These studies generally have dealt with criminal justice policy implications of undercover operations; little attention has focused on the effects of undercover work on the officers themselves (Girodo, 1984; 1985).

From the *Journal of Criminal Justice*, Vol. 21, pp. 383–94, 1993. Reprinted by permission of Elsevier Science, Ltd., Oxford, England.

In this study undercover work was defined as assignments of police officers to investigative roles in which they adopt fictitious civilian identities for a sustained period of time in order to discover criminal activities that are not usually reported to police or to infiltrate criminal groups that are normally difficult to access (see Miller, 1992). This study examined the consequences of working undercover for police officers. Focusing on role dynamics and situated identity in undercover assignments, it explored the impact of work experiences on officers with respect to their interaction with informants and suspects, interpersonal relations with family and friends, and readjustment to routine police activities.

The Nature of Undercover Work

Assignments to undercover units are avidly sought and highly valued. The selection process typically is intense and very competitive. Most undercover police units require interested officers to make application in the form of a request to transfer, which is followed by a series of rigorous interviews and assessments to screen out all but the best qualified for the specialized unit. Since an elite few are actually selected for undercover assignments, these officers enjoy a professional mystique associated with the unique nature of their work.

Undercover assignments allow officers wide discretionary and procedural latitude in their covert roles. This latitude, coupled with minimal departmental supervision, allows the undercover agent to operate with fewer constraints, exercise more personal initiative, and enjoy greater professional autonomy than regular patrol officers. Manning (1980) cautioned that such conditions may lessen officer accountability, lower adherence to procedural due process, and undermine normative subscription to the rule of law.

Marx (1988) further argued that police subcultural norms of suspicion and solidarity may take a conspiratorial turn as undercover agents adopt a protective code of silence not unlike that characteristic of organized crime. Covert intelligence gathering procedures and processes become highly insular, almost peripheral to routine police operations. There develops a need-to-know doctrine in which information is strictly guarded and selectively shared. The secrecy required for clandestine police work offers rich opportunities for self-aggrandizement, with many agents developing an exaggerated sense of power. As Marx (1988:161) concluded, "the work has an addictive quality as [officers] come to enjoy the power, intrigue, excitement and their protected contact with illegality."

The undercover agent typically must operate alone; moreover, the deeper the level of cover required in the investigation, the more isolated the officer becomes (Williams and Guess, 1981). Direct and sustained management of covert activities is practically impossible because of the solitary nature of the work. When supervision is lax or nonexistent, undercover officers are prone to cut corners, which may lead to an end-justifies-the-means type of attitude (Manning, 1980). In addition to the inadequate supervision, often there are no written departmental policy guidelines covering undercover operations for officers to rely on in lieu of direct supervisory control. Even when policies are explicated in departmental operations manuals, typically they are neither known nor followed by officers (Farkas, 1986).

Lack of supervision and effective policy guidelines diminish operational accountability and responsibility at the department level, leaving officers in the field to fend for themselves. Consequently, undercover agents often devise their own operational procedures in order to accomplish unit objectives. These officers develop individualized styles of working, relying on personal expertise and judgment (Marx, 1985; 1988).

Methods

Three federal law enforcement agencies and eight municipal police departments located in the greater Denver metropolitan area participated in the present study. The researchers approached each agency with a request to obtain the names of officers who were presently or formerly assigned to undercover operations and who would be available for personal interviews with the researchers. Utilizing the lists of study volunteers provided by the respective agencies, the researchers contacted each officer initially to determine his or her length of undercover experience and present assignment. The officers were then stratified according to these two variables so that a wide range of work experiences, from entry to termination of undercover work, would be tapped. Next, 20 officers who currently were working undercover were selected—ten having less than three years and ten having three or more years of undercover experience, and 20 officers who were not presently assigned to undercover operations also were selected—ten having less than three years and ten having three or more years of prior undercover experience. The sample of

40 officers was comprised of 35 men and 5 women. Their ages ranged from 28 to 45 (mean = 37), and their undercover experience ranged from one to seven years (mean = 4).

All interviews were conducted at the respective agencies in either subject offices, private conference rooms, or interrogation rooms. Each interview lasted approximately two hours and was tape-recorded with the subject's consent. An unstructured in-depth interview format was used, which relied on sequential probes to pursue leads provided by subjects. This allowed the subjects to identify and elaborate on important domains they perceived to characterize their experiences in undercover work, rather than the researchers eliciting responses to structured questions. The interview tapes were subsequently transcribed for qualitative data analysis.

Qualitative data analysis involved a search for general statements about relationships among categories of observations. As Schatzman and Strauss (1973:110) noted, "the most fundamental operation in the analysis of qualitative data is that of discovering significant classes of things, persons or events and the properties that characterize them." Employing grounded theory techniques similar to those suggested by Glaser and Strauss (1967), the researchers categorized the data into primary conceptual themes to reflect the experiential domains of undercover work identified by the officers.

The Impact of Undercover Work

Informant Relations

Since officers must learn to operate on their own much of the time and since undercover work is proactive, one of the most critical requirements is the ability to cultivate informants for information on illegal activities and for contacts with active criminals. The relationship between an officer and an informant is to a great extent symbiotic, for they come to rely upon one another for services they can obtain only from each other. The cooperation of informants in supplying information is fundamental in most police intelligence-gathering operations. Deals and bargains must be struck and honored for cases to be made. Informant relations are really exchange relations. For example, Skolnick (1975) noted that at each link in the chain of a narcotics investigation officers must make arrangements with suspects in order to move to the next higher level in the criminal organization responsible for the purchase, manufacture, and distribution of the narcotics. According to one federal agent,

> An informant is the easiest, quickest way to do police work. . . . [He] can walk you in the front door and take you directly to the crook and introduce you face-to-face.

Officers must develop and maintain stable relations with informants who can provide reliable information over time. The incentives that officers can offer informants to secure their cooperation or compliance often involve a carrot-and-stick approach. One officer provided several examples of the tactics he has used with his informants:

> Getting cases dropped . . . or dealing with probation officers for not going hard on them. Lobbying district attorneys or city attorneys about the cases or getting bonds reduced so that they can bond out of jail. . . . Getting their cars released from the pound so they can get their wheels back. I have even loaned them money out of my own pocket.

The handling of informants may be highly individualized. Since interpersonal styles vary, relations with informants may be idiosyncratic and thus not transferable across officers.

> I developed my own informants who got to trust me and take me at my word. My word was gospel to them. . . . They literally wouldn't talk to anybody else. When they got into trouble, they called me. And they would do anything for me.

Left to their own personal devices in working with informants, however, some officers may resort to questionable practices:

> We would have the person arrested by other officers, not knowing why they were involved. They usually were arrested for misdemeanor warrants. We would then get them out of jail in return for information. It would appear to the informant that we were doing him a favor.

A related problem involves officers' discretion to overlook illegal activities of informants in order to preserve access to information. This practice may cause agents to lose their sense of perspective regarding the relative importance of their operations in crime control; that is, these officers may come to believe that the types of crimes they are fighting pose a greater public safety concern than the offenses committed by their informants. The immediate justice meted out through arrests of informants for their crimes seems to be far outweighed by the long-term crime control benefits that may be realized only through the use of information these individuals provide. This utilitarian view may be advanced even by police administrators, who emphasize the larger public safety view of crime control;

that is, these administrators convey the view that the activities of street criminals may be ignored for the purpose of getting at the "heavy hitters" who run criminal organizations. As one officer observed,

> You see captains and lieutenants using people and not putting them in jail for certain warrants so that they can get more information. . . . You see there is no problem doing it even though it was a violation of the operations manual. We feel if the captain can do it, and do it in front of us like that, then we can do it.

This reliance on active criminals for information about other active and ostensibly more serious criminals creates a variety of challenges to the integrity of police work. For example, informants are not bound by procedural due process constraints. Moreover, the tolerance of informant lawlessness by law enforcement officials in the interest of securing information may blur the line between legal and illegal police practices.

> [Informants] . . . are going to screw up, so you've got to cover their ass. I've had to do things on several occasions, like setting up some guy, just to clear an informant. . . . You just know that when they screw up . . . they're always able to turn around and offer something that makes up for that.

On the other hand, many officers are sensitive to the risks involved in depending on informants for information to do their jobs. Informant information may be faulty and, if acted upon, could jeopardize, compromise, or embarrass the officer. One federal agent illustrated the problem:

> The main basis for our intelligence and what we go by in initiating investigations usually is a confidential informant, who are criminals themselves, which makes their motives suspect. I have seen cases where we were sure as we could be about a suspect, and we have been wrong. Our information came from an informant who had been corroborated in the past and had been pretty trustworthy, and you still get burned.

The officer-informant relationship is driven by reciprocity but grounded in deceit. Both the agent and the informant must create illusions in the dual roles they play—both pretend to be people they are not. Credibility and reliability are tenuous commodities where misrepresentation of self is the key to continued relations.

Informants, as active participants in illicit enterprises, are part of the cover that affords police access to criminals (Manning, 1980); however, the illegal activities informants engage in while working for the police pose a problem of control. Police undercover operations must not disrupt routine criminal processes, which include illegal behavior by informants. Thus, it is not uncommon for informants to take advantage of their protected status by pursuing more criminal opportunities. For police, it is imperative that informants' motivations for cooperation be judged and their roles in undercover operations be monitored. Assessing informant motivation and directing informant participation are critical in managing undercover operations. The observations of three officers typify this perspective:

> A guy that is motivated by money is pretty easy to control. The ones that are into revenge are also easy to control, because if they think they are getting back at someone, or as long as you keep them thinking that you are doing this to get back at so-and-so, they are okay. . . . The hard ones to control are the ones who are doing it because it's fun or a game to them. They think they are smarter than you. . . . You control snitches by strength of personality—letting them know your rules and . . . knowing their motivation.

> The trick is being able to place the proper weight on the informant's credibility. What is his motive? That's the rule in dealing with these people.

> You never take anything they [informants] do for granted. I put myself in their position and ask, "What's in it for me?" You then get a feeling for what they're doing and why. What you don't want is surprises.

As Levine (1990:45) noted, "'Never trust a snitch' . . . is one of the most important proverbs in the unwritten bible of a narc." Many undercover officers have echoed this sentiment, often adding that informants do not deserve to be treated well. After all, informants typically commit a range of criminal acts, and they may be perceived as no different than the offenders who are being targeted. Two agents sized up their informants as follows:

> [Y]ou can't turn your back on them for a second or they will bite you. They lie to you all the time. They are untrustworthy. They have the morals of an alley cat.

> [I]nformants are some of the sorriest excuses for human beings imaginable—like sociopaths, no conscience. They're just looking out for themselves. . . . I have dealt with some real scum bags, and you can feel awfully dirty later on. . . .

Informants are generally considered a necessary evil. This view is typified in the observation that it often "takes a crook to catch a crook." The work ideology prevailing among undercover officers reflects a rather matter-of-fact dissonance reduction in managing relationships with informants, as the following two accounts illustrate:

> You'll always have informants in this kind of work. There's just no other way . . . to do the job. . . . [T]hat old saying, "You can't live with 'em, you can't live without 'em"— I think it applies to informants as well.

> We're not dealing with saints here. We see it all . . ., so you get used to just about anything after awhile. . . . [Y]ou can't let it get to you, because if you do, then you have a big problem. . . . What's important is control—you have to be able to control your informant. You must be a good manipulator.

From such sentiments arise purely utilitarian justifications for the manipulation of informants and their treatment as disposable byproducts of undercover operations. For example, several officers noted that it would be counterproductive to become too concerned about the personal well-being of an informant simply because informants are expendable; that is, once a police operation concludes, an informant may be cut off from the department or, in some cases, arrested and prosecuted. For many veteran officers, informants become almost invisible, blending into the background of the criminal environment. There is no affect associated with their dealings with informants; personal relations are feigned for instrumental purposes. One officer summed up this approach:

> Informants can appear to be our friends and we can appear to be theirs; however, they are a necessary tool of our trade and must be treated that way. . . .

In contrast, some officers experience genuine feelings of concern for informants as individuals. They point out that they frequently must establish and nurture relationships with key informants over extended periods of time. Such relations inevitably lead to a mutual exchange of personal information. It is not surprising that these relationships may foster conflicting emotions among officers:

> I have sympathy for some of my informants. . . . You spend a great deal of time working with them and listening to their problems. Basically, you are their keeper while they are working for you. You start to feel responsible for what they do. You wonder why their life is such a mess. I try to keep that separate, but you really can't. . . .

While relations with informants pose significant problems for officers, close association with targeted criminals heightens the challenges of the undercover role considerably. As the next section shows, the stakes are higher and the costs of deception are greater.

Identification with Criminals

As noted previously in this article, undercover infiltration into criminal networks requires the use of techniques that include presenting a false identity in interaction with offenders in their environment. However, the agent is not feigning his or her entire presentation of self. Much of his or her genuine self is actually incorporated into the false identity created. After all, he or she is playing a role, and, like a method actor, the officer actually strives to identify personally with the part:

> You have to learn to be an actor because you're pretending to be somebody you're not. . . . [Y]ou re pretending to be a crook, and the crook thinks you're a crook, so you must rely on personal experience.

The officer's job is actually made easier through incorporating much of himself or herself into the performance. As one undercover agent observed.

> It's best to tell as few lies as possible. The fewer lies you tell, the easier the lies are to remember and keep straight. And your lies should be related to your personal life experiences. This makes recall easier. . . . You should not attempt to change your life history . . . because you are likely to confuse what you said to each crook.

Undercover officers who must sustain a deceptive front over extended periods of time face increased risk of stress-induced illness, physical harm, or corruption (Girodo, 1991; Carter, 1990; Manning and Redlinger, 1991). For example, Girodo (1991) noted that the more undercover assignments undertaken, the more drug, alcohol, and disciplinary problems experienced by federal agents during their careers. In a report on drug trafficking and police corruption, the International Association of Chiefs of Police (1989:74–75) warned of the negative impact on officers working covert narcotics operations:

> [O]fficers who do come into continuous contact with criminals while in an undercover capacity are more vulnerable to temptation. In most cases, long-term undercover assignments . . . are not worthwhile, considering the jeopardy to an officer's well being.

Most subjects in the present study readily identified a host of temptations endemic to undercover work. As one officer attested,

> It's unlike anything else in law enforcement. There is a great deal of hours that are spent alone. There is a great deal of pressure. . . . There are a great many temptations out there involving money, narcotics, alcohol . . . [and] women.

In a Federal Bureau of Investigation study of its special agents who were involved in deep undercover operations, many operatives were found to experience profound changes in their value systems, often resulting in overidentification with criminals and a questioning of certain criminal statutes they were sworn to enforce (U.S. Department of Justice, Federal Bureau of Investigation, 1978). Two federal agents in the present study reported these types of problems in their long-term undercover assignments:

> I identified very strongly with the bad guys. . . . Even though these people were breaking the law, they had some fairly good reasons for doing it. . . . I realized everything wasn't black and white. Everything became kind of gray. . . .

> It didn't take me long to get into the way of thinking like the crooks I was running with. I started identifying with these people very quickly. . . . [P]art of it was identifying with them and part of it was trying to fit in with them.

The deep undercover operative who lives under false pretenses for months or years necessarily forms close relationships with those under investigation, as well as with their associates, friends, or families. There are subtle assimilation processes involved in undercover work since officers must adjust and adapt to an unfamiliar criminal subculture; consequently, officers may take on, in greater or lesser degree, the folkways, mores, and customs of that criminal subculture. For some, the net result is having their conventional outlook undermined and conventional bonds of social control weakened. Such processes free the officer to engage in nonconventional activities characteristic of the criminal primary group with which he or she affiliates, as illustrated in the following two reports:

> You get into a case where you are undercover for a very long period of time, where you are acting like a puke-ball for a year or more in order to make a huge case. I mean, you start hanging around these guys and start picking up their bad habits . . ., doing things that are not really related to the case and hanging out with people you shouldn't be with.

> I had an undercover apartment where I would stay a good amount of time. I soon met and started to run around with some groups. They were a segment of society that I didn't have a whole lot of experience with. All of a sudden they became the whole focus of my life. They were my social life. They were my work life. They were everything.

Undercover operatives come to share many experiences with those under investigation in order to be perceived as authentic. While this sharing heightens officer credibility, it also promotes bonding, which in turn fosters understanding of and sympathy for the targeted individuals.

> You are only human and you get to know and like a lot of people. When you're a year with these people, they become your friends. You share your problems with them . . . [and] they make sacrifices for you. . . .

Prolonged and intense interaction within a criminal network leads to emotional conflicts. Since deception requires a dual self-identity for the agent, there is constant tension between loyalty and betrayal in performing an undercover role and an uneasy moral ambiguity, as revealed in the following remarks of two narcotics officers:

> There are cases that you don't want to see come to an end because you don't want to arrest them. You like the people. You hate to see their lives ruined. You hate to think about what they are going to think about you. . . . You would like to just slide out of the picture and never be seen again.

> I can remember very distinctly going out and arresting these same people that had become my friends. I can't even talk about it now without getting emotional. They had trusted me. And all of a sudden I was the police and I'm testifying in court . . . against them. It took a long time to get over that.

The observations of the next two officers indicate that they felt morally tainted by the undercover experience.

> It is something that you have to live with that just doesn't go away. It nags and eats at you. You feel really bad about it—all the people that got caught up . . . [in the operation], and their lives were ruined and their kids' lives.

> Knowing what I know now, I don't think I could ever work narcotics again. . . . I know I've changed. Certainly more cynical about what we're doing. . . . And for what? To dirty ourselves like the crooks?

The work orientations and habits developed by undercover officers often have spillover effects on their interpersonal relations with family and friends. These problems are described in the next section.

Relations with Family and Friends

Undercover assignments may disrupt or interfere with an officer's family relationships and activities. As Marx (1988:166–67) observed, undercover work exerts pressure on interpersonal relations because of "the odd hours, days, weeks away from home, unpredictability of work schedules, concern over safety, late night temptations and partying that the role may bring, and personality and life style changes that the agent may undergo."

Some undercover officers have difficulty separating the traits and attributes associated with their deceptive criminal roles from their normal demeanor in conventional social roles. They experience role strain in shifting between the criminal identity at work and the conventional identity at home.

> Trying to be what the crooks were caused me some real problems with my wife right off the bat. We would go to a social gathering and I would end up off in some corner staring into the back yard and probably drinking too much, because I didn't like the pressure. People would come up and ask me what I did for a living and I had some cocka-mamie story I would give . . .; it was always some lie.

For some officers, adopting a deceptive criminal identity for an undercover assignment essentially precludes their assuming their conventional identity while off-duty. As a veteran agent observed,

> There are a lot of guys who I don't think have been able to put their undercover role aside when they go home. When they work under-cover, they are always undercover.

One officer who apparently adopted this work strategy provided additional insight into the demands of the undercover role:

> For me, at least, working undercover is not something that can easily be turned on and off again at will. You get into character and start thinking and acting like the crooks you're hanging with. . . . You can't afford to be yourself because it's hard to keep who you are and your stories straight. . . . I think it's dangerous if you let yourself slip back and forth.

In Farkas's (1986) study of former and current undercover police officers in Honolulu, 41 percent reported adverse changes in inter-personal relations with family and friends, 37 percent experienced stress in associating with family and friends in public, and 33 percent expressed anxiety over not being able to discuss their assign-ments with family and friends. In the following observations, officers in the present study have provided first-hand accounts of the types of problems revealed in the research by Farkas (1986). First, an officer described some of the disruptive effects of his work on family rela-tionships:

> [A] lot of times I was involved in undercover operations where I would spend so much time away from home. . . . Then you go home grumpy. You don't feel like doing anything with the family. They want to go out for a burger. I just got through eating fifty burgers in the last two weeks. . . . The last thing I want to do is go out and get in the car. So, undercover work messes up your family life a lot.

Second, being in an active undercover role often can cause officers to worry about the safety of their families when they are with them in public; there is concern about the possibility of chance encounters with suspects or criminal associates who know the officers by undercover identities:

> [W]e may have gone to a shopping mall or somewhere with my family and see somebody who may be involved in a case or may know who you are, so you wouldn't want your family to be part of it. So, I found myself limiting my activities . . . to pretty much just staying at home with the family. Or when I did go out, not taking them with me. This isolation was definitely stressful for all of us.

Third, the need to maintain secrecy in covert operations restricts communication with family and friends, heightening feelings of uncertainty and danger associated with the work:

> I was totally isolated from my family and friends. I couldn't tell them where I was. . . . how [I was] doing or what [I was] working on. . . . [It] was extremely painful and upsetting [and frightening] to them. . . . My whole family really took a beating over that period of time.

Law enforcement organizations rarely prepare officers or their families for the kinds of interpersonal problems they are likely to face as a result of an undercover assignment. Two former narcotics officers in the present study lamented the negative effects in hindsight:

> I would give anything if prior to working undercover I would have known some of the pitfalls and some of the pressures that were going to be put on my family situation.

> Things got kind of crazy . . ., out of control, really. I lost perspective on a lot of things, including my wife and kids, and she ended up divorcing me. . . . I should have seen it coming, but I was so into my work that it didn't matter at the time. Nothing mattered at the time.

A common theme of undercover work that runs through the dramatic life-style changes revealed above is a "separation of self." Undercover work typically requires officers to adopt a criminal persona, distancing themselves from a conventional life style. This transformation involves isolation from police peers, family members, and friends, as well as from conventional places where activities with these individuals normally occur. These people and places provide the emotional, psychological, social, and moral bearings for conventional living. To a great extent, these bearings reflect and reinforce one's personality, a part of the self; thus, the separation of that part of the self is akin to a loss of identity. Officers working undercover are expected to seem to be people they are not through role-playing;

however, their isolation in those roles actually may foster real changes in attitudes, values, beliefs, manner, habits, demeanor, character, and identity (Strauss, 1988). Operatives may begin to think and feel like the criminals they are impersonating. Who they are, or are becoming, may be confusing to family, friends, and colleagues. These individuals are perceived as different. The relational landscapes are altered, and the situations are disorienting.

Return to Routine Police Work

Ending an undercover assignment and returning to patrol duty can be awkward for many officers. These former operatives often experience difficulty in adjusting to the everyday routine of traditional police work. Farkas (1986) reported that former undercover agents frequently suffer from such emotional problems as anxiety, loneliness, and suspiciousness; moreover, they experience disruptions in marital relations. Similarly, Girodo (1984) noted that the return to regular police duties after a lengthy assignment as an undercover operative is analogous to coming down from an emotional high. Officers in this situation often report feeling lethargic and depressed as well as experiencing self-estrangement in their new assignments. After six years in an undercover unit, this former narcotics agent described his adjustment problems:

> I was well trained for something else. What am I doing here? At times it hits you hard. For three months on graves I didn't want to hear about vice and narcotics. I didn't want to see them, hear about them, or know anything about them. I just didn't want any contact because it was painful. . . . I don't blame anybody. I knew I was going to be rotated out . . ., but yet I feel cheated somehow.

Two former undercover officers commented on the psychological impact of being transferred back to patrol:

> I was really pissed off. I had a short fuse and would go off for no reason at all. I guess I was even trying to provoke some sort of response. . . .

> I was bored and restless and resented what I was doing. I just didn't feel good about myself and was mad at everybody. I didn't feel anybody understood what I was going through because they hadn't done the things I had.

Many of the problems associated with reassignment to patrol duties can be attributed to decreased autonomy and diminished personal initiative in job performance. For example, working a certain geographic area of the community, responding primarily to radio-dispatched calls for service, handling noncriminal cases, and being subject to closer supervisory monitoring of activities all make for less exciting work experiences than those enjoyed in undercover assignments (Marx, 1988). A veteran officer reflected upon what he missed the most following his transfer to patrol after five years in an undercover unit:

> The excitement in undercover work is, to me, the ultimate. An officer is actually doing something and creating things that are happening. He comes back on the street and back to a daily routine. . . . I still miss the closeknit unit and having the kind of freedom and control we did.

Former undercover agents generally see themselves as having developed and honed special skills as a result of their undercover experiences; consequently, they feel that their talents and abilities are wasted in routine assignments. As the following comments show, officers view their return to patrol as the functional equivalent of a demotion:

> It's like stepping backwards. I mean, you have accomplished a lot of things . . . [in] seven years in undercover. You get better and better over time and suddenly you're sent back to where you were seven years ago—right back at the bottom.

> Narcotics is not a glamorous job. You got to be tough mentally. You get that only from experience. . . . Narcotics officers should be assigned on a permanent basis and not rotated out after a set number of years. . . . I'll never be able to adjust to patrol; my career is ruined.

For several former narcotics officers, the return to routine police duties was even more devastating; they expressed deeply held personal beliefs and commitment concerning the societal importance of their undercover work. As undercover narcotics agents, they saw themselves not just on the "front lines" fighting the war on drugs; they felt they had assumed even greater risks by going undercover "behind enemy lines" to infiltrate and destroy criminal networks. Their experiences were intense, inherently dangerous, and exciting. Some of these officers actually perceived themselves as engaged in a perverse form of trench warfare, as soldiers whose mission was to win the war on drugs one dealer at a time. The following comment is representative of this sentiment:

> Highly committed members of an elite narcotics unit want no part of ordinary police duties . . ., handling DUIs, domestics, and noise complaints. . . . Drugs are our number one problem, and I got tremendous satisfaction getting drug traffickers off the street. . . . There is a drug war going on out there, and it bothers me a lot I'm no longer . . . doing my part.

Finally, Girodo (1985) noted that some attributes thought to be beneficial in an undercover assignment (e.g., deceptive, manipulative, inclined toward risk taking) may have adverse consequences in routine police work. For example, ex-undercover officers tend to adopt a more proactive approach to policing, with an emphasis on the "strategic management" of suspects. As one former undercover investigator explained:

> I talk to arrestees differently. I am always looking for what information they can give me as opposed to throwing them in jail and forgetting about them like I did before I was in undercover. Now all I think about is, "Can I get something out of them?"

Undercover officers are likely to have developed a different working style and demeanor—often characterized by heightened suspicion, cynicism, and caution—that may escalate conflict in interaction with suspects or undermine citizen satisfaction and confidence in service calls. Such consequences have led several officers to stress the need for a decompression period; that is, former operatives need time off for gradual reentry into their new assignments:

> I think it's extremely dangerous to go back on the street in uniform and deal with citizen complaints just off a long undercover assignment. You're just not ready to handle those types of problems. . . . I mean, you're not comfortable or as confident as you should be. And I guess you try to make up for that with a lot of bravado. . . . You really need some time away to get things straight again.

For many officers, an understanding of the dramatic changes they have undergone as a result of their undercover experiences arises only in retrospect, after they have had time to appreciate the stark contrast between the demands of their former and present work assignments fully.

Conclusions

Unlike police officers with conventional assignments, undercover agents tend to operate primarily within criminal networks. The agent's ability to blend in—to resemble and be accepted by criminals—is critical for any undercover operation. Deception is continuous and must be adhered to consistently for the illusion to be maintained; that is, the officer's appearance and demeanor must seem natural and genuine.

An operative is required to adopt an alternate identity. The undercover officer must be a good improviser in order to perform convincingly in accordance with the role demands of a false identity. When a person's identity is changed, even for the temporary purpose of acting a part, the individual comes to view himself or herself differently; he or she is not the same person as before. This identity transformation helps the officer to fit in with those of the criminal world in which he or she now operates. It is not unexpected, then, that prolonged participation in a criminal subculture may create role conflicts for the officer.

In addition, the officer must manage a split between conventional and nonconventional identities. Typically, undercover work requires the officer to obtain new identification documents, to change appearance (e.g., clothes, hair style, beard, made-up, etc.), and to alter demeanor. speech, and life-style in order to fit in with suspects. Over an extended period of time, undercover pursuits tend to isolate the officer from contact with friends and relatives, thus limiting or precluding participation in conventional activities. The undercover officer is often far removed, both physically and emotionally, from support systems and institutional symbols that serve to define his or her conventional self. Without such relational ties to reinforce his or her normal identity, sustained interaction with law violators threatens to undermine the maintenance of a conventional self concept. The line separating the self concept associated with the role of an undercover cop and the self concept tied to the responses of deviant others who reinforce the role performances becomes increasingly blurred. The norms of police ethics may thus be turned upside down in undercover work.

Undercover operatives face both professional and personal risks in the deceptive roles they assume in their assignments. From an operational standpoint, police administrators must formulate and implement organizational guidelines and procedures to monitor the activities of undercover agents within the rules and regulations of the department and the laws governing the jurisdiction. First, these procedures will promote constitutional due process protections. Second, these procedures will govern the parameters of the investigation, the assessment of intelligence information, and the gathering of evidence, and thus they will minimize tactical and legal pitfalls that could threaten the success of the operation. Third, these procedures will gauge the impact of undercover work experiences on the operative.

The monitoring of an undercover officer throughout an assignment requires regular supervisory meetings with the agent to discuss problems or issues that arise. These concerns may involve the array of adverse consequences identified in the present study, which have been shown to pose various moral, ethical, legal, professional, and personal dilemmas related to the unique roles officers have assumed in particular undercover operations or to reentering traditional assignments. Moreover, debriefing sessions may be made mandatory following the termination of every undercover assignment or as part of a periodic rotation out of undercover assignments or part of a reorientation training in preparation for the transition from operative to traditional police officer. The emphasis shifts from managing undercover activities to monitoring the ability of operatives to function within the undercover role and to return as normal, functional members of the department and the community, that is, to ensure their capacity to resume their responsibilities as law enforcement officers, spouses, parents, friends, etc.—the whole complex of roles and identities that make them who they really are, not who they have pretended to be.

References

Carter, D. L. (1990). An overview of drug-related misconduct of police officers: Drug abuse and narcotics corruption. In *Drugs, crime and the criminal justice system*, ed. R. Weisheit. Cincinnati, OH: Anderson Publishing Co.

Farkas, G. (1986). Stress in undercover policing. In *Psychological services for law enforcement*, ed. J. T. Reese and H. A. Goldstein. Washington, DC: U.S. Government Printing Office.

Girodo, M. (1984). Entry and re-entry strain in undercover agents. In *Role transitions: Explorations and explanations*, ed. V. L. Allen and E. van de Vliert. New York: Plenum Press.

———. (1985). Health and legal issues in narcotics investigations: Misrepresented evidence. *Behavioral Sciences & the Law* 3:299–308.

———. (1991). Drug corruption in undercover agents: Measuring the risk. *Behavioral Sciences & the Law* 9:361–70.

Glaser, B. G., and Strauss, A. L. (1967). *The discovery of grounded theory: Strategies for qualitative research*. Chicago: Aldine Publishing Co.

International Association of Chiefs of Police (1989). *Building integrity and reducing drug corruption in police departments*. Gaithersburg, MD: IACP.

Levine, M. (1990). *Deep cover*. New York: Delacorte Press.

Manning, P. K. (1980). *The narc's game: Organizational and informational limits on drug enforcement*. Cambridge, MA: MIT Press.

Manning, P. K., and Redlinger, L. J. (1991). Invitational edges. In *Thinking about police*, ed. C. B. Klockars and S. Mastrofski. New York: McGraw-Hill.

Marx, G. T. (1985). Who really gets stung? Some issues raised by the new police undercover work. In *Moral issues in police work*, ed. F. A. Elliston and M. Feldberg. Totowa, NJ: Rowman and Allanheld.

———. (1988). *Undercover: Police surveillance in America.* Berkeley: University of California Press.

Miller, G. I. (1987). Observations on police undercover work. *Criminology,* 25(1): 27–46.

Pogrebin, M. R., and Atkins, B. (1979). Some perspectives on police corruption. In *Legality, morality and ethics in criminal justice*, ed. N. N. Kittrie and J. Susman. New York: Praeger Publishers.

Schatzman, L., and Strauss, A. L. (1973). *Field research: Strategies for a natural sociology.* Englewood Cliffs, NJ: Prentice-Hall.

Schoeman, F. (1986). Undercover operations: Some moral questions about S. 804. *Crim Just Ethics* 5:16–22.

Skolnick, J. H. (1975). *Justice without trial: Law enforcement in democratic society*, 2nd ed. New York: John Wiley and Sons.

———. (1982). Deception by police. *Crim Just Ethics* 1:40–54.

Stitt, B. G., and James, G. (1985). Entrapment: An ethical analysis. In *Moral issues in police work*, ed. F. A. Elliston and M. Feldberg. Totowa, NJ: Rowman and Allanheld.

Strauss, A. L. (1988). Turning points in identity. In *Social interaction*, ed. C. Clark and H. Robboy. New York: St. Martin's Press.

U.S. Department of Justice, Federal Bureau of Investigation (1978). *The special agent in undercover investigations.* Washington, DC: U.S. Department of Justice.

Williams, J., and Guess, L. (1981). The informant: A narcotics enforcement dilemma. *Journal of Psychoactive Research* 13:235–45.

8

Reflections on Police Corruption

James W. Birch

I've given a great deal of thought to policing since leaving the Philadelphia Police Department four years ago. So many questions still go unanswered, and I often wonder if any of the inequities and corrupt ways will ever change—or if anyone really wants them to change.

For seven years I worked uniform patrol in a high crime district in a major metropolitan area and met some of the best and worst police officers society has to offer. We shared many good times, some bad times, and, of course, we shared the everyday sacrifices of loss of privacy and identity so common to police work. Being a cop was like living in a fish bowl with everyone watching and judging your every move. The public was consistently ready to forget the good job you did the minute they saw what they thought was a bad job. The public was so quick to condemn!

From *Criminal Justice Ethics,* 1983, Vol. 2.2, beginning on page 2. Reprinted by permission.

But the hardest feelings to reconcile are the feelings of deep bitterness and disappointment I still feel toward many of my former fellow officers and supervisors. Why did so many of the police seem to feel that sleeping, drinking, and on-duty sexual activity were perquisites of the job? It always dumbfounded me that cops would resent those few supervisors who actually tried to run straight squads. And why was the ward leader always the one to see for favored assignments and transfers, rather than having the assignments and transfers awarded on merit—that is, on earning them?

If the public only knew how much the marriage between local politics and police really cost them in inefficiency and quality of service! And corruption—why did city officials keep talking about the few "rotten apples" when every officer and citizen knew police corruption was a system problem? Didn't the city hear everyone laughing?

It's corruption that I found hardest to endure. Always the daily decisions of whether to take or not to take. The free coffee and meals, formal pads, and peer pressure all worked to blur ethics. Why did it seem that every citizen had something a little extra they wanted you to do or to overlook? I can remember headlines of corruption investigations, especially the Knapp Commission, which identified the "meat-eaters"—those corrupt, greedy cops in city after city who always wanted more and finally got caught. I was prepared for the big bribes; it would be easy to turn those down. An old adage I believe in states, "A man thinking about committing a sin would do well to first imagine reading about it as if it were public." I had no intention of making those headlines. But somebody should have emphasized the "grass eaters"—those legions of cops who simply take what comes their way. Somebody should have mentioned that from the moment you hit the street, you're faced with decisions regarding corruption.

Corruption starts with the free cup of coffee and slowly builds into a ladder of opportunities, with each rung becoming more and more serious. I remember all the little tests everyone had for you. Your partners, supervisors, and the public were constantly watching and making assumptions about what kind of cop you were going to be based on which favors you accepted and which you turned down.

I remember well my first day on the street, working a wagon with a veteran cop—I remember all the questions I wanted to ask, all the pride and enthusiasm that swelled inside me. What would we do first? Where would we patrol? For two weeks we worked together and for two weeks our first stop was always at the same diner. After all, you never began a tour without first getting some coffee! My partner always "bought" the coffee, but one day, after much persistence on my part (and reluctance on his) he said, "OK kid, you go this time." I walked to the counter, ordered two to go, and handed the owner some money. "That's OK officer, no charge." "No, I insist, how much is it?" "Really, officer, don't worry about it." I pushed the change toward him and he pushed it back. The scene was comical, yet absurd. I finally got in the last push and turned to leave. I couldn't believe it when he actually threw the coins at me. By this time everyone in the diner was looking and I felt absolutely ridiculous. Would I ever get used to being in the fish bowl? My partner laughed hysterically when I told him what happened. I wasn't sure if I'd passed my first test or not!

Coffee, free meals, haircuts—everywhere you went the public insisted on giving a special "police discount." No police solicitation; just enter a store, offer to pay full price and wait for the inevitable discount. It was so common that even the most idealistic, straight guys would secretly resent the few stores which didn't participate. Everyone had their own reasons for giving. Some had relatives who were cops, some were police buffs, some were intimidated by the uniform and felt they had to do something. But most were buying "insurance"; they expected a quick response if they ever needed the police. I don't know any officer who didn't feel comfortable taking at least some of these minor favors. But this is precisely what makes the coffee, etc., a problem—the vast police participation tends to legitimize the behavior to both the police and the public. Also, it sets the stage for increased involvement on the corruption ladder.

Maybe this is why I wasn't completely offended or caught off-guard when it was my turn to make some club checks and found the owners willing to barter for letting them stay open. By then I was aware that members of the public offered things for their own self-interest. It was obvious that few bars or private clubs in any area were ready to close at the legally prescribed hour. The public didn't want to leave their favorite watering holes by such unrealistic hours and, in many cases, off-duty cops were doing the drinking which prompted the old double standard rule. However, when you were working midnights, it was a requirement to make "appearances" at these establishments to ensure that all customers were gone, and to complete a report saying so. It didn't take a genius to quickly figure out that the emphasis was on those "appearances." Seldom were the places actually closed. As long as the report was submitted stating the customers were gone and the door was locked, no one would verify it.

I remember, when I was still considered a rookie, working a sector for the first time where I was required to close a club. I decided I'd better do it by the book in spite of all the advice from my fellow cops just to stick my head in the door and then write a report saying the club was closed. At the prescribed time I made the first of two required visits just to let the club owner know that I would be back in thirty minutes to be sure all customers had gone. The bartender seemed cooperative—"Sure, Officer, don't worry, we always close on time." The problem occurred when I returned and found more customers than before and a much brisker business. The bartender was still cordial, "What can I get you—a beer? mixed drink?" Everybody was always trying to give you something and change the subject! When I strongly suggested he immediately stop sales and close the club, and when he knew I wasn't kidding, he suggested I'd better get a supervisor right away. It was really hard to do things by the book. . . . After relating the events to a supervisor, he gave me the typical "Good job" and sent me away. He would handle the situation personally. I never did go back to see if the club actually closed. It was just amazing to realize the extent of the barter system in which police operate. Each day brought new opportunities to compromise ideals and principles. "I'll give you free drinks and x amount of dollars and you give me under-enforcement of all laws regarding my customers!" Anyway, it was a long time before I worked a route that had a club on it.

When I joined the police department in 1971, all eyes were on the problems New York City was having relative to the Knapp Commission. Police were always watching other departments to compare pay, benefits, and working conditions. But this was a little different. Could that type of major corruption investigation ever happen here? I don't remember any Serpicos in my department. Few cops would ever risk exposing the system the way Serpico did. More often than not, a live and let live attitude existed. By the time I, or any cop, got a steady car or beat, ground rules would already have been established. Without ever having to say anything, it was known which cops would and which wouldn't get involved with any of the unofficial arrangements between the public and police. Supervisors had a good idea of which rung you were on and how high on the corruption ladder you were likely to climb. But it was interesting to compare departments. We spent many an hour assigning "meat eater" and "grass eater" labels to cops we knew. Even though we couldn't think of any Serpicos, it was easy to identify the other career paths cops followed. You participated in the unofficial arrangements either by actively soliciting or simply taking what the public offered; or you didn't participate at all, but in that case, you also didn't tell. It was always clearcut. Obviously the choice Serpico made was out of the question, and resigning from the department because of ideals was laughable. "Don't make waves" seemed to be the cop's favorite cliche.

It still amazes me when I think how difficult it was to avoid corrupt situations. You could always be sure that some citizen would find you and make you an offer you couldn't refuse. I could stop a car for running a light, for instance, and have the operator beg me to take $20 to forget the ticket. Or, better yet, the driver might throw the $20 in my window because he knows it's the going rate in the district. So many things can go through an officer's mind, so many ways to rationalize the corruption. If I saw nothing wrong with the free coffee or in allowing clubs to stay open beyond legal closing times, then why not make this motorist happy too? After all, he made the offer and, in essence, I'm here to serve the community. Then again, I could arrest him for bribery—but who wants to face the inside crew? The grief you receive from some cops for making such a petty arrest is merciless. Or, I could really make the guy angry by telling him what to do with his $20 and give him the ticket. What a system!

The magnitude of the problem really hit home one day when I was working a car with a young cop who had spent about two years on the force and who had acquired the reputation of being really aggressive. A supervisor "gave us a meet" at a certain intersection and, naturally, we responded supposing we were to have our log signed. Instead, the cop was summoned into the supervisor's car and they talked for a long time. Later that day the young cop told me how happy he was to have been finally accepted by the squad. The supervisor had told him he was a good cop, trustworthy, made good arrests and showed up at most squad parties. In fact, he fit in so much that he was now officially in on those unofficial arrangements which guaranteed him a second income. He was so happy to be accepted that he had to tell someone and he figured it was OK to tell me because he knew I wasn't the Serpico type!

I didn't know many greedy "meat eater" cops. There really weren't that many. There was no need to break away and get involved with high risk vices like narcotics when the public was so willing to provide everything from free coffee up to formal payments to overlook gambling and liquor violations. My department was the target of a corruption investigation in 1973. It was embarrassing and humiliating to read about how the city refused to cooperate and how they kept insisting that corruption wasn't a system problem—just a problem of a few "rotten apples." I agree that the "meat eaters" are the "rottenest" of the apples. But why does everyone ignore how they became that way? They didn't become cops one day and start dealing narcotics the next. They were weaned through their careers by a public willing to pay for favors, cops willing to take, and public officials refusing to admit that these "rotten apples" actually live in a very "rotten barrel"!

I wish police departments and city officials would admit that police corruption results from a system where honest police recruits are placed into a dishonest police subculture. The police system is typical of the bartering and favor-peddling which pervades the entire justice system and society as well. Public officials would only be telling the public what they already know, but in admitting to the extent of the problem, officials could also share responsibility for it with the public, as they properly should. Why shouldn't the public be told that they are part of the problem and that corruption in the police department will only end when the public wants it to end? Let the police department identify and eliminate the greedy "meat eaters," but tell the public they are responsible for eliminating "minor perks," payments for bar closing, ticket-fixing, and formalized pads—that is, for eliminating the minor bribes that create the climate for "meat eaters."

The hypocrisy that exists now is pitiful. I marvel at the mentality behind some of the ways departments attempt to pacify the public. For instance, as one boss told me, it is a well-known fact that if vice arrest quotas aren't assigned to officers, then few if any vice arrests will be made because police officers are citizens who also enjoy playing numbers and drinking after hours and don't really view these activities as illegal. So, given the choice, they wouldn't make arrests for this type of vice activity. Typically, the department responds by assigning a fixed number of arrests each month for vice. They fear that without the quota the total vice arrests will be so low that the public, knowing vice exists, will assume the police are taking payoffs and are corrupt. Consequently, each month the required arrests are made to try to persuade the public that the department isn't corrupt. Unbelievable!

I often wonder if we need vice units at all. The level of corruption in any area is determined by the community, not police enforcement. Just take two cops, give them a small office, and tell the public that due to limited manpower and their obvious desire for some corruption, the police will only respond to citizen complaints. Then we could take the squads currently assigned to vice and place them in activities where they have public support.

We must stop worrying about appearances and politics. Tell the people they are responsible for much of the corruption, and the police will not expend any more manpower fighting a losing battle. We must also admit to ourselves that a system of vice opportunities presents itself to all officers at all ranks. We should start with new police applicants and explain to them that inherent in the job is the constant temptation to make "little extras" ranging from free meals to regular monthly payoffs. We must tell the applicant that some officers can't take the pressure and some end up behind bars. We must continually emphasize to police academy classes that as soon as they receive their first assignments, they will be unofficially and officially watched and tested by the community and their peers alike to see how they do on the ladder of corruption. I remember vividly the instructors at my police academy stating "there is no systematic corruption in this department—only those few 'rotten apples'"! If the instructors had told the truth, perhaps hundreds of new officers would have been prepared for the rude awakening of the real world. We must continually have in-service classes for veteran officers and supervisors so that the veterans can learn about and discuss the findings of the various commission investigations throughout the country. We should formulate programs which continually educate both the public and police that corruption is a system problem.

There is so much that needs to be done. Wouldn't it be refreshing if police departments would finally do something innovative, and finally stand up and admit that each department has a corruption problem—rather than repeating the traditional "rotten apple" rhetoric?

I will continue giving a great deal of thought to policing. Since leaving the department I've had the opportunity to soul-search and to work with many police departments in many states. These experiences, plus personal research, have increased my desire to see change. While operations may differ among departments, I've found the basics are always evident—a system of public and police corruption, police politics, and an aversion to innovation. I'm looking forward to and will work toward the day when the public and police will overcome this system.

Section III

Confrontation and Compromise: The Courts

The criminal courts are steeped in myth and surrounded by controversy. Myths abound because many citizens have ignored their rights and neglected their duties with regard to the courts. The potential for access, as recognized in the U.S. Constitution, and which extends to each citizen the opportunity to observe the criminal process in open court, has been ignored. Moreover, the duty to participate in and contribute to a more efficient and effective court system through service on grand and petit juries has been neglected. The notice to appear for jury duty often results in the development of a host of excuses why one cannot serve. Without firsthand experiences, then, we should not be surprised that most Americans have relied on the media for information about the court process. For the most part, contributions made by movies, television and popular novels have not been positive and constructive in that reality is often distorted. Further, where the public does follow an actual case, it is often one in which the case is sensational and/or the defendant is wealthy. These celebrated cases can be very entertaining to watch, but they usually have little resemblance to the manner in which most cases are handled.

We have been led to believe that the criminal trial is a frequent and highly dramatic event which takes place in an emotion-filled courtroom packed by spectators and the press. We are surprised to learn that most cases do not go to trial. When a trial does occur, courtrooms are often empty or are utilized by a very few individuals engaged in the tedious business that makes up everyday reality for judges and lawyers. Contrary to popular conceptions, most cases are plea bargained, a somewhat complex process through which a charge against the defendant is reduced in exchange for a plea of guilty, thereby avoiding a costly and time-consuming trial. Nothing in our media experience has prepared us for the attorney who is incompetent or so terribly disinterested in a case that justice is denied. The wise and dispassionate judge we see on television cannot always be found in the courtroom. Sometimes the judge we observe seems to be ignorant and prejudiced. Finally, we often overlook the fact that it is the prosecutor who ultimately determines the actual charges the defendant must face; it is the prosecutor who accepts or rejects a plea bargain and decides whether a case will go to trial.

Given the gravity of the tasks performed by the criminal courts, we should not be surprised that court operations are surrounded by controversy. Our courts function in an adversarial setting and are subjected to intense and conflicting pressures. The need to protect individual rights often appears to collide with society's legitimate demand for protection. The volume of litigation has increased considerably over the past ten years, and persons accused of crimes have an increased number of rights. The result is delay in the court process and crowded dockets which judges must eventually clear while providing both the substance and appearance of justice. Because many citizens are suspicious of the courts, there is an unwillingness to invest the needed financial allocations for this aspect of the criminal justice system. Courts have enjoyed autonomy for many years. They have been ignored, and in their isolation have developed a host of problems which defy simple solutions. In the following section a number of these problems have been addressed.

Although the criminal justice system is supposed to consider each case on its own merits, this becomes less likely as the burden on the system increases. In "Maintaining the Myth of Individualized Justice," John Rosecrance illustrates how the sentencing recommendations of probation officers are based on a few relatively fixed criteria, but are written to provide the illusion that recommendations are based on a careful consideration of the individual characteristics of the offender. This again illustrates the system's continuing tension between bureaucratic efficiency and justice.

Bureaucratic efficiency is also illustrated in Mike McConville and Chester Mirsky's "Guilty Plea Courts," which examines the way in which the judge puts pressure on defendants to enter a guilty plea. Cases resolved through a guilty plea can be disposed of quickly. Since there is no trial in such cases, improper police searches and other facts of the case that might raise questions about the guilt of the accused will never be brought to light. This is particularly likely when the defendant is poor and relatively powerless. Bureaucratic efficiency is achieved with the appearance that justice has been served.

In "The Practice of Law as a Con Game," Abraham Blumberg focuses on the role of defense attorney. Blumberg contends that the image of an aggressive defense attorney fighting for the protection of his or her client's rights is a myth. The defense attorney is very much a part of the informal court organization. As a result, he or she tends to be cooperative with the prosecutor, rather than combative. By contributing to the negotiated plea both parties benefit—the defense attorney receives a fee for very little work and the prosecutor avoids an expensive trial. The defendant, of course, has a great deal to lose. The right to counsel established by the United States Supreme Court becomes meaningless as a result of these informal relationships and hidden agendas.

Milton Heumann addresses a related issue in his article "Adapting to Plea Bargaining: Prosecutors." Plea bargaining is central to the operation of our criminal courts. It is the final plea bargain agreed upon by the prosecutor and the defense attorney that will determine the sentence, a fact often ignored by those who focus solely on the judiciary in studying the sentencing process. By providing excerpts of conversations between prosecutors and other court personnel, Heumann gives a first-person account of the realities of plea bargaining and the politics and conflicts which are a part of the bargaining process. The distinction between prosecutor and judge become blurred as the prosecutor comes to expect that he or she will exercise sentencing powers.

Finally, in "Convicted but Innocent," Ronald Huff, Arye Rattner, and Edward Sagarin examine a fascinating but seldom discussed problem, the wrongful conviction of innocent people. They estimate how often this might occur and show how it is possible, even in a system where accused individuals have a large number of rights and procedural safeguards. Several things about these wrongful convictions are particularly disturbing. First is the situation in which people who are actually innocent are persuaded to enter a plea of guilty.

Second is the willingness of some prosecutors to ignore evidence that might prove the defendant's innocence. Third is the frequency with which innocent people are convicted on the basis of faulty eyewitness testimony. Increasing defendants' rights may somewhat reduce the incidence of wrongful conviction, but it would also increase the number of guilty who are set free. Finding a proper balance between these competing interests is essential to the very notion of justice.

9

Maintaining the Myth of Individualized Justice
Probation Presentence Reports

John Rosecrance

The Justice Department estimates that over one million probation presentence reports are submitted annually to criminal courts in the United States (Allen and Simonsen 1986: 111). The role of probation officers in the presentence process traditionally has been considered important. After examining criminal courts in the United States, a panel of investigators concluded: "Probation officers are attached to most modern felony courts; presentence reports containing their recommendations are commonly provided and these recommendations are usually followed" (Blumstein, Martin, and Holt 1983). Judges view presentence reports as an integral part of sentencing, calling them "the best guide to intelligent sentencing" (Murrah 1963: 67) and "one of the

From *Justice Quarterly*, 5(2):235–256. Reprinted with permission of the Academy of Criminal Justice Sciences.

most important developments in criminal law during the 20th century" (Hogarth 1971: 246).

Researchers agree that a strong correlation exists between probation recommendations (contained in presentence reports) and judicial sentencing. In a seminal study of judicial decision making, Carter and Wilkins (1967) found 95 percent agreement between probation recommendation and sentence disposition when the officer recommended probation and 88 percent agreement when the officer opposed probation.

Although there is no controversy about the correlation between probation recommendation and judicial outcome, scholars disagree as to the actual influence of probation officers in the sentencing process. That is, there is no consensus regarding the importance of the presentence investigator in influencing sentencing outcomes. On the one hand, Myers (1979: 538) contends that the "important role played by probation officer recommendation argues for greater theoretical and empirical attention to these officers." Walsh (1985: 363) concludes that "judges lean heavily on the professional advice of probation." On the other hand, Kingsnorth and Rizzo (1979) report that probation recommendations have been supplanted by plea bargaining and that the probation officer is "largely superfluous." Hagan, Hewitt, and Alwin (1979), after reporting a direct correlation between recommendation and sentence, contend that the "influence of the probation officer in the presentence process is subordinate to that of the prosecutor" and that probation involvement is "often ceremonial."

My research builds on the latter perspective, and suggests that probation presentence reports do not influence judicial sentencing significantly but serve to maintain the myth that criminal courts dispense individualized justice. On the basis of an analysis of probation practices in California, I will demonstrate that the presentence report, long considered an instrument for the promotion of individualized sentencing by the court, actually deemphasizes individual characteristics and affirms the primacy of instant offense and prior criminal record as sentencing determinants. The present study was concerned with probation in California; whether its findings can be applied to other jurisdictions is not known. California's probation system is the nation's largest, however (Petersilia, Turner, Kahan, and Peterson 1985), and the experiences of that system could prove instructive to other jurisdictions.

In many California counties (as in other jurisdictions throughout the United States) crowded court calendars, determinate sentencing guidelines, and increasingly conservative philosophies have made it difficult for judges to consider individual offenders' characteristics thoroughly. Thus judges, working in tandem with district attorneys, emphasize the legal variables of offense and criminal record at sentencing (see, for example, Forer 1980; Lotz and Hewitt 1977; Tinker, Quiring, and Pimentel 1985). Probation officers function as employees of the court; generally they respond to judicial cues and emphasize similar variables in their presentence investigations. The probation officers' relationship to the court is ancillary; their status in relation to judges and other attorneys is subordinate. This does not mean that probation officers are completely passive; individual styles and personal philosophies influence their reports. Idiosyncratic approaches, however, usually are reserved for a few special cases. The vast majority of "normal" (Sudnow 1965) cases are handled in a manner that follows relatively uniform patterns.

Hughes's (1958) work provides a useful perspective for understanding the relationship between probation officers' status and their presentence duties. According to Hughes, occupational duties within institutions often serve to maintain symbiotic status relationships as those in higher-status positions pass on lesser duties to subordinates. Other researchers (Blumberg 1967; Neubauer 1974; Rosecrance 1985) have demonstrated that although judges may give lip service to the significance of presentence investigations, they remain suspicious of the probation officers' lack of legal training and the hearsay nature of the reports. Walker (1985) maintains that in highly visible cases judges tend to disregard the probation reports entirely. Thus the judiciary, by delegating the collection of routine information to probation officers, reaffirms its authority and legitimacy. In this context, the responsibility for compiling presentence reports can be considered a "dirty work" assignment (Hagan 1975) that is devalued by the judiciary. Judges expect probation officers to submit noncontroversial reports that provide a facade of information, accompanied by bottom-line recommendations that do not deviate significantly from a consideration of offense and prior record. The research findings in this paper will show how probation officers work to achieve this goal.

In view of the large number of presentence reports submitted, it is surprising that so little information about the presentence investigation process is available. The factors used in arriving at a sentencing recommendation, the decision to include certain information, and the methods used in collecting data have not been described. The world of presentence investigators has not been explored by social science researchers. We lack research about the officers who prepare presentence reports, and hardly understand how they think and feel about those reports. The organizational dynamics and the status positions that influence presentence investigators have not been identified prominently (see, for example, Shover 1979). In this article I intend to place probation officers' actions within a framework that will increase the existing knowledge of the presentence process. My research is informed by 15 years of experience as a probation officer, during which time I submitted hundreds of presentence reports.

Although numerous studies of probation practices have been conducted, an ethnographic perspective rarely has been included in this body of research, particularly in regard to research dealing with presentence investigations. Although questionnaire techniques (Katz 1982), survey data (Hagan et al. 1979), and decision-making experiments (Carter 1967) have provided some information about presentence reports, qualitative data, which often are available only through an insider's perspective,[1] are notably lacking. The subtle strategies and informal practices used routinely in preparing presentence reports often are hidden from outside researchers.

The research findings emphasize the importance of *typing* in the compilation of public documents (presentence reports). In this paper "typing" refers to "the process by which one person (the agent) arrives at a private definition of another (the target)" (Prus 1975: 81). A related activity, *designating*, occurs when "the typing agent reveals his attributions of the target to others" (Prus and Stratten 1976:48). In the case of presentence investigations, private typings become designations when they are made part of an official court report. I will show that presentence recommendations are developed through a typing process in which individual offenders are subsumed into general dispositional categories. This process is influenced largely by probation officers' perceptions of factors that judicial figures consider appropriate; probation officers are aware that the ultimate purpose of their reports is to please the court. These perceptions are based on prior experience and are reinforced through judicial feedback.

Methods

The major sources of data used in this study were drawn from interviews with probation officers. Prior experience facilitated my ability to interpret the data. Interviews were conducted in two three-week periods during 1984 and 1985 in two medium-sized California counties. Both jurisdictions were governed by state determinate sentencing policies; in each, the district attorney's office remained active during sentencing and generally offered specific recommendations. I did not conduct a random sample but tried instead to interview all those who compiled adult presentence reports. In the two counties in question, officers who compiled presentence reports did not supervise defendants.[2]

Not all presentence writers agreed to talk with me; they cited busy schedules, lack of interest, or fear that I was a spy for the administration. Even so, I was able to interview 37 presentence investigators, approximately 75 percent of the total number of such employees in the two counties.[3] The officers interviewed included eight women and 29 men with a median age of 38.5 years, whose probation experience ranged from one year to 27 years. Their educational background generally included a bachelor's degree in a liberal arts subject (four had degrees in criminal justice, one in social work). Typically the officers regarded probation work as a "job" rather than a profession. With only a few exceptions, they did not read professional journals or attend probation association conventions.

The respondents generally were supportive of my research, and frequently commented that probation work had never been described adequately. My status as a former probation officer enhanced the interview process greatly. Because I could identify with their experiences, officers were candid, and I was able to collect qualitative data that reflected accurately the participants' perspectives. During the interviews I attempted to discover how probation officers conducted their presentence investigations. I wanted to know when a sentencing recommendation was decided, to ascertain which variables influenced a sentencing recommendation decision, and to learn how probation officers defined their role in the sentencing process.

Although the interviews were informal, I asked each of the probation officers the following questions:

1. What steps do you take in compiling a presentence report?
2. What is the first thing you do upon receiving a referral?
3. What do you learn from interviews with the defendant?
4. Which part of the process (in your opinion) is the most important?
5. Who reads your reports?
6. Which part of the report do the judges feel is most important?
7. How do your reports influence the judge?
8. What feedback do you get from the judge, the district attorney, the defense attorney, the defendant, your supervisor?

In addition to interviewing probation officers, I questioned six probation supervisors and seven judges on their views about how presentence reports were conducted.

The procedure I used to analyze the collected data was similar to the grounded theory method advocated by Glaser and Strauss (1967).

This method seeks to develop analyses that are generated from the data themselves (Blumer 1979). Thus in the beginning of the study I maintained a flexible and unstructured approach. This flexibility was particularly important because I wanted to ensure that my years in the field had not left me with a preconceived conceptual model and that my research was not an attempt to justify conclusions already reached. By facing the issue of possible subjectivity at each stage of the investigation, I let the data lead me rather than the other way around. As the data accumulated and as theories and propositions emerged, they were modified and compared, and in turn formed the groundwork for further data collection. Initially, for example, I attempted to frame the presentence process in the context of factors related to the individual officer (reporting style, experience, or criminal justice philosophy). I could not discern a regular pattern, however, so I analyzed other factors.

Findings

In the great majority of presentence investigations, the variables of present offense and prior criminal record determine the probation officer's final sentencing recommendation. The influence of these variables is so dominant that other considerations have minimal influence on probation recommendations. The chief rationale for this approach is "That's the way the judges want it." There are other styles of investigation; some officers attempt to consider factors in the defendant's social history, to reserve sentencing judgment until their investigation is complete, or to interject personal opinions. Elsewhere (Rosecrance 1987), I have developed a typology of presentence investigators which describes individual styles; these types include self-explanatory categories such as hard-liners, bleeding-heart liberals, and team players as well as mossbacks (those who are merely putting in their time) and mavericks (those who strive continually for independence).

All types of probation officers, however, seek to develop credibility with the court. Such reputation building is similar to that reported by McCleary (1978) in his study of parole officers. In order to develop rapport with the court, probation officers must submit reports that facilitate a smooth work flow. Probation officers assume that in the great majority of cases they can accomplish this goal by emphasizing offense and criminal record. Once the officers have established reputations as "producers," they have "earned" the right to some degree of discretion in their reporting. One investigation officer described this process succinctly: "When you've paid your dues, you're allowed some slack." Such discretion, however, is limited to a minority of cases, and in these "deviant" cases probation officers frequently allow social variables to influence their recommendation. In one report an experienced officer recommended probation for a convicted felon with a long prior record because the defendant's father agreed to pay for an intensive drug treatment program. In another case a probation officer decided that a first-time shoplifter had a "very bad attitude" and therefore recommended a stiff jail sentence rather than probation. Although these variations from normal procedure are interesting and important, they should not detract from our examination of an investigation process that is used in most cases.

On the basis of the research data, I found that the following patterns occur with sufficient regularity to be considered "typical." After considering offense and criminal record, probation officers place defendants into categories that represent the eventual court recommendation. This typing process occurs early in the course of presentence inquiry; the balance of the investigation is used to reaffirm the private typings that later will become official designations. In order to clarify the decision-making processes used by probation officers I will delineate the three stages in a presentence investigation: 1) typing the defendant, 2) gathering further information, and 3) filing the report.

Typing the Defendant

A presentence investigation is initiated when the court orders the probation department to prepare a report on a criminal defendant. Usually the initial court referral contains such information as police reports, charges against the defendant, court proceedings, plea-bargaining agreements (if any), offenses in which the defendant has pleaded or has been found guilty, and the defendant's prior criminal record. Probation officers regard such information as relatively unambiguous[4] and as part of the "official" record. The comment of a presentence investigator reflects the probation officer's perspective on the court referral:

> I consider the information in the court referral hard data. It tells me what I need to know about a case, without a lot of bullshit. I mean the guy has pled guilty to a certain offense—he can't get out of that. He has such and such a prior record—there's no changing that. So much of the stuff we put in these reports is subjective and open to interpretation. It's good to have some solid information.

Armed with information in the court referral, probation officers begin to type the defendants assigned for presentence investigation.

Defendants are classified into general types based on possible sentence recommendations; a probation officer's statement indicates that this process begins early in a presentence investigation.

> Bottom line; it's the sentence recommendation that's important. That's what the judges and everybody wants to see. I start thinking about the recommendation as soon as I pick up the court referral. Why wait? The basic facts aren't going to change. Oh, I know some POs will tell you they weigh all the facts before coming up with a recommendation. But that's propaganda—we all start thinking recommendation right from the get-go.

At this stage in the investigation the factors known to probation officers are mainly legally relevant variables. The defendant's unique characteristics and special circumstances generally are unknown at this time. Although probation officers may know the offender's age, sex, and race, the relationship of these variables to the case is not yet apparent.

These initial typings are private definitions (Prus 1975) based on the officer's experience and knowledge of the court system. On occasion, officers discuss the case informally with their colleagues or supervisors when they are not sure of a particular typing. Until the report is complete, their typing remains a private designation. In most cases the probation officers type defendants by considering the known and relatively irrefutable variables of offense and prior record. Probation officers are convinced that judges and district attorneys are most concerned with that part of their reports. I heard the following comment (or versions thereof) on many occasions: "Judges read the offense section, glance at the prior record, and then flip to the back and see what we recommend." Officers indicated that during informal discussions with judges it was made clear that offense and prior record are the determinants of sentencing in most cases. In some instances judges consider extralegal variables, but the officers indicated that this occurs only in "unusual" cases with "special" circumstances. One such case involved a probation grant for a woman who killed her husband after she had been a victim of spouse battering.

Probation investigators are in regular contact with district attorneys, and frequently discuss their investigations with them. In addition, district attorneys seem to have no compunction about calling the probation administration to complain about what they consider an inappropriate recommendation. Investigators agreed unanimously that district attorneys typically dismiss a defendant's social history as "immaterial" and want probation officers to stick to the legal facts.

Using offense and prior record as criteria, probation officers place defendants into dispositional (based on recommendation) types. In describing these types[5] I have retained the terms used by probation officers themselves in the typing process. The following typology is community (rather than researcher) designated (Emerson 1983; Spradley 1970): (1) deal case, (2) diversion case, (3) joint case, (4) probation case with some jail time, (5) straight probation case. Within each of these dispositional types, probation officers designate the severity of punishment by labeling the case either lightweight or heavy-duty.

A designation of "lightweight" means that the defendant will be accorded some measure of leniency because the offense was minor, because the offender had no prior criminal record, or because the criminal activity (regardless of the penal code violation) was relatively innocuous. Heavy-duty cases receive more severe penalties because the offense, the offender, or the circumstances of the offense are deemed particularly serious. Diversion and straight probation types generally are considered lightweight, while the majority of joint cases are considered heavy-duty. Cases involving personal violence invariably are designated as heavy-duty. Most misdemeanor cases in which the defendant has no prior criminal record or a relatively minor record are termed lightweight. If the defendant has an extensive criminal record, however, even misdemeanor cases can call for stiff penalties; therefore such cases are considered heavy-duty. Certain felony cases can be regarded as lightweight if there was no violence, if the victim's loss was minimal, or if the defendant had no prior convictions. On occasion, even an offense like armed robbery can be considered lightweight. The following example (taken from an actual report) is one such instance: a first-time offender with a simulated gun held up a Seven-Eleven store and then returned to the scene, gave back the money, and asked the store employees to call the police.

The typings are general recommendations; specifics such as terms and conditions of probation or diversion and length of incarceration are worked out later in the investigation. The following discussion will clarify some of the criteria for arriving at a typing.

Deal cases involve situations in which a plea bargain exists. In California, many plea bargains specify specific sentencing stipulations; probation officers rarely recommend dispositions contrary to those stipulated in plea-bargaining agreements. Although probation officers allegedly are free to recommend a sentence different from that contained in the plea bargain, they have learned that such an action is unrealistic (and often counter-productive to their own interests) because judges inevitably uphold the primacy of sentence agreements. The following observation represents the probation officers' view of plea-bargaining deals:

> It's stupid to try and bust a deal. What's the percentage? Who needs the hassle? The judge always honors the deal—after all, he was part of

it. Everyone, including the defendant, has already agreed. It's all nice and neat, all wrapped up. We are supposed to rubber-stamp the pack-age— and we do. Everyone is better off that way.

Diversion cases typically involve relatively minor offenses com-mitted by those with no prior record, and are considered "a snap" by probation officers. In most cases, those referred for diversion have been screened already by the district attorney's office; the probation investigator merely agrees that they are eligible and therefore should be granted diversionary relief (and eventual dismissal of charges). In rare instances when there has been an oversight and the defendant is ineligible (because of prior criminal convictions), the probation officer informs the court, and criminal proceedings are resumed. Either sit-uation involves minimal decision making by probation officers about what disposition to recommend. Presentence investigators approach diversion cases in a perfunctory, almost mechanical manner.

The last three typings generally refer to cases in which the sen-tencing recommendations are ambiguous and some decision making is required of probation officers. These types represent the major con-sequences of criminal sentencing: incarceration and/or probation. Those categorized as joint (prison) cases are denied probation; instead the investigator recommends an appropriate prison sentence. In certain instances the nature of the offense (e.g., rape, murder, or arson) renders defendants legally ineligible for probation. In other sit-uations, the defendants' prior record (especially felony convictions) makes it impossible to grant probation (see, e.g., Neubauer 1974: 240). In many cases the length of prison sentences has been set by legal statute and can be increased or decreased only marginally (depending on the aggravating or mitigating circumstances of the case).

In California, the majority of defendants sentenced to prison receive a middle term (between minimum and maximum); the length of time varies with the offense. Those cases that fall outside the middle term usually do so for reasons related to the offense (e.g., using a weapon) or to the criminal record (prior felony convictions or, con-versely, no prior criminal record). Those typed originally as joint cases are treated differently from other probation applicants: con-cerns with rehabilitation or with the defendant's life situation are no longer relevant, and proper punishment becomes the focal point of inquiry. This perspective was described as follows by a probation officer respondent: "Once I know so-and-so is a heavy-duty joint case I don't think in terms of rehabilitation or social planning. It becomes a matter of how long to salt the sucker away, and that's covered by the code."

For those who are typed as probation cases, the issue for the investigator becomes whether to recommend some time in jail as a condition of probation. This decision is made with reference to whether the case is lightweight or heavy-duty. Straight probation usually is reserved for those convicted of relatively innocuous offenses or for those without a prior criminal record (first-timers). Some probation officers admitted candidly that all things being equal, middle-class defendants are more likely than other social classes to receive straight probation. The split sentence (probation and jail time) has become popular and is a consideration in most misdemeanor and felony cases, especially when the defendant has a prior criminal record. In addition, there is a feeling that drug offenders should receive a jail sentence as part of probation to deter them from future drug use.

Once a probation officer has decided that "some jail time is in order," the ultimate recommendation includes that condition. Although the actual amount of time frequently is determined late in the case, the probation officer's opinion that a jail sentence should be imposed remains constant. The following comment typifies the sentiments of probation officers whom I have observed and also illustrates the imprecision of recommending a period of time in custody:

> It's not hard to figure out who needs some jail. The referral sheet can tell you that. What's hard to know is exactly how much time. Ninety days or six months—who knows what's fair? We put down some number but it is usually an arbitrary figure. No one has come up with a chart that correlates rehabilitation with jail time.

Compiling Further Information

Once an initial typing has been completed, the next investigative stage involves collecting further information about the defendant. During this stage most of the data to be collected consists of extralegal considerations. The defendant is interviewed and his or her social history is delineated. Probation officers frequently contact collateral sources such as school officials, victims, doctors, counselors, and relatives to learn more about the defendant's individual circumstances. This aspect of the presentence investigation involves considerable time and effort on the part of probation officers. Such information is gathered primarily to legitimate earlier probation officer typings or to satisfy judicial requirements; recommendations seldom are changed during this stage. A similar pattern was described by a presentence investigator:

> Interviewing these defendants and working up a social history takes time. In most cases it's really unnecessary since I've already decided

what I am going to do. We all know that a recommendation is governed by the offense and prior record. All the rest is just stuffing to fill out the court report, to make the judge look like he's got all the facts.

Presentence interviews with defendants (a required part of the investigation) frequently are routine interactions that were described by a probation officer as "anticlimactic." These interviews invariably are conducted in settings familiar to probation officers, such as jail interviewing rooms or probation department offices. Because the participants lack trust in each other, discussions rarely are candid and open. Probation officers are afraid of being conned or manipulated because they assume that defendants "will say anything to save themselves." Defendants are trying to present themselves in a favorable light and are wary of divulging any information that might be used against them.

It is assumed implicitly in the interview process that probation officers act as interrogators and defendants as respondents. Because presentence investigators select the questions, they control the course of the interview and elicit the kind of responses that serve to substantiate their original defendant typings. A probationer described his presentence interview to me as follows:

I knew what the P.O. wanted me to say. She had me pegged as a nice middle-class kid who had fallen in with a bad crowd. So that's how I came off. I was contrite, a real boy scout who had learned his lesson. What an acting job! I figured if I didn't act up I'd get probation.

A probation officer related how she conducted presentence interviews:

I'm always in charge during the interviews. I know what questions to ask in order to fill out my report. The defendants respond just about the way I expect them to. They hardly ever surprise me.

On occasion, prospective probationers refuse to go along with structured presentence interviews. Some offenders either attempt to control the interview or are openly hostile to probation officers. Defendants who try to dominate interviews often can be dissuaded by reminders such as "I don't think you really appreciate the seriousness of your situation" or "I'm the one who asks the questions here." Some defendants, however, show blatant disrespect for the court process by flaunting a disregard for possible sanctions.

Most probation officers have interviewed some defendants who simply don't seem to care what happens to them. A defendant once informed an investigation officer: "I don't give a fuck what you motherfuckers try and do to me. I'm going to do what I fuckin' well please. Take your probation and stick it." Another defendant told her probation officer: "I'm going to shoot up every chance I get, I need my fix more than I need probation." Probation officers categorize belligerent defendants and those unwilling to "play the probation game" as dangerous or irrational (see, e.g., McCleary 1978). Frequently in these situations the investigator's initial typing is no longer valid, and probation either will be denied or will be structured stringently. Most interviews, however, proceed in a predictable manner as probation officers collect information that will be included in the section of the report termed "defendant's statement."

Although some defendants submit written comments, most of their statements actually are formulated by the probation officer. In a sociological sense, the defendant's statement can be considered an "account" (Scott and Lyman 1968). While conducting presentence-interviews, probation officers typically attempt to shape the defendant's account to fit their own preconceived typing. Many probation officers believe that the defendant's attitude toward the offense and toward the future prospects for leading a law-abiding life are the most important parts of the statement. In most presentence investigations the probation investigator identifies and interprets the defendant's subjective attitudes and then incorporates them into the report. Using this procedure, probation officers look for and can report attitudes that "logically fit" with their final sentencing recommendation (see, for example, Davis 1983).

Defendants who have been typed as prison cases typically are portrayed as holding socially unacceptable attitudes about their criminal actions and unrealistic or negative attitudes about future prospects for living an upright life. Conversely, those who have been typed as probation material are described as having acceptable attitudes, such as contriteness about the present offense and optimism about their ability to lead a crime-free life. The structuring of accounts about defendant attitudes was described by a presentence investigator in the following manner:

> When POs talk about the defendant's attitude we really mean how that attitude relates to the case. Naturally I'm not going to write about what a wonderful attitude the guy has—how sincere he seems—and then recommend sending him to the joint. That wouldn't make sense. The judges want consistency. If a guy has a shitty attitude but is going to get probation anyway, there's no percentage in playing up his attitude problem.

In most cases the presentence interview is the only contact between the investigating officer and the defendant. The brevity of this contact and the lack of post-report interaction foster a legalistic perspective. Investigators are concerned mainly with "getting the case through court" rather than with special problems related to supervising probationers on a long-term basis. One-time-only interviews rarely allow probation officers to become emotionally involved with their cases; the personal and individual aspects of the defendant's personality generally are not manifested during a half-hour presentence interview. For many probation officers the emotional distance from offenders is one of the benefits of working in presentence units. Such an opinion was expressed by an investigation officer: "I really like the one-shot-only part of this job. I don't have time to get caught up with the clients. I can deal with facts and not worry about individual personalities."

The probation officer has wide discretion in the type of collateral information that is collected from sources other than the defendant or the official record. Although a defendant's social history must be sketched in the presentence report, the supplementation of that history is left to individual investigators. There are few established guidelines for the investigating officer to follow, except that the psychiatric or psychological reports should be submitted when there is compelling evidence that the offender is mentally disturbed. Informal guidelines, however, specify that in misdemeanor cases reports should be shorter and more concise than in felony cases. The officers indicated that reports for municipal court (all misdemeanor cases) should range from four to six pages in length, while superior court reports (felony cases) were expected to be six to nine pages long. In controversial cases (to which only the most experienced officers are assigned) presentence reports are expected to be longer and to include considerable social data. Reports in these cases have been as long as 30 pages.

Although probation officers learn what general types of information to include through experience and feedback from judges and supervisors, they are allowed considerable leeway in deciding exactly what to put in their reports (outside of the offense and prior record sections). Because investigators decide what collateral sources are germane to the case, they tend to include information that will reflect favorably on their sentencing recommendation. In this context the observation of one probation officer is understandable: "I pick from the mass of possible sources just which ones to put in the report. Do you think I'm going to pick people who make my recommendation look weak? No way!"

Filing the Report

The final stage in the investigation includes dictating the report, having it approved by a probation supervisor, and appearing in court. All three of these activities serve to reinforce the importance of prior record and offense in sentencing recommendations. At the time of dictation, probation officers determine what to include in the report and how to phrase their remarks. For the first time in the investigation, they receive formal feedback from official sources. Presentence reports are read by three groups important to the probation officers: probation supervisors, district attorneys, and judges. Probation officers recognize that for varying reasons, all these groups emphasize the legally relevant variables of offense and prior criminal record when considering an appropriate sentencing recommendation.[6] Such considerations reaffirm the probation officer's initial private typing.

A probation investigator described this process:

> After I've talked to the defendants I think maybe some of them deserve to get special consideration. But when I remember who's going to look at the reports. My supervisor, the DA, the judge; they don't care about all the personal details. When all is said and done, what's really important to them is the offense and the defendant's prior record. I know that stuff from the start. It makes me wonder why we have to jack ourselves around to do long reports.

Probation officers assume that their credibility as presentence investigators will be enhanced if their sentencing recommendations meet with the approval of probation supervisors, district attorneys, and judges. On the other hand, officers whose recommendations are consistently "out of line" are subject to censure or transfer, or they find themselves engaged in "running battles" (Shover 1974: 357) with court officials. During the last stage of the investigation probation officers must consider how to ensure that their reports will go through court without "undue personal hassle." Most investigation officers have learned that presentence recommendations based on a consideration of prior record and offense can achieve that goal.

Although occupational self-interest is an important component in deciding how to conduct a presentence investigation, other factors also are involved. Many probation officers agree with the idea of using legally relevant variables as determinants of recommendations. These officers embrace the retributive value of this concept and see it as an equitable method for framing their investigation. Other officers reported that probation officers' discretion had been "short-circuited" by determinate sentencing guidelines and that they were reduced to "merely going through the motions" in conducting their investigations. Still other officers view the use of legal variables to structure recommendations as an acceptable bureaucratic shortcut to compensate partially for large case assignments. One probation officer stated, "If the department wants us to keep pumping out presentence reports we can't consider social factors—we just don't have time." Although probation officers are influenced by various dynamics, there seems little doubt that in California, the social history which once was considered the "heart and soul" of presentence probation reports (Reckless 1967: 673) has been largely devalued.

Summary and Conclusions

In this study I provide a description and an analysis of the processes used by probation investigators in preparing presentence reports. The research findings based on interview data indicate that probation officers tend to deemphasize individual defendants' characteristics and that their probation recommendations are not influenced directly by factors such as sex, age, race, socioeconomic status, or work record. Instead, probation officers emphasize the variables of instant offense and prior criminal record. The finding that offense and prior record are the main considerations of probation officers with regard to sentence recommendations agrees with a substantial body of research (Bankston 1983; Carter and Wilkins 1967; Dawson 1969; Lotz and Hewitt 1977; Robinson, Carter, and Wahl 1969; Wallace 1974; Walsh 1985).

My particular contribution has been to supply the ethnographic observations and the data that explain this phenomenon. I have identified the process whereby offense and prior record come to occupy the central role in decision making by probation officers. This identification underscores the significance of private typings in determining official designations. An analysis of probation practices suggests that the function of the presentence investigation is more ceremonial than instrumental (Hagan 1985).

I show that early in the investigation probation officers, using offense and prior record as guidelines, classify defendants into types; when the typing process is complete, probation officers essentially have decided on the sentence recommendation that will be recorded later in their official designation. The subsequent course of investigations is determined largely by this initial private typing. Further data collection is influenced by a sentence recommendation that already has been firmly established. This finding answers affirmatively the research question posed by Carter (1967: 211):

> Do probation officers, after "deciding" on a recommendation early in the presentence investigation, seek further information which justifies the decision, rather than information which might lead to modification or rejection of that recommendation?

The type of information and observation contained in the final presentence report is generated to support the original recommendation decision. Probation officers do not regard defendant typings as tentative hypotheses to be disproved through inquiry but rather as firm conclusions to be justified in the body of the report.

Although the presentence interview has been considered an important part of the investigation (Spencer 1983), I demonstrate that it does not significantly alter probation officers' perceptions. In most cases probation officers dominate presentence interviews; interaction between the participants is guarded. The nature of interviews between defendants and probation officers is important in itself; further research is needed to identify the dynamics that prevail in these interactions.

Attitudes attributed to defendants often are structured by probation officers to reaffirm the recommendation already formulated. The defendant's social history, long considered an integral part of the presentence report, in reality has little bearing on sentencing considerations. In most cases the presentence is no longer a vehicle for social inquiry but rather a typing process which considers mainly the defendant's prior criminal record and the seriousness of the criminal offense. Private attorneys in growing numbers have become disenchanted with the quality of probation investigations and have commissioned presentence probation reports privately (Rodgers, Gitchoff, and Paur 1984). At present, however, such a practice is generally available only for wealthy defendants.

The presentence process that I have described is used in the great majority of cases; it is the "normal" procedure. Even so, probation officers are not entirely passive actors in this process. On occasion they will give serious consideration to social variables in arriving at a sentencing recommendation. In special circumstances officers will allow individual defendants' characteristics to influence their report. In addition, probation officers who have developed credibility with the court are allowed some discretion in compiling presentence reports. This discretion is not unlimited, however; it is based on a prior record of producing reports that meet the court's approval, and is contingent on continuing to do so. A presentence writer said, "You can only afford to go to bat for defendants in a few select cases; if you try to do it too much, you get a reputation as being 'out of step.'"

This research raises the issue of probation officers' autonomy. Although I depict presentence investigators as having limited autonomy, other researchers (Hagan 1975; Myers 1979; Walsh 1985) contend that probation officers have considerable leeway in recommendation. This contradictory evidence can be explained in large part by the type of sentencing structure, the professionalism of probation workers, and the role of the district attorney at sentencing. Walsh's study (1985), for example, which views probation officers as important actors in the presentence process, was conducted in a jurisdiction with indeterminate sentencing, where the probation officers demonstrated a high degree of professionalism and the prosecutors "rarely made sentencing recommendations." A very different situation existed in the California counties that I studied: determinate sentencing was enforced, probation officers were not organized professionally, and the district attorneys routinely made specific court recommendations. It seems apparent that probation officers' autonomy must be considered with reference to judicial jurisdiction.

In view of the primacy of offense and prior record in sentencing considerations, the efficacy of current presentence investigation practices is doubtful. It seems ineffective and wasteful to continue to collect a mass of social data of uncertain relevance. Yet an analysis of courtroom culture suggests that the presentence investigation helps maintain judicial mythology as well as probation officer legitimacy. Although judges generally do not have the time or the inclination to consider individual variables thoroughly, the performance of a presentence investigation perpetuates the myth of individualized sentences. Including a presentence report in the court file gives the appearance of individualization without influencing sentencing practices significantly.

Even in a state like California, where determinate sentencing allegedly has replaced individualized justice, the judicial system feels obligated to maintain the appearance of individualization. After observing the court system in California for several years I am convinced that a major reason for maintaining such a practice is to make it easier for criminal defendants to accept their sentences. The presentence report allows defendants to feel that their case at least has received a considered decision. One judge admitted candidly that the "real purpose" of the presentence investigation was to convince defendants that they were not getting "the fast shuffle." He observed further that if defendants were sentenced without such investigations, many would complain and would file "endless appeals" over what seems to them a hasty sentencing decision. Even though judges typically consider only offense and prior record in a sentencing decision, they want defendants to believe that their cases are being judged individually. The presentence investigation allows this assumption to be maintained. In addition, some judges use the probation officer's report as an excuse for a particular type of sentence. In some instances they deny responsibility for the sentence, implying that their "hands were tied" by the recommendation. Thus judges are taken "off the hook" for meting out an unpopular sentence. Further research is needed to substantiate the significance of these latent functions of the presentence investigation.

The presentence report is a major component in the legitimacy of the probation movement; several factors support the probation officers' stake in maintaining their role in these investigations. Historically, probation has been wedded to the concept of individualized treatment. In theory, the presentence report is suited ideally to reporting on defendants' individual circumstances. From a historical perspective (Rothman 1980) this ideal has always been more symbolic than substantive, but if the legitimacy of the presentence report is questioned, so then is the entire purpose of probation.

Regardless of its usefulness (or lack of usefulness), it is doubtful that probation officials would consider the diminution or abolition of presentence reports. The number of probation workers assigned to presentence investigations is substantial, and their numbers represent an obvious source of bureaucratic power. Conducting presentence investigations allows probation officers to remain visible with the court and the public. The media often report on controversial probation cases, and presentence writers generally have more contact and more association with judges than do others in the probation department.

As ancillary court workers, probation officers are assigned the dirty work of collecting largely irrelevant data on offenders (Hagan 1975; Hughes 1958). Investigation officers have learned that emphasizing offense and prior record in their reports will enhance relationships with judges and district attorneys, as well as improving their occupational standing within probation departments. Thus the presentence investigation serves to maintain the court's claim of individualized concern while preserving the probation officer's role, although a subordinate role, in the court system.[7]

The myth of individualization serves various functions, but it also raises serious questions. In an era of severe budget restrictions (Schumacher 1985) should scarce resources be allocated to compiling predictable presentence reports of dubious value? If social variables are considered only in a few cases, should courts continue routinely to require presentence reports in all felony matters (as is the practice in California)? In summary, we should address the issue of whether the criminal justice system can afford the ceremony of a probation presentence investigation.

Notes

[1]For a full discussion of the insider-outsider perspective in criminal justice see Marquart (1986).

[2]In a few jurisdictions, officers who prepare investigations also supervise the defendants after probation has been granted, but, this procedure is becoming

less prevalent in contemporary probation (Clear and Cole 1986). It is possible that extralegal variables play a significant role in the supervision process, but this paper is concerned specifically with presentence investigations.

[3]There was no exact way to determine whether the 25 percent of the officers I was unable to interview conducted their presentence investigations significantly differently from those I interviewed. Personal observation, however, and the comments of the officers I interviewed (with whom I discussed this issue) indicated that those who refused used similar methods in processing their presentence reports.

[4]On occasion police reports are written vaguely and are subject to various interpretations; rap sheets are not always clear, especially when some of the final dispositions have not been recorded.

[5]I did not include terminal misdemeanor dispositions, in which probation is denied in favor of fines or jail sentences, in this typology. Such dispositions are comparatively rare and relatively insignificant.

[6]Although defense attorneys also read the presentence reports, their reactions generally do not affect the probation officers' occupational standing (McHugh 1973; Rosecrance 1985).

[7]I did not discuss the role of presentence reports in the prison system. Traditionally, probation reports were part of an inmate's jacket or file and were used as a basis for classification and treatment. The position of probation officers was legitimated further by the fact that prison officials also used the presentence report. I would suggest, however, that the advent of prison overcrowding and the accompanying security concerns have rendered presentence reports relatively meaningless. This contention needs to be substantiated before presentence reports are abandoned completely.

References

Allen, Harry E. and Clifford E. Simonsen. 1986. *Corrections in America*. New York: Macmillan.

Bankston, William B. 1983. "Legal and Extralegal Offender Traits and Decision-Making in the Criminal Justice System." *Sociological Spectrum*, 3: 1–18.

Blumberg, Abraham. 1967. *Criminal Justice*. Chicago: Quadrangle.

Blumer, Martin. 1979. "Concepts in the Analysis of Qualitative Data." *Sociological Review*, 27:651–77.

Blumstein, Alfred J., S. Martin and N. Holt. 1983. *Research on Sentencing: The Search for Reform*. Washington, DC: National Academy Press.

Carter, Robert M. 1967. "The Presentence Report and the Decision-Making Process." *Journal of Research in Crime and Delinquency*, 4:203–11.

Carter, Robert M. and Leslie T. Wilkins. 1967. "Some Factors in Sentencing Policy." *Journal of Criminal Law, Criminology, and Police Science*, 58: 503–14.

Clear, Todd and George Cole. 1986. *American Corrections*. Monterey, CA: Brooks/Cole.

Davis, James R. 1983. "Academic and Practical Aspects of Probation: A Comparison." *Federal Probation*, 47:7–10.

Dawson, Robert. 1969. *Sentencing*. Boston: Little, Brown.

Emerson, Robert M. 1983 (reissued 1988). "Ethnography and Understanding Members' Worlds." In Robert M. Emerson (ed.), *Contemporary Field Research: A Collection of Readings.* Prospect Heights, IL: Waveland Press.

Forer, Lois G. 1980. *Criminals and Victims.* New York: Norton.

Glaser, Barney and Anselm Strauss. 1967. *The Discovery of Grounded Theory.* Chicago: Aldine.

Goldsborough, E. and E. Burbank. 1968. "The Probation Officer and His Personality." In Charles L. Newman (ed.), *Sourcebook on Probation, Parole, and Pardons.* Springfield, IL: Charles C Thomas, pp. 104–12.

Hagan, John. 1975. "The Social and Legal Construction of Criminal Justice: A Study of the Presentence Process." *Social Problems,* 22:620–37.

———. 1977. "Criminal Justice in Rural and Urban Communities: A Study of the Bureaucratization of Justice." *Social Forces,* 55:597–612.

———. 1985. *Modern Criminology: Crime, Criminal Behavior, and its Control.* New York: McGraw-Hill.

Hagan, John, John Hewitt and Duane Alwin. 1979. "Ceremonial Justice: Crime and Punishment in a Loosely Coupled System." *Social Forces,* 58:506–25.

Hogarth, John. 1971. *Sentencing as a Human Process.* Toronto: University of Toronto Press.

Hughes, Everett C. 1958. *Men and Their Work.* New York: Free Press.

Katz, Janet. 1982. "The Attitudes and Decisions of Probation Officers." *Criminal Justice and Behavior,* 9:455–75.

Kingsnorth, Rodney and Louis Rizzo. 1979. "Decision-Making in the Criminal Courts: Continuities and Discontinuities." *Criminology,* 17:3–14.

Lotz, Ray and John Hewitt. 1977. "The Influence of Legally Irrelevant Factors on Felony Sentencing." *Sociological Inquiry,* 47:39–48.

Marquart, James W. 1986. "Outsiders as Insiders: Participant Observation in the Role of a Prison Guard." *Justice Quarterly,* 3:15–32.

McCleary, Richard. 1978. *Dangerous Men.* Beverly Hills: Sage.

McCleary, Richard, Barbara Nienstadt and James Erven. 1982. "Uniform Crime Reports as Organizational Outcomes: Three Time Series Experiments." *Social Problems,* 29:361–73.

McHugh, John J. 1973. "Some Comments on Natural Conflict between Counsel and Probation Officer." *American Journal of Corrections,* 3: 15–32.

Michalowski, Raymond J. 1985. *Order, Law and Crime.* New York: Random House.

Murrah, A. 1963. "Prison or Probation?" In B. Kay and C. Veddar (eds.), *Probation and Parole.* Springfield, IL: Charles C Thomas, pp. 63–78.

Myers, Martha A. 1979. "Offended Parties and Official Reactions: Victims and the Sentencing of Criminal Defendants." *Sociological Quarterly,* 20:529–46.

Neubauer, David. 1974. *Criminal Justice in Middle America.* Morristown, NJ: General Learning.

Petersilia, Joan, Susan Turner, James Kahan and Joyce Peterson. 1985. "Executive Summary of Rand's Study, Granting Felons Probation." *Crime and Delinquency,* 31:379–92.

Prus, Robert. 1975. "Labeling Theory: A Statement on Typing." *Sociological Focus*, 8:79–96.

Prus, Robert and John Stratten. 1976. "Factors in the Decision-Making of North Carolina Probation Officers." *Federal Probation*, 40:48–53.

Reckless, Walter C. 1967. *The Crime Problem*. New York: Appleton.

Robinson, James, Robert Carter and A. Wahl. 1969. *The San Francisco Project*. Berkeley: University of California School of Criminology.

Rodgers, T. A., G. T. Gitchoff and I. Paur. 1984. "The Privately Commissioned Presentence Report." In Robert M. Carter, Daniel Glaser, and Leslie T. Wilkins (eds.), *Probation, Parole, and Community Corrections*. New York: Wiley, pp. 21–30.

Rosecrance, John. 1985. "The Probation Officers' Search for Credibility: Ball Park Recommendations." *Crime and Delinquency*, 31:539–54.

———. 1987. "A Typology of Presentence Probation Investigators." *International Journal of Offender Therapy and Comparative Criminology*, 31:163–77.

Rothman, David. 1980. *Conscience and Convenience: The Asylum and its Alternatives in Progressive America*. Boston: Little. Brown.

Schumacher, Michael A. 1985. "Implementation of a Client Classification and Case Management System: A Practitioner's View." *Crime and Delinquency*, 31:445–55.

Scott, Marvin and Stanford Lyman. 1968. "Accounts." *American Sociological Review*, 33:46–62.

Shover, Neal. 1974. "Experts and Diagnosis in Correctional Agencies." *Crime and Delinquency*, 20:347–58.

———. 1979. *A Sociology of American Corrections*. Homewood, IL: Dorsey.

Spencer, Jack W. 1983. "Accounts, Attitudes and Solutions: Probation Officer-Defendant Negotiations of Subjective Orientations." *Social Problems*, 30:570–81.

Spradley, Joseph P. 1970. *You Owe Yourself a Drunk: An Ethnography of Urban Nomads*. Boston: Little, Brown.

Sudnow, David. 1965. "Normal Crimes: Sociological Features of the Penal Code." *Social Problems*, 12:255–76.

Tinker, John N., John Quiring and Yvonne Pimentel. 1985. "Ethnic Bias in California Courts: A Case Study of Chicano and Anglo Felony Defendants." *Sociological Inquiry*, 55:83–96.

Walker, Samuel. 1985. *Sense and Nonsense About Crime*. Monterey, CA: Brooks/Cole.

Wallace, John. 1974. "Probation Administration." In Daniel Glaser (ed.), *Handbook of Criminology*. Chicago: Rand-McNally, pp. 940–70.

Walsh, Anthony. 1985. "The Role of the Probation Officer in the Sentencing Process." *Criminal Justice and Behavior*, 12:289–303.

10

The Practice of Law as a Con Game

Abraham S. Blumberg

A recurring theme in the growing dialogue between sociology and law has been the great need for a joint effort of the two disciplines to illuminate urgent social and legal issues. Having uttered fervent public pronouncements in this vein, however, the respective practitioners often go their separate ways. Academic spokesmen for the legal profession are somewhat critical of sociologists of law because of what they perceive as the sociologist's preoccupation with the application of theory and methodology to the examination of legal phenomena, without regard to the solution of legal problems. Further, it is felt that "contemporary writing in the sociology of law . . . betrays the existence

From *Law and Society Review*. (June, 1967), pp. 15–39. Reprinted by permission of the author.

of painfully unsophisticated notions about the day-to-day operations of courts, legislatures and law offices."[1] Regardless of the merit of such criticism, scant attention—apart from explorations of the legal profession itself—has been given to the sociological examination of legal institutions, or their supporting ideological assumptions. Thus, for example, very little sociological effort is expended to ascertain the validity and viability of important court decisions, which may rest on wholly erroneous assumptions about the contextual realities of social structure. A particular decision may rest upon a legally impeccable rationale; at the same time it may be rendered nugatory or self-defeating by contingencies imposed by aspects of social reality of which the lawmakers are themselves unaware.

Within this context, I wish to question the impact of three landmark decisions of the United States Supreme Court; each hailed as destined to effect profound changes in the future of criminal law administration and enforcement in America. The first of these, *Gideon vs. Wainwright*, 372 U.S. 335 (1963) required states and localities henceforth to furnish counsel in the case of indigent persons charged with a felony.[2] The Gideon ruling left several major issues unsettled, among them the vital question: What is the precise point in time at which a suspect is entitled to counsel?[3] The answer came relatively quickly in *Escobedo v. Illinois*, 378 U.S. 478 (1964), which has aroused a storm of controversy. Danny Escobedo confessed to the murder of his brother-in-law after the police had refused to permit retained counsel to see him, although his lawyer was present in the station house and asked to confer with his client. In a 5–4 decision, the court asserted that counsel must be permitted when the process of police investigative effort shifts from merely investigatory to that of accusatory: "When its focus is on the accused and its purpose is to elicit a confession—our adversary system begins to operate, and, under the circumstances here, the accused must be permitted to consult with his lawyer."

As a consequence, Escobedo's confession was rendered inadmissible. The decision triggered a national debate among police, district attorneys, judges, lawyers, and other law enforcement officials, which continues unabated, as to the value and propriety of confessions in criminal cases.[4] On June 13, 1966, the Supreme Court in a 5–4 decision underscored the principle enunciated in *Escobedo* in the case of *Miranda v. Arizona*.[5] Police interrogation of any suspect in custody, without his consent, unless a defense attorney is present, is prohibited by the self-incrimination provision of the Fifth Amendment. Regardless of the relative merit of the various shades of opinion about the role of counsel in criminal cases, the issues generated thereby will be in part resolved as additional cases move toward decision in the

Supreme Court in the near future. They are of peripheral interest and not of immediate concern in this paper. However, the *Gideon*, *Escobedo*, and *Miranda* cases pose interesting questions. In all three decisions, the Supreme Court reiterates the traditional legal conception of a defense lawyer based on the ideological perception of a criminal case as an *adversary, combative* proceeding, in which counsel for the defense assiduously musters all the admittedly limited resources at his command to *defend* the accused.[6] The fundamental question remains to be answered: Does the Supreme Court's conception of the role of counsel in a criminal case square with social reality?

The task of this paper is to furnish some preliminary evidence toward the illumination of that question. Little empirical understanding of the function of defense counsel exists; only some ideologically oriented generalizations and commitments. This paper is based upon observations made by the writer during many years of legal practice in the criminal courts of a large metropolitan area. No claim is made as to its methodological rigor, although it does reflect a conscious and sustained effort for participant observations.

Court Structure Defines Role of Defense Lawyer

The overwhelming majority of convictions in criminal cases (usually over 90 per cent) are not the product of a combative, trial-by-jury process at all, but instead merely involve the sentencing of the individual after a negotiated, bargained-for plea of guilty has been entered.[7] Although more recently the overzealous role of police and prosecutors in producing pretrial confessions and admissions has achieved a good deal of notoriety, scant attention has been paid to the organizational structure and personnel of the criminal court itself. Indeed, the extremely high conviction rate produced without the features of an adversary trial in our courts would tend to suggest that the "trial" becomes a perfunctory reiteration and validation of the pretrial interrogation and investigation.[8]

The institutional setting of the court defines a role for the defense counsel in a criminal case radically different from the one traditionally depicted.[9] Sociologists and others have focused their attention on the deprivations and social disabilities of such variables as race, ethnicity, and social class as being the source of an accused person's defeat in a criminal court. Largely overlooked is the variable of the court organization itself, which possesses a thrust, purpose, and direction of its own. It is grounded in pragmatic values, bureaucratic priorities, and administrative instruments. These exalt maximum production and the particularistic career designs of organizational incumbents, whose occupational and career commitments tend to generate a set of priorities. These priorities exert a higher claim than the stated ideological goals of "due process of law," and are often inconsistent with them.

Organizational goals and discipline impose a set of demands and conditions of practice on the respective professions in the criminal court, to which they respond by abandoning their ideological and professional commitments to the accused client, in the service of these higher claims of the court organization. All court personnel, including the accused's own lawyer, tend to be coopted to become agent-mediators[10] who help the accused redefine his situation and restructure his perceptions concomitant with a plea of guilty.

Of all the occupational roles in the court the only private individual who is officially recognized as having a special status and concomitant obligations is the lawyer. His legal status is that of "an officer of the court" and he is held to a standard of ethical performance and duty to his client as well as to the court. This obligation is thought to be far higher than that expected of ordinary individuals occupying the various occupational statuses in the court community. However, lawyers, whether privately retained or of the legal-aid, public defender variety, have close and continuing relations with the prosecuting office and the court itself through discreet relations with the judges via their law secretaries or "confidential" assistants. Indeed, lines of communication, influence and contact with those offices, as well as with the Office of the Clerk of the court, Probation Division, and with the press, are essential to present and prospective requirements of criminal law practice. Similarly, the subtle involvement of the press and other mass media in the court's organizational network is not readily discernible to the casual observer. Accused persons come and go in the court system schema, but the structure and its occupational incumbents remain to carry on their respective career, occupational and organizational enterprises. The individual stridencies, tensions, and conflicts a given accused person's case may present to all the participants are overcome, because the formal and informal relations of all the groups in the court setting require it. The probability of continued future relations and interactions must be preserved at all costs.

This is particularly true of the "lawyer regulars" i.e., those defense lawyers, who by virtue of their continuous appearances in behalf of defendants, tend to represent the bulk of a criminal court's non-indigent case workload, and those lawyers who are not "regulars," who appear almost casually in behalf of an occasional client. Some of the "lawyer regulars" are highly visible as one moves about the major urban centers of the nation, their offices line the back streets of the courthouses, at times sharing space with bondsmen. Their political "visibility" in terms of local club house ties, reaching into the judge's chambers and prosecutor's office, are also deemed essential to successful practitioners. Previous research has indicated that the "lawyer regulars" make no effort to conceal their dependence upon police, bondsmen, jail personnel. Nor do they conceal the necessity for maintaining intimate relations with all levels of personnel in the court setting as a means of obtaining, maintaining, and building their practice. These informal relations are the *sine qua non* not only of retaining a practice, but also in the negotiation of pleas and sentences.[11]

The client, then, is a secondary figure in the court system as in certain other bureaucratic settings.[12] He becomes a means to other ends of the organization's incumbents. He may present doubts, contingencies, and pressures which challenge existing informal arrangements or disrupt them; but these tend to be resolved in favor of the continuance of the organization and its relations as before. There is a greater community of interest among all the principal organizational structures and their incumbents than exists elsewhere in other settings. The accused's lawyer has far greater professional, economic, intellectual and other ties to the various elements of the court system than he does to his own client. In short, the court is a closed community.

This is more than just the case of the usual "secrets" of bureaucracy which are fanatically defended from an outside view. Even all elements of the press are zealously determined to report on that which will not offend the board of judges, the prosecutor, probation, legal-aid, or other officials, in return for privileges and courtesies granted in the past and to be granted in the future. Rather than any view of the matter in terms of some variation of a "conspiracy" hypothesis, the simple explanation is one of an ongoing system handling delicate tensions, managing the trauma produced by law enforcement and administration, and requiring almost pathological distrust of "outsiders" bordering on group paranoia.

The hostile attitude toward "outsiders" is in large measure engendered by a defensiveness itself produced by the inherent deficiencies of assembly line justice, so characteristic of our major criminal courts. Intolerably large caseloads of defendants which must be disposed of in an organizational context of limited resources and personnel, potentially subject the participants in the court community to harsh scrutiny from appellate courts, and other public and private sources of condemnation. As a consequence, an almost irreconcilable conflict is posed in terms of intense pressures to process large numbers of cases on the one hand, and the stringent ideological and legal requirements of "due process of law," on the other hand. A rather tenuous resolution of the dilemma has emerged in the shape of a large variety of bureaucratically ordained and controlled "work crimes," short cuts, deviations, and outright rule violations adopted as court practice in order to meet production norms. Fearfully anticipating criticism on ethical as well as legal grounds, all the significant participants in the court's social structure are bound into an organized system of complicity. This consists of a work arrangement in which the patterned, covert, informal breaches, and evasions of "due process" are institutionalized, but are nevertheless denied to exist.

These institutionalized evasions will be found to occur to some degree, in all criminal courts. Their nature, scope and complexity are largely determined by the size of the court, and the character of the community in which it is located, e.g., whether it is a large, urban institution, or a relatively small rural county court. In addition, idiosyncratic, local conditions may contribute to a unique flavor in the character and quality of the criminal law's administration in a particular community. However, in most instances a variety of stratagems are employed—some subtle, some crude, in effectively disposing of what are often too large caseloads. A wide variety of coercive devices are employed against an accused-client, couched in a depersonalized, instrumental, bureaucratic version of due process of law, and which are in reality a perfunctory obeisance to the ideology of due process. These include some very explicit pressures which are exerted in some measure by all court personnel, including judges, to plead guilty and avoid trial. In many instances the sanction of a potentially harsh sentence is utilized as the visible alternative to pleading guilty, in the case of recalcitrants. Probation and psychiatric reports are "tailored" to organizational needs, or are at least responsive to the court organization's requirements for the refurbishment of a defendant's social biography, consonant with his new status. A resourceful judge can, through his subtle domination of the proceedings, impose his will on the final outcome of a trial. Stenographers and clerks, in their function as record keepers, are on occasion pressed into service in support of a judicial need to "rewrite" the record of a courtroom event. Bail practices are usually employed for purposes other than simply assuring a defendant's presence on the date of a hearing in connection with his case. Too often, the discretionary power as to bail is part of the arsenal of weapons available to collapse the resistance of an accused person. The foregoing is a most cursory examination of some of the more prominent "short cuts" available to any court organization. There are numerous other procedural strategies constituting due process deviations, which tend to become the work style artifacts of a court's personnel. Thus, only court "regulars" who are "bound in" are really accepted; others are treated routinely and in almost a coldly correct manner.

The defense attorneys, therefore, whether of the legal-aid, public defender variety, or privately retained, although operating in terms of pressures specific to their respective role and organizational obligations, ultimately are concerned with strategies which tend to lead to a plea. It is the rational, impersonal elements involving economies of time, labor, expense and a superior commitment of the defense counsel to these rationalistic values of maximum production[13] of court organization that prevail, in his relationship with a client. The lawyer "regulars" are frequently former staff members of the prosecutor's office and utilize the prestige, know-how and contacts of their former affiliation as part of their stock in trade. Close and continuing relations between the lawyer "regular" and his former colleagues in the prosecutor's office generally overshadow the relationship between the regular and his client. The continuing colleagueship of supposedly adversary counsel rests on real professional and organizational needs of a *quid pro quo*, which goes beyond the limits of an accommodation or *modus vivendi* one might ordinarily expect under the circumstances of an otherwise seemingly adversary relationship. Indeed, the adversary features which are manifest are for the most part muted and exist even in their attenuated form largely for external consumption. The principals, lawyer and assistant district attorney, rely upon one another's cooperation for their continued professional existence, and so the bargaining between them tends usually to be "reasonable" rather than fierce.

Fee Collection and Fixing

The real key to understanding the role of defense counsel in a criminal case is to be found in the area of the fixing of the fee to be charged and its collection. The problem of fixing and collecting the fee tends to influence to a significant degree the criminal court process itself, and not just the relationship of the lawyer and his client. In essence, a lawyer-client "confidence game" is played. A true confidence game is unlike the case of the emperor's new clothes wherein that monarch's nakedness was a result of inordinate gullibility and credulity. In a genuine confidence game, the perpetrator manipulates the basic dishonesty of his partner, the victim or mark, toward his own (the confidence operator's) ends. Thus, "the victim of a con scheme must have some larceny in his heart."[14]

Legal service lends itself particularly well to confidence games. Usually, a plumber will be able to demonstrate empirically that he has performed a service by clearing up the stuffed drain, repairing the leaky faucet or pipe—and therefore merits his fee. He has rendered, when summoned, a visible, tangible boon for his client in return for the requested fee. A physician, who has not performed some visible surgery or otherwise engaged in some readily discernible procedure in connection with a patient, may be deemed by the patient to have "done nothing" for him. As a consequence, medical practitioners may simply prescribe or administer by injection a placebo to overcome a patient's potential reluctance or dissatisfaction in paying a requested fee, "for nothing."

In the practice of law there is a special problem in this regard, no matter what the level of the practitioner or his place in the hierarchy of prestige. Much legal work is intangible either because it is simply a few words of advice, some preventive action, a telephone call, negotiation of some kind, a form filled out and filed, a hurried conference with another attorney or an official of a government agency, a letter or opinion written, or a countless variety of seemingly innocuous, and even prosaic procedures and actions. These are the basic activities, apart from any possible court appearance, of almost all lawyers, at all levels of practice. Much of the activity is not in the nature of the exercise of the traditional, precise professional skills of attorney such as library research and oral argument in connection with appellate briefs, court motions, trial work, drafting of opinions, memoranda, contracts, and other complex documents and agreements. Instead, much legal activity, whether it is at the lowest or highest "white shoe" law firm levels, is of the brokerage, agent, sales representative, lobbyist type of activity, in which the lawyer acts for someone else in pursuing the latter's interests and designs. The service is intangible.[15]

The large scale law firm may not speak as openly of the "contacts," their "fixing" abilities, as does the lower level lawyer. They trade instead upon a facade of thick carpeting, walnut panelling, genteel low pressure, and superficialities of traditional legal professionalism. There are occasions when even the large firm is on the defensive in connection with the fees they charge because the services rendered or results obtained do not appear to merit the fee asked.[16] Therefore, there is a recurrent problem in the legal profession in fixing the amount of fee, and in justifying the basis for the requested fee.

Although the fee at times amounts to what the traffic and the conscience of the lawyer will bear, one further observation must be made with regard to the size of the fee and its collection. The defendant in a criminal case and the material gain he may have acquired during the course of his illicit activities are soon parted. Not infrequently the ill gotten fruits of the various modes of larceny are sequestered by a defense lawyer in payment of his fee. Inexorably, the amount of the fee is a function of the dollar value of the crime committed, and is frequently set with meticulous precision at a sum which bears an uncanny relationship to that of the net proceeds of the particular offense involved. On occasion, defendants have been known to commit additional offenses while at liberty on bail, in order to secure the requisite funds with which to meet their obligations for payment of legal fees. Defense lawyers condition even the most obtuse clients to recognize that there is a firm interconnection between fee payment and the zealous exercise of professional expertise, secret knowledge, and organizational "connections" in their behalf. Lawyers, therefore, seek to keep their clients in a proper state of tension, and to arouse in them the precise edge of anxiety which is calculated to encourage prompt fee payment. Consequently, the client attitude in the relationship between defense counsel and an accused is in many instances a precarious admixture of hostility, mistrust, dependence, and sycophancy. By keeping his client's anxieties aroused to the proper pitch, and establishing a seemingly causal relationship between a requested fee and the accused's ultimate extrication from his onerous difficulties, the lawyer will have established the necessary preliminary groundwork to assure a minimum of haggling over the fee and its eventual payment.

In varying degrees, as a consequence, all law practice involves a manipulation of the client and a stage management of the lawyer-client relationship so that at least an *appearance* of help and service will be forthcoming. This is accomplished in a variety of ways, often exercised in combination with each other. At the outset, the lawyer-professional employs with suitable variation a measure of sales-puff which may range from an air of unbounding self-confidence, adequacy, and dominion over events, to that of complete arrogance. This will be supplemented by the affectation of a studied, faultless mode of personal attire. In the larger firms, the furnishings and office trappings will serve as the backdrop to help in impression management and client intimidation. In all firms, solo or large scale, an access to secret knowledge, and to the seats of power and influence is inferred, or presumed to a varying degree as the basic vendible commodity of the practitioners.

The lack of visible end product offers a special complication in the course of the professional life of the criminal court lawyer with respect to his fee and in his relations with his client. The plain fact is that an accused in a criminal case always "loses" even when he has been exonerated by an acquittal, discharge, or dismissal of his case. The hostility of an accused which follows as a consequence of his arrest, incarceration, possible loss of job, expense and other traumas connected with his case is directed, by means of displacement, toward his lawyer. It is in this sense that it may be said that a criminal lawyer never really "wins" a case. The really satisfied client is rare, since in the very nature of the situation even an accused's vindication leaves him with some degree of dissatisfaction and hostility. It is this state of affairs that makes for a lawyer-client relationship in the criminal court which tends to be a somewhat exaggerated version of the usual lawyer-client confidence game.

At the outset, because there are great risks of nonpayment of the fee, due to the impecuniousness of his clients, and the fact that a man who is sentenced to jail may be a singularly unappreciative client, the criminal lawyer collects his fee *in advance*. Often, because the lawyer and the accused both have questionable designs of their own upon each other, the confidence game can be played. The criminal lawyer must serve three major functions, or stated another way, he must solve three problems. First, he must arrange for his fee; second, he must prepare and then, if necessary, "cool out" his client in case of defeat[17] (a highly likely contingency); third, he must satisfy the court organization that he has performed adequately in the process of negotiating the plea, so as to preclude the possibility of any sort of embarrassing incident which may serve to invite "outside" scrutiny.

In assuring the attainment of one of his primary objectives, his fee, the criminal lawyer will very often enter into negotiations with the accused's kin, including collateral relatives. In many instances, the accused himself is unable to pay any sort of fee or anything more than a token fee. It then becomes important to involve as many of the accused's kin as possible in the situation. This is especially so if the attorney hopes to collect a significant part of a proposed substantial fee. It is not uncommon for several relatives to contribute toward the fee. The larger the group, the greater the possibility that the lawyer will collect a sizable fee by getting contributions from each.

A fee for a felony case which ultimately results in a plea, rather than a trail, may ordinarily range anywhere from $500 to $1,500. Should the case go to trial, the fee will be proportionately larger, depending upon the length of the trial. But the larger the fee the lawyer wishes to exact, the more impressive his performance must be, in terms of his stage managed image as a personage of great influence and power in the court organization. Court personnel are keenly aware of the extent to which a lawyer's stock in trade involves the precarious stage management of an image which goes beyond the usual professional flamboyance, and for this reason alone the lawyer is "bound in" to the authority system of the court's organizational discipline. Therefore, to some extent, court personnel will aid the lawyer in the creation and maintenance of that impression. There is a tacit commitment to the lawyer by the court organization, apart from formal etiquette, to aid him in this. Such augmentation of the lawyer's stage managed image as this affords, is the partial basis for the *quid pro quo* which exists between the lawyer and the court organization. It tends to serve as the continuing basis for the higher loyalty of the lawyer to the organization; his relationship with his client, in contrast is transient, ephemeral and often superficial.

Defense Lawyer as Double Agent

The lawyer has often been accused of stirring up unnecessary litigation, especially in the field of negligence. He is said to acquire a vested interest in a cause of action or claim which was initially his client's. The strong incentive of possible fee motivates the lawyer to promote litigation which would otherwise never have developed. However, the criminal lawyer develops a vested interest of an entirely different nature in his client's case: to limit its scope and duration rather than do battle. Only in this way can a case be "profitable." Thus, he enlists the aid of relatives not only to assure payment of his fee, but he will also rely on these persons to help him in his agent-mediator role of convincing the accused to plead guilty, and ultimately to help in "cooling out" the accused if necessary.

It is at this point that an accused-defendant may experience his first sense of "betrayal." While he had perhaps perceived the police and prosecutor to be adversaries, or possibly even the judge, the accused is wholly unprepared for his counsel's role performance as an agent-mediator. In the same vein, it is even less likely to occur to an accused that members of his own family or other kin may become agents, albeit at the behest and urging of other agents or mediators, acting on the principle that they are in reality helping an accused negotiate the best possible plea arrangement under the circumstances. Usually, it will be the lawyer who will activate next of kin in this role, his ostensible motive being to arrange for his fee. But soon latent and unstated motives will assert themselves, with entreaties by counsel to the accused's next of kin, to appeal to the accused to "help himself" by pleading. *Gemeinschaft* sentiments are to this extent exploited by a defense lawyer (or even at times by a district attorney) to achieve specific secular ends, that is, of concluding a particular matter with all possible dispatch.

The fee is often collected in stages, each installment usually payable prior to a necessary court appearance required during the course of an accused's career journey. At each stage, in his interviews and communications with the accused, or in addition, with members of his family, if they are helping with the fee payment, the lawyer employs an air of professional confidence and "inside-dopesterism" in order to assuage anxieties on all sides. He makes the necessary bland assurances, and in effect manipulates his client, who is usually willing to do and say the things, true or not, which will help his attorney extricate him. Since the dimensions of what he is essentially selling, organizational influence and expertise, are not technically and precisely measurable, the lawyer can make extravagant claims of influence and secret knowledge with impunity. Thus, lawyers frequently claim to have inside knowledge in connection with information in the hands of the D.A., police, probation officials or to have access to these functionaries. Factually, they often do, and need only to exaggerate the nature of their relationships with them to obtain the desired effective impression upon the client. But, as in the genuine confidence game, the victim who has participated is loath to do anything which will upset the lesser plea which his lawyer has "conned" him into accepting.[18]

In effect, in his role as double agent, the criminal lawyer performs an extremely vital and delicate mission for the court organization and the accused. Both principals are anxious to terminate the litigation with a minimum of expense and damage to each other. There is no other personage or role incumbent in the total court structure more strategically located, who by training and in terms of his own requirements, is more ideally suited to do so than the lawyer. In recognition of this, judges will cooperate with attorneys in many important ways. For example, they will adjourn the case of an accused in jail awaiting plea or sentence if the attorney requests such action. While explicitly this may be done for some innocuous and seemingly valid reason, the tacit purpose is that pressure is being applied by the attorney for the collection of his fee, which he knows will probably not be forthcoming if the case is concluded. Judges are aware of this tactic on the part of lawyers, who, by requesting an adjournment, keep an accused incarcerated awhile longer as a not too subtle method of dunning a client for payment. However, the judges will go along with this, on the ground that important ends are being served. Often, the only end served is to protect a lawyer's fee.

The judge will help an accused's lawyer in still another way. He will lend the official aura of his office and courtroom so that a lawyer can stage manage an impression of an "all out" performance for the accused in justification of his fee. The judge and other court personnel will serve as a backdrop for a scene charged with dramatic fire, in which the accused's lawyer makes a stirring appeal in his behalf. With a show of restrained passion, the lawyer will intone the virtues of the accused and recite the social deprivations which have reduced him to his present state. The speech varies somewhat, depending on whether the accused has been convicted after trial or has pleaded guilty. In the main, however, the incongruity, superficiality, and ritualistic character of the total performance is underscored by a visibly impassive, almost bored reaction on the part of the judge and other members of the court retinue.

Afterward, there is a hearty exchange of pleasantries between the lawyer and district attorney, wholly out of context in terms of the supposed adversary nature of the preceding events. The fiery passion in defense of his client is gone, and the lawyers for both sides resume their offstage relations, chatting amiably and perhaps including the judge in their restrained banter. No other aspect of their visible conduct so effectively serves to put even a casual observer on notice, that these individuals have claims upon each other. These seemingly innocuous actions are indicative of continuing organizational and informal relations, which, in their intricacy and depth, range far beyond any priorities or claims a particular defendant my have.[19]

Criminal law practice is a unique form of private law practice since it really only appears to be private practice.[20] Actually it is bureaucratic practice, because of the legal practitioner's enmeshment in the authority, discipline, and perspectives of the court organization. Private practice, supposedly, in a professional sense, involves the maintenance of an organized, disciplined body of knowledge and learning; the individual practitioners are imbued with a spirit of autonomy and service, the earning of a livelihood being incidental. In the sense that the lawyer in the criminal court serves as a double agent, serving higher organizational rather than professional ends, he may be deemed to be engaged in bureaucratic rather than private practice. To some extent the lawyer-client "confidence game," in addition to its other functions, serves to conceal this fact.

The Client's Perception

The "cop-out" ceremony, in which the court process culminates, is not only invaluable for redefining the accused's perspectives of himself, but also in reiterating publicly in a formally structured ritual the accused person's guilt for the benefit of significant "others" who are observing. The accused not only is made to assert publicly his guilt of a specific crime, but also a complete recital of its details. He is further made to indicate that he is entering his plea of guilty freely, willingly, and voluntarily, and that he is not doing so because of any promises or in consideration of any commitments that may have been made to him by anyone. This last is intended as a blanket statement to shield the participants from any possible charges of "coercion" or undue influence that may have been exerted in violation of due process requirements. Its function is to preclude any later review by an appellate court on these grounds, and also to obviate any second thoughts an accused may develop in connection with his plea.

However, for the accused, the conception of self as a guilty person is in large measure a temporary role adaptation. His career socialization as an accused, if it is successful, eventuates in his acceptance and redefinition of himself as a guilty person.[21] However, the transformation is ephemeral, in that he will, in private, quickly reassert his innocence. Of importance is that he accept his defeat, publicly proclaim it, and find some measure of pacification in it.[22] Almost immediately after his plea, a defendant will generally be interviewed by a representative of the probation division in connection with a presentence report which is to be prepared. The very first question to be asked of him by the probation officer is: "Are you guilty of the crime to which you pleaded?" This is by way of double affirmation of the defendant's guilt. Should the defendant now begin to make bold assertions of his innocence, despite his plea of guilty, he will be asked to withdraw his plea and stand trial on the original charges. Such a threatened possibility is, in most instances, sufficient to cause an accused to let the plea stand and to request the probation officer to overlook his exclamations of innocence. Table I that follows is a breakdown of the categorized responses of a random sample of male defendants in Metropolitan Court[23] during 1962, 1963, and 1964 in connection with their statements during presentence probation interviews following their plea of guilty.

It would be well to observe at the outset, that of the 724 defendants who pleaded guilty before trial, only 43 (5.94 per cent) of the total group had confessed prior to their indictment. Thus, the ultimate judicial process was predicated upon evidence independent of any confession of the accused.[24]

As the data indicate, only a relatively small number (95) out of the total number of defendants actually will even admit their guilt, following the "cop-out" ceremony. However, even though they have affirmed their guilt, many of these defendants felt that they should have been able to negotiate a more favorable plea. The largest aggregate of defendants (373) were those who reasserted their "innocence" following their public profession of guilt during the "cop-out" ceremony. These defendants employed differential degrees of fervor, solemnity and credibility, ranging from really mild, wavering assertions of innocence which were embroidered with a variety of stock explanations and rationalizations, to those of an adamant, "framed" nature. Thus, the "Innocent" group, for the most part, were largely concerned with underscoring for their probation interviewer their essential "goodness" and "worthiness," despite their formal plea of guilty. Assertion of his innocence at the post-plea stage, resurrects a more respectable and acceptable self concept for the accused defendant who has pleaded guilty. A recital of the structural exigencies which precipitated his plea of guilt, serves to embellish a newly proffered claim of innocence, which many defendants mistakenly feel will stand them in good stead at the time of sentence, or ultimately with probation or parole authorities.

Table I Defendant Responses as to Guilt or Innocence after Pleading Guilty

N = 724   Years—1962, 1963, 1964

Nature of Response	N of Defendants	
Innocent (Manipulated)	The "lawyer or judge, police or D.A. 'conned me'"	86
Innocent (Pragmatic)	"Wanted to get it over with" "You can't beat the system" "They have you over a barrel when you have a record"	147
Innocent (Advice of cousel)	"Followed my lawyer's advice"	92
Innocent (Defiant)	"Framed"— "Betrayed by 'Complainant,' 'Police,' 'Squealers,' 'Lawyer,' 'Friends,' 'Wife,' 'Girlfriend'"	33
Innocent (Adverse social data)	Blames probation officer or psychiatrist for "Bad Report," in cases where there was pre-pleading investigation	15
Guilty	"But I should have gotten a better deal" Blames lawyer, D.A., Police, Judge	74
Guilty	Won't say anything further	21
Fatalistic (Doesn't press his "Innocence," won't admit "Guilt")	"I did it for convenience" "My lawyer told me it was only thing I could do" "I did it because it was the best way out"	248
No Response		8
Total		724

Relatively few (33) maintained their innocence in terms of having been "framed" by some person or agent-mediator, although a larger number (86) indicated that they had been manipulated or "conned" by an agent-mediator to plead guilty, but as indicated, their assertions of innocence were relatively mild.

A rather substantial group (147) preferred to stress the pragmatic aspects of their plea of guilty. They would only perfunctorily assert their innocence and would in general refer to some adverse aspect of their situation which they believed tended to negatively affect their bargaining leverage, including in some instances a prior criminal record.

One group of defendants (92), while maintaining their innocence, simply employed some variation of a theme of following "the advice of counsel" as a covering response, to explain their guilty plea in the light of their new affirmation of innocence.

The largest single group of defendants (248) were basically fatalistic. They often verbalized weak suggestions of their innocence in rather halting terms, wholly without conviction. By the same token, they would not admit guilt readily and were generally evasive as to guilt or innocence, preferring to stress aspects of their stoic submission in their decision to plead. This sizable group of defendants appeared to perceive the total court process as being caught up in a monstrous organizational apparatus, in which the defendant role expectancies were not clearly defined. Reluctant to offend anyone in authority, fearful that clear-cut statements on their part as to their guilt or innocence would be negatively construed, they adopted a stance of passivity, resignation and acceptance. Interestingly, they would in most instances invoke their lawyer as being the one who crystallized the available alternatives for them, and who was therefore the critical element in their decision-making process.

In order to determine which agent-mediator was most influential in altering the accused's perspectives as to his decision of plead or go to trial (regardless of the proposed basis of the plea), the same sample of defendants were asked to indicate the person who first suggested to them that they plead guilty. They were also asked to indicate which of the persons or officials who made such suggestion, was most influential in affecting their final decision to plead.

The following table indicates the breakdown of the responses to the two questions:

It is popularly assumed that the police, through forced confessions, and the district attorney, employing still other pressures, are most instrumental in the inducement of an accused to plead guilty.[25] As Table II indicates, it is actually the defendant's own counsel who is most effective in this role. Further, this phenomenon tends to reinforce the extremely rational nature of criminal law administration, for an organization could not rely upon the sort of idiosyncratic measures employed by the police to induce confessions and maintain its efficiency, high production and overall rational-legal character. The defense counsel becomes the ideal agent-mediator since, as "officer of the court" and confidant of the accused and his kin, he lives astride both worlds and can serve the ends of the two as well as his own.[26]

Table II Role of Agent-mediators in Defendant's Guilty Plea

Person or Official	First Suggested Plea of Guilty	Influenced the Accused Most in His Final Decision to Plead
Judge	4	26
District attorney	67	116
Defense counsel	407	411
Probation officer	14	3
Psychiatrist	8	1
Wife	34	120
Friends and kin	21	14
Police	14	4
Fellow inmates	119	14
Others	28	5
No response	8	10
Total	724	724

While an accused's wife, for example, may be influential in making him more amenable to a plea, her agent-mediator role has, nevertheless, usually been sparked and initiated by defense counsel. Further, although a number of first suggestions of a plea came from an accused's fellow jail inmates, he tended to rely largely on his counsel as an ultimate source of influence in his final decision. The defense counsel, being a crucial figure in the total organizational scheme in constituting a new set of perspectives for the accused, the same sample of defendants were asked to indicate at which stage of their contact with counsel was the suggestion of a plea made. There are three basic kinds of defense counsel available in Metropolitan Court: Legal-aid, privately retained counsel, and counsel assigned by the court (but may eventually be privately retained by the accused).

The overwhelming majority of accused persons, regardless of type of counsel, related a specific incident which indicated an urging or suggestion, either during the course of the first or second contact, that they plead guilty to a lesser charge if this could be arranged. Of all the agent-mediators, it is the lawyer who is most effective in manipulating an accused's perspectives, notwithstanding pressures that may have been previously applied by police, district attorney, judge or any of the agent-mediators that may have been activated by them. Legal-aid and assigned counsel would apparently be more likely to suggest a possible plea at the point of initial interview as response to pressures of time. In the case of the assigned counsel, the strong possibility that there is no fee involved, may be an added impetus to such a suggestion at the first contact.

In addition, there is some further evidence in Table III of the perfunctory, ministerial character of the system in Metropolitan Court and similar criminal courts. There is little real effort to individualize, and the lawyer's role as agent-mediator may be seen as unique in that he is in effect a double agent. Although, as "officer of the court" he mediates between the court organization and the defendant, his roles with respect to each are rent by conflicts of interest. Too often these must be resolved in favor of the organization which provides him with the means for his professional existence. Consequently, in order to reduce the strains and conflicts imposed in what is ultimately an overdemanding role obligation for him, the lawyer engages in the lawyer-client "confidence game" so as to structure more favorably an otherwise onerous role system.[27]

Table III   Stage at Which Counsel Suggested Accused to Plead

N= 724

	Counsel Type							
Contact	Privately Retained		Legal-aid		Assigned		Total	
	N	%	N	%	N	%	N	%
First	66	35	237	49	28	60	331	46
Second	83	44	142	29	8	17	233	32
Third	29	15	63	13	4	9	96	13
Fourth or more	12	6	31	7	5	11	48	7
No response	0	0	14	3	2	4	16	2
Total	190	100	487	101	47	101	724	100

Conclusion

Recent decisions of the Supreme Court, in the area of criminal law administration and defendant's rights, fail to take into account three crucial aspects of social structure which may tend to render the more libertarian rules as nugatory. The decisions overlook (1) the nature of courts as formal organization; (2) the relationship that the lawyer-regular *actually* has with the court organization; and (3) the character of the lawyer-client relationship in the criminal court (the routine relationships, not those unusual ones that are described in "heroic" terms in novels, movies, and TV).

Courts, like many other modern large-scale organizations, possess a monstrous appetite for the cooptation of entire professional groups as well as individuals.[28] Almost all those who come within the ambit of organizational authority, find that their definitions, perceptions and values have been refurbished, largely in terms favorable to the particular organization and its goals. As a result, recent Supreme Court decisions may have a long range effect which is radically different from that intended or anticipated. The more libertarian rules will tend to produce the rather ironic end result of augmenting the *existing* organizational arrangements, enriching court organizations with more personnel and elaborate structure, which in turn will maximize organizational goals of "efficiency" and production. Thus, many defendants will find that courts will possess an even more sophisticated apparatus for processing them toward a guilty plea!

Notes

[1] H. W. Jones, *A View From the Bridge*, Law and Society: Supplement to Summer, 1965 Issue of Social Problems, p. 42 (1965). See G. Geis, *Sociology, Criminology, and Criminal Law*, 7 Social Problems, pp. 40–47 (1959); N. S. Timasheff, *Growth and Scope of Sociology of Law*, in *Modern Sociological Theory in Continuity and Change*, pp. 424–49 (H. Becker & A. Boskoff, eds. 1957), for further evaluation of the strained relations between sociology and law.

[2] This decision represented the climax of a line of cases which had begun to chip away at the notion that the Sixth Amendment of the Constitution (right to assistance of counsel) applied only to the federal government, and could not be held to run against the states through the Fourteenth Amendment. An exhaustive historical analysis of the Fourteenth Amendment and the Bill of Rights will be found in C. Fairman, *Does the Fourteenth Amendment Incorporate the Bill of Rights? The Original Understanding*, 2 Stan. L. Rev., pp. 5–139 (1949). Since the Gideon decision, there is already evidence that its effect will ultimately extend to indigent persons charged with misdemeanors—and perhaps ultimately even traffic cases and other minor offenses. For a popular account of this important development in connection with the right to assistance of counsel, see A. Lewis, *Gideon's Trumpet* (1964). For a scholarly historical analysis of the right to counsel see W. M. Beaney, *The Right to Counsel in American Courts* (1955). For a more recent comprehensive review and discussion of the right to counsel and its development, see Note, *Counsel at Interrogation*, 73 Yale L.J., pp. 1000–57 (1964).

With the passage of the Criminal Justice Act of 1964, indigent accused persons in the federal courts will be defended by federally paid legal counsel. For a general discussion of the nature and extent of public and private legal aid in the United States prior to the Gideon case. see E. A. Brownell, *Legal Aid in the United States* (1961); also R. B. van Mehren, et al., *Equal Justice for the Accused* (1959).

[3]In the case of federal defendants the issue is clear. In *Mallory v. United States*, 354 U.S. 449 (1957), the Supreme Court unequivocally indicated that a person under federal arrest must be taken "without any unnecessary delay" before a U.S. commissioner where he will receive information as to his rights to remain silent and to assistance of counsel which will be furnished, in the event he is indigent, under the Criminal Justice Act of 1964. For a most interesting and richly documented work in connection with the general area of the Bill of Rights. see C. R. Sowle, *Police Power and Individual Freedom* (1962).

[4]See N. Y. Times, Nov. 20, 1965, p. 1, for Justice Nathan R. Sobel's statement to the effect that based on his study of 1,000 indictments in Brooklyn, NY from February-April, 1965, fewer than 10% involved confessions. Sobel's detailed analysis will be found in six articles which appeared in the New York Law Journal, beginning November 15, 1965, through November 21, 1965, titled *The Exclusionary Rules in the Law of Confessions: A Legal Perspective—A Practical Perspective*. Most law enforcement officials believe that the majority of convictions in criminal cases are based upon confessions obtained by police. For example, the District Attorney of New York County (a jurisdiction which has the largest volume of cases in the United States), Frank S. Hogan, reports that confessions are crucial and indicates "if a suspect is entitled to have a lawyer during preliminary questioning . . . any lawyer worth his fee will tell him to keep his mouth shut," N.Y. Times, Dec. 2, 1965, p. 1. Concise discussions of the issue are to be found in D. Robinson, Jr. *Massiah, Escobedo and Rationales for the Exclusion of Confessions*, 56 *J. Crim. L.C. & P.S.*, pp. 412–31 (1965); D.C. Dowling, *Escobedo and Beyond: The Need for a Fourteenth Amendment Code of Criminal Procedure*, 56 *J. Crim. L.C. & P.S.*, pp. 143–57 (1965).

[5]*Miranda v. Arizona*, 384 U.S. 436 (1966).

[6]Even under optimal circumstances a criminal case is a very much one-sided affair, the parties to the "contest" being decidedly unequal in strength and resources. See A. S. Goldstein, *The State and the Accused: Balance of Advantage in Criminal Procedure*, 69 Yale L.J., pp. 1149–99 (1960).

[7]F. J. Davis et al., *Society and the Law: New Meanings for an Old Profession* 301 (1962); L. Orfield, *Criminal Procedure from Arrest to Appeal, p.* 297 (1947). D. J. Newman, *Pleading Guilty for Considerations: A Study of Bargain Justice*, 46 *J. Crim. L.C. & P.S.*, pp. 780–90 (1954). Newman's data covered only one year, 1954, in a midwestern community, however, it is in general confirmed by my own data drawn from a far more populous area, and from what is one of the major criminal courts in the country, for a period of fifteen years from 1950 to 1964 inclusive. The English experience tends also to confirm American data, see N. Walker, *Crime and Punishment in Britain: An Analysis of the Penal System* (1965). See also D. J. Newman, *Conviction: The Determination of Guilt or Innocence Without Trial* (1966), for a comprehensive legalistic study of the guilty plea sponsored by the American Bar Foundation. The criminal court as a social system, an analysis of "bargaining" and its functions in the criminal court's organizational structure, are examined in my

forthcoming book, *The Criminal Court: A Sociological Perspective*, to be published by Quadrangle Books, Chicago.

[8]G. Feifer, *Justice in Moscow* (1965). The Soviet trial has been termed "an appeal from the pretrial investigation" and Feifer notes that the Soviet "trial" is simply a recapitulation of the data collected by the pretrial investigator. The notions of a trial being a "tabula rasa" and presumptions of innocence are wholly alien to Soviet notions of justice. ". . . the closer the investigation resembles the finished script, the better. . . ." *Id*. at 86.

[9]For a concise statement of the constitutional and economic aspects of the right to legal assistance, see M. G. Paulsen, *Equal Justice for the Poor Man* (1964); for a brief traditional description of the legal profession see P. A. Freund, *The Legal Profession*, Daedalus, pp. 689–700 (1963).

[10]I use the concept in the general sense that Erving Goffman employed it in his *Asylums: Essays on the Social Situation of Mental Patients and Other Inmates* (1961).

[11]A. L. Wood, *Informal Relations in the Practice of Criminal Law*, 62 Am. J. Soc., pp. 48–55 (1956); J. E. Carlin, *Lawyers on Their Own*, pp. 105–109 (1962); R. Goldfarb, *Ransom—A Critique of the American Bail System*, pp. 114–15 (1965). Relatively recent data as to recruitment to the legal profession, and variables involved in the type of practice engaged in, will be found in J. Ladinsky, *Careers of Lawyers, Law Practice, and Legal Institutions*, 28 Am. Soc. Rev., pp. 47–54 (1963). See also S. Warkov & J. Zelan, *Lawyers in the Making* (1965).

[12]There is a real question to be raised as to whether in certain organizational settings, a complete reversal of the bureaucratic-ideal has not occurred. That is, it would seem, in some instances the organization appears to exist to serve the needs of its various occupational incumbents, rather than its clients. A. Etzioni, *Modern Organizations*, pp. 94–104 (1964).

[13]Three relatively recent items reported in the New York Times, tend to underscore this point as it has manifested itself in one of the major criminal courts. In one instance the Bronx County Bar Association condemned "mass assembly-line justice," which "was rushing defendants into pleas of guilty and into convictions, in violation of their legal rights." N.Y. Times, March 10, 1965, p. 51. Another item, appearing somewhat later that year reports a judge criticizing his own court system (the New York Criminal Court), that "pressure to set statistical records in disposing of cases had hurt the administration of justice." N.Y. Times, Nov. 4, 1965, p. 49. A third, and most unusual recent public discussion in the press was a statement by a leading New York appellate judge decrying "instant justice" which is employed to reduce court calendar congestion "converting our courthouses into counting houses . . ., as in most big cities where the volume of business tends to overpower court facilities." N.Y. Times, Feb. 5, 1966, p. 58.

[14]R. L. Gasser, *The Confidence Game*, 27 Fed. Prob. 47 (1963).

[15]C. W. Mills, *White Collar*, pp. 121–29 (1951); J. E. Carlin, *supra*, note 11.

[16]E. O. Smigel, *The Wall Street Lawyer*, (New York: The Free Press of Glencoe, 1964), p. 309.

[17]Talcott Parsons indicates that the social role and function of the lawyer can be therapeutic, helping his client psychologically in giving him necessary emotional support at critical times. The lawyer is also said to be acting as an agent of social control in the counseling of his client and in the influencing of his course of conduct. See T. Parsons, *Essays in Sociological Theory*, 382 et seq. (1954); E.

Goffman, *On Cooling the Mark Out: Some Aspects of Adaptations to Failure*, in *Human Behavior and Social Processes*, pp. 482–505 (A. Rose ed., 1962). Goffman's "cooling out" analysis is especially relevant in the lawyer-accused client relationship.

[18]The question has never been raised as to whether "bargain justice," "copping a plea," or justice by negotiations is a constitutional process. Although it has become the most central aspect of the process of criminal law administration, it has received virtually no close scrutiny by the appellate courts. As a consequence, it is relatively free of legal control and supervision. But, apart from any questions of the legality of bargaining, in terms of the pressures and devices that are employed which tend to violate due process of law, there remain ethical and practical questions. The system of bargain-counter justice is like the proverbial iceberg, much of its danger is concealed in secret negotiations and its least alarming feature, the final plea, being the one presented to public view. See A. S. Trebach, *The Rationing of Justice*, pp. 74–94 (1964); Note, *Guilty Plea Bargaining: Compromises by Prosecutors to Secure Guilty Pleas*, 112 U. Pa. L. Rev., pp. 865–95 (1964).

[19]For a conventional summary statement of some of the inevitable conflicting loyalties encountered in the practice of law, see E. E. Cheatham, *Cases and Materials on the Legal Profession*, pp. 70–79 (2d ed., 1955).

[20]Some lawyers at either end of the continuum of law practice appear to have grave doubts as to whether it is indeed a profession at all. J. E. Carlin, *op. cit., supra*, note 11, at 192; E. O. Smigel, *supra*, note 16 at 304–305. Increasingly, it is perceived as a business with widespread evasion of the Canons of Ethics, duplicity and chicanery being practiced in an effort to get and keep business. The poet, Carl Sandburg, epitomized this notion in the following vignette: "Have you a criminal lawyer in this burg?" "We think so but we haven't been able to prove it on him." C. Sandburg, *The People, Yes*, 154 (1936).

Thus, while there is considerable amount of dishonesty present in law practice involving fee splitting, thefts from clients, influence peddling, fixing, questionable use of favors and gifts to obtain business or influence others, this sort of activity is most often attributed to the "solo," private practice lawyer. See A. L. Wood, *Professional Ethics Among Criminal Lawyers*, Social Problems (1959). However, to some degree, large scale "downtown" elite firms also engage in these dubious activities. The difference is that the latter firms enjoy a good deal of immunity from these harsh charges because of their institutional and organizational advantages, in terms of near monopoly over more desirable types of practice, as well as exerting great influence in the political, economic and professional realms of power.

[21]This does not mean that most of those who plead guilty are innocent of any crime. Indeed, in many instances those who have been able to negotiate a lesser plea, have done so willingly and eagerly. The system of justice-by-negotiation, without trial, probably tends to better serve the interests and requirements of guilty persons, who are thereby presented with formal alternatives of "half a loaf," in terms of, at worst, possibilities of a lesser plea and a concomitant shorter sentence as compensation for their acquiescence and participation. Having observed the prescriptive etiquette in compliance with the defendant role expectancies in this setting, he is rewarded. An innocent person, on the other hand, is confronted with the same set of role prescriptions, structures and legal

alternatives, and in any event, for him this mode of justice is often an ineluctable bind.

[22]Any communicative network between persons whereby the public identity of an actor is transformed into something looked on as lower in the local scheme of social types will be called a "status degradation ceremony." H. Garfinkel, *Conditions of Successful Degradation Ceremonies*, 61 Am. J. Soc., pp. 420–24 (1956). But contrary to the conception of the "cop out" as a "status degradation ceremony," is the fact that it is in reality a charade, during the course of which an accused must project an appropriate and acceptable amount of guilt, penitence and remorse. Having adequately feigned the role of the "guilty person," his hearers will engage in the fantasy that he is contrite, and thereby merits a lesser plea. It is one of the essential functions of the criminal lawyer that he coach and direct his accused-client in that role performance. Thus, what is actually involved is not a "degradation" process at all, but is instead, a highly structured system of exchange cloaked in the rituals of legalism and public professions of guilt and repentance.

[23]The name is of course fictitious. However, the actual court which served as the universe from which the data were drawn, is one of the largest criminal courts in the United States, dealing with felonies only. Female defendants in the years 1950 through 1964 constituted from 7–10% of the totals for each year.

[24]My own data in this connection would appear to support Sobel's conclusion (see note 4 *supra*), and appears to be at variance with the prevalent view, which stresses the importance of confessions in law enforcement and prosecution. All the persons in my sample were originally charged with felonies ranging from homicide to forgery; in most instances the original felony charges were reduced to misdemeanors by way of a negotiated lesser plea. The vast range of crime categories which are available facilitates the patterned court process of plea reduction to a lesser offense, which is also usually a socially less opprobrious crime. For an illustration of this feature of the bargaining process in a court utilizing a public defender office, see D. Sudnow, *Normal Crimes: Sociological Features of the Penal Code in a Public Defender Office*, 12 Social Problems, pp. 255–76 (1964).

[25]Failures, shortcomings and oppressive features of our system of criminal justice have been attributed to a variety of sources including "lawless" police, overzealous district attorneys, "hanging" juries, corruption and political connivance, incompetent judges, inadequacy or lack of counsel, and poverty or other social disabilities of the defendant. See A. Barth, *Law Enforcement versus the Law* (1963), for a journalist's account embodying this point of view; J. H. Skolnick, *Justice without Trial: Law Enforcement in Democratic Society* (1966), for a sociologist's study of the role of the police in criminal law administration. For a somewhat more detailed, albeit legalistic and somewhat technical discussion of American police procedures, see W. R. LaFave, *Arrest: The Decision to Take a Suspect into Custody* (1965).

[26]Aspects of the lawyer's ambivalences with regard to the expectancies of the various groups who have claims upon him, are discussed in H. J. O'Gorman, *The Ambivalence of Lawyers*, paper presented at the Eastern Sociological Association meetings, April 10, 1965.

[27]W. J. Goode, *A Theory of Role Strain*, 25 Am. Soc. Rev., pp. 483–96 (1960); J. D. Snok, *Role Strain in Diversified Role Sets*, 71 Am. J. Soc., pp. 363–72 (1966).

[28]Some of the resources which have become an integral part of our courts. e.g., psychiatry, social work and probation, were originally intended as part of an ameliorative, therapeutic effort to individualize offenders. However, there is some evidence that a quite different result obtains, than the one originally intended. The ameliorative instruments have been coopted by the court in order to more "efficiently" deal with a court's caseload, often to the legal disadvantage of an accused person. See F. A. Allen, *The Borderland of Criminal Justice* (1964); T. S. Szasz, *Law, Liberty and Psychiatry* (1963) and also Szasz's most recent, *Psychiatric Justice* (1965); L. Diana, "The Rights of Juvenile Delinquents: An Appraisal of Juvenile Court Procedures," 47 *J. Crim. L. C. & P.S.*, pp. 561–69 (1957).

11

Adapting to Plea Bargaining
Prosecutors

Milton Heumann

The new prosecutor shares many of the general expectations that his counterpart for the defense brings to the court. He expects factually and legally disputable issues, and the preliminary hearings and trials associated with these. If his expectations differ at all from the naive "Perry Mason" orientation, it is only to the extent that he anticipates greater success than the hapless Hamilton Burger of Perry Mason fame.

The new prosecutor's views about plea bargaining parallel those of the defense attorney. He views plea bargaining as an expedient employed in crowded urban courts by harried and/or poorly motivated prosecutors. He views the trial as "what the system is really about," and plea bargaining as a necessary evil dictated by case volume. The following exchange with a newly appointed prosecutor is illustrative.

Reprinted from *Plea Bargaining* by Milton Heumann with permission of the University of Chicago Press and the author. © 1978 by the University of Chicago Press.

Q: Let's say they removed the effects of case pressure, provided you with more manpower. You wouldn't have that many cases. . . .

A: Then everybody should go to trial.

Q: Everybody should go to trial?

A: Yeah.

Q: Why?

A: Because supposedly if they're guilty they'll be found guilty. If they're not guilty they'll be found not guilty. That's the fairest way . . . judged by a group of your peers, supposedly.

Q: So you think that plea bargaining is a necessary evil?

A: Yeah.

Q: Would justice be better served if all cases went to trial?

A: That's the way it's supposed to be set up. Sure. Why wouldn't it?

Q: Would prosecutors be more satisfied?

A: Probably.

Q: If cases went to trial?

A: Sure.

Q: Why?

A: Because they could talk in front of twelve people and act like a lawyer. Right. Play the role.

It should be emphasized that these expectations and preferences of the new prosecutor are founded on the minimal law school preparation discussed earlier [in *Plea Bargaining*, from which this is excerpted]. The newcomers simply do not know very much about the criminal justice system.

Unlike defense attorneys, however, the new prosecutor is likely to receive some form of structured assistance when he begins his job. The chief prosecutor or chief state's attorney may provide this aid, if the prosecutor's office is staffed by a number of prosecutors or state's attorneys—that is, if the newcomer is not the only assistant prosecutor—it is more common for the chief prosecutor to assign to one or more of his experienced assistants the responsibility for helping the newcomer adjust. Since the newcomer's actions reflect on the office as a whole, it is not surprising that this effort is made.

The assistance the newcomer receives can be described as a form of structured observation. For roughly two weeks, he accompanies an experienced prosecutor to court and to plea bargaining sessions and observes him in action. The proximity of the veteran prosecutor—and his designation as the newcomer's mentor—facilitate communication between the two. The experienced prosecutor can readily explain or justify his actions, and the newcomer can ask any and all relevant questions. Certainly, this is a more structured form of assistance than defense attorneys receive.

However, new prosecutors still feel confused and overwhelmed during this initial period. Notwithstanding the assistance they receive, they are disoriented by the multitude of tasks performed by the prosecutor and by the environment in which he operates. This is particularly true in the circuit court, where the seemingly endless shuffling of files, the parade of defendants before the court and around the courtroom, the hurried, early morning plea bargaining sessions all come as a surprise to the new prosecutor.

Q: What were your initial impressions of the court during this "orientation period?"

A: The first time I came down here was a Monday morning at the arraignments. Let's face it, the majority of people here, you don't expect courts to be as crowded as they are. You don't expect thirty to thirty-five people to come out of the cell block who have been arrested over the weekend. It was . . . you sit in court the first few days, you didn't realize the court was run like this. All you see, you see Perry Mason on TV, or pictures of the Supreme Court, or you see six judges up there in a spotless courtroom, everyone well dressed, well manicured, and you come to court and find people coming in their everyday clothes, coming up drunk, some are high on drugs, it's . . . it's an experience to say the least.

Q: Could you describe your first days when you came down here? What are your recollections? Anything strike you as strange?

A: Just the volume of business and all the stuff the prosecutor had to do. For the first week or two, I went to court with guys who had been here. Just sat there and watched. What struck me was the amount of things he [the prosecutor] has to do in the courtroom. The prosecutor runs the courtroom. Although the judge is theoretically in charge, we're standing there plea bargaining and calling the cases at the same time and chewing gum and telling people to quiet down and setting bonds, and that's what amazed me. I never thought I would learn all the terms. What bothered me also was the paperwork. Not the Supreme Court decisions, not the *mens rea* or any of this other stuff, but the amount of junk that's in those files that you have to know. We never heard about this crap in law school.

As suggested in the second excerpt, the new prosecutor is also surprised by the relative insignificance of the judge. He observes that the prosecutor assumes—through plea bargaining—responsibility for the disposition of many cases. Contrary to his expectations of being an adversary in a dispute moderated by the judge, he finds that often the prosecutor performs the judge's function.

It is precisely this responsibility for resolving disputes that is most vexing to the new superior court state's attorney. Unlike his circuit court counterpart, he does not generally find hurried conferences, crowded courts, and so on. But he observes that, as in the circuit court, the state's attorney negotiates cases, and in the superior court far more serious issues and periods of incarceration are involved in these negotiations. For the novice state's attorney, the notion that he will in short order be responsible for resolving these disputes is particularly disturbing.

Q: What were your initial impressions of your job here [as a state's attorney]?

A: Well, I was frightened of the increased responsibility. I knew the stakes were high here. . . . I didn't really know what to expect, and I would say it took me a good deal of time to adapt here.

Q: Adapt in which way?

A: To the higher responsibilities. Here you're dealing with felonies, serious felonies all the way up to homicides, and I had never been involved in that particular type of situation. . . . I didn't believe that I was prepared to handle the type of job that I'd been hired to do. I looked around me and I saw the serious charges, the types of cases, and the experienced defense counsel on the one hand and the inexperience on my part on the other, and I was, well. . . .

Q: Did you study up on your own?

A: No more than. . . . Before I came over here I had done some research and made a few notes, et cetera, about the procedures. I think I was prepared from the book end of things to take the job, but, again, it was the practical aspects that you're not taught in law school and that you can only learn from experience that I didn't have, and that's what I was apprehensive about.

These first weeks in the court, then, serve to familiarize the newcomer with the general patterns of case resolution. He is not immediately thrust into the court but is able to spend some time simply observing the way matters are handled. The result, though, is to increase his anxiety. The confusion of the circuit court and the responsibilities of a state's attorney in the superior court were not anticipated. The newcomer expects to be able to prepare cases leisurely and to rely on the skills learned in law school. Yet he finds that his colleagues seem to have neither the time nor the inclination to operate in this fashion. As the informal period of orientation draws to a close, the newcomer has a better perspective on the way the system operates, but still is on very uneasy footing about how to proceed when the responsibility for the case is his alone. In short, he is somewhat disoriented by his orientation.

The Prosecutor on His Own
Initial Firmness and Resistance to Plea Bargaining

Within a few weeks after starting his job, the prosecutor and the state's attorney are expected to handle cases on their own. Experienced personnel are still available for advice, and the newcomer is told that he can turn to them with his problems. But the cases are now the newcomer's, and, with one exception, he is under no obligation to ask anyone for anything.

The new prosecutor is confronted by a stream of defense attorneys asking for a particular plea bargain in a case. If the prosecutor agrees, his decision is irreversible. It would be a violation of all the unwritten folkways of the criminal court for either a defense attorney or a prosecutor to break his word. On the other hand, if the prosecutor does not plea bargain, offers nothing in exchange for a plea, he at least does not commit himself to an outcome that may eventually prove to be a poor decision on his part. However, a refusal to plea bargain also places him "out of step" with his colleagues and with the general expectation of experienced defense attorneys.

Like the new attorney, the new prosecutor is in no hurry to dispose of the case. He is (1) inclined toward an adversary resolution of the case through formal hearings and trial, (2) disinclined to plea bargain in general, and (3) unsure about what constitutes an appropriate plea bargain for a particular case. Yet he is faced with demands by defense attorneys to resolve the case through plea bargaining. The new defense attorney has the luxury of postponing his decision for any given case. He can seek the advice of others before committing himself to a particular plea bargain in a particular case. For the new prosecutor, this is more difficult, since he is immediately faced with the demands of a number of attorneys in a number of different cases.

When the new prosecutor begins to handle his own cases, then, he lacks confidence about how to proceed in his dealings with defense attorneys. He often masks his insecurity in this period with an outward air of firmness. He is convinced that he must appear confident and tough, lest experienced attorneys think they can take advantage of him.

Q: What happened during your first few days of handling cases on your own?

A: Well, as a prosecutor, first of all, people try to cater to you because they want you to do favors for them. If you let a lawyer run all over you, you are dead. I had criminal the first day, on a Monday, and I'm in there [in the room where cases are negotiated], and a guy comes in, and I was talking to some lawyer on his file, and he's just standing there. Then I was talking to a second guy, and he was about fourth or fifth. So he looked at me and says: "When the hell you going to get to me?" So I says: "You wait your fucking turn. I'll get to you when I'm ready. If you don't like it, get out." It's sad that you have to swear at people, but it's the only language they understand—especially lawyers. Lawyers are the most obstinate, arrogant, belligerent bastards you will ever meet. Believe me. They come into this court—first of all—and we are really the asshole of the judicial system [circuit court], and they come in here and don't really have any respect for you. They'll come in here and be nice to you, because they feel you'll give them a *nolle*. That's all. Lawyers do not respect this court. I don't know if I can blame them or not blame them. You can come in here and see the facilities here; you see how things are handled; you see how it's like a zoo pushing people in and out. . . . When they do come here, lawyers have two approaches. One, they try to soft soap you and kiss your ass if you give them a *nolle*. Two, they'll come in here and try to ride roughshod over you and try to push you to a corner. Like that lawyer that first day. I had to swear at him and show him I wasn't going to take that shit, and that's that. The problem of dealing with lawyers is that you can't let them bullshit you. So, when I first started out I tried to be. . . . It's like the new kid on the block. He comes to a new neighborhood, and you've got to prove yourself. If you're a patsy, you're going to live with that as long as you're in court. If you let a couple of lawyers run over you, word will get around to go to _____, he's a pushover. Before you know it, they're running all over you. So you have to draw a line so they will respect you.

At first I was very tough because I didn't know what I was doing. In other words, you have to be very wary. These guys, some of them, have been practicing in this court for forty years. And they'll take you to the cleaners. You have to be pretty damn careful.

The new prosecutor couples this outward show of firmness toward attorneys with a fairly rigid plea bargaining posture. His reluctance to offer incentives to the defendant for a plea or to reward the defendant who chooses to plead is, at this point in the prosecutor's career, as much a function of his lack of confidence as it is a reflection of his antipathy toward plea bargaining. During this very early stage he is simply afraid to make concessions. Experienced court personnel are well aware that new prosecutors adopt this rigid stance.

Q: Have you noticed any differences between new prosecutors and prosecutors that have been around awhile?

A: Oh, yes. First of all, a new prosecutor is more likely to be less flexible in changing charges. He's afraid. He's cautious. He doesn't

know his business. He doesn't know the liars. He can't tell when
he's lying or exaggerating. He doesn't know all the ramifications.
He doesn't know how tough it is sometimes to prove the case to
juries. He hasn't got the experience, so that more likely than not
he will be less flexible. He is also more easily fooled. [circuit court
judge]

I can only answer that question in a general way. It does seem to
me that the old workhorses [experienced prosecutors] are more
flexible than the young stallions. [superior court judge]

Q: You were saying about the kids, the new prosecutors, the new
state's attorneys. Are they kind of more hard-assed?

A: They tend to be more nervous. They tend to have a less well-defined
idea of what they can do and what they can't do without being criticized. So, to the extent that they are more nervous, they tend to
be more hard-assed. [private criminal attorney]

Q: What about new prosecutors? Do they differ significantly from
prosecutors who have been around awhile?

A: Initially a new prosecutor is going to be reluctant to *nolle*, reluctant
to give too good a deal because he is scared. He is afraid of being
taken advantage of. And if you are talking about the circuit court,
they've got the problem that they can't even talk it over with anybody. They've got a hundred fifty cases or whatever, and they make
an offer or don't make an offer, that's it. Maybe at the end of the
day they may get a chance to talk it over and say: "Gee, did I do the
right thing?" The defense attorney, when the offer is made, has the
opportunity to talk to somebody plus his client before making a
decision. So I think it takes the prosecutor a longer time to come
around and work under the system. [legal aid attorney]

It is not difficult to understand why the new prosecutor is reluctant
to plea bargain and why he appears rigid to court veterans. Set aside
for the moment the prosecutor's personal preference for an adversary resolution and consider only the nature of the demands being
made on him. Experienced attorneys want charges dropped, sentence recommendations, and *nolles*. They approach him with the
standard argument about the wonderful personal traits of the defendant, the minor nature of the crime, the futility of incarceration, and
so on. When the new prosecutor picks up the file, he finds that the
defendant probably has an extensive prior criminal record and,
often, that he has committed a crime that does not sound minor at
all. Under the statute for the crime involved, it is likely that the defendant faces a substantial period of incarceration, yet in almost all circuit court cases and in many superior court cases, the attorneys are
talking about a no-time disposition. What to the new prosecutor fre-

quently seems like a serious matter is treated as a relatively inconsequential offense by defense attorneys. And, because the newcomer views the matter as serious, his resolve to remain firm—or, conversely, his insecurity about reducing charges—is reinforced.

Illustrations of this propensity for the new prosecutor or state's attorney to be "outraged" by the facts of the case, and to be disinclined to offer "sweet" deals, are plentiful. The following comments by two circuit court prosecutors and a superior court state's attorney, respectively, illustrate the extent to which the newcomer's appraisal of a case differed from that of the defense attorney and from that of his own colleagues.

Q: You used to go to____ [chief prosecutor] for help on early cases. Were his recommendations out of line with what you thought should be done with the case?

A: Let's say a guy came in with a serious crime. . . a crime that I thought was serious at one time, anyway. Take fighting on ____ Avenue [a depressed area of Arborville]. He got twenty-five stitches in the head and is charged with aggravated assault. One guy got twenty-five stitches, the other fifteen. And the attorneys would want me to reduce it. I'd go and talk to____ [chief prosecutor]. He'd say: "They both are drunk, and both got head wounds. Let them plead to breach of peace, and the judge will give them a money fine." Things like that I didn't feel right about doing, since, to me, right out of law school, middle class, you figure twenty-five stitches in the head, Jesus Christ.

Q: How did you learn what a case was worth?

A: What do you mean, what it's worth?

Q: In terms of plea bargaining. What the going rate. . . .

A: From the prosecutors and defense attorneys who would look at me dumbfounded when I would tell them that I would not reduce this charge. And then they would go running to my boss and he'd say, "Well, it's up to him." Some would even go running to the judge, screaming. One guy claimed surprise when I intended to go to trial for assault in second, which is a Class D felony. Two counts of that and two misdemeanor counts. It was set for jury trial. His witnesses were there. His experience in this court, he said, having handled two or three hundred cases, was that none has ever gone to trial. So he claimed surprise the day of trial. He just couldn't believe it.

Q: Were you in any way out of step with the way things were done here when you first began handling cases on your own?

A: In one respect I was. I evaluated a case by what I felt a proper recommendation should be, and my recommendations were almost always in terms of longer time. I found that the other guys in the office were breaking things down more than I expected. As a citizen, I couldn't be too complacent about an old lady getting knocked down, stuff like that. I thought more time should be recommended. I might think five to ten, six to twelve, while the other guys felt that three to seven was enough.

Implicit in these remarks are the seeds of an explanation for a prosecutor's gradually becoming more willing to plea bargain. One can hypothesize that as his experience with handling cases increases, he will feel less outraged by the crime, and thus will be more willing to work out a negotiated settlement. One assistant state's attorney likened his change in attitude to that of a nurse in an emergency room.

It's like nurses in emergency rooms. You get so used to armed robbery that you treat it as routine, not as morally upsetting. In the emergency room, the biggest emergency is treated as routine. And it's happening to me. The nature of the offense doesn't cause the reaction in me that it would cause in the average citizen. Maybe this is a good thing; maybe it isn't.

Though there is merit in this argument—prosecutors do become accustomed to crime—it is hardly a sufficient explanation of prosecutorial adaptation to plea bargaining. Other factors, often far more subtle, must be considered if we are to understand how and why the novice prosecutor becomes a seasoned plea bargainer.

Learning about Plea Bargaining

In the preceding sections I have portrayed the new prosecutor as being predisposed toward an adversary resolution of a case, uncertain about his responsibilities, rigid in his relations with defense attorneys, reluctant to drop charges and to plea bargain in cases that he considers serious, and anxious to try out the skills he learned in law school. This characterization of the newcomer contrasts sharply with that of the veteran prosecutor portrayed earlier [again in *Plea Bargaining*]. The veteran prosecutor was described as taking an active role in plea bargaining—urging, cajoling, and threatening the defense attorney to share in the benefits of a negotiated disposition. How is the veteran prosecutor to be reconciled with the new prosecutor of the preceding section?

The answer lies in what the prosecutor learns and is taught about plea bargaining. His education, like the defense attorney's, is not structured and systematic. Instead, he works his way through cases, testing the adversary and plea bargaining approaches. He learns piecemeal the costs and benefits of these approaches, and only over a period of time does he develop an appreciation for the relative benefits of a negotiated disposition.

Rather than proceed with a sequential discussion of the newcomer's experience, I think it more profitable at this point to distill from his experiences those central concerns that best explain his adaptation to the plea bargaining system. Some of the "flavor" of the adaptation process is sacrificed by proceeding in this fashion, but, in terms of clarity of presentation, I think it is a justifiable sacrifice. Thus, I will discuss separately the considerations that move the prosecutor in the plea bargaining direction, and later tie these together into an overall perspective on prosecutorial adaptation.

The Defendant's Factual and Legal Guilt

Prosecutors and state's attorneys learn their roles primarily entail the processing of factually guilty defendants. Contrary to their expectations that problems of establishing factual guilt would be central to their job, they find that in most cases the evidence in the file is sufficient to conclude (and prove) that the defendant is factually guilty. For those cases where there is a substantial question as to factual guilt, the prosecutor has the power—and is inclined to exercise it—to *nolle* or dismiss the case. If he himself does not believe the defendant to be factually guilty, it is part of his formal responsibilities to filter the case out. But, of the cases that remain after the initial screening, the prosecutor believes the majority of defendants to be factually guilty.

Furthermore, he finds that defense attorneys only infrequently contest the prosecutor's own conclusion that the defendant is guilty. In their initial approach to the prosecutor they may raise the possibility that the defendant is factually innocent, but in most subsequent discussions their advances focus on disposition and not on the problem of factual guilt. Thus, from the prosecutor's own reading of the file (after screening) and from the comments of his "adversary," he learns that he begins with the upper hand; more often than not, the factual guilt of the defendant is not really disputable.

Q: Are most of the defendants who come to this court guilty?

A: Yeah, or else we wouldn't have charged them. You know, that's something that people don't understand. Basically the people that are brought here are believed very definitely to be guilty or we wouldn't go on with the prosecution. We would *nolle* the case, and, you know, that is something, when people say, "Well, do you really believe. . . ." Yeah. I do. I really do, and if I didn't and we can clear them, then we *nolle* it, there's no question about it.

But most cases are good, solid cases, and in most of them the defendant is guilty. We have them cold-cocked. And they plead guilty because they are guilty. . . a guy might have been caught in a package store with bottles. Now, he wasn't there to warm his hands. The defendant may try some excuse, but they are guilty and they know they are guilty. And we'll give them a break when they plead guilty. I don't think we should throw away the key on the guy just because we got him cold-cocked. We've got good cases, we give them what we think the case is worth from our point of view, allowing the defendant's mitigating circumstances to enter.

Q: The fact that you're willing to offer a pretty good bargain in negotiations might lead a person to plead guilty even if he had a chance to beat it at trial. But if he was found guilty at the trial he might not get the same result?

A: That's possible. I mean, only the accused person knows whether or not he's committed the crime, and. . . . It's an amazing thing, where, on any number of occasions, you will sit down to negotiate with an accused's attorney . . . and you know [he will say]: "No, no, he's not guilty, he wants his trial." But then if he develops a weakness in the case, or points out a weakness to you, and then you come back and say: "Well, we'll take a suspended sentence and probation," suddenly he says, "Yes, I'm guilty." So it leads you to conclude that, well, all these people who are proclaiming innocence are really not innocent. They're just looking for the right disposition. Now, from my point of view, the ideal situation might be if the person is not guilty, that he pleads not guilty, and we'll give him his trial and let the jury decide. But most people who are in court don't want a trial. I'm not the person who seeks them out and says, "I will drop this charge" or "I will reduce this charge, I will reduce the amount of time you have to do." They come to us, so, you know, the conclusion I think is there that any reasonable person could draw, that these people are guilty, that they are just looking for the best disposition possible. Very few people ask for a speedy trial.

In addition to learning of the factual culpability of most defendants, the prosecutor also learns that defendants would be hard-pressed to raise legal challenges to the state's case. As was discussed earlier, most cases are simply barren of any contestable legal issue, and nothing in the prosecutor's file or the defense attorney's arguments leads the prosecutor to conclude otherwise.

The new prosecutor or state's attorney, then, learns that in most cases the problem of establishing the defendant's factual and legal guilt, is nonexistent. Typically, he begins with a very solid case, and, contrary to his expectations, he finds that few issues are in need of resolution at an adversary hearing or trial. The defendant's guilt is not generally problematic; it is conceded by the defense attorney. What remains problematic is the sentence the defendant will receive.

Distinguishing Among the Guilty Defendants

Formally, the prosecutor has some powers that bear directly on sentence. He has the option to reduce or eliminate charges leveled against the defendant; the responsibility for the indictment is his, and his alone. Thus, if he *nolles* some of the charges against the defendant, he can reduce the maximum exposure the defendant faces or insure that the defendant is sentenced only on a misdemeanor (if he *nolles* a felony), and so forth. Beyond these actions on charges, the formal powers of the prosecutor cease. The judge is responsible for sentencing. He is supposed to decide the conditions of probation, the length of incarceration, and so on. Notwithstanding this formal dichotomy of responsibility, prosecutors find that defense attorneys approach them about both charge and sentence reduction.

Since charge reduction bears on sentence reduction, it is only a small step for defense attorneys to inquire specifically about sentences; and, because there is often an interdependence between charge and sentence, prosecutors are compelled at least to listen to the attorney's arguments. Thus, the prosecutor finds attorneys parading before him asking for charge and sentence reduction, and, in a sense, he is obligated to hear them out.

It is one thing to say that prosecutors and state's attorneys must listen to defense attorneys' requests about disposition and another to say that they must cooperate with these attorneys. As already indicated, new prosecutors feel acutely uneasy about charge and sentence reduction. They have neither the confidence nor the inclination to usurp what they view as primarily the judge's responsibility. Furthermore, one would think that their resolve not to become involved in this area would be strengthened by their learning that most defendants are factually and legally guilty. Why should they discuss dispositions in cases in which they "hold all the cards?"

This query presupposes that prosecutors continue to conceive of themselves as adversaries, whose exclusive task is to establish the defendant's guilt or innocence. But what happens is that as prosecutors gain greater experience handling cases, they gradually develop certain standards for evaluating cases, standards that bear not just on the defendant's guilt or innocence, but, more importantly, on the disposition of the defendant's case. These standards better explain prosecutorial behavior in negotiating dispositions than does the simple notion of establishing guilt or innocence.

Specifically prosecutors come to distinguish between serious and nonserious cases, and between cases in which they are looking for time and cases in which they are not looking for time. These standards or distinctions evolve after the prosecutor has processed a substantial number of factually and legally guilty defendants. They provide a means of sorting the raw material—the guilty defendants. Indeed, one can argue that the adversary component of the prosecutor's job is shifted from establishing guilt or innocence to determining the seriousness of the defendant's guilt and whether he should receive time. The guilt of the defendant is assumed, but the problem of disposition remains to be informally argued.

Prosecutors and state's attorneys draw sharp distinctions between serious and nonserious cases. In both instances, they assume the defendant guilty, but they are looking for different types of dispositions, dependent upon their classification of the case. If it is a nonserious matter, they are amenable to defense requests for a small fine in the circuit court, some short, suspended sentence, or some brief period of probation; similarly, in a nonserious superior court matter the state's attorney is willing to work out a combination suspended sentence and probation. The central concern with these nonserious cases is to dispose of them quickly. If the defense attorney requests some sort of no-time disposition that is dependent upon either a prosecutorial reduction of charges or a sentence recommendation, the prosecutor and state's attorney are likely to agree. They have no incentive to refuse the attorney's request, since the attorney's desire comports with what they are "looking for." The case is simply not worth the effort to press for greater penalty.

On the other hand, if the case is serious, the prosecutor and state's attorney are likely to be looking for time. The serious case cannot be quickly disposed of by a no-time alternative. These are cases in which we would expect more involved and lengthy plea bargaining negotiations.

Whether the case is viewed as serious or nonserious depends on factors other than the formal charges the defendant faces. For example, these nonformal considerations might include the degree of harm done the victim, the amount of violence employed by the defendant, the defendant's prior record, the characteristics of the victim and defendant, the defendant's motive; all are somewhat independent of formal charge, and yet all weigh heavily in the prosecutor's judgment of the seriousness of the case. Defendants facing the same formal charges, then, may find that prosecutors sort their cases into different categories. Two defendants charged with robbery with violence may find that in one instance the state's attorney is willing to reduce the charge and recommend probation, while in the second case he is looking for a substantial period of incarceration. In the former case, the defendant may have simply brushed against the victim (still technically robbery with violence), whereas in the second, he may have dealt the victim a severe blow. Or possibly, the first defendant was a junkie supporting his habit, whereas the second was operating on the profit motive. These are, of course, imperfect illustrations, but the point is that the determination as to whether a case is serious or not serious only partially reflects the charges against the defendant. Often the determination is based on a standard that develops with experience in the court, and operates, for the most part, independently of formal statutory penalties.

The following excerpts convey a sense of the serious/nonserious dichotomy and also support the argument that charge does not necessarily indicate seriousness.

Q: How did you learn what cases were worth?

A: You mean sentences.

Q: Yeah.

A: Well, that's a hit-or-miss kind of an experience. You take a first offender; any first offender in a nonviolent crime certainly is not going to jail for a nonviolent crime. And a second offender, well, it depends again on the type of crime, and maybe there should be some supervision, some probation. And a third time, you say, well now this is a guy who maybe you should treat a little more strictly. Now, a violent crime, I would treat differently. How did I learn to? I learned because there were a few other guys around with experience, and I got experience, and they had good judgments, workable approaches, and you pick it up like that. In other words, you watch others, you talk to others, you handle a lot of cases yourself.

Q: Does anybody, the public, put pressure on you to be tougher?

A: Not really.

Q: Wouldn't these sentences be pretty difficult for the public to understand?

A: Yeah, somewhat. . . . Sure, we are pretty easy on a lot of these cases except that. . . . We are tough on mugging and crimes by violence. Say an old lady is grabbed by a kid and knocked to the ground and her pocketbook taken as she is waiting for the bus. We'd be as tough as anybody on that one, whether you call it a breach of peace or a robbery. We'd be very tough. And in this case there would be a good likelihood of the first offender going to jail, whatever the charge we give him. The name of the charge isn't important. We'd had the facts regardless.

Q: So you think you have changed? You give away more than you used to?

A: I don't give away more. I think that I have reached the point where. . . . When I started I was trying to be too fair, if you want to say that, you know, to see that justice was done, and I was severe. But, you know, like ____ [head prosecutor] says, you need to look for justice tempered with mercy, you know, substantial justice, and that's what I do now. When I was new, a guy cut [knifed] someone he had to go to jail. But now I look for substantial justice—if two guys have been drinking and one guy got cut, I'm not giving anything away, but a fine, that's enough there.

Q: But you are easier now? I mean, you could look for time?

A: Look, if I get a guy that I feel belongs in jail, I try to sentence bargain and get him in jail. We had this one guy, ____. He was charged with breach of peace. We knew he had been selling drugs but we couldn't prove anything. He hits this girl in ____'s parking lot [large department store], and tried to take her purse. She screams and he runs. This was a real son-of-a-bitch, been pimping for his own wife. On breach of peace I wanted the full year, and eventually got nine months. Cases like that I won't give an inch on. And the lawyer first wanted him to plead to suspended sentence and a money fine. I said this guy is a goddamned animal. Anybody who lets his wife screw and then gets proceeds from it, and deals in drugs. . . well, if you can catch the bastard on it, he belongs behind bars.

The second standard used by prosecutors and state's attorneys in processing factually and legally guilty defendants is the time/no-time distinction. There is an obvious relationship between the serious/nonserious standard and this one: in the serious case time is generally the goal; whereas in the nonserious case, a no-time disposition is satisfactory to the prosecutor. But this simple relationship does not always hold, and it is important for us to consider the exceptions.

In some serious cases, the prosecutor or state's attorney may not be looking for time. Generally, these are cases in which the prosecutor has a problem establishing either the factual or legal guilt of the defendant, and thus is willing to settle for a plea to the charge and offer a recommendation of a suspended sentence. The logic is simple: the prosecutor feels the defendant is guilty of the offense but fears that if he insists on time, the defense attorney will go to trial and uncover the factual or legal defects of the state's case. Thus, the prosecutor "sweetens the deal" to extract a guilty plea and to decrease the likelihood that the attorney will gamble on complete vindication.

Of the prosecutors I interviewed, a handful expressed disenchantment with plea bargaining. They felt that their associates were being too lenient, giving away too much in return for the defendant's plea. They argued that the prosecutor's office should stay firm and go to trial if necessary in order to obtain higher sentences. They were personally inclined to act this way: they "didn't like plea bargaining." But when pushed a bit, it became clear that their antipathy to plea bargaining was not without its exceptions. In the serious case with factual or legal defects they felt very strongly that plea bargaining was appropriate. The sentiments of such an "opponent" to plea bargaining are presented below.

Q: So you are saying that you only like some kinds of plea bargaining?

A: I like to negotiate cases where I have a problem with the case. I know the guy is guilty, but I have some legal problem, or unavailability of a witness that the defendant doesn't know about that will make it difficult for us to put the case on. I would have trouble with the case. Then it is in my interest to bargain; even in serious cases with these problems, it is in the best interests of the state to get the guy to plead, even if it's to a felony with suspended sentence.

Q: If there was no plea bargaining, then the state would lose out?

A: Yes, in cases like these. These would be cases that without plea bargaining we would have trouble convicting the defendant. But this has nothing to do with the defendant's guilt or innocence. Yet we might have to let him go. It is just to plea bargain in cases like this. It is fair to get the plea from the defendant, since he is guilty. Now, there is another situation; whereas in the first situation, I have no philosophical problems with plea bargaining. We may have a weak case factually. Maybe the case depends on one witness, and I have talked to the witness and realized how the witness would appear in court. Maybe the witness would be a flop when he testifies. If I feel the defendant is guilty, but the witness is really bad, then I know that we won't win the case at trial, that we won't win a big concession in plea bargaining. So I will evaluate the case, and I will be predisposed to talking about a more lenient disposition.

The other unexpected cross between the standards—nonserious case/looking for time—occurs in several types of situations. First, there is the case in which the defendant has a long history of nonserious offenses, and it is felt that a short period of incarceration will "teach him a lesson," or at least indicate that there are limits beyond which prosecutors cannot be pushed. Second, there is the situation where the prosecutor holds the defense attorney in disdain and is determined to teach the attorney a lesson. Thus, though the defendant's offense is nonserious, the prosecutor would generally be amenable to a no-time disposition, the prosecutor chooses to hold firm. It is precisely in these borderline cases that the prosecutor can be most successful in exercising sanctions against the uncooperative defense attorney. The formal penalties associated with the charges against the defendant give him ample sentencing range, and by refusing to agree to a no-time disposition, the costs to the defense attorney become great. The attorney is not able to meet his client's demands for no time, and yet he must be leery about trial, given the even greater exposure the defendant faces. These borderline decisions by prosecutors, then, are fertile grounds for exploring sanctions against defense attorneys. It is here that we can expect the cooperative defense attorneys to benefit most, and the recalcitrant defense attorney to suffer the most. Relatedly, one can also expect prosecutors to be looking for time in nonserious offenses in which the defendant or his counsel insists on raising motions and going to trial. These adversary activities may be just enough to tip the prosecutor into looking for time.

In addition to its relationship to the serious/nonserious standard, the time/no-time standard bears on prosecutorial plea bargaining behavior in another way. As prosecutors gain experience in the plea bargaining system, they tend to stress "certainty of time" rather than "amount of time." This is to say that they become less concerned about extracting maximum penalties from defendants and more concerned with insuring that in cases in which they are looking for time, the defendant actually receives some time. Obviously, there are limits to the prosecutor's largesse—in a serious case thirty days will not be considered sufficient time. But prosecutors are willing to consider periods of incarceration substantially shorter than the maximum sentence allowable for a particular crime. In return, though, prosecutors want a guarantee of sorts that the defendant will receive time. They want to decrease the likelihood that the defendant, by some means or other, will obtain a suspended sentence. Thus, they will "take" a fixed amount of time if the defendant agrees not to try to "pitch" for a lower sentence, or if the defendant pleads to a charge in which all participants know some time will be meted out by the judge. In the latter instance, the attorney may be free to "pitch," but court personnel know his effort is more a charade for the defendant than a realistic effort to obtain a no-time disposition. The following excerpts illustrate prosecutorial willingness to trade off years of time for certainty of time.

> I don't believe in giving away things. In fact _____ [a public defender] approached me; there's this kid _____, he has two robberies, one first degree, one second, and three minor cases. Now,

this kid I made out an affidavit myself for tampering with a witness. This kid is just n.g. _____ came to me and said, "We'll plead out, two to five." He'll go to state's prison. I agreed to that—both these offenses are bindovers. These kids belong in jail. I'd rather take two to five here than bind them over to superior court and take a chance on what will happen there. At least my two to five will be a year and three-quarters in state's prison. The thing is, if I want to get a guy in jail for a year, I'll plea bargain with him, and I'll take six months if I can get it, because the guy belongs in jail, and if I can get him to jail for six months why should I fool around with that case, and maybe get a year if I am lucky? If I can put a guy away for six months I might be cheated out of six months, but at least the guy is doing six months in jail.

What is a proper time? It never bothers me if we could have gotten seven years and instead we got five. In this case, there was no violence; minor stuff was stolen. We got time out of him. That is the important thing.

A: It makes no difference to me really if a man does five to ten or four to eight. The important thing is he's off the street, not a menace to society for a period of time, and the year or two less is not going to make that great a difference. If you do get time, I think it's . . . you know, many prosecutors I know feel this way. They have achieved confinement, that's what they're here for.

Q: Let's take another example. Yesterday an attorney walked in here when I was present on that gambling case. He asked you if it could be settled without time?

A: And I said no. That ended the discussion.

Q: What will he do now?

A: He'll file certain motions that he really doesn't have to file. All the facts of our case were spelled out; he knows as much about our cases as he'll ever know. So his motions will just delay things: There'll come a point, though, when he'll have to face trial; and he'll come in to speak with us, and ask if we still have the same position. We'll have the same position. We'll still be looking for one to three. His record goes back to 1923, he's served two or three terms for narcotics, and he's been fined five times for gambling. So we'd be looking for one to three and a fine. Even though he's in his sixties, he's been a criminal all his life, since 1923. . . .

Q: But if the attorney pushes and says, "Now look. He's an old guy. He's sixty-two years old, how about six months?"

A: I might be inclined to accept it because, again, confinement would be involved. I think our ends would be met. It would show his compadres that there's no longer any immunity for gambling, that there is confinement involved. So the end result would be achieved.

> Justice Holmes, who is supposed to be the big sage in American jurisprudence, said it isn't the extent of the punishment but the certainty of it. This is my basic philosophy. If the guy faces twelve years in state's prison, I'm satisfied if on a plea of guilty he'll go to state's prison for two or three years.

The experienced prosecutor, then, looks beyond the defendant's guilt when evaluating a case. He learns—from a reading of the file and from the defense attorney's entreaties—that most defendants are factually and legally guilty and that he generally holds the upper hand. As he gains experience in processing these cases, he gradually begins to draw distinctions within this pool of guilty defendants. Some of the cases appear not to be serious, and the prosecutor becomes willing to go along with the defense attorney's request for no-time dispositions. The cases simply do not warrant a firmer prosecutorial posture. In serious cases, when he feels time is in order, he often finds defense attorneys in agreement on the need for some incarceration.

In a sense, the prosecutor redefines his professional goals. He learns that the statutes fail to distinguish adequately among guilty defendants, that they "sweep too broadly," and give short shrift to the specific facts of the offense, to the defendant's prior record, to the degree of contributory culpability of the victim, and so on. Possessing more information about the defendant than the judge does, the prosecutor—probably unconsciously—comes to believe that it is his professional responsibility to develop standards that distinguish among defendants and lead to "equitable" dispositions. Over time, the prosecutor comes to feel that if he does not develop these standards, if he does not make these professional judgments, no one else will.

The prosecutor seems almost to drift into plea bargaining. When he begins his job he observes that his colleagues plea bargain routinely and quickly finds that defense attorneys expect him to do the same. Independent of any rewards, sanctions, or pressures, he learns the strengths of his cases, and learns to distinguish the serious from the nonserious ones. After an initial period of reluctance to plea bargain at all (he is fearful of being taken advantage of by defense attorneys), the prosecutor finds that he is engaged almost unwittingly in daily decisions concerning the disposition of cases. His obligation to consider alternative charges paves the way for the defense attorney's advances; it is only a small jump to move to sentence discussions. And as he plea bargains more and more cases, the serious/nonserious and time/no-time standards begin to hold sway in his judgments. He feels confident about the disposition he is looking for, and if a satisfactory plea bargain in line with his goals can be negotiated, he comes to feel that there is little point to following a more formal adversary process.

Case Pressure and Potential Backlog

Though they may do so during the first few weeks, the newcomer's peers and superiors do not generally pressure him to move cases because of volume. Instead, he is thrust in the fray largely on his own and is allowed to work out his own style of case disposition. Contrary to the "conspiratorial perspective" of the adaptation process, he is not coerced to cooperate in processing "onerously large case loads."

The newcomer's plea bargaining behavior is conditioned by his reactions to particular cases he handles or learns about and not by caseload problems of the office. The chief prosecutor within the jurisdiction may worry about his court's volume and the speed with which cases are disposed, but he does not generally interfere with his assistant's decision about how to proceed in a case. The newcomer is left to learn about plea bargaining on his own, and for the reason already discussed, he learns and is taught the value of negotiating many of his cases. The absence of a direct relationship between prosecutor plea bargaining and case pressure is suggested in the following remarks.

Q: Is it case pressure that leads you to negotiate?

A: I don't believe it's the case pressure at all. In every court, whether there are five cases or one hundred cases, we should try to settle it. It's good for both sides. If I were a public defender I'd try to settle all the cases for my guilty clients. By negotiating you are bound to do better. Now take this case. [He reviewed the facts of a case in which an elderly man was charged with raping a seven-year-old girl. The defendant claimed he could not remember what happened, that he was drunk, and that, though the girl might have been in the bed with him, he did not think he raped her.] I think I gave the defense attorney a fair deal. The relatives say she was raped, but the doctors couldn't conclusively establish that. I offered him a plea to a lesser charge, one dealing with advances toward minors, but excluding the sex act. If he takes it, he'll be able to walk away with time served [the defendant had not posted bail and had spent several months in jail]. It's the defendant's option though. He can go through trial if he wants, but if he makes that choice, the kid and her relatives will have to be dragged through the agonies of trial also. Then I would be disposed to look for a higher sentence for the defendant. So I think my offer is fair, and the offer has nothing to do with the volume of this court. It's the way I think the case—all things considered—should be resolved.

Q: You say the docket wasn't as crowded in 1966, and yet there was plea bargaining. If I had begun this interview by saying why is there plea bargaining here. . . .

A: I couldn't use the reason there's plea bargaining because there are a lot of cases. That's not so: that's not so at all. If we had only ten cases down for tomorrow and an attorney walked in and wanted to discuss a case with me, I'd sit down and discuss it with him. In effect, that's plea bargaining. Whether it's for the charge or for an agreed recommendation or reduction of the charge or what have you, it's still plea bargaining. It's part of the process that has been going on for quite a long time.

Q: And you say it's not because of the crowded docket, but if I gave you a list of reasons for why there was plea bargaining and asked you to pick the most important. . . .

A: I never really thought about the. . . . You talk about the necessity for plea bargaining, and you say, well, it's necessary, and one of the reasons is because we have a crowded docket, but even if we didn't we still would plea bargain.

Q: Why?

A: Well, it has been working throughout the years, and the way I look at it, it's beneficial to the defendant, it's beneficial to the court, and not just in saving time but in avoiding police officers coming to court, witnesses being subpoenaed in, and usually things can be discussed between prosecutors and defense counsel which won't be said in the open court and on the record. There are many times that the defense counsel will speak confidentially with the prosecutor about his client or about the facts or about the complainant or a number of things. So I don't know if I can justify plea bargaining other than by speaking of the necessity of plea bargaining. If there were only ten cases down for one day, it still would be something that would be done.

Maybe in places like New York they plea bargain because of case pressure. I don't know. But here it is different. We dispose of cases on the basis of what is fair to both sides. You can get a fair settlement by plea bargaining. If you don't try to settle a case quickly, it gets stale. In New York the volume probably is so bad that it becomes a matter of "getting rid of cases." In Connecticut, we have some pretty big dockets in some cities, but in other areas—here, for example—we don't have that kind of pressure. Sure, I feel some pressure, but you can't say that we negotiate our cases out to clear the docket. And you probably can't say that even about the big cities in Connecticut either.

Prosecutors, then, do not view their propensity to plea bargain as a direct outcome of case pressure. Instead, they speak of "mutually satisfactory outcomes," "fair dispositions," "reducing police overcharging," and so on. We need not here evaluate their claims in detail; what is important is that collectively their arguments militate against according case pressure the "top billing" it so often receives in the literature.

Another way to conceptualize the relationship between case pressure and plea bargaining is to introduce the notion of a "potential backlog." Some prosecutors maintain that if fewer cases were plea bargained, or if plea bargaining were eliminated, a backlog of cases to be disposed of would quickly clog their calendars. A potential backlog, then, lurks as a possibility in every jurisdiction. Even in a low volume jurisdiction, one complex trial could back up cases for weeks, or even months. If all those delayed cases also had to be tried, the prosecutor feels he would face two not so enviable options. He could become further backlogged by trying as many of them as was feasible, or he could reduce his backlog by outright dismissal of cases. The following comments are typical of the potential backlog argument.

Q: Some people have suggested that plea bargaining not be allowed in the court. All cases would go to trial before a judge or jury and . . .

A: Something like that would double, triple, and quadruple the backlog. Reduce that 90 percent of people pleading guilty, and even if you were to try a bare minimum of those cases, you quadruple your backlog. It's feasible.

Well, right now we don't have a backlog. But if we were to try even 10 percent of our cases, take them to a jury, we'd be so backed up that we couldn't even move. We'd be very much in the position of . . . some traffic director in New York once said that there will come a time that there will be one car too many coming into New York and nobody will be able to move. Well, we can get ourselves into that kind of situation if we are going to go ahead and refuse to plea bargain even in the serious cases.

Though a potential backlog is an ever-present possibility, it should be stressed that most prosecutors develop this argument more as a prediction as to the outcome of a rule decreasing or eliminating plea bargaining than as an explanation for why they engage in plea bargaining. If plea bargaining were eliminated, a backlog would develop; but awareness of this outcome does not explain why they plea bargain.

Furthermore, prosecutors tend to view the very notion of eliminating plea bargaining as a fake issue, a straw-man proposition. It is simply inconceivable to them that plea bargaining could or would be eliminated. They maintain that no court system could try all of its cases, even if huge increases in personnel levels were made; trials consume more time than any realistic increase in personnel levels could manage. They were willing to speculate on the outcome of a rule proscribing plea bargaining, but the argument based on court backlog that they evoked was not a salient consideration in understanding their day-in, day-out plea bargaining behavior.

It is, of course, impossible to refute with complete certainty an argument that prosecutors plea bargain because failure to do so would cause a backlog of unmanageable proportions to develop. However, the interviews indicate other more compelling ways to conceptualize prosecutorial adaptation to plea bargaining, and these do not depend on a potential backlog that always can be conjured up. Though the backlog may loom as a consequence of a failure to plea bargain, it—like its case-pressure cousin—is neither a necessary nor sufficient explanatory vehicle for understanding the core aspects of prosecutorial plea bargaining behavior.

A Perspective on Prosecutorial Adaptation

Perhaps the most important outcome of the prosecutor's adaptation is that he evidences a major shift in his own presumption about how to proceed with a case. As a newcomer, he feels it to be his responsibility to establish the defendant's guilt at trial, and he sees no need to justify a decision to go to trial. However, as he processes more and more cases, as he drifts into plea bargaining, and as he is taught the risks associated with trials, his own assumption about how to proceed with a case changes. He approaches every case with plea bargaining in mind, that is, he presumes that the case will be plea bargained. If it is a "nonserious" matter, he expects it to be quickly resolved; if it is "serious" he generally expects to negotiate time as part of the disposition. In both instances, he anticipates that the case will eventually be resolved by a negotiated disposition and not by a trial. When a plea bargain does not materialize, and the case goes to trial, the prosecutor feels compelled to justify his failure to reach an accord. He no longer is content to simply assert that it is the role of the prosecutor to establish the defendant's guilt at trial. This adversary component of the prosecutor's role has been replaced by a self-imposed burden to justify why he chose to go to trial, particularly if a certain conviction—and, for serious cases, a period of incarceration—could have been obtained by means of a negotiated disposition.

Relatedly, the prosecutor grows accustomed to the power he exercises in these plea bargaining negotiations. As a newcomer, he argued that his job was to be an advocate for the state and that it was the judge's responsibility to sentence defendants. But, having in fact "sentenced" most of the defendants whose files he plea bargained, the distinction between prosecutor and judge becomes blurred in his own mind. Though he did not set out to usurp judicial prerogatives—indeed, he resisted efforts to engage him in the plea bargaining process—he gradually comes to expect that he will exercise sentencing powers. There is no fixed point in time when he makes a calculated choice to become adjudicator as well as adversary. In a sense, it simply "happens"; the more cases he resolves (either by charge reduction or sentence recommendations), the greater the likelihood that he will lose sight of the distinction between the roles of judge and prosecutor.

12

Guilty Plea Courts
A Social Disciplinary Model
of Criminal Justice

Mike McConville
Chester Mirsky

Introduction

The majority of routine felony cases, the day-to-day workload of criminal courts, are settled by guilty pleas.[1] Traditional accounts assume that those actually guilty of criminal acts adopt a cost-efficient method of confronting their guilt, make deals, and plead guilty (Alschuler 1976). Implicit in these accounts is the notion that the decision

From *Social Problems*, Vol. 42, No. 2, pp. 216–34, copyright © 1995. Reprinted by permission.

to offer or accept a plea is based on the weight of the evidence against the accused and the presence or absence of a viable legal defense (Walker 1993). Nardulli, Eisenstein, and Flemming (1988:210) contend, for example, that the "absence of factual ambiguity in most cases looms large as an explanation for the defendant's decision to plead guilty." The guilty plea is usually both inevitable and just (Feeley 1979; Maynard 1984).

Defenders and supporters of the system recognize that, without a trial, there is a risk that rights guaranteed to a criminal defendant may not be protected and that the factually innocent may be convicted. The assignment of legal counsel to all criminal defendants, guaranteed by *Gideon vs. Wainwright* (1963), is supposed to ensure the protection of individual rights and adequate scrutiny of the police evidence against a criminal defendant. In spite of legal representation, most criminal defendants still plead guilty because "[c]ourt personnel simply recognize the factual culpability of many defendants and the fruitlessness, at least in terms of case outcome, of going to trial" (Heumann 1978:156).

Indeed, many courtroom observers who defend the current system point to colloquies such as the following (which ended one of the cases discussed below), in which judges question defendants before allowing them to plead guilty, to show that factually guilty defendants' legal rights are respected and protected, even as they forego a public trial. (All names in this paper are pseudonyms.)

Q: "Have you had an opportunity to consult with your lawyer, Mr. Gartenstein, and to discuss the matter with him before choosing to plead guilty?"

A: "Yes."

Q: "Do you understand that by pleading guilty you have given up your right to trial by jury?"

A: "Yes."

Q: "Do you understand that by pleading guilty you have given up your right to confront and cross-examine witnesses against you, to testify, and to call witnesses on your own behalf?"

A: "Yes."

Q: "Do you understand that you have given up your right to remain silent and your privilege against self-incrimination?"

A: "Yes."

Q: "Do you understand that at a trial you are presumed innocent and that the prosecution has to prove your guilt beyond a reasonable doubt?"

A: "Yes."

Q: "Has anybody threatened or coerced you?"

A: "No."

Q: "Is your plea voluntary and of your own free will?"

A: "Yes."

Q: "Do you understand that in pleading guilty you have given up all these rights and that the conviction entered is the same as a conviction after trial?"

A: "Yes."

Q: "Did you along with McBride and Hervey forcibly steal property from the person of the complaining witness and possess what appeared to be a gun?"

A: "Yes."[2]

The research reported in this paper comes to a different conclusion. We conclude that in large urban areas guilty pleas are part of a vertically integrated system of imposing control and discipline on highly visible sections of society, those who are perceived as dangerous because of their lack of involvement in an acceptable labor market and the intensity of their involvement with the criminal justice system. This system often begins with proactive "sweeps" by specialized police units (such as narcotics control units); it extends through the system of assigning counsel to indigent defendants, and it concludes with a highly coercive drama in which defendants are first shown (by being made to watch others) that they will suffer greatly increased penalties if they refuse to plead guilty, and in which they are then given their 15 seconds to accept or reject the pleas and sentences offered to them by calendar judges.

We call this a social disciplinary model, a form of substantive rationality committed to achieving order through surveillance and control of the urban underclass (Simon 1993; Smith and Visher 1981; Smith, Visher, and Davidson 1984). A social disciplinary model, concerned with containment rather than crime control (Simon 1993), imposes judgments of conviction without restraint on how police power may be exercised against the individual.

In this paper we first describe our research methods and our perhaps unusual way of presenting our results. We then turn to 1) the significance of proactive policing; 2) the relation between the assigned counsel and the indigent criminal defendant; and 3) the educational and disciplinary scripts of pleading guilty.

Research Methods

This essay is part of a study of the provision of defense services to the poor in New York City. In 1984 and 1985, with the permission of the court and the parties, we observed 236 defendants in more than 150 felony cases in guilty plea court, i.e., calendar "parts" (Luskin 1989) as they are called in New York, where cases can only be resolved through non-trial dispositions. We observed more than 650 court appearances along with the activities at central booking and at lawyer interviews in the court pens. We received a copy of all relevant court papers for each case, and we interviewed the prosecutors, judges, defense attorneys, and, whenever possible, the defendants in each case. We recorded all our observations in field notes made during or immediately after a court proceeding. In 1986 and 1987, we supplemented our sample with an additional 100 felony cases.

In addition to these qualitative materials, we analyzed the statistical reports put out by the Office of Court Administration from 1986 through 1993. These contain monthly ratings that show the number of guilty plea dispositions achieved by all judges as well as detailed comparisons among judges. We also assembled quantitative data on the vouchers submitted for payment by assigned counsel that indicated how frequently court-appointed lawyers claimed expenses for investigation and for witness interviews. The historical and quantitative aspects of our research have been reported earlier (McConville and Mirsky 1986–87, 1988, 1989, 1990).

In one brief article it is not possible to present more than a minute sample from our body of qualitative data. Our aim is to present observations that both 1) reveal the fundamental processes at work in the guilty plea system, and 2) represent the central tendencies or model case from our data. Here we focus on one defense lawyer, Emerson, one Criminal defendant, Roberto Santiago, and the events, including other cases heard that Emerson represented or that Santiago observed, that preceded Santiago's decision to plead guilty. A closer look at these actors and their cases produces a deeper understanding of the social disciplinary processes at work than a more circumscribed sample of data from a slightly larger number of cases.

Roberto Santiago was arrested as he left his apartment at 1:30 A.M. by police officers engaged in a sweep of the neighborhood. Before the arrest, undercover officers toured Santiago's neighborhood and radioed descriptions of suspected drug dealers to backup units whose officers swept the street for people they believed fit the descriptions. The sweep occurred once the police had decided to complete an operation in which undercover officers, posing as gypsy cab drivers, purchased cocaine and other drugs from street-level dealers. When Santiago was held later in a precinct, an undercover officer, looking through a two-way mirror, identified him as a person from whom the officer had purchased cocaine six months earlier.

By 1989, with the advent of the crack epidemic, drug arrests, often initiated by nonindividuated sweeps, produced more than 50 percent of all superior court indictments in New York City. Santiago, along with more than 56 percent of those arrested who were indicted, pleaded guilty after appearing only before a calendar judge.[3] Santiago was a person of color, and, during our observations, more than 80 percent of all arrested defendants were people of color. Santiago was 21, and more than half of all arrested defendants were below age 30. Santiago, with more than three-quarters of arrested defendants, was represented by a court-assigned lawyer. Santiago, along with more than half of the arrested defendants we observed, was represented by a number of different court-assigned attorneys during several months.

Proactive Police Work

Increasingly, police work seeks to impose order in areas of the inner city that the police and the wider society view as dangerous (Pepinsky 1975; Wilson 1987; Jaynes and Williams 1988). When the generation of criminal cases is part of the quest to impose order, arrests and guilty pleas become symbolic tests of police authority (Mann 1993; Balbus 1973). In this model, the police work proactively. They reach out into the community, creating and discovering crimes through sting operations and buys and sells, to which police officers and undercover agents are almost invariably the only witnesses. In New York City, sweeps directed at drug dealers and prostitutes have become increasingly common in many areas. The occupants and inhabitants of these "public" spaces are generically placed at risk.

Proactive policing influences how the justice system as a whole responds to crime. When proactive cases become the typical and then the model case, the system itself, regardless of the nature of the case, abandons the traditional assumption that expects police to respond to crimes reported by the public in which 1) the major witnesses are either the victims or other members of the public, and 2) questions regarding witness reliability, and the sufficiency and persuasiveness of the evidence, are legitimately subject to testing.

In the enterprise of social discipline, based on proactive policing, the only credibility contest pits a team of undercover police officers against people of color who are ghetto dwellers. Here the outcome is predetermined and the message is understood by everyone. Judges, under great pressure to clear their calendars, do not tolerate "obstructive" lawyers who pursue "technical defenses" or insist upon trials (McConville and Mirsky 1986–87:837–38). Defense lawyers rarely conduct in-depth interviews with their clients. In one of the cases discussed here, when the defendant, Hickson, protested that he had not sold any narcotics, his lawyer replied:

> I'm not interested in that. Do you understand? It doesn't matter whether you are innocent or guilty: It doesn't matter because the cops are making out a case.

This was the lawyer's way of saying that when the only potential witnesses are police officers, the idea of denying the charge or insisting upon a hearing or trial is not worth considering.

For the same reason, defense lawyers rarely make independent investigations or use the services of investigators. Court-appointed lawyers may request expense money for conducting investigations and interviewing potential witnesses. However, our analysis of a sample of vouchers submitted by assigned counsel in felony cases showed that they rarely do this. There are no vouchers submitted at all for investigation in 73 percent of all homicide cases. The figure was 88 percent for all other felonies. No witness interviews were claimed in 80 percent of all homicides or 90 percent of all other felonies. No motions were filed in 75 percent of all homicide cases or 90 percent for other felonies (McConville and Mirsky 1986–87).

The court papers assembled in the case of *People vs. Santiago* contained the only "facts" (Smith 1974:8) upon which his case would be decided. The uniformed officer who signed Roberto Santiago's complaint lacked personal knowledge of the allegations. What the uniformed officer swore to was a conclusion based upon statements made by the undercover officer after viewing the defendant at the precinct. No police officer questioned Santiago or asked him to provide an explanation of his conduct. The complaint contained no information regarding the undercover officer's opportunity to observe the person selling drugs, how the officer later came to identify the defendant, or the presence of any corroborating evidence.

The remaining court papers, prepared at central booking, included the "RAP sheet," a narcotics addiction form, a "wanted statement," and the Pre-Trial Services Agency form. The RAP sheet, a computerized print-out of a defendant's prior criminal record, generated from a fingerprint comparison, revealed that Santiago did not have any previous arrests, while the narcotics form (from physical observations) indicated only that he was not a drug user. The wanted statement, based upon a name and date-of-birth comparison, however, indicated that someone by the name of Santiageles, with the same date of birth as Santiago, was wanted by the Navy for desertion.

The Pre-Trial Services Agency form indicated that Santiago had "insufficient community ties" and therefore was a risk of flight. At central booking, Santiago had informed an agency representative that he was employed, that he had lived with his mother and sister at his current address for the past ten years and at his previous address for ten years, and that he had never been arrested before. The agency could not verify the information Santiago provided, because Santiago's family did not have a telephone and his employment was "off-the-books."

The Assignment of Counsel

Once Roberto Santiago's court papers were assembled, he was transferred to a holding cell behind the arraignment court to await the assignment of an attorney. A copy of the papers was first placed in a basket designated for the Legal Aid Society, the City's public defender agency (McConville and Mirsky 1986–87). The uneven work patterns of the Legal Aid Society staff attorneys, the number of staff attorneys at arraignment, and the availability of "18–B attorneys,"[4] however, often provoked judges to assign Legal Aid cases to 18–B regulars. These lawyers represented almost as many indicted defendants (roughly 30 percent) as the Legal Aid Society (roughly 40 percent) (McConville and Mirsky 1986–87). The regulars were solo practitioners; some subsisted on court assignments, while others prospered on these cases, earning more than $100,000 from court assignments (McConville and Mirsky 1986–87; Assael 1989; Fritsch and Purdy 1994). They stationed themselves in the court building, expecting to obtain case assignments on a moment's notice.

While Roberto Santiago sat in the court pen, the sight of Legal Aid staff attorneys in court chatting among themselves provoked Judge Lorraine to order the court captain to "find an 18–B who can help clear the docket." Lorraine was a Criminal (inferior) Court calendar judge who routinely processed more than 100 cases in an eight-hour arraignment shift, disposing of 50 percent through guilty pleas.

At the court captain's instigation, Emerson, the 18–B attorney assigned for the day to conflict cases, began to thumb through cases the clerk had placed in the basket. Emerson picked out some case files, briefly looked at the names and said: "I'm not interested in this, it's a burglary, and this is a robbery, a chain snatch. I can't stand these robberies, it's a horrible crime. I like narcotics, let's see." Then he found a case file that attracted him, looked through it quickly, and said, "I'll take this one." Soon, he had gathered three cases and walked away from the Legal Aid basket. Emerson had chosen the cases of Danny James, Monroe Hickson, and Roberto Santiago.

Emerson began to work on the case of Roberto Santiago. As Santiago pulled on a cigarette and nervously moved around the pen, he looked drawn and frightened.

Emerson: "Okay. They say you sold some cocaine but here's the good news."

A voice from inside the pen intervened and said:
"It's your first offense."

Emerson: "That's right it's your first offense, and second, it happened six months ago. No there is no way in which you are going to be convicted by any jury on this. What happened, did you just get picked up? Were they just flushing the area?"

Santiago: "I don't know what happened, man. Oh, man! I was just coming out of my building and I was just grabbed, told to stand up against the wall. I've been here three days. . ."

Emerson: "Okay. So you were just grabbed. They grabbed everyone right?"

The "voice" appeared again (a white male aged about 35, blond with a mustache) and said:
"Look, they picked up the whole neighborhood."

Emerson then left to telephone Santiago's aunt to verify the information Santiago had provided concerning his employment and ties to the community. But the line was always busy and Emerson returned to speak with Santiago again. As he was speaking he flicked through the papers; he suddenly stopped and yelled, "What the fuck is this? There's a warrant out for you."

Santiago: "A warrant? It's not for me. Oh, no!"

Emerson: "The Navy, the Navy wants you. You are wanted by the Navy on a warrant. Did you quit before you did your time with them?"

Santiago: "I've never been in the Navy."

Emerson: "It must be a mistake. There are lots of Santiagos, but it will have to be checked. I'll go and see."

Emerson's interviews with Hickson and Santiago were perfunctory and public. Emerson spoke through the cell bars in the presence of other defendants and uniformed officers. As he returned to court after speaking to Santiago, Emerson said to us: "This [the Navy warrant] could screw it up today but he'll get an acquittal. They will never convict on this evidence." Emerson did not review the physical description of Santiageles to determine whether the warrant referred to someone else.[5]

Nor did Emerson obtain information from Santiago regarding his community ties and whether his family or friends had the capacity to post bail. Similarly, when a cell mate emphasized the non-individuated nature of Santiago's arrest, Emerson responded by referring to the date of the alleged sale as the important factor in determining whether the case would result in a conviction. Emerson never questioned the outcome of a case; he was able to attempt a guilty plea within moments of meeting a defendant or to adjourn cases without further delay.

Arraignment—The Commencement of Judicial Review

At arraignment, his first appearance before a judge, Roberto Santiago saw the futility of any legal challenge to the police case. When Santiago was produced before Judge Lorraine, Emerson's first act was to respond affirmatively to the court officer's request: "Do you waive the reading of the rights and charges?" Lorraine then asked the Assistant District Attorney (ADA) to address Santiago's release status:

ADA: "This case involves a sale of cocaine. The sale was hand to hand. It is a B felony, quite serious, and the Pre-Trial Services sheet indicates that this defendant has insufficient community ties to warrant parole at this point without a substantial cash bail. Therefore the People ask $3,000 cash bail."

Lorraine: "Mr. Emerson, you may be heard."

Emerson: "This is like when you go into a store to buy olives and someone tells you that there might be more than one quality of olives. You can get big olives or you can get giant olives or you can get absolutely colossal huge olives. Here the District Attorney's office is telling you they have giant olives, but in reality the olives in this case are very small ones. In fact I don't see how they are going to prosecute at all in this case because the sale took place so long ago. The sale took place almost six months ago, and I simply don't see how the state will bring charges successfully in this case. The identification evidence will never stand up. How are they going to produce a lab test? He has no prior arrests. I called his home phone number and it was busy."

Lorraine: "You obviously don't know anything about the Special Narcotics Prosecutor's Office."

Emerson: "They'll never make 180.80."[6]

Lorraine: "I don't think you understand how an undercover investigation works, Mr. Emerson. This is not abnormal at all. In fact, most undercover investigations work like this when the arrest occurs some time after the original sale. But you can keep the case and fight it as much as you want. I'll set bail at $1,500 cash or bond."

Lorraine set bail in an amount that a defendant requiring the assignment of counsel would be unlikely to post (Nagel 1983) without inquiring into the factual-legal basis for the undercover officer's identification, i.e., the opportunity to observe the person selling drugs, the cause for delay in arrest, or its effect on the reliability of the undercover officer's later identification of Santiago. Neither Emerson nor the judge made any reference to Roberto Santiago's community ties, and Emerson failed to challenge the ADA's repetition of the Pre-Trial Services finding of "insufficient community ties," other than to state that Santiago's phone was busy.

Emerson never discussed with Santiago the rights that attach to arraignment. Nor did Lorraine inform the defendant that he had a right to remain silent, the right to a prompt hearing on the charges, the right to counsel, or the right to proceed without a lawyer and to represent himself. Instead, Emerson's presence satisfied legal formalism; it signified that a lawyer had so advised the defendant, that the defendant had asserted his right to silence and had requested the assignment of counsel, and that Emerson had agreed to act as the attorney-of-record.

Unless the ADA reduced the charge to a misdemeanor, Lorraine lacked jurisdiction to accept a guilty plea in Santiago's case. However, she could have required the ADA to amend the complaint to provide some basis for the undercover officer's identification. She also could have inquired into Santiago's community ties and employment history to determine whether Santiago should be released or detained. In addition, she could have refused to continue Emerson as Santiago's attorney, had she concluded that the lawyer's understanding was so flawed as to disable him from providing competent representation. Instead, Lorraine made no effort to expand the record or to provide a legal basis for her actions. Lorraine adjourned the case to another date without delay.

While in jail following the arraignment, Santiago called a neighbor who made contact with his family. His mother responded and, within a day, posted $1,500 to obtain his release. Santiago thereafter made three court appearances with a family member. Each time he waited until mid-afternoon to discover that the judge had adjourned his case because the grand jury had not yet indicted him. When the grand jury did act, the indictment alleged that the drug sale occurred *eighteen months*, not sixth months, before Santiago's arrest. However, Emerson had not attempted to reconstruct the events in question through an in-depth interview with the defendant, nor had he undertaken any independent factual and legal inquiry.

Public Education in the Courtroom and Guilty Plea Scripts

When Roberto Santiago first appeared in Supreme, Court, 20 months had expired between the alleged incident and the filing of the indictment. Under formal legal rationality, the delay in arrest and indictment was reason enough to dismiss the charges, upon a showing that the delay was intentional, attributable to the police, and prejudicial to the defendant (*United States vs. Lovasco* 1977). Should Santiago refuse to plead guilty and insist upon litigating the propriety of the delay, however, Judge Roger, a calendar judge in guilty plea court with an intolerance for "dilatory tactics" would rule on the challenge. Roger was the calendar judge with the highest rate of dispositions and the largest caseload; his daily calendar often contained more than 50 indicted defendants.

All judges are rated according to their ability to dispose of large caseloads without hearing or trial. The calendar judges we observed in guilty plea court were those with the highest rate of disposition measured in terms of total caseload.[7] These judges were fixtures in guilty plea court, while judges who compared unfavorably were routinely assigned to hearing and trial courts (Luskin 1989; Heydebrand and Seron 1987). During a one-year period of our observations, six calendar judges disposed of approximately 11,600 indictments, of which 4,126 (35 percent) were disposed of within 60 days and 3,581 (31 percent) between 61 and 135 days (Office of Court Administration 1984–85). These judges educated defendants and others present in their courtroom that the opportunity to contest the police case was limited.

As Roberto Santiago waited for his case to be called, he, along with other defendants, lawyers, and families and friends assembled, listened to the bench conferences Judge Roger conducted with prosecutors and defense attorneys, most of which led to guilty pleas. To be sure Roger appeared to comply with formal legal rationality, the defendants "voluntarily" waived their rights on the record. However, Roger relied upon police interrogation practices to ensure that defendants would become compliant. He manipulated the bail status of released defendants[8] by jailing those defendants who refused to plead guilty, despite the fact that a defendant who had been released at arraignment had voluntarily appeared on several adjourned dates. By contrast, Roger rewarded defendants who pleaded guilty by allowing them to remain free on bail, although they were now convicted and awaiting sentence. Roger raised the stakes on defendants who refused to admit guilt by threatening them with a greater sentence on any subsequent adjourned date. Initial offers of probation, if refused, would later become fixed jail time, whereas offers of jail time once refused, would be increased into indeterminate state prison sentences. In the event of a conviction after a trial, Roger would impose a sentence that greatly exceeded the last guilty plea offer made.

These encounters, which Roger described to the authors as "tests of strength," placed a premium on the defendant's resolve, pitted against the judge's power to control the outcome. At these conferences, Roger reduced cases to skeletal outlines—a "chain snatch," and "undercover drug sale," a "break-in." All conversations at the bench and all statements made by Roger to lawyers and defendants were "off-the-record." Only the formal setting of bail, the adjourn date, and the entry of the guilty plea and sentence were "on-the-record."[9]

Roger first read a write-up of the state's evidence supplied by the ADA. The central feature of the summary sheet was the prosecution's charge and sentence offer. Should the offer be acceptable to Roger, he would immediately repeat it to the defense lawyer. If Roger believed that the prosecution's offer failed to serve as adequate inducement for a plea, or if he believed it to be too generous, Roger would alter either the charge or the sentence. Should the ADA object, Roger would threaten the prosecution with an immediate trial (for which police and civilian witnesses were never immediately available), or he would insist that the ADA who presented the case to the grand jury or a supervisor immediately appear in court to defend the original offer. When confronted with Roger's displeasure, the ADA usually agreed to Roger's demands, after which Roger would describe the offer to the defense lawyer. Roger then would tell the lawyer to speak to the defendant about pleading guilty.

In Judge Roger's court, the advice that lawyers gave their clients occurred under the judge's watchful eye, at the defense table some 15 feet from the bench. Should the defendant exhibit a facial grimace or utter a hostile response, Roger would raise the guilty plea offer and jail the defendant, while loudly repeating to those assembled the consequences that flow from such resistance. This display of force enabled Roberto Santiago and other defendants sitting in the courtroom to appreciate Roger's displeasure at recalcitrance and the power that the judge could bring to bear on any person who persisted in pleading not guilty (Dumm 1990).

The next case demonstrated how respect for law became a function of the extent to which Roger was capable of instilling fear in the individual. Here, Roger threatened to increase the sentence to show defendants that law is "a compelling and powerful force." As the court clerk called out the names of Leng, McBride, and Hervey, the defendants, who appeared to be about age 18, were escorted by officers from the court pen to stand behind the defense table. As they did so, three lawyers, Sherr, a Legal Aid attorney, and Gartenstein and Rucker, 18–B attorneys, entered the well of the courtroom and stood facing Roger. The ADA addressed Roger saying: "May we approach the bench?" Roger told all the lawyers to come up. The ADA then handed Roger a sheet that contained a short summary of the charges, the guilty plea and sentence offer, and a recommendation to continue to detain the defendants in lieu of $10,000 bail.

Roger read aloud the one-line statements of facts disclosed in the prosecutor's summary. As soon as the reading was completed, Roger glanced at the defendants' RAP sheets and made the following remark off the record: "Here's the offer." Before he said anything further, Gartenstein said: "Judge, he [Leng] said he made YO.[10]"

Roger: "It is not so on the sheet."

Gartenstein: "He tells me he did or at least I think that's what he says."

Roger: "Check it out."

Gartenstein went to speak to Leng and resumed a few seconds later saying: "I've checked and he did make YO." Roger continued: "Here's the offer. McBride 4 to 8 [years] [mandatory minimum sentence for a predicate felon], Leng and Hervey [not predicate felons] 1 to 4 and no YO." All three attorneys went back to inform their clients of the likely consequences of refusing Roger's guilty plea offer.

When Sherr told his client of Roger's offer, McBride recoiled, frowned, and made a dismissive gesture towards Sherr. Roger noticed this immediately and spoke in resonant off-the-record tones to the whole courtroom. Roger's speech enabled Roberto Santiago and others present to hear his contempt for the defendant's response, while it demonstrated that in Roger's court, a lawyer is little more than a formal appendage whose function is easily made redundant:

> McBride doesn't appear to like it. Tell him, Mr. Sherr, that I remember him and it's not good for a calendar judge to remember someone. Tell him it is going to go up next time, 6 to 12. It is not going to stay. It is going up. McBride is going to get 4 to 8 if he is smart, 6 to 12 if he is dumb. [McBride put his face into a nervous smile] I like his attitude.

Tell McBride it is *now* 6 to 12 [Rogers emphasis]. If he wants to play hard ball, let's play hard ball. Tell the others it will go to 3 to 9 if they don't want the offer.

Within a few seconds, the lawyers resumed to the bench and stated that the defendants were unwilling to accept the judge's offer. Thereafter, Roger showed everyone that the judge, as chief constable and jailer, was neither neutral with regard to the question of guilt or innocence nor powerless to ensure a guilty plea. Roger, speaking over the lawyers and directly to the defendants said: "All right, the offers are now 6 to 12 for McBride and 3 to 9 for Leng and Hervey." The effectiveness of Roger's actions was vividly demonstrated when Leng returned from the court pens moments later and pleaded guilty.

After the court officers had escorted the defendants to the court pen, Gartenstein had further opportunity to speak with Leng. He then asked the clerk to recall Leng's case so that Leng could accept Roger's initial offer of 1 to 4 years. Upon Gartenstein's statement that Leng was now willing to accept the offer, Roger spoke to Leng on the record, allowing him to waive his rights and to plead guilty. The transcript of this colloquy was quoted in the introduction to the article.

Santiago's Guilty Plea

Unknown to Roberto Santiago, Roger had decided to replace Emerson with another attorney, should Emerson appear again before him. Roger's decision was based upon Emerson's performance in an earlier case, when the lawyer had rejected, out-of-hand, Roger's guilty plea offer and had insisted that the defendant could not be convicted on the identification of a stranger. Roger later informed one of the authors that Emerson was an "incompetent lawyer" who acted "obstructively" when confronted with evidence which, in Roger's view, was sufficient to convict the defendant.

When the court clerk called out Roberto Santiago's name, Emerson entered the well of the courtroom along with the defendant. The clerk informed Santiago that he had been indicted for the sale of cocaine and asked Santiago: "How do you plead?" Santiago responded immediately and firmly: "Not guilty." Roger than asked Emerson to approach the bench and said: "I do not want you to appear again in my court. I am going to relieve you of this assignment." Emerson turned and left the courtroom, leaving Santiago standing alone at the defense table.

Roger's dismissal of Emerson demonized the only individual the court had earlier assigned to protect Santiago. Roger did this without consulting Santiago. To ensure the entry of Santiago's guilty plea, Roger continued the process without a moment's hesitation. He asked Richard Sartag to "accept the court's assignment" and to substitute for Emerson. Sartag, an 18–B regular who had positioned himself in the first row of the courtroom, nodded his assent. Thereafter, he approached the bench, after which Roger read the prosecution's summary of the case:

> Roger: "The defendant is a first offender who was one of a group of people who sold drugs to an undercover officer over an 18–month period. The officer positively identified the defendant at the precinct after he was arrested."

Roger then turned to Sartag and stated the offer:

> Roger: "Tell him in return for a plea to attempted criminal sale of a controlled substance in the third degree, I'll give him a split sentence [time already served and five years probation].[11] Tell him should he go to trial and be convicted of the sale, he would be facing at least 2 to 6 years."

Neither Roger nor Sartag said anything about whether the twenty-month delay in indictment had prejudiced the defendant's opportunity to receive a fair trial, the reliability of the undercover officer's identification, or the availability of any corroborative evidence to independently connect the defendant to the drug sale. No reference was made to the original allegation that the sale occurred six months before Roberto Santiago's arrest. Instead, Sartag conveyed Roger's offer to Santiago in a momentary conversation. Thereafter, Sartag advised Santiago to "plead guilty in return for a promise of probation." Santiago agreed, after which the formal guilty plea colloquy ensued, on the record. When Roger solicited Santiago's waiver of the rights associated with a jury trial, Santiago responded "yes" to each of the judge's inquiries. Thereafter, Roger asked Santiago two leading questions to provide a *prima facie* basis, in law, to legitimate the entry of the guilty plea:

> Q: "Did you, on May 27 (past year), near the northeast corner of 106 Street and Amsterdam Ave., sell a controlled substance, to-wit crack cocaine, to an individual then known to you?"
>
> A: "Yes."
>
> Q: "Did you, in exchange, receive $100 in U.S. currency?"
>
> A: "Yes."

Roger directed the court clerk to enter Santiago's guilty plea and to adjourn the case for sentencing, while he rewarded Santiago by permitting him to remain free on bail. Sartag returned to the court benches.

After the court appearance, Santiago stood in the hallway of the courthouse visibly upset. When one of the authors asked him why he pleaded guilty, Santiago said he was "frightened" and that he feared he would have to "flee to Puerto Rico or some other island" to avoid "getting sent to prison." Santiago approached Emerson, who remained in the hallway, and asked: "What is going to happen next?" Emerson replied: "I am no longer your lawyer, and I don't know."

Conclusion: Legal and Social Order

Our research shows that guilty pleas in New York City are a part of a vertical process: What will happen later at the court stage influences what happens earlier at the police stage. Routine case processing in court, through guilty pleas, reinforces the actions and expectations of the police and defendants, thereby encouraging sweeps, dragnets and other non-individuated arrests. This integral feedback loop, in which facts are of little consequence and in which witnesses are not called at either hearings or trials (and the propriety of policing and the reliability of police evidence are untested), institutionalizes domination. Subordination and degradation are thereafter employed to reinforce the substantive objectives of proactive policing.

Each stage of the criminal process, from arrest and court papers to arraignment and guilty plea court, displays the contrast between social discipline and a crime control system based upon factual or legal guilt. In a social disciplinary process, defendants charged with felonies, whom a judge has detained, may be released later because the setting of bail relates only to the initiating acts of the police and omits consideration of the sufficiency and persuasiveness of the evidence or the circumstances of the accused. Thereafter, while the subsequent entry of a guilty plea, even with the carrot of probation, may ensure social discipline, it is without any assurance that criminal activity occurred in the first instance or will cease thereafter.

In this setting, the judges, rather than the lawyers translate the demands of social discipline into the language of the street—and to thereby persuade defendants, through their lawyers, of the desirability and inevitability of pleading guilty. If judges are key courtroom actors in securing guilty pleas, defense lawyers are structurally unable to exercise a meaningful influence on the process, except in relation to defendants. While it is the lawyer's task to convey to the defendant, in no uncertain terms, the wishes of the court, should the defendant reject the offer, the judge may speak directly to the defendant, further marginalizing the attorney. This hierarchy of power reduces what some commentators in other settings describe as a consensus model (Nardulli, Flemming, and Eisenstein 1985) to a formalistic canopy.

In New York City and other large urban settings, reliance on guilty pleas occurs because of three major structural features endemic to the justice system itself. First, judges proceeded on the assumption that their courtroom practices, while at variance with due process, were consonant with the perceived wishes of the wider society. While the general public observed guilty plea court at a distance, its impressions are created through accounts associated with the "common knowledge" that those arrested are guilty, and that when confronted with the moment of truth they will confess their guilt. Second, disciplinary practices regularly occurred in the presence of disempowered people, who expect nothing more from a system in which the objectives of policing define the process. It is this audience that was first "taught . . . [the] lesson" (Garland 1991:202). Third, in employing domination, the actors exploited the political space provided by malleable legal rules in an attempt to validate the initiating acts of the police, and to thereby overcome law's perceived failure to arrive at a satisfactory strategy for social control.

In achieving wider social disciplinary objectives, however, the actors discarded the criminal justice system's crime control objectives, except in so far as they happened to have been fulfilled by the police at the arrest stage. In guilty plea courts, law and legality took on a meaning separate from a crime control system based upon factual guilt or principles of proof associated with legal guilt. Law became redefined and reordered to validate substantive outcomes obtained through methods that subordinate and maintain order over groups society has labeled dangerous.

Notes

[1] In the United States, more than 90 percent of state criminal cases and 85 percent of all federal cases are disposed of without trial, mostly through guilty pleas (United States Department of Justice 1990).

[2] The leading question is directed to the definition of robbery in the second degree as contained in Penal Law Sec. 160.10 (1973). It tracks the elements of the offense and it provides a factual basis for the guilty plea. Upon the defendant's response, Judge Roger instructed the clerk to enter defendant Leng's guilty plea in the court record.

[3] In New York City, between 1984 and 1990, guilty pleas accounted for between 76 and 84 percent of all dispositions. Trials account for between 7 and 10 percent and dismissals for between 8 and 10 percent.

[4]Under New York City's scheme, should a Legal Aid lawyer decline the assignment because of a professional conflict of interest (usually involving representation of more than one defendant in the same case), a court officer would assign a private lawyer compensated by the city. These are known as "18–B attorneys" because of the law that provides for their appointment and compensation (McConville and Mirsky 1986–87).

[5]Before the case was called, the ADA reviewed the Navy warrant and determined, from a comparison of the physical descriptions, that Santiago and Santiageles were not the same person. Thereafter, no further mention was made of the warrant.

[6]The section of the Criminal Procedure Law (1982) requires the prosecution to present the case to a grand jury within 120 hours of the time of arrest or, if witnesses were unavailable or memories unrefreshed, to release the defendant.

[7]Monthly ratings are published that show the number of guilty plea dispositions for all judges over an equivalent number of judge work days, and all judges are compared against the judge with the highest disposition rate and the largest case load.

[8]Roger's use of the power to detain individuals, in lieu of money bail, occurred despite New York's statutory scheme, which first required a finding that the conditions of pre-trial release set by the arraignment judge were inadequate to secure the defendant's further appearance.

[9]Off-the-record remarks were publicly uttered and audible to all but were not transcribed by the court stenographer, who waited for something official to occur before placing any words on the record.

[10]People who are judged Youth Offenders (YO) have not been convicted of a crime despite the fact that they may have committed a criminal act. Hence, they may not be sentenced as predicate felons.

[11]Criminal sale of a controlled substance is a class B felony with a maximum term of 8-1/3 to 25 years. However, a defendant, like Santiago, pleading guilty to an attempt (a lesser class C felony) may receive a split sentence of imprisonment not in excess of 60 days followed by probation of 5 years.

Cases

Gideon vs. Wainwright, 372 U.S. 335 (1963)
United States vs. Lovasco, 431 U.S. 783 (1977)
Wong Sun vs. United States, 371 U.S. 471 (1963)

References

Alschuler, Albert W. 1976. "The trial judge's role in plea bargaining." *Columbia Law Review* 76:1059.

Assael, Shawn. 1989. "18–B counsel made $17.5 million in '88." *Manhattan Lawyer* 49:1.

Balbus, Isaac. 1973. *The Dialectics of Legal Repression.* New York: Russell Sage.

Feeley, Malcolm. 1979. *The Process Is The Punishment.* New York: Russell Sage.

Feeley, Malcolm. 1982. "Plea bargaining and the structure of the criminal process." *Justice System Journal* 7:338.

Freeman, Jody. 1993. "The disciplinary function of race representation: Lessons from the Kennedy Smith and Tyson trials." *Law and Social Inquiry* 517–46.

Fritsch, Jane, and Matthew Purdy. 1994. "Lawyers for New York poor: A program with no monitor." *New York Times* CXLIII:1.

Garland, David. 1991. "Punishment in culture: The symbolic dimension of criminal justice." In *Studies in Law, Politics and Society*, eds. Austin Sarat and Susan Silbey, 11:191. Greenwich, CT: JAI Press.

Garfinkel, Harold. 1956. "Conditions of successful degradation ceremonies." *American Journal of Sociology* 61:420.

Gilboy, Janet, and John R. Schmidt. 1979. "Replacing lawyers: A case study of the sequential representation of criminal defendants." *Journal of Criminal Law and Criminology* 70:1.

Heumann, Milton. 1978. *Plea Bargaining: The Experiences of Prosecutors, Judges and Defense Attorneys*. Chicago: University of Chicago Press.

Heydebrand, Wolf, and Carol Seron. 1987. "The organizational structure of courts: Toward the technocratic administration of justice." *International Review of Sociology* 2:63.

Jaynes, Gerald D., and Robbin Williams, Jr., eds. 1988. *A Common Destiny: Blacks in American Society*. Washington, DC: National Academy Press.

Luskin, Marie. 1989. "Making sense of calendaring system: A reconsideration of concept and measurement." *Justice System Journal* 13:240.

Mann, Coramae Richey. 1993. *Unequal Justice*. Bloomington: Indiana University Press.

McConville, Michael, and Chester L. Mirsky. 1986–87. "Criminal defense of the poor in New York City." *Review of Law and Social Change* 15:582.

———. 1988. "The state, the legal profession and the defense of the poor." *Journal of Law and Society* 15: No. 4.

———. 1989. "Criminal defense of the poor in New York City." In *Occasional Papers From the Center for Research in Crime and Justice*, ed. Graham Hughes, 1–42. New York: New York University School of Law.

———. 1990. "Understanding defense of the poor in state courts: The sociolegal context of nonadversarial advocacy." In *Studies in Law, Politics and Society*, eds. Austin Sarat and Susan Silbey, 10:217. Greenwich, CT: JAI Press.

Nagel, Ilene. 1983. "The legal/extra-legal controversy: Judicial decisions in pre-trial release." *Law and Society Review* 17:481–515.

Nardulli, Peter F., Roy B. Flemming, and James Eisenstein. 1985. "Criminal courts and bureaucratic justice: Concessions and consensus in the guilty plea process." *Criminal Law and Criminology* 79:1103–31.

Nardulli, Peter F., James Eisenstein, and Roy B. Flemming. 1988. *The Tenor of Justice*. Chicago: University of Illinois Press.

Nonet, Philippe, and Philip Selznick. 1978. *Law and Society in Transition: Toward Responsive Law*. New York: Octagon Books.

Pepinsky, Harold E. 1975. "Police decision-making." In *Decision in the Criminal Justice System*, ed. Donald M. Gottfredson, Washington, DC: U.S. Government Printing Office.

Simon, Jonathan S. 1993. *Poor Discipline: Parole and the Social Control of the Underclass*. Chicago: University of Chicago Press.

Smith, Dorothy. 1974. "Women's perspective as a radical critique of sociology." *Sociological Inquiry* 44:7–14.

Smith, Douglas A., and Christy A. Visher. 1981. "Street level justice: Situational determinants of police arrest decisions." *Social Problems* 29:167–77.

Smith, Douglas A., Christy A. Visher, and Laura A. Davidson. 1984. "Equity and discretionary justice: The influence of race on police arrest decisions." *Journal of Criminal Law and Criminology* 75:234–49.

Teubner, Gunther. 1987. "Juridification: Concepts, aspects, limits, solutions." In *Juridification of Social Spheres: A Comparative Analysis in the Areas of Labor, Corporate, Antitrust and Social Welfare Law*, ed. Gunther Teubner, 3–48. Berlin/NY: Walter de Gruyter.

United States Department of Justice. 1990. *Sourcebook of Criminal Justice Statistics*, eds. Kathleen McGuire and Timothy J. Fannagan. Washington, DC: United States Government Printing Office.

Walker, Samuel. 1993. *Taming the System: The Control of Discretion in Criminal Justice 1950–1990*. New York: Oxford University Press.

Wilson, William J. 1987. *The Truly Disadvantaged The Inner City, The Underclass, and Public Policy*. Chicago: University of Chicago Press.

13

Convicted *But* Innocent
Wrongful Conviction and Public Policy

C. Ronald Huff
Arye Rattner
Edward Sagarin

During the 1980s and early 1990s, the American conscience was shaken by a number of instances that cast doubt on a cherished belief—that innocent people are seldom, if ever, convicted and imprisoned, and they are certainly not executed. Almost as if orchestrated in the way they came to public attention, completely unrelated cases of miscarriage of justice, not in which the guilty were freed but in which the totally innocent were severely punished, became front-page news and the subject of frequent discussion on television. Nor were the charges trivial: Most of the convictions were for murder or rape.

From *Convicted But Innocent: Wrongful Conviction and Public Policy* by C. Ronald Huff, Arye Rattner, and Edward Sagarin, © 1996 Sage Publications, Inc. Reprinted by permission.

Defining the Convicted Innocents

We have carved out for study in this work a group that is not easy to define and that excludes many who are wrongfully incarcerated. This is not about injustice broadly defined, but about one special aspect of injustice, the conviction of an innocent person.

Convicted innocents, as defined here, are people who have been arrested on criminal charges, although not necessarily armed robbery, rape, or murder; who have either pleaded guilty to the charge or have been tried and found guilty; and who, notwithstanding plea or verdict, are in fact innocent. Although we shall present estimates of the extent of this phenomenon among felony cases, our discussions and conclusions will revolve around those who have been clearly exculpated, either because the alleged crime was never committed or, more frequently, the convicted person was not the perpetrator. Many convicted innocents have committed other crimes, but are nonetheless innocent of the specific charges of which they have been accused and convicted.

This definition excludes from our discussion several important groups. From the viewpoint of injustice, the most significant of these groups consists of people who have been held before trial for considerable periods of time, many months or even years, and then exonerated, with their innocence either admitted by the prosecution and the police or so clearly established as to be beyond question. Matzner and English (1973) have written about a case in which four people were held in a New Jersey jail on murder charges for which the evidence was utterly absurd, but because the charge was first-degree murder, punishable by death, no bail was allowed. Two of the individuals held were a couple, middle-class publishers of a local community newspaper; the third was one of their employees, and the fourth was a fairly high-ranking police officer who was arrested and charged with the murder when he objected to the manner in which the investigation was being handled. The case involved false arrest, prosecutorial and police improprieties, and incarceration without crime. But despite the suffering imposed on these four people and their families, their case does not fall within the purview of our study, because our major interest is in the factors that contribute to the malfunctioning of a legal system that results in false *conviction* (including the false plea of guilty).

Our definition excludes those found not guilty in a second trial, or on appeal, because of the exclusion of crucial evidence stemming from illegal searches and seizures or other violations of suspects' rights. To be sure, such people were once convicted and today stand legally not guilty, but there is a significant difference between being found "not guilty" according to the standards of our legal system and establishing complete innocence. In many of these cases complete exoneration cannot be inferred from subsequent acquittals or reversals. So it is with the case of Claus von Bulow, which provides an excellent example of the difference between having a conviction reversed on appeal and the establishment of innocence. Convicted on two counts of attempting to murder his wealthy and socially prominent wife, Martha (Sunny) von Bulow, of Newport, Rhode Island, von Bulow had his conviction overturned in 1984 by the Rhode Island Supreme Court, which ruled that there had been an illegal search that resulted in toxicological testing and that the subsequent expert testimony by the state's toxicologist was therefore inadmissible. In making this ruling, the Rhode Island Supreme Court argued that the language of the Rhode Island Constitution permitted the application of a more exacting standard than that required by the U.S. Constitution as interpreted by the U.S. Supreme Court.

Miranda and Escobedo both had their guilty verdicts overturned, but neither of them qualifies for inclusion in this study of convicted innocents, any more than would someone who was found not guilty by reason of insanity at a second trial. These are people whose factual guilt, rather than legally established guilt, has not been effectively disputed. But this is not the place to discuss the rationale of a criminal justice system that will free a person generally or almost universally believed to be guilty of a major crime because of procedural defects rather than substantive error. In such instances, it is not the innocence of the accused that has been established, but the unfairness governing his or her arrest and conviction. It is that unfairness the courts seek to deter by overturning convictions reached through violations of the rights of the accused.

Like many others, we are concerned with the many guilty persons who "beat the rap" because of good lawyers or fine technicalities or intimidation of witnesses, who then fear to testify against them. These persons far outnumber the convicted innocents, of that we are certain. They are examples of justice gone wrong, sometimes for defensible reasons (as when a true confession is excluded because it was obtained by illegal trickery or force), but more often for reasons that dismay those who recognize the enormity of the crime problem, especially in the United States. In fact, when we first began our research on wrongful conviction, we surveyed judges and other public officials and received this reply from one Ohio judge: "I am deeply disappointed that my old university is even remotely involved in this type of venture. Aren't there more pressing topics in this world that your efforts can be funneled to?" (Huff, Rattner, & Sagarin, 1986, p. 522).

Why, then, concentrate on what is probably the small percentage of convicted innocents and ignore the far more numerous and, in some respects, more threatening problem of the opposite, the judicially released guilty? There are many answers to this question. Both sides of the coin deserve attention, but the one we focus on has received it only in unrelated stories that have hit the newspapers. Both problems deserve study to determine what can be done to reduce injustice and undeserved pain and suffering; here we focus on one, and others will concentrate elsewhere. Finally, as we will argue in our concluding chapter, we believe that the two problems are interrelated in two important ways: (a) The conviction of the innocent leaves the guilty free to commit more crimes, thus threatening public safety; and (b) each instance of the conviction of an innocent enhances the possibility that there will be more not-guilty verdicts against the truly guilty.

How Could This Have Happened?

Quite clearly, there is no accurate, scientific way to determine how many innocent people are convicted, or, put another way, how many of those convicted of crimes are innocent. When we include, as is appropriate, those who plead guilty to crimes they have not committed, the problem becomes more complex, for it is relatively rare for suspects to plead guilty to serious crimes, relatively rare for innocent persons to be given prison terms, and relatively rare for such impropriety and errors to gain the attention of the mass media.

Lacking any figures, those who have written on the subject, or who have given it serious thought, have relied on newspaper accounts that surface, not infrequently but in numbers sufficiently small to make one believe that the prisons are overwhelmingly filled with the guilty; yet not so infrequently that the problem can be disregarded as a tragedy so ominous as to touch the nerve centers and the basic tenets of a criminal justice system.

These newspaper accounts have been collected by several authors, who have usually added other cases gleaned from such sources as interviews with attorneys, court records, interviews with victims of false conviction, and even interviews with victims of crime. Their works almost always consist of a series of anecdotes, with each case a small horror story in itself, yet they provide no data that might give us an estimate of the magnitude of the occurrence, or legal analysis that might show its sources. For one thing, the cases collected are not seriously or sufficiently detailed; often one learns little more than that an innocent person, whose name is given, was arrested for forgery or embezzlement and that after his or her arrest, authorities noted that the events continued to occur, leading them finally to the right culprit and to the exoneration of the wrong one.

In one classic book, Borchard (1932) discusses 60 cases, with an average of only three or four pages devoted to each; other authors have included somewhat fewer cases. Added to these works, of which we have made ample use in our studies (their shortcomings notwithstanding), are extremely interesting book-length accounts of individual cases, the authors of which are convinced that innocent persons have been convicted and either put to death or given lengthy prison terms.

To determine the prevalence of the phenomenon of wrongful conviction, we initially set out to study the perception of its prevalence by criminal justice personnel; it should be noted that the sample of personnel we queried was stacked in favor of obtaining conservative estimates, rather than those who might be more easily persuaded that mistakes are made by "the system." We regard our result, then, as a conservative prevalence estimation made by a largely conservative sample, most members of which have every reason to defend the system's accuracy and underestimate error. Public defenders, who might be expected to hold a relatively critical view of the system, represented only 9% of respondents.

Concentrating on those closest to the trial process, we asked for respondents' perceptions of the problem both in their own experience and in their own jurisdictions, and as they saw it to exist on a national scale. We mailed 353 questionnaires and received 229 responses (a response rate of approximately 65%).

How people perceive a fact, and particularly how they perceive its frequency and prevalence, cannot be a substitute for more objective tests of a quantitative or even a qualitative nature. People may believe that the majority of people in prison are there because they have been convicted of violent crimes, and a study may or may not come up with the same conclusion. Hence, one might well ask, why utilize perception at all, when studies can give us much more accurate results? We believe, however, that there are specific reasons perception is an important ingredient in the present study.

First, on the issue of wrongful conviction we know of no better way to approach the question of prevalence than through observation. When the actors involved are likely to be the most knowledgeable, to be closest to the situation at hand, we believe that they can come up with data close enough to objective truth to be usable. It is our conclusion that a survey of the perceptions of the types of persons in our sample concerning the prevalence of false positives offers at least a conservative baseline estimate of how these people see the problem.

Perception has a second usefulness, as pointed out by a long line of prestigious sociologists, from Simmel and Thomas to Merton and Goffman. How people perceive a phenomenon will be one of the determinants of how they act: Perception is a cause of behavior and a key to its understanding. Criminologists have shown that widespread fear of crime—individuals' perception that they are vulnerable—makes a major contribution to behavior on the streets, in our homes, and in our everyday lives. If people believe that many innocents are found guilty, this can have a devastating effect on our criminal justice system, and specifically on jury behavior.

We know of no previous study that has attempted to quantify the phenomenon of wrongful conviction, but we were able to clarify the issue to some degree by examining the work of Kalven and Zeisel (1966), who conducted one of the classic studies of the American jury. In drawing upon this work, we had to do some speculating, but Kalven and Zeisel's data, when extrapolated, brought us to approximately the same conclusion as that we drew from our survey of the perceptions of criminal justice personnel.

Now, let us look at how our own sample of judges, prosecutors, public defenders, and others saw this situation. In our questionnaire, we made no effort to raise the problem of innocent suspects making guilty pleas, and it is not at all certain whether or not the respondents took this issue into account in making their estimates of the pervasiveness of false conviction, as they perceive it. The estimates we received ranged from zero (an unbelievable figure, in light of what was on the front pages of Ohio newspapers at the time) up to 5% of all cases, with most responses hovering near the 1% mark. With these figures before us, and side by side with the experience of Kalven and Zeisel (1966), we decided to see what the magnitude of the problem would appear to be if we cut the 1% figure in half, on the grounds that most of our respondents selected the category "less than 1%," thereby indicating that they believed wrongful conviction does occur (they rejected "never"), but also indicating that it occurs in less than 1% of all felony convictions. Given that the midpoint between zero and 1% is 0.5%, we felt justified in using that figure.

We are left with what appears to be an impressive figure for accuracy and justice: 99.5% of all guilty verdicts in felony cases are handed down on people who did indeed commit the crimes of which they have been accused. But in terms of real numbers, this figure is more disheartening. According to the U.S. Department of Justice's Bureau of Justice Statistics (1995, p. 374), the estimated total number of persons arrested and charged with index crimes in 1993 was 2,848,400.[1]

Conviction rates vary from state to state and by type of offense, but based on the best available data, an analysis of the likelihood of felony conviction in the nation's 75 largest counties, we can reasonably assume that about 70% of all felony arrests result in conviction (U.S. Department of Justice, 1995, p. 497). Now, if we go to our survey data and to the study of the American jury, and assume that 70% of those arrested for index crimes are convicted, this would yield the following estimate of wrongful conviction for the eight crimes in the FBI index only:

1990 arrests for index crimes	2848,400
x conviction rate (70%)	x 0.7
1990 convictions for index crimes	1,993,880
x wrongful conviction rate (0.5%)	x .005
Estimated number of wrongful convictions	9,969

Thus, if these apparently conservative estimates are reasonable, we are facing an interesting dilemma: A high volume of prosecutions, even if 99.5% accurate when guilty verdicts are rendered, can still generate about 10,000 erroneous convictions for index crimes in a single year. And this figure does not include the many erroneous convictions that occur in cases involving crimes not in the index; when these are added to the 10,000 "index false positives," the result is even more sobering.

Why do such cases occur? What are the sources of these errors in the criminal justice system? If we had to isolate a single "system dynamic" that pervades large numbers of these cases, we would probably describe it as *police and prosecutorial overzealousness*: the anxiety to solve a case; the ease with which one having such anxiety is willing to believe, on the slightest evidence of the most negligible nature, that the culprit is in hand; the willingness to use improper, unethical, and illegal means to obtain a conviction when one believes that the person at the bar is guilty.

Drawing from both the analysis of the database and the extensive analysis of more recent cases, from which we were able to glean a great deal of information, we discovered that it was increasingly obvious that several factors were often simultaneously at work. In fact, these "interaction effects" are so important that isolating any one individual factor misses the point—we typically see, in these cases, system failure, with more than one error occurring.

Furthermore, although we have since had an opportunity to review reports of several hundred more recent cases reported in the mass media and in scholarly publications, this review has not produced any new factors that were not present in our original database. The pat-

terns are distressingly similar, with eyewitness error, police and prosecutorial overzealousness, and perjury interacting to produce system
failure. Moreover, these elements interact in such complex ways that
any simple tabular listing of cases by "types of errors" would be a gross
oversimplification and would be misleading. We have decided not to
present such a table, because our sources typically lack the detailed
case-level information necessary to understand these interaction
effects.

How Does It Happen?

How can an innocent defendant be convicted? What would possibly induce an innocent person to plead guilty? What goes wrong with
a criminal justice system that has created an elaborate system of safeguards to protect the rights of suspects and defendants—a system that
gave us *Powell* (1932), *Mapp* (1961), *Gideon* (1963), and *Miranda*
(1966), among many others?

By interviewing convicted innocents, attorneys, and other key
informants, and by analyzing hundreds of individual cases, mostly of
relatively recent vintage, we were able to add considerably to the cases
that made up our original database. Despite assessing more than 500
acknowledged false positives (with more called to our attention each
month), we remain convinced that in these cases, police and prosecutorial overzealousness and eyewitness error (usually unintentional),
along with perjury, are pervasive, and that the most likely scenario is
one in which these factors interact to produce system failure, resulting
in the conviction of an innocent person.

Eyewitness Error

We believe that the single most important factor leading to
wrongful conviction in the United States and England (Brandon &
Davies, 1973) is eyewitness misidentification, to which we could add,
in good faith. This is shown not only in our database, but in the
responses to our questionnaire, where nearly 8 out of 10 ranked witness error (primarily witness misidentification, but also including
some less frequent types of witness error) as by far the most frequent
type of error leading to false conviction. Other studies have also

emphasized the importance of eyewitness error (but see Bedau & Radelet, 1987, p. 61; Radelet & Bedau, 1992).

Intermingled with eyewitness error is the question of rewards. Is a person likely to be more positive, on the witness stand, that a given defendant is the person he or she saw if the witness has either a financial incentive (reward) or plea-bargaining/sentencing incentive? A number of jurisdictions have begun to scrutinize the use of informants, especially jailhouse "snitches" and narcotics informants, because such testimony has often been linked with wrongful conviction. Race plays an important role in eyewitness identification, and this is probably as true of relatively unprejudiced witnesses as it is of more prejudiced witnesses.

In 1967, the U.S. Supreme Court handed down decisions in three landmark cases involving eyewitness identification, in which the Court sought to establish effective constitutional safeguards and guidelines governing the admission of such evidence in federal and state criminal trials. In *United States v. Wade* (1967), the Court decided that the postindictment lineup (or police parade, as it is known in England) is a critical stage at which an accused is entitled to the aid of counsel. The Court noted the great possibility of unfairness in a lineup at which counsel is not present. In the *Wade* case, bank employees who had witnessed the robbery of their bank were allowed to see the accused in the custody of the FBI before the lineup began.

On the same day the *Wade* decision was handed down, the Court also decided *Gilbert v. California* (1967), a case involving the murder of a police officer during an armed robbery. Again, there was a lineup, this time 16 days after the appointment of counsel, who was not notified. In-court identifications were made by witnesses who were present at the lineup, and the Court determined that the accused had been deprived of the right to counsel.

In the last case of the trilogy handed down that day, *Stovall v. Denno* (1967), a murder suspect had been taken to the hospital bedside of the slain man's widow for her to make an identification. The widow identified him as the killer, and the accused was convicted. The Court upheld the legality of this identification, ruling that there was no denial of due process, because the widow was the only person who could exonerate the suspect, she could not go to the police station for the usual lineup, and there was no way of knowing how long she might live. This was a decision that elicited strong dissent. It would appear that it might have been more appropriate to bring several possible suspects, or the equivalent of a lineup, to the widow's bedside, so that she could have chosen from among them; whether this would have been more stressful to the ailing and grieving woman, and whether such stress must take precedence over the rights of a defendant or an accused, would be arguable.

Although jurors attach great significance to eyewitness testimony, experts and judges increasingly share the view of Judge Lumbard of the Second Circuit, who has observed:

> Centuries of experience in the administration of criminal justice have shown that convictions based solely on testimony that identifies a defendant previously unknown to the witness is highly suspect. Of the various kinds of evidence it is the least reliable, especially where unsupported by corroborating evidence. (*Jackson v. Fogg*, 1978)

Despite the steps taken by the Supreme Court to establish safeguards against eyewitness misidentification, such errors continue to surface. In 1982, a Texas prisoner, Howard Mosley of Galveston, who had been convicted in a stabbing death and sentenced to a life term, was exonerated after new evidence indicated that the crime had been committed by a man who also admitted killing 10 others ("Monday Finally Comes," 1982). In a highly publicized Ohio case where great weight was placed on eyewitness identification by the victims of rape, William Jackson spent nearly 5 years in prison for rapes that he did not commit. He was released from prison after a grand jury indicted another Ohio man (also named Jackson, but unrelated) on 36 counts of rape and 46 counts of aggravated burglary ("Freed Jackson's Advice," 1982; "Ohio Doctor Accused," 1982).

In the Jackson case, both the innocent and the guilty defendants were black, and the innocent one had been identified by several white eyewitnesses, an indication of the special difficulties in interracial identification. Nonetheless, there were some similarities in resemblance: The two Jacksons were of approximately the same height, both wore Afro hairstyles, and their facial shapes and mustaches were similar as well. By contrast, in the Texas case, Mosley was fully a foot taller than Watts, the actual offender, but was misidentified by witnesses to the point where the jury did not have a reasonable doubt.

Accounts of eyewitness error are myriad, and sometimes bizarre. In one incredible case, Jeffrey Streeter was convicted without even having been arrested. Streeter had been sitting outside a courtroom and was asked by a defense attorney if he would sit next to him as a way of testing the credibility of the eyewitnesses. The defense attorney failed to inform the judge of the switch. Despite the fact that the actual defendant was also in the courtroom at the time, three eyewitnesses unflinchingly pointed to the startled Streeter, seated next to the defense attorney, as the criminal. Streeter was convicted and sentenced to a year in jail for assaulting an elderly man. However, he spent only one night in jail before being released on his own recognizance, and his conviction was subsequently reversed ("Court Stand-in Is Convicted," 1980).

In another case, Robert Duncan, president of the Missouri Association of Criminal Defense Lawyers, was representing a Mexican American defendant who had been arrested after being identified by a woman who was raped by "an Italian-looking man." When a second suspect was brought in, she identified him, too, as the same guilty offender. She reportedly told authorities, "I'm getting tired of coming down here to identify this man." According to the defense attorney, "The second guy didn't look anything at all like my client" ("When Nightmare of False Arrest," 1984, p. 46).

Prosecutorial and Police Misconduct and Errors

Far too many cases come from the states to the Supreme Court presenting dismal pictures of official lawlessness, of illegal searches and seizures, illegal detentions attended by prolonged interrogation and coerced admissions of guilt, of the denial of counsel, and downright brutality.

William J. Brennan, *The Bill of Rights and the States*, 1961

Some of the improprieties committed by police and prosecutors are directed against guilty people, but this makes them no more legal or proper; many of the most famous landmark cases brought before the Supreme Court concerning such improprieties have resulted in the freeing of blatantly culpable individuals. This was true of Miranda and Escobedo, for example, but not of Ozzie Powell and the other Scottsboro defendants, or of Bradley Cox in Ohio. The reasons for police and prosecutorial misconduct should be distinguished from the types of misconduct that occur. The reason generally given for such misconduct is the firm belief that the person in custody, or under suspicion, is guilty, and it is therefore a public service to get him or her into the slammer, or even executed, even if that might involve bending the rules, flexing authoritarian muscles, suppressing some evidence, or other acts of wrongdoing.

Overzealousness is a term often applied to this type of investigation and prosecution, and although we do not dispute that such a factor can exist, it is not simple. Overzealousness itself might not arise from so noble a motive as generally stated; it might come from a desire to add points to a scorecard, to enhance a reputation as a tough and successful prosecutor because of an impending election, or to receive commendation and promotion in the police department for having nabbed a vicious criminal and solved a difficult case. Overzealousness might also conceal bigotry and racism, or sometimes greed. In England, a chief detective secretly divided the reward money that was given to the major prosecution witness in one of the cases described by Ludovic Kennedy. The detective himself went to prison eventually, although the men he had helped to convict were not freed; they even met on one occasion in a prison yard.

Largely overlooked in previous discussions of overzealousness has been the possibility that it may sometimes derive from the inability, unwillingness, or lack of funds and personnel available to police to make true and proper investigations. It is clearly easier to close a case where there is grave doubt about the suspect's guilt than to continue to pursue it until there is sufficient reason to be confident the accused is guilty and to gather enough legally acceptable evidence to prove that in court. Caseload pressure, the need to close cases and move on to others, is powerful, and many law enforcement officials have privately (and sometimes publicly) acknowledged this problem.

Police and prosecutorial improprieties take on several different forms: coaching witnesses at lineups but denying such coaching under oath; obtaining confessions through brutality, threat, force, or guile, and denying any such actions in court; planting evidence, such as a gun or drugs, that will militate against the accused; making threats against potential witnesses for the accused; using rewards and offers of immunity to entice those willing to testify; and suppressing exculpatory evidence even after motions for discovery have been made.

Item: A prosecutor brings as evidence a pair of men's undershorts found a mile from the crime scene. Alleging that these shorts belong to the accused and are heavily stained with blood that is the same type as the victim's, the prosecutor calls a chemist, who verifies this incriminating information. The defense requests, and is denied, an opportunity to examine the shorts (a judicial error that will subsequently be corrected by a higher court). Despite the defendant's denial that the shorts—the only link in a chain of rather meager evidence—are his, the jury brings in a verdict of guilty. The convicted prisoner subsequently petitions the Supreme Court for a writ of habeas corpus. The shorts are produced, by order of the Court, and a microanalyst appears for the petitioner and testifies that they are stained not with blood, but with red paint. The prosecutor later admits having known that the stains were paint—a fact not only unrevealed to the jury and defense, but deliberately misrepresented in a manner that comes perilously close to subornation of perjury by the prosecutor (*Miller v. Pate*, 1967).

Item: Two men are arrested and convicted of armed robbery and first-degree murder, and are sentenced to life imprisonment without eligibility for parole. Sullivan admits his part in the crime, but claims that Reissfelder was not his partner. After spending 16 years in prison, never wavering in his protestation of innocence, Reissfelder is exonerated. Five policemen, an FBI agent, and a probation officer submit statements indicating that the authorities conducting the original investigation knew at the time of the trial and conviction that Reissfelder was not a party to the crime ("16 Years in Jail," 1983). The law is clear—the defense is entitled to have any evidence that might prove exculpatory—but in this case, again, prosecutors knew they had the wrong man and yet were intent on continuing the prosecution. Although the prosecutor's job is to seek justice, and not just convictions, in some cases winning the conviction clearly takes precedence.

A duplicate of the above case occurred in California, where two defendants were convicted of murdering a 65-year-old man. One confessed to the murder, but the other, Juan Venegas, spent 2-1/2 years in prison following conviction, protesting his innocence. When finally released and exonerated, he mounted a civil suit against the state and was awarded $1 million (an award that was later reduced substantially). Evidence at the civil trial showed that the police intimidated witnesses to perjure themselves and to orchestrate a frame-up of Venegas (Granelli, 1980; "Innocent Prisoner," 1980).

Plea Bargaining

Many innocent defendants are convicted after entering guilty pleas. For most people, these may be the most puzzling of all cases of convicted innocents (for guilty pleas must be counted as convictions). After all, why would a perfectly innocent person plead guilty? This is one of the least publicized dynamics of wrongful conviction. One of the reasons for the lack of publicity is that most—although not all—of these "bargains" result in immediate freedom, suspended sentences, or perhaps probation, and hence in these cases there is no continued aftermath, no investigation, no exoneration. The revocation of a guilty plea is legally permitted only under limited conditions; for example, when a judge refuses to abide by a bargain that has been made between the defendant, through counsel, and the prosecution. Ordinarily, a plea bargain closes the case.

There are ample reasons some innocent persons plead guilty. In a social psychological experiment utilizing role playing, Gregory, Mowen, and Linder (1978) found that innocent persons, playing the role of defendants, were more likely to accept plea bargains when they faced a number of charges or when the probable severity of punishment, as they perceived and feared it, was great. Such experiments are particularly relevant in an era when executions have been resumed in the United States and are frequent in certain states, such as Florida and Texas. When their lives are at stake, innocent persons who have been wrongly identified or who have been victims of perjury and forged documentation that their defense attorneys are unable to combat are greatly tempted to make deals. Even though they might be facing long prison terms, they live with the hope that eventually the truth will be discovered and they will be freed.

Such was the situation in Richmond, Virginia, when Harry Siegler, who maintained his innocence throughout his trial, sat and watched an alarmingly strong case being made against him. Siegler was charged with first-degree murder, and, as Virginia is among the states that have capital punishment laws that have been upheld as constitutional by the U.S. Supreme Court, he feared the jury would find him guilty and sentence him to death by electrocution. While awaiting the jury's verdict, the defendant, in desperation, changed his plea to guilty in a bargain that would result in a term of life imprisonment. A few minutes later, the jury came in with its verdict: not guilty. We cite this case not because we are certain of Siegler's innocence (we are not), but because it illustrates the potential importance of severe punishments, such as execution, in inducing defendants, some of whom may be innocent, to plead guilty (but see Bedau & Radelet, 1987, p. 63).

In cases involving less serious charges, a defendant who is unable to make bail and is offered, in exchange for a plea of guilty, immediate release with nothing more consequential than a minor criminal record (a typical scenario in communities where such records are not uncommon and not highly stigmatizing) cannot easily resist the lure of a guilty plea. Even if the defendant knows him- or herself to be guiltless, a finding of not guilty is not at all certain if a case goes to trial.

For those caught up in the criminal justice system, and whose incomes do not qualify them for assistance from public defenders or legal aid organizations, legal fees are extraordinarily high. If a person is charged with disorderly conduct, simple assault, or resisting arrest (the completely innocent, in their outrage, often do resist arrest), he or she may be most eager to have the episode over with, and to walk out of court with a guilty plea, rather than return for many more court appearances and pay additional funds to an attorney. Those who believe that, having established their innocence, they will be able to turn around and file civil suits for costs and compensation for pain and humiliation are, with few exceptions, indulging in pipe dreams.

A guilty plea is usually accompanied by a ritualistic colloquy between the judge and the accused, in which the judge may subtly compel the defendant to confess to his or her guilt. Insofar as there has been a bargain, the judge does not wish to clutter the record with the suspicion that an innocent person has been compelled to plead guilty. There is an interesting point of distinction that is often over-looked: A plea of not guilty is not considered a denial of guilt, but rather a prayer to the court that one be found not guilty, and an expression that one chooses to go to trial to emerge with such a finding; a plea of guilty, on the other hand, is almost always thought of as a confession of guilt. That it might be entered into for reasons other than a defendant's culpability is given scant attention.

Community Pressure for Conviction

In periods of high crime rates and great public outcry against criminals, and when group pressures are felt in the courtroom, conviction rates may be higher than at other times. Groups united by some common bond are, in fact, often referred to as pressure groups, and it is undeniable that efforts to influence what is happening in the world often extend to the courtroom. Groups that have sought to have such influence include ethnic and racial groups, women's groups, and homosexual and antihomosexual groups, as well as others. In the famous rape case in New Bedford, Massachusetts, in which both the victim and the defendants were of Portuguese descent, the Portuguese American community attempted to exert pressure before, during, and after the trial, while feminist groups and their allies were fighting with equal vigor on the other side. It is possible that the increase in the number of instances of false imprisonment in rape cases that have come to light since the early 1970s may be due in part to increased pressure to obtain convictions in rape cases; by contrast, the majority of rape charges in the earlier part of the century were almost invariably directed against blacks, and were a manifestation of racist community pressure.

When community and group pressure and prejudice against an accused individual are high, the situation is sometimes handled by a call for a change of venue. The court must allow a change of venue at defense request if mob violence threatens (*Blevins v. State*, 1963) or it if appears or proves to be impossible to select an impartial jury in the original venue (*People v. Harris*, 1981). The court must consider all relevant factors, including the scope and source of publicity, the nature and gravity of the offense, the size of the community and the defendant's status therein, the popularity and prominence of the victims, inconvenience to the prosecution and to the administration of justice if the venue is changed, and the likelihood of finding a substantially better or fairer jury panel elsewhere (*State v. Engel*, 1980). Even when changes of venue are granted, the results are not always trials that are free from pressures; witness the Scottsboro case, where the change of venue from Scottsboro to Decatur, another small, rural Alabama town with an equal amount of prejudice in the 1930s, proved fruitless in diminishing community pressure to convict the innocent.

Pressure from the public, sometimes intensified by news media coverage, can be an expression of democratic participation in the criminal justice process. It can sometimes make the system more responsive to the social needs, values, and feelings of large numbers of citizens. It can serve as a watchdog, lest corruption and malfeasance in the system go unnoticed or the rich and powerful who deserve some form of punishment remain unindicted. Such a spotlight on the courts may thus result in the prosecution of cases that warrant pursuit, but that might otherwise be dropped because of the standing and influence of accused perpetrators and their families, or in appropriate findings of not guilty. It is difficult to believe that Joanne Little or Angela Davis would have been found anything other than guilty had it not been for public pressure. When members of the Black Panthers and other militants were arrested, the president of Yale University startled the country by stating that he doubted if a black person could receive a fair trial in America, a statement that probably acted as a self-fulfilling prophecy. Likewise, absent national and even international pressure, how many arrests and successful prosecutions would have occurred in the case of the three civil rights workers who were murdered in Mississippi in 1964?

Public pressure, then, is a two-edged sword. In some cases it may force courts to deal more fairly with certain suspects than they otherwise might have, but it may also simply reflect the public's fears and desires for vengeance, feelings that are easily manipulated by demagogues who are ready and willing to oblige.

Inadequacy of Counsel

The right to counsel is now well established in the United States. Despite the Bill of Rights, which sets out this right quite clearly, it took several cases to establish it in some states; important in this regard are the cases of *Powell v. Alabama* (1932), *Gideon v. Wainwright* (1963), and *Argersinger v. Hamlin* (1972). In the conviction of the innocent, an important factor is not the right to counsel, but the counsel's adequacy. In fact, that was the issue in the case of Ozzie Powell, one of the Scottsboro boys, who was represented, in a half-hearted and blatantly incompetent manner, by counsel barely interested in Powell's case, much less his welfare. It was only because this was a capital case that the Supreme Court ruled that Powell had been deprived of due process of law, as guaranteed by the Fourteenth Amendment.

That some people are convicted because their lawyers have little experience, caseloads that are too large, and inadequate budgets to carry out excellent investigations is evident. Counsel for Bradley Cox (falsely convicted of rapes actually committed by Jon Simonis, "the ski mask rapist") worked hard, but he was a harried public defender who gave Cox permission to take a polygraph test without counsel present, who missed at least one major opportunity for a mistrial, and whose cross-examination of the detectives who had obtained the false confession was anything but hard-hitting.

Few cases are overturned on the basis of inadequacy or incompetence of counsel; exoneration seldom comes because of such an appeal being upheld, but because of other developments. The rationale that the original defense counsel, for whatever reasons, did not adequately represent the client's interests in the case makes the appeal difficult to win. Collegial relationships within the legal profession, though pitting lawyer against lawyer as adversaries, generally stop short of promoting the idea of attacking colleagues for mishandling cases, just as doctors are not eager to testify against other doctors, police against police, and so forth. Lawyers assigned anew, or on appeal, are not eager to pursue this line to gain reversals, preferring to characterize as "new" evidence anything that was previously overlooked.

Errors that defense attorneys may make include failing to make discovery motions and to pursue them vigorously; using poor judgment in deciding whether or not to put a defendant on the stand; allowing a defendant to take a polygraph test, especially in the absence of the defense counsel; and failing to challenge vigorously the contentions made by the prosecution in court (Finer, 1973).

Accusations Against the Innocent by the Guilty

Item: Nathaniel Carter is arrested for murder in the stabbing death of Clarice Herndon. Carter's chief accuser is his estranged wife, who testifies that she watched helplessly as Carter attacked her foster mother with a knife, inflicting 23 stab wounds. Carter is sentenced to a prison term of 25 years to life, his flawless record notwithstanding, on the basis of the accusation of one self-stated eyewitness weighted against his own denial and verifiable alibi. After he has served 2 years in prison, his ex-wife, under complete immunity, admits that she, in fact, was the one who killed her foster mother. The police explain that the cuts on Mrs. Carter's hands at the time of the crime led them to believe that she, too, had been attacked by her former husband. If she seemed to be the perfect witness, the police were far from perfect investigators ("How Errors Convicted," 1984).

In the two cases explored by Ludovic Kennedy in his books about miscarriages of justice in Great Britain, the killer was the chief witness against the innocent accused, and each case rested almost entirely on the actual murderer's perjured testimony. Such was true of Timothy Evans, whose hanging for the murders committed by his accuser, Christie, is described in *Ten Rillington Place* (Kennedy, 1961/1985b). In a case in which three men were convicted (one later to be freed because of the impregnability of his alibi) for the murder of a postmaster, the man who pointed the finger at the three innocent people was himself the murderer (he also collected a part of the reward for helping to solve the crime). When it became known that the convictions were based almost solely on the accusation of the actual murderer, one judge found this nearly impossible to believe, saying that to allow innocent people to go to prison for long terms because of what one has oneself committed is to be "wicked beyond belief" (a phrase used as the title of one of Kennedy's books). Such a statement from a judge who had been handling criminal cases for many years is, we believe, an indication of naïveté beyond belief.

There is yet another type of false accusation, in which the chief witness against the accused is not the one who committed the crime, but one who falsely claims victimization in a crime that never took place. An example is the accuser of Robert Daniels, who was a student who lived in a coed dormitory. While he was talking to a female student in the dorm hallway, a door to one of the rooms off the hall opened and the room's occupant asked Daniels and the woman to speak more quietly. The woman he was speaking to then invited Daniels into her room, where they continued their conversation and later went to bed together. A few hours afterward, Daniels got up and dressed, went to his own room for a little more sleep, then spent the day attending classes, as did the woman with whom he had passed a few hours the evening before. Her day was different from his in one respect, however: At the end of her school day, she went to the police and reported that she had been raped. That evening, Daniels was arrested. The alleged victim's word was the only evidence against Daniels's denial, but weighing against him was that he had a criminal past and the woman appeared to be the epitome of everything righteous and proper. Daniels was convicted and sent to prison. His innocence did not come to light until the complaining witness in his case was arrested for arson and claimed that she was committing such acts because of the trauma of the rape. A suspicious prosecutor delved deeper into the woman's life and found that she had a history of mental illness and was under a therapist's care. The therapist later admitted that he knew of the false charge of rape and of Daniels's imprisonment, but claimed that he could say nothing because of the confidentiality of the doctor-patient relationship.

Accusations regarding crimes that never occurred are not limited to rape, child molestation, and other sex cases. There have been several cases in which men have served prison terms for murders that never took place; the putative victims simply disappeared, knowing full well that particular individuals would spend many years in prison for their "murders." Some people have served long terms in prison for murder only to have their "victims" turn up eventually, alive and well.

Criminal Records

A major factor in the conviction of the innocent is that such defendants often have criminal records. In the case of Robert Daniels, his record probably swayed opinion against him, although it is still difficult to understand how a jury could have found the weight of the evidence so strongly against him that the jurors felt his guilt was established beyond a reasonable doubt. Daniels's case also raises other issues, such as whether the rules of confidentiality should extend to the toleration of so severe a social evil as sending an innocent person to prison—would the therapist have remained silent and allowed the defendant, whom he knew was not guilty, to be executed? If so, this would be ironic, in that physicians are precluded from directly assisting in the execution (even by lethal injection) of guilty offenders, yet a "therapist," claiming "ethical obligations," might remain silent while an innocent man is executed.

A criminal record places a person's picture in police files, where it might possibly be picked out by crime victims. A record also makes an individual more vulnerable to police interrogation and to making false confessions. An innocent defendant with a criminal record is less likely to take the stand to testify in his or her own behalf, because this opens up the possibility that the record will be brought out during cross-examination. If the innocent defendant does not take the stand, he or she is deprived of a witness who can deny the defendant's involvement in the crime. Further, no matter what judges may tell jurors to the contrary, most jurors take a defendant's failure to take the witness stand to be a sign of guilt. Finally, a criminal record makes a witness/defendant suspect once he or she is on the stand. Jurors not only tend to disbelieve a person with a record, they often feel that it is not crucial to determine such a person's guilt or innocence in a given case, because it is good to sweep the bad guys off the streets.

In our source documents, the question of previous criminal record was not mentioned in a sufficient number of cases for us to make a reliable computation, but from following newspaper stories of recent years and from reading books and trial transcripts that go into cases in detail, we know that many convicted innocents have had records that made them vulnerable, and that contributed, with other factors, to their becoming victims of the criminal justice system.

Race as a Factor

Many convicted innocents are white, some are even middle-class, but a disproportionate number are black or Hispanic. Some have been convicted of crimes by all-white, handpicked juries. In the case of George Whitmore, the first conviction of this innocent man was by an all-white jury, and it was only when a journalist heard a rumor, later confirmed in court, that racist language was used in the jury room that the conviction was thrown out. Aside from the prejudices of police, prosecutors, and jurors, being of a race different from that of witnesses may increase the possibility of misidentification.

A miscellany of other factors can work to create convicted innocents. Some are less prevalent and some less investigated than others. These include judicial errors, bias, and neglect of duty; unintentional and sometimes even intentional errors on the part of criminal investigators, medical examiners, and forensic science experts; incompetence of the accused to assist in his or her own defense; and, finally, simple coincidence. All of these factors and others duplicate and overlap one another and synergistically act together. It is a tribute to the criminal justice system if in fact convicted innocents constitute only one-half of 1% of the total number of people convicted each year. It is possible, however, through study, analysis, and proper social policy, to reduce this figure, and it is our contention, that in so doing the criminal justice system will be able to increase the percentage of the guilty who are convicted as well.

The manner in which numerous factors work simultaneously to keep innocent individuals behind bars is dramatically illustrated by an obscure case that surfaced on the front page of the *New York Times* on November 30, 1985. Willie Jones was a 33-year-old black man who had been in minor trouble for lawbreaking in the past, when he was arrested for opening the gate to a New York subway station and attempting to get a ride without paying the fare. Hardly a serious charge, and one might expect that a criminal justice system that had been extraordinarily lenient, almost apologetic, to a white-collar commuter from Connecticut who had been using his Connecticut highway tokens to cheat the New York subways might show a little compassion. But Willie Jones, remanded to jail and referred to legal aid (New York's equivalent of the public defender) for counsel, was confronted with a "rap sheet" that showed a long list of serious crimes, including the revelation that he was now wanted for jumping $3,500 bail.

Over and over, Jones complained to the people at legal aid that the rap sheet was not his, although it bore his name and a physical description not terribly unlike his own. There was no picture and there were no fingerprints, and no one took the trouble to try to obtain these, because everyone knew that the defendant was lying. A plea bargain was arranged between legal aid and the prosecution, but, to the consternation of his attorneys, the accused turned it down, saying that he would not plead guilty to a crime he had not committed. For 3 months, Jones languished in a local jail, until finally the day of his trial arrived. When he came to court, he was greeted by a happy and smiling legal aid counsel who told him that it was all a mistake—he was not the Willie Jones the police (and his own attorneys) had thought he was.

Why did this case take on the form that it did? First, although the charge on which Jones was picked up was very minor, even trivial, the fact was that he was not a model citizen, and although the record the authorities confronted him with was not his own, he did have a previous arrest record. In addition, he was black, and prejudice came into play. There was an assumption that this lower-class black man was making up absurd stories to protest his innocence, when everyone knew he was guilty. Third, he had inadequate counsel, people overburdened with caseloads, anxious to make as many deals as possible in order to get on to their next cases. They had neither the facilities nor the motivation to investigate, demand fingerprints, and look into such a simple matter as the possible difference in social security numbers between two men having the name of Willie Jones. Fourth, he was a victim of plea-bargaining pressure—cop a plea and get the thing over with; move the case through the system; push the widget along the conveyor belt. Fifth, he was a victim of sloppy work, although not malicious, in the police and prosecutorial stages. And sixth, coincidence in part led to Jones's predicament—coincidence plays a part in many cases.

Only one thing separates Willie Jones from the other individuals we discuss. He was never convicted. In his case, the error was discovered before the trial. He was "only" jailed, that's all. A happy ending? Anyone who thinks so has never spent any time in a cramped jail cell with a randomly assigned roommate.

Notes

[1] The term *index crimes* refers to eight serious crimes that are used as an index of criminality in the United States. Not all serious crimes are considered index crimes, because they are not considered to be reliably reported and are not seen as useful in constructing such an index. The index crimes are as follows: murder and nonnegligent manslaughter, forcible rape, aggravated assault, robbery, burglary, larceny-theft, motor vehicle theft, and arson.

Cases

Argersinger v. Hamlin, 407 U.S. 25 (1972).
Blevins v. State, 108 Ga. App. 738, 134 S.E.2d (1963)
Gideon v. Wainwright, 372 U.S. 335 (1963)
Gilbert v. California, 388 U.S. 263 (1967).
Jackson v. Fogg, 589 F.2d 108 (2d Cir. 1978).
Mapp v. Ohio, 367 U.S. 643 (1961).
Miller v. Pate, 386 U.S. 1 (1967).
Miranda v. Arizona, 384 U.S. 436 (1966).
People v. Harris, 28 Cal. 3d 935, 623 P.2d 240 (1981).
Powell v. Alabama, 287 U.S. 45 (1932).
State v. Engel, 289 N.W.2d 204 (N.D. 1980).
Stovall v. Denno, 388 U.S. 293 (1967).
United States v. Wade, 388 U.S. 218 (1967).

References

Bedau, H. A., and Radelet, M. L. 1987. Miscarriages of justice in potentially capital cases. *Stanford Law Review, 40*, 21–179.

Borchard, E. M. 1932. *Convicting the innocent: Sixty-five actual errors of criminal justice.* Garden City, NY: Doubleday.

Brandon, R., and Davies, C. 1973. *Wrongful imprisonment: Mistaken convictions and their consequences.* London: Allen & Unwin.

Court stand-in is convicted of crime he didn't commit. 1980, July 17. *Atlanta Constitution,* p. 12A.

Finer, J. J. 1973. Ineffective assistance of counsel. *Cornell Law Review, 58,* 1077–120.

Freed Jackson's advice for wrongfully accused is to get venue change. 1982, September 25. *Columbus Citizen-Journal.*

Granelli, J. S. 1980, December 15. Trials—and errors. *National Law Journal,* p. 1.

Gregory, W. L., Mowen, J. C., and Linder, D. E. 1978. Social psychology and plea bargaining: Applications, methodology and theory. *Journal of Personality and Social Psychology, 36,* 1521–1530.

How errors convicted the wrong man. 1984, March 15. *New York Times,* p. B1.

Huff, C. R., Rattner, A., and Sagarin, E. 1986. Guilty until proved innocent: Wrongful conviction and public policy. *Crime & Delinquency, 32,* 518-544.

Innocent prisoner gets $1 million. 1980, September 4. *San Francisco Chronicle,* p. 38.

Kalven, H., and Zeisel, H. 1966. *The American jury.* Boston, Little, Brown.

Kennedy, L. 1985b. *Ten Rillington Place.* New York: Avon. (Original work published 1961).

Matzner, D., and English, M. 1973. *Victims of justice.* New York: Atheneum.

Monday finally comes for weekend killer. 1982, August 15. *Houston Chronicle,* p. 1.

Ohio doctor accused of 36 rapes: Man jailed for two of them is freed. 1982, September 24. *New York Times.*

Radelet, M. L., and Bedau, H. G. 1992. *In spite of innocence: Erroneous convictions in capital cases.* Boston: Northeastern University Press.

16 years in jail, case dismissed. 1983, August 31. *Atlanta Constitution,* p. 1A.

U.S. Department of Justice, Bureau of Justice Statistics. 1995. *Sourcebook of criminal justice statistics, 1994.* Washington, DC: Government Printing Office.

When nightmare of false arrest comes true. 1984, December 17. *U.S. News & World Report,* 45–47.

Section IV

Change without Progress
Corrections

Corrections is in need of reforms which are unlikely to occur. Many of the problems facing corrections can be attributed to philosophical and operational conflicts. There is a lack of consensus regarding the purpose of punishment. On the one hand we inflict punishment as a revenge for the wrongs suffered by victims. On the other hand we hope that our intervention will prevent criminal behavior from occurring in the future. Millions of dollars are spent each year in a large variety of rehabilitation and treatment programs. Many of these programs have proven to be of questionable value, and some are not appreciated by the participating offenders.

Because there is little agreement regarding the purpose of corrections, there is much debate in the legislative process as part of an effort to make certain that one or another perspective dominates. As a result, approaches to corrections often move like a pendulum from one extreme to another. Many aspects of corrections are seen as confused and purposeless.

Public attitudes toward corrections are also inconsistent. Many Americans believe that persons convicted of crimes should spend longer periods of time incarcerated in prison—though politicians are under considerable pressure to not increase funding for prisons to keep pace with the desired increases in prison populations. At the same time, the public is also likely to believe that prisons do not rehabilitate and that some offenders are more dangerous *after* incarceration in one of our overpopulated violent prisons. We want to continue relying on the kinds of punishment mechanisms used in the past even though we readily acknowledge they have not worked.

While there are a number of topics and issues in the field of corrections, this section focuses on boot camps, incarceration, inmate subcultures, and using the death penalty. Incarceration in a maximum security prison can be a terribly degrading experience. Overpopulated and understaffed, a number of prisons have become unmanageable as inmate gangs control major aspects of institutional life. Narcotics traffic flourishes in many prisons, and homosexual rape is a common occurrence as the weak succumb to the strong in this human jungle. While prison riots have called public attention to the degrading and dehumanizing experience of incarceration, there is an abundance of public apathy and hostility that overwhelms any short-term concern.

In "A Critical Look at the Idea of Boot Camp as Correctional Reform," Merry Morash and Lila Rucker examine a trend toward institutions modeled after harsh and degrading military boot camps of the past. Ironically, this strategy was tried in the past with little luck, and the military itself is moving away from this model because it too often does more harm than good. It is also noted that such approaches glorify and officially sanction machismo and a reliance on brute force, which often is what led to the incarceration in the first place.

In "Changes in Prison Culture," Geoffrey Hunt and his associates discuss changes in prison life which have occurred in recent years. These changes included a substantial influx of young violent offenders who were not familiar with existing prison routines and had little respect for them. Ironically, this disruption in prison culture was made worse by the efforts of prison officials to contain the influence of gangs in prison. Where gangs were contained, these youthful violent offenders moved into the vacuum in power. Complicating matters is the growing problem of prison crowding and the increasing link between gang activity on the street and gang activity in prison. As a result of these changes in prison culture, even long-time inmates had difficulty knowing how to deal with the new informal rules of prison life.

Lawmakers responded to the public's demand for greater use of imprisonment and longer sentences for those sent to prison with an unparalleled increase in prison construction. Expenditures for building and maintaining prisons have grown dramatically, often cutting into state budgets for such things as education. In "Fear, Politics, and the Prison-Industrial Complex," Steven Donziger argues that the crime problem has been greatly exaggerated and distorted. Some of this comes from politicians who can make substantial political capital by arguing for more prisons. Other pressures come from the many interest groups who stand to gain by expanded prison capacity. Given the amounts of money involved, the stakes are high. In contrast, there is little incentive to promote reducing the rate of imprisonment or the rate of new prison construction. Donziger makes a convincing case that prisons are part of an industry that can be very lucrative for private businesses. Unfortunately, the gains to private industry are an economic loss to taxpayers who must finance the drain on state and federal budgets brought about by this industry.

Finally, while much has been written about the moral and practical issues surrounding the death penalty, surprisingly little work has focused on the execution process. Robert Johnson's "This Man Has Expired" presents a stark firsthand account of how a modern death team operates and the process by which the offender is psychologically "dead" well before the execution.

14

A Critical Look at the Idea
of Boot Camp as a
Correctional Reform

Merry Morash
Lila Rucker

Introduction
The Boot Camp Idea

In several states, correctional boot camps have been used as an alternative to prison in order to deal with the problem of prison overcrowding and public demands for severe treatment (Parent, 1988). Correctional boot camps are styled after the military model for basic training, and, similar to basic training, the participants are primarily

From *Crime and Delinquency*, Vol. 36, No. 2 (April 1990), pp. 204–22. Copyright © 1990 by Sage Publications, Inc.

young males. However, the "recruits" are offenders, though usually nonviolent and first-time ones (Parent, 1988). Boot camps vary in their purpose, but even when they are instituted primarily to reduce overcrowding, the implicit assumption is that their programs are of equal or greater deterrent or rehabilitative value than a longer prison sentence.

By the end of 1988, boot camps were operating in one county (Orleans Parish, Louisiana) and in eight states (Georgia, Oklahoma, Mississippi, Louisiana, South Carolina, New York, Florida, and Michigan), they were planned in three states (North Carolina, Kansas, and New Hampshire), and they were being considered in at least nine other states (Parent, 1988). The model was also being considered for a large number of youthful Detroit offenders. And in the summer of 1989, the boot camp model was put forth by the House Crime Subcommittee chairman as a potential national strategy for treating drug abusers (Gannett News Service, 1989).

The National Institute of Justice is supporting evaluations of correctional boot camp programs, and other evaluations without federal support are also underway. Such formal evaluations will no doubt provide invaluable evidence of the effect of the programs on participants and, in some cases, on the correctional system (e.g., the resulting diversion of offenders from more restrictive environments). The purpose of this article is to provide another type of assessment, specifically, a critical analysis of the history and assumptions underlying the use of a military model in a correctional setting.

The popular image of military boot camp stresses strict and even cruel discipline, hard work, and authoritarian decision making and control by a drill sergeant. It should be noted that this image does not necessarily conform to either current practices in the U.S. military or to all adaptations of boot camp in correctional settings. However, in a survey of existing correctional boot camp programs, Parent (1988) found commonality in the use of strict discipline, physical training, drill and ceremony, military bearing and courtesy, physical labor, and summary punishment for minor misconduct. Some programs have combined selected elements of the military boot camp model with more traditional forms of rehabilitation. In Oklahoma, for example, the paramilitary structure, including the use of regimentation, has been only one aspect of an otherwise "helping, supportive environment" that is considered by the administration to be a prerequisite if "change is to last or have any carry over" (Kaiser, 1988). In Michigan, the major emphasis has been on developing the "work ethic" by utilizing various motivational tactics (e.g., chants), strong discipline, and rehabilitation (Hengish, 1988). All participants work from 8:00 AM to 3:30 PM daily; evenings involve educational and therapeutic programs.

When more traditional methods of rehabilitation are included, a consideration of the boot camp idea is more complex, requiring an analysis of both the costs and benefits of mixing the imagery or the reality of a boot camp approach with other measures.

Regardless of the actual degree to which a militaristic, basic training model has been emphasized, the press has taken this emphasis as primary and usually has portrayed it in a positive light. Numerous stories have been printed under titles such as "Boot Camp—In Prison: An Experiment Worth Watching" (Raspberry, 1987, p. H21), "New York Tests a Boot Camp for Inmates" (Martin, 1988), "'Squeeze You Like a Grape': In Georgia, A Prison Boot Camp Sets Kids Straight" (*Life*, 1988), and "Some Young US Offenders Go To 'Boot Camp'—Others Are Put in Adult Jails" (Sitomer, 1987, p. 1). The text similarly has reflected a positive evaluation of the approach. For example, Raspberry (1987) wrote of the Louisiana boot camp that "[t]he idea [is] to turn a score of lawbreakers into disciplined, authority-respecting men." He quoted the warden: "[W]e're giving an inmate a chance to get out of prison in 90 days instead of seven years. But you're making him work for it. . . . We keep them busy from the time they wake up until they fall asleep with chores that include such sillinesses as cleaning latrines with a toothbrush." The warden concluded that the approach "teaches them self-discipline and self-control, something many of these men have never had" (Raspberry, 1987). Similarly, Martin (1988, p. 15) wrote about the New York program:

> Days are 16 hours long, and two-mile runs and calisthenics on cold asphalt are daily staples. Work is chopping down trees or worse. The discipline recalls Parris Island. . . . those who err may be given what is genteelly termed 'a learning experience,' something like carrying large logs around with them everywhere they go or, perhaps, wearing baby bottles around their necks.

Life's (1988, p. 82) coverage of the Georgia program included the following statement by one of the sergeants: "[Here] being scared is the point. You have to hit a mule between the eyes with a two-by-four to get his attention . . . and that's exactly what we're doing with this Program."

The journalistic accounts of boot camps in corrections have celebrated a popular image of a relatively dehumanizing experience that is marked by hard, often meaningless, physical labor. The inmate has been portrayed as deficient, requiring something akin to being beaten over the head in order to become "a man."

The imagery of the people that we send to boot camp as deserving of dehumanizing treatment is in itself troubling, but even more so in light of the fact that the inmates are disproportionately minorities and underclass members. The boot camp idea also raises the disturbing question: Why would a method that has been developed to prepare people to go into war, and as a tool to manage legal violence, be considered as having such potential in deterring or rehabilitating offenders? Wamsley (1972, p. 401) concluded from a review of officers' manuals and prior research that military basic training is designed to promote fundamental values of military subculture, including

> (1) acceptance of all-pervasive hierarchy and deference patterns; (2) extreme emphasis on dress, bearing, and grooming; (3) specialized vocabulary; (4) emphasis on honor, integrity, and professional responsibility; (5) emphasis on brotherhood; (6) fighter spirit marked by aggressive enthusiasm; and (7) special reverence for history and traditions.

In another summary of the values stressed in military basic training, Merryfinch (1981, p. 9) identified "a commitment to organized violence as the most effective way to resolve conflicts, a glorification of 'hard' emotions (aggression, hatred, brutality) and a strict channeling of 'soft' emotions (compassion, love, suffering). . . ." Clearly, many of the objectives of military basic training are not shared by the policymakers who promote correctional boot camps. What is even more striking is that none of them make sense as a means to promote either rehabilitation or deterrence, and the emphasis on unquestioned obedience to authority and aggression is inconsistent with prosocial behavior.

What Has Been Tried and What Works in Corrections?

The correctional boot camp model has been touted as a new idea. However, militarism, the use of hard labor, and efforts to frighten offenders—most recently surfacing in the "Scared Straight" programs—have a long history in prison settings. We will focus first on militarism. In 1821, John Cray, the deputy keeper of the newly constructed Auburn Prison, moved away from the use of solitary confinement when suicides and mental breakdowns increased. As an alternative, he instituted a military regime to maintain order in overcrowded prisons (McKelvey, 1977, p. 14). The regime, which was based in part on his experiences as a Canadian army officer, required downcast eyes, lockstep marching, no talking or other communication among prisoners, and constant activity under close supervision

(McKelvey, 1977). The issue for Cray and his contemporaries was the prevention of crime "through fear of punishment; the reformation of offenders being of minor consideration" (Lewis, 1983, p. 26).

Neither Cray's attempts nor those of his Pennsylvania cohorts, however, achieved either deterrence or reform (Cole, 1986, p. 497). During the Progressive Era, there was a shift away from the sole emphasis on punishment. At Elmira Reformatory, Zebulon Brockway added a new twist to Cray's militaristic regulations, certain of which (lockstep marching and rules of silence) had fallen into disrepute because they were now seen as debasing, humiliating, and destructive of initiative (Cole, 1986, p. 497). By 1896, the industrial reformatory at Elmira had ". . . well coordinated discipline which centered around the grading and marking system, an honest application of the indeterminate sentence, trade and academic schools, military organization and calisthenic exercises" (McKelvey, 1977, p. 137). Similar to many of the contemporary boot camps, at Elmira the philosophy was to combine both rehabilitation approaches and work with military discipline and physical activity to, among other things, improve self-esteem. However, the legacy of Brockway's Elmira Reformatory was not a move toward rehabilitation (Johnson, 1987, p. 41). Instead, the militaristic atmosphere set the stage for abusive punishment, and the contradiction between military discipline and rehabilitation was apparent (Pisciotta, 1983, pp. 620–21).

Some might counter the argument that the militaristic approach opens the door for abusive punishment by pointing out that in contemporary correctional settings, physical punishment and harm are eliminated. However, as Johnson (1987, p. 48; see also Christie, 1981) noted, nonphysical abuse can be viewed as a "civilized" substitute. Also, in some cases physical abuse is a matter of definition, as is seen in the accounts of dropouts from one contemporary boot camp. They reported being treated like "scum," working 18–hour days, being refused permission to use the bathroom, being provoked to aggression by drill instructors, being forced to push a bar of soap along the floor with their noses, and being forced to participate in an exercise called "air raids" in which trainees run and dive face down, landing on their chests with arms stretched out to their sides (Bellew, 1988, p. 10). At least in some settings, the military model has provided a legitimization of severe punishment. It has opened the door for psychological and even physical abuse that would be rejected as cruel and unusual punishment in other correctional settings.

Turning now to work in correctional settings, its persistent use has been supported by its congruence with alternative objectives, including punishment, incapacitation, rehabilitation, and control inside the institution (Lejins, 1970, pp. 309–10). However, the form of work at a particular time has not been influenced just by ideals and objectives, but by basic economic forces (Rusche and Kirchheimer, 1939). For example, in order to protect private enterprise, the tread-mill was used to occupy offenders following prohibitions against the use of prison labor (Morse, 1973, p. 33; see also Morash and Anderson, 1978). Also, in the nineteenth century, a major purpose of imprisonment was to teach the regular work habits demanded by employers (Rusche and Kirchheimer, 1939; Melossi and Pavarini, 1981). In contemporary discussions of correctional boot camp pro-grams, work has been justified as both punitive and rehabilitative, as both exemplifying the harsh result of breaking the law and teaching the "work ethic." However, the economic constraints imposed by lim-ited budgeting for rehabilitation efforts and the shrinking number of jobs for unskilled workers have shaped the form of work. Thus, hard physical labor, which has no transfer to the contemporary job market, has been the choice in correctional boot camps.

Further criticism of the form of work used in the boot camp set-tings rests on empirical research. The literature on work programs in general has not supported the conclusion that they produce a decrease in recidivism (Taggart, 1972; Fogel, 1975, pp. 114–16; Lipton, Mar-tinson, and Wilks, 1975). Especially pertinent to the present analysis, in a recent article Maguire, Flanagan, and Thornberry (1988) showed that labor in a correctional institution was unrelated to recidivism after prisoner differences were taken into account. The exception was work programs that actually provided employment (e.g., Jeffrey and Woolpert, 1974; Rudolf and Esselstyn, 1973). Based on an extensive review of the literature, Gendreau and Ross (1987, p. 380; see also Walter and Mills, 1980) further specified the characteristics of correc-tional work programs that were related to lower recidivism: "Work programs must enhance practical skills, develop interpersonal skills, minimize prisonization, and ensure that work is not punishment alone." Clearly, the evaluation literature contradicts the idea that hard, often meaningless, labor in the boot camp setting has some pos-itive effect.

Moreover, although negative attitudes and lack of the work ethic might be one influence on the choice of economic crime instead of a job, structural arguments have provided alternative explanations. For example, Wilson (1987) documented that low-skilled minorities have been hardest hit by deindustrialization of the national labor force and changes in the geographic location of industries. The labor surplus in low-technology fields, and the strength of general social and psycho-logical factors thought to cause criminal behavior, have been found to counteract most offender work programs (Maguire et al., 1988, p. 16). In a supporting ethnography, Sullivan (1983) showed that the slightly greater availability of jobs in white, working-class neighborhoods explained residents' lesser criminality; in black, lower class neighborhoods where there were no work opportunities, males in their late teens used robbery as a regular source of income. Altering men's attitudes toward work does nothing to combat these structural deficiencies.

The "Scared Straight" programs, a contemporary version of correctional efforts intended to deter offenders through fright, also are not supported by empirical research. In a San Quentin program of this type, older adolescent participants were arrested less often but for more serious crimes than a comparison group (Lewis, 1983). An evaluation of a similar New Jersey program showed that participants were more seriously delinquent than a control group (Finckenauer, 1982). On the surface, an evaluation of a "tough" detention regime in British detention centers suggests that though there were no increases in recidivism, there also were no decreases (Thornton et al., 1984). However, although the British detention center programs incorporated such "military" approaches as strict discipline, drill, and parades, a primary focus was on staff being personally helpful to the youth. Also, humiliating and punitive staff reactions were prohibited by general guidelines. Thus, the British detention center model departed markedly from many of the U.S. models. In general, then, the program elements of militarism, hard labor, and fear engendered by severe conditions do not hold much promise, and they appear to set the stage for abuse of authority.

Military Boot Camps

The idea of boot camp as applied in correctional settings is often a simplification and exaggeration of an outdated system of military training that has been examined and rejected as unsatisfactory by many experts and scholars and by the military establishment itself. The difficulties that the military has discovered with the traditional boot camp model, and the resulting implications for reforms, could be instructive to people in search of positive correctional measures.

A number of difficulties with what will be referred to as the "traditional" military boot camp approach that is now mimicked in correctional settings were uncovered by a task force appointed in the 1970s (Raupp, 1978; Faris, 1975). The first difficulty with the traditional boot camp approach involved inconsistent philosophies, policies, and procedures. Ten years after the task force report was published, a follow-up study provided further insight into the problem of inconsistency and the related patterns of unreasonable leadership and contrived stressful situations. The study documented the "severe effects" of lack of predictability in such areas as standards for cleanliness and how cadence was called (Marlowe et al., 1988, p. 10). According to the study, "predictability and reasonableness contribute to trainee self-esteem, sense of being valued by the unit and commitment to the organization." Further, "when authority is arbitrarily imposed, or when leaders lead strictly by virtue of their power or authority, the result is often anger and disrespect" (Marlowe et al., 1988, pp. 11–12). Also, "dysfunctional stress [which results when work is irrelevant or contrived], heightens tensions, shortens tempers, and increases the probability of abuse while generally degrading the effectiveness of training" (Raupp, 1978, p. 99). By contrast, "functional" stress is legitimate and work-related, resulting from such instances as "the mental and physical stress of a tactical road march (Raupp, 1978, p. 98)."

The second difficulty that the task force identified with traditional boot camp training was a widespread "we-versus-they" attitude and the related view that trainees were deserving of degrading treatment (Raupp, 1978, p. 9). The we-versus-they attitude was manifested by different behavioral and/or dress standards for trainees and for other personnel. Specifically, trainees were given "skin-head" haircuts and were prohibited from swearing and shouting, and physical training was used as punishment.

Aside from the investigative reports sponsored by the military, empirical studies of the effects of military boot camps, the effects of physical training (which is a major component of many correctional boot camp programs), and learning in general have provided relevant findings. Empirical evidence regarding the psychological impact of traditional military basic training on young recruits between the ages of 18 and 22 has demonstrated that "there was no increase in scores on ego-strength, or any other evidence of beneficial psychological effects accruing from basic training" (Ekman, Friesen, and Lutzker, 1962, p. 103). Administration of the MMPI to recruits revealed that "the change in the shape of the [MMPI] profiles suggests that aggressive, impulsive, and energetic features became slightly more prominent" (Ekman et al., 1962, p. 103). The authors concluded that the changes on the subscales imply that

> more callous attitudes, a tendency to ignore the needs of others, and feelings of self-importance increase slightly during basic training. The recruits appear less prone to examine their own responsibility for conflicts, and more ready to react aggressively. (Ekman et al., 1962, p. 104)

The importance of this finding is heightened by the conclusion of Gendreau, Grant, and Leipciger (1979, p. 71) that components of self-esteem that were good predictors of recidivism include the very same characteristics, namely, "self-centered, exploitive of others, easily led, and anxious to please." Sonkin and Walker (1985; see also Walker, 1983; Eisenberg and Micklow, 1979) also speculated that basic training in the military can result in the transfer of violent solutions to family settings. Eisenberg and Micklow (1979, p. 50) therefore proposed that military basic training be modified to include classes on "communication skills, stress reduction, and anger management." Although correctional boot camps do not provide training in the use of weapons or physical assault, they promote an aggressive model of leadership and a conflict-dominated style of interaction that could exacerbate tendencies toward aggression.

In another empirical study of military basic training, Wamsley (1972) contrasted the effects of Air Force Aviation Cadet Pre-Flight Training School with Air Force Officer's Training School. The Cadet School employed harsh techniques—including such activities as head shaving, marching miles in stiff shoes, and impromptu exercises as physical punishment—to inculcate basic values and eliminate the "unfit." After one week, 33% of recruits left. Wamsley (1972, p. 401) wrote that "Those with low capacities for anxiety, insufficient self-esteem to withstand and discredit abuse, inability to control or suppress anger, or those with latent neuroses or psychoses literally 'cracked' under the stress, and attempted suicides and psychiatric referrals were not uncommon." The purpose of constant exhortations to "get eager, mister" or "get proud, Raunch" was to promote an aggressive fighter spirit, and the "common misery and despair created a bond" among the trainees.

Increased aggression and a bond among inmates are not desired outcomes of correctional boot camps, so again the efficacy of using the military boot camp model is in question. Moreover, it is unlikely that the offenders in correctional boot camps are more mentally healthy than Air Force recruits. What is the effect of using such techniques when there is no escape valve through dropping out of the program? And, if only the best-adjusted stay, what is accomplished by the program? The contrast of the Cadet School with the Officer's Training School, which did not use humiliation and severe physical conditions and punishment, provides convincing evidence of the ineffectiveness of such an approach to training people. Wamsley (1972, p. 418) concluded that there was a "lack of a clear utility for Pre-Flight's intense socialization" and that the "socialization process was brutally expensive in human terms and produced exaggerated forms of behavior which were not clearly related to effective task accomplishments."

Additional research has shown that positive improvements in self-esteem result from physical training primarily when the environment is supportive. For example, Hilyer and Mitchell (1979, p. 430) demonstrated that college students with low self-concepts who received physical fitness training in a helpful, facilitative, supportive environment demonstrated an increase in self-concept scores. The improvement was two and one-half times as great as that of low-concept peers who received physical fitness training and no support.

Also contradicting the negatively oriented training strategy that is characteristic of the old-style military boot camp model, virtually no empirically supported criminological theories have suggested that aggressive and unpredictable reactions by authority figures encourage prosocial behavior. The opposite has been promulgated by most learning theorists. For instance, Satir (1973, p. 13) concluded that learning happens only when a person feels valued and is valued, when he or she feels like a connected part of the human race (see also Rogers, 1975, p. 6). Feelings of self-worth can only flourish in an atmosphere in which individual differences are appreciated and mistakes are tolerated; communication is direct, clear, specific, and honest; rules are flexible, human, appropriate, and subject to change; and links to society are open (Satir, 1972, p. 4–6). Finally, there has been considerable theory and research showing that antisocial behavior is increased when authority figures provide aggressive models for behavior (e.g., Bandura, 1973, pp. 252–53). Research in the sociology of sport has provided further evidence that physical training under the direction of an authoritarian trainer increases aggression (Coakley, 1986).

There is no systematic evidence of the degree to which the problems in traditional-style military boot camps are manifested in correctional settings, but there is evidence that they do occur. The introductory descriptions of the correctional boot camp model clearly reveal a tendency for some of the "drill sergeants" to use negative leadership. Telephone interviews with representatives of nine correctional boot camps show a tendency to focus on "tearing down the individuals and then building them back up." Reflective of this philosophy are negative strategies alluded to earlier, such as the utilization of debasing "welcoming speeches," the "chair position," and "learning experiences" that require men to wear baby bottles around their necks or to carry tree limbs with them all day.

Correctional boot camps also provide settings conducive to high levels of unpredictability and contrived stress. In one program (Bellew, 1988, p. 5), dropouts, current trainees, and parolees who had completed the program all reported that "differences between DI [drill instructor] styles made it tough to avoid trouble. Trainees' beds may be made to satisfy DI 'A,' but at shift change, if DI 'B' doesn't approve of that particular style, trainees are punished." As further illustration, another inmate reported that on the first day of participation in the boot camp, he was told that he had quit and could not participate. When the inmate sat down for the rest of the day, he was reportedly "kicked out for sitting down," and his having left the program was listed as voluntary. The inmate reported that he had tried to participate but that the drill instructor kept telling him that he had quit. The interviewer reported that at the time of the interview, the offender was "still confused as to what actually had happened that day" (Bellew, 1988, p. 10).

It is true that, as proponents of correctional boot camps claim, many military recruits feel that their survival of basic training is evidence of maturity and a major achievement in their lives (Gottlieb, 1980, pp. 166–67). However, the sense of achievement is linked to the notion that the experience is the first step in preparing them for the unique role of a soldier. Moreover, military boot camp is intended as just a prelude to acquaint the recruits with their new environment, in which they will take more control of their lives (Rabinowitz, 1982, p. 1084). It is not obvious that the boot camp experience alone, including elements of capricious and dehumanizing treatment, would be seen in such a positive light by inmate participants.

Clearly, the view that boot camp is just the first step in a socialization process has not been carried over into the correctional setting. While nearly all programs reported either regular or intensive probation or parole periods following release (Parent, 1988), none of the postrelease programs have had the capability to provide the continuous and multifaceted support network inherent in being a member of the military "family" or process. Postrelease programs are not designed to provide either the tightly knit structure or the guaranteed work that characterize military life.

It could be argued that the purpose of correctional boot camp is not to bind soldiers to their leaders or to develop group solidarity. Thus, the failure of the outmoded military boot camp model to achieve these results may not be a serious concern. Even if we accept this argument, the research on military basic training raises serious questions about the potential for undesirable outcomes, including increased aggression.

Stereotypes of Masculinity and Correctional Measures

The very idea of using physically and verbally aggressive tactics in an effort to "train" people to act in a prosocial manner is fraught with contradiction. The idea rests on the assumption that forceful control is to be valued. The other unstated assumption is that alternative methods for promoting prosocial behavior, such as the development of empathy or a stake in conformity (e.g., through employment), are not equally valued. Feminist theorists (Eichler, 1980; Bernard, 1975) have noted the societywide valuation of the stereotypically masculine characteristics of forcefulness and aggression and the related devaluation of the stereotypically feminine characteristics of empathy and cooperative group behavior. Heidensohn (1987, p. 25) specifically wrote that programs like boot camp have been "designed to reinforce conventional male behaviour" and that they range from "quasi-militaristic short, sharp shocks to adventure training."

There is little doubt that the military is a male-dominated institution (*Defense*, 1987) and that there is a military ideology that rejects both women and stereotypically female characteristics (Yuval-Davis, 1985; Yudkin, 1982; Larwood, Glasser, and McDonald, 1980; Stiehm, 1981, p. 57, 1989, p. 226; Enloe, 1983). As Enloe (1983, p. 7; see also Ruddick, 1983; O'Brien, 1979) wrote, there is a common assumption that "the military . . . is a *male* preserve, run by men and for men according to masculine ideas and relying solely on *man* power." In some military settings, terms such as "little girl," "woman," and "wife" have been routinely used to negatively label a trainee who is viewed as having failed in some way (Eisenhart, 1975; Stiehm, 1982, p. 371). Traditional marching chants have included degrading comments about women, and sexist terms for women and their body parts have been common in military settings (Ruddick, 1983, p. 231). Stiehm (1981, p. 257) concluded from her research that even after the mandated inclusion of women in the U.S. Military Academy, considerable derogatory name calling and ridicule of women were common. The implication is that to fail is to be female, or, conversely, to succeed is to be aggressive, dominant, and therefore unquestionably "male."

One might argue that name calling is not used in correctional settings. Given the military background of many correctional staff involved in the reforms and the popular image of boot camp experiences, the degree to which such an antiwoman attitude exists is an important empirical question. Aside from overt rejection of women and femaleness, the boot camp model, with its emphasis on unquestioned authority and aggressive interactions and its deemphasis on group cooperation and empathy, promotes a limited image of the "true man."

It is not surprising that few have questioned the distorted image of masculinity embodied in the idea of boot camp, for this imagery is implicit in the assumptions of many criminological theories (Naffine, 1987), and it is shared by many offenders. Focusing on criminologists, Naffine (1987) showed how several major theories have presented male offenders' aggression and assertiveness in a positive light while they have devalued characteristics associated with women. To be more specific, major theories have accepted the stereotypical characteristics of men as normal and have presented women as dependent, noncompetitive, and passive. Naffine's (1987, p. 126) analysis revealed the "curious result of extolling the virtues of the male, as a good criminal, and treating conforming women as if they were the socially deviant group." This result has been echoed in the use of a military model that similarly extols the virtues that are often associated with both masculinity and aggression in our society.

Writing about images of masculinity among economically marginalized men, who are overrepresented in the offender population, Messerschmidt (1986, p. 59) built on the notion that in our society "both masculinity and power are linked with aggression/violence while femininity and powerlessness are linked with nonviolence" (also see Schwendinger and Schwendinger, 1985, p. 161). He went on to note that as a result of the unavailability of jobs that are not degrading, powerless men seek out alternative avenues through which to exercise their masculinity. Other supports of criminality include an orientation toward "exploitative individualism," as opposed to any caring ties to group members, and male bonding, which is the ritual rejection of "weakness" associated with femininity. This rejection is demonstrated through activities like gang fights. Again, there is a parallel with the stereotype of masculinity embodied in the boot camp model. Specifically, Eisenhart (1975) has described military training's emphasis on self-sufficiency and the avoidance of attachment to others.

The irony in emphasizing an aggressive model of masculinity in a correctional setting is that these very characteristics may explain criminality. Theorists working in the area of crime causation have focused on both the identification with male stereotypical traits and roles, which are consistent with illegal behavior (Oakley, 1972, p. 72; see also Tolson, 1977), and the frustration that males feel when they cannot achieve these stereotypes because of low social status (Messerschmidt, 1986, pp. 59–68). The empirical support to link stereotypical masculinity with criminality has been inconsistent (Cullen, Golden, and Cullen, 1979; Norland, James, and Shover, 1978; Thornton and James, 1979; Loy and Norland, 1981). There is some evidence, however, that female stereotypical characteristics predict prosocial behavior (Morash, 1983; Gilligan, 1982; Hoffman, 1975; Eisenberg and Miller, 1987).

An additional irony is found in the inclusion of women in correctional boot camps. Holm (1982, p. 273) observed that in the military, "women . . . suffered from role identification problems when put through military training programs designed traditionally 'to make men out of boys,'" programs that had "more to do with the rites of manhood than the requirements of service jobs." There is serious doubt about the efficacy of placing women in a militaristic environment that emphasizes masculinity and aggressiveness and that in some cases rejects essentially prosocial images and related patterns of interaction associated with the stereotype of femininity.

Alternative Models in Corrections

Correctional policymakers and program staff are not alone in their application of the traditional boot camp model as an approach for training people outside of military settings. Looking again at news reports, we see that the boot camp type of training has been accepted in a variety of organizations as a means to increase the productivity, skill levels, efficiency, and effectiveness of participants. Such enterprises are as diverse as the Electronic Data Systems Corporation (Klausner, 1984, p. 17), the Nick Bollettieri Tennis Academy (Arias, 1986, p. 107), and Japan's Managers' Training School (Bueil, 1983). In keeping with the boot camp model, participants are made to endure humiliation so that a bond can develop with the teacher (Klausner, 1984, p. 17). There appear to be social forces supporting acceptance of the general idea that the boot camp model is appropriate as a method for promoting training and human development. In spite of the societal pressures to use such a model, our assessment has a number of negative implications for the application of boot camps in correctional settings.

The first implication is based on the research on boot camp and the development of human potential in a military setting. At certain times and in certain geographic locations, military personnel have been charged with training and employing populations that are not markedly dissimilar from the economically marginalized young men and women that populate the prisons. They also have been engaged in the imprisonment of people for the violation of criminal laws. A continued examination of their techniques and outcomes could provide further instruction. As a starting point, it might be noted that in the military, the version of boot camp used in correctional settings is not commonly viewed as an effective correctional measure. Furthermore, through *Project 10,000*, the military has been successful in integrating poorly educated recruits into their own workforce, though often in relatively low-skill positions that restricted transfer to the civilian workforce (Sticht et al., 1987). Contrary to critics' anticipation of disciplinary problems with poorly educated recruits, less than 5% of the participants failed to conform to military rules and regulations. The approach to integration involved traditional methods of literacy training coupled with individualized teaching geared to a specific job assignment. This approach is consistent with the findings that we have reviewed on effective work programs in correctional settings.

A second implication of our analysis of the idea of boot camp is that we need to reconsider correctional alternatives. Harris (1983, p. 166) wrote that the "development of a more humane, caring and benevolent society involves a continuing quest for higher standards of decency and good will and an ever decreasing resort to . . . degrading sanctions." For her, the continued and fundamental interdependence of self and other is primary, and she thinks in terms of "persuasion, nonviolent action, positive reinforcement, personal example, peer support and the provision of life-sustaining and life-enhancing services and opportunities" (Harris, 1983, p. 166). It is noteworthy that the rehabilitation models of corrections that many experts have publicly rejected reflect a deemphasis on the questionable stereotypes of "how to be a man" that are promoted by the boot camp model.

A third implication has to do with the evaluation of existing and planned boot camp programs. A number of potential, negative outcomes of a boot camp environment have been identified. One of these is increased aggression, including physical and nonphysical punishment, directed against offenders by prison staff. Also included are increased offender aggression, a devaluation of women and so-called "feminine traits" (e.g., sensitivity), and other negative effects of an unpredictable, authoritarian atmosphere. In addition to considering these effects directly, program evaluation should monitor the degree to which the environment is characterized by inconsistent standards and expectations, dysfunctional stress, a we-versus-they attitude, and negative leadership styles. Furthermore, because correctional boot camp programs mix the elements of a military model with less coercive methods of human change, it is important to design research that reveals the actual program elements that produce both desired and undesired program outcomes.

Our review and analysis suggest that even when the elements of the military boot camp model are mixed with traditional rehabilitative approaches, there can be negative outcomes. Thus, the boot camp model is unlikely to provide a panacea for the needs of rehabilitation or for the pressures arising from the problems of both prison overcrowding and public demands for severe punishment. Whether the point is to provide rehabilitation, to deter, or to divert people from prison, alternatives other than boot camp should be given careful consideration.

296   Section IV—Change without Progress: Corrections

References

Arias, Ron. 1986. "At Nick Bollettieri's Florida Boot Camp, Tennis Is Played Only One way, To Win." *People Weekly*, October 20:107.

Bandura, Albert. 1973. *Aggression: A Social Learning Analysis.* Englewood Cliffs, NJ: Prentice-Hall.

Bellew, Deena C. 1988. *An Evaluation of IMPACT Using Intensive Interviews: The Inmate Perspective.* Unpublished manuscript. Baton Rouge: Louisiana State University.

Bernard, Jesse. 1975. *Women, Wives, Mothers: Values and Options.* Chicago: Aldine.

Bueil, Barbara. 1983. "Corporate Boot Camp in Japan." *Life*, September:40.

Christie, Nils. 1981. *Limits to Pain.* Oxford: Mattin Robertson.

Coakley, Jay J. 1986. *Sport in Society: Issues and Controversies.* St. Louis, MO: Mosby.

Cole, George F. 1986. *The American System of Criminal Justice.* Monterey, CA: Brooks/Cole.

Cullen, Francis T., Kathryn M. Golden and John B. Cullen. 1979. "Sex and Delinquency: A Partial Test of the Masculinity Hypothesis." *Criminology*, 17:301–10.

Defense. 1987. "Almanac: People in Active Duty." September/October:32.

Eichler, Margrit. 1980. *The Double Standard: A Feminist Critique of Feminist Social Science.* New York: St. Martin's Press.

Eisenberg, Nancy and Paul A. Miller. 1987. "The Relation of Empathy to Prosocial and Related Behaviors." *Psychological Bulletin*, 101:91–119.

Eisenberg, Sue E. and Patricia L. Micklow. 1979. "The Assaulted Wife: 'Catch 22' Revisited." *Women's Rights Law Reporter*, 3:138–61.

Eisenhart, R. Wayne. 1975. "You Can't Hack It Little Girl: A Discussion of the Covert Psychological Agenda of Modern Combat Training." *Journal of Social Issues*, 31:13–23.

Ekman, Paul, Wallace V. Friesen and Daniel R. Lutzker. 1962. "Psychological Reactions to Infantry Basic Training." *Journal of Consulting Psychology*, 26:103–04.

Enloe, Cynthia. 1983. *Does Khaki Become You? The Militarization of Women's Lives.* Boston: South End.

Faris, John H. 1975. "The Impact of Basic Combat Training: The Role of the Drill Sergeant." Pp. 13–24 in *The Social Psychology of Military Service*, edited by E. Goldman and D. R. Segal. Beverly Hills: Sage.

Finckenauer, James O. 1982. *Scared Straight and the Panacea Phenomenon.* Englewood Cliffs, NJ: Prentice-Hall.

Fogel, David. 1975. . . . *We Are the Living Proof* . . . Cincinnati: Anderson.

Gannett News Service. 1989. "Boot Camp Prisons." *Lansing State Journal*, 135 (June 19): 11.

Gendreau, Paul, Brian A. Grant and Mary Leipciger. 1979. "Self-Esteem, Incarceration, and Recidivism." *Criminal Justice and Behavior*, 6:67–75.

Gendreau, Paul and Robert R. Ross. 1987. "Revivification of Rehabilitation: Evidence from the 1980s." *Justice Quarterly*, 4:349–96.

Gilligan, Carol. 1982. *In a Different Voice*. Cambridge: Harvard University Press.

Gottlieb, David. 1980. *Babes in Arms: Youth in the Army*. Beverly Hills: Sage.

Harris, M. Kay. 1983. "Strategies, Values, and the Emerging Generation of Alternatives to Incarceration." *Review of Law and Social Change*, 12: 141–70.

Heidensohn, Francis. 1987. "Women and Crime: Questions for Criminology." Pp. 16–27 in *Gender, Crime and Justice*, edited by P. Carlen and A. Worral. Milton Keynes, England: Open University Press.

Hengish, Donald. 1988. Michigan Bureau of Correctional Facilities, Community Alternatives Program. Telephone interview, December 1.

Hilyer, James S., Jr. and William Mitchell. 1979. "Effects of Systematic Physical Fitness Training Combined with Counseling on the Self-Concept of College Students." *Journal of Counseling Psychology*, 26:427–36.

Hoffman, Martin L. 1975. "Sex Differences in Moral Internalization and Values." *Journal of Personality and Social Psychology*, 32:720–29.

Holm, Jeanne. 1982. *Women in the Military*. Novato, CA: Presidio.

Jeffrey, Ray and Stephen Woolpert. 1974. "Work Furlough as an Alternative to Incarceration: An Assessment of its Effects on Recidivism and Social Cost." *Journal of Criminal Law and Criminology*, 65:404–15.

Johnson, Robert. 1987. *Hard Time*. Monterey, CA: Brooks/Cole.

Kaiser, Steven. 1988. Warden, Lexington Assessment and Reception Center, Lexington, Oklahoma. Telephone interview, November 16.

Klausner, Michael. 1984. "Perot's Boot Camp." *Wall Street Journal*, August 3:17.

Larwood, Laurie, Eric Glasser and Robert McDonald. 1980. "Attitudes of Male and Female Cadets Toward Military Sex Integration." *Sex Roles*, 6: 381–90.

Lejins, Peter P. 1970. "Ideas Which Have Moved Corrections." *Proceedings of the One Hundredth Annual Congress of Corrections of the American Correctional Association*: 308–22.

Lewis, Roy V. 1983. "Scared Straight—California Style: Evaluation of the San Quentin Squire Program." *Criminal Justice and Behavior*, 10:209–26.

Life. 1988. "'Squeeze You Like a Grape': In Georgia, A Prison Boot Camp Sets Kids Straight," July: 82.

Lipton, Douglas, Robert Martinson and Judith Wills. 1975. *The Effectiveness of Correctional Treatment*. New York: Praeger.

Loy, Pamela and Stephen Norland. 1981. "Gender Convergence and Delinquency." *Sociological Quarterly*, 22:275–83.

Maguire, Kathleen E., Timothy J. Flanagan and Terence P. Thornberry. 1988. "Prison Labor and Recidivism." *Journal of Quantitative Criminology*, 4: 3–18.

Marlowe, David H., James A. Martin, Robert I. Schneider, Larry Ingraham, Mark A. Vaitkus and Paul Bartone. 1988. *A Look at Army Training Centers: The Human Dimensions of Leadership and Training*. Washington, DC: Department of Military Psychiatry, Walter Reed Army Institute of Research.

Martin, Douglas. 1988. "New York Tests a Boot Camp for Inmates." *New York Times*, March 4:15.

McKelvey, Blake. 1977. *American Prisons: A History of Good Intentions.* Montclair, NJ: Patterson Smith.

Melossi, Dario and Massimo Pavarini. 1981. *The Prison and the Factory: Origins of the Penitentiary System.* London: Macmillan.

Merryfinch, Lesley. 1981. "Militarization/Civilization." Pp. 9–13 in *Loaded Questions: Women in the Military*, edited by W. Chapkis. Washington, DC: Transnational Institute.

Messerschmidt, James W. 1986. *Capitalism, Patriarchy, and Crime: Toward a Socialist Feminist Criminology.* Totowa, NJ: Rowman and Littlefield.

Morash, Merry. 1983. "An Explanation of Juvenile Delinquency: The Integration of Moral-Reasoning Theory and Sociological Knowledge." Pp. 385–410 in *Personality Theory, Moral Development, and Criminal Behavior*, edited by W. S. Laufer and J. M. Day. Lexington, MA: Lexington Books.

Morash, Merry and Etta Anderson. 1978. "Liberal Thinking on Rehabilitation: A Work-Able Solution to Crime?" *Social Problems*, 25:556–63.

Morse, Wayne. 1973. "The Attorney General's Survey of Release Procedures." Pp. 23–53 in *Penology: The Evolution of Corrections in America*, edited by G. C. Killinger and P. F. Cromwell, Jr. St. Paul, MN: West.

Naffine, Ngaire. 1987. *Female Crime: The Construction of Women in Criminology.* Sydney: Allen and Unwin.

Norland, Stephen, Jennifer James and Neal Shover. 1978. "Gender Role Expectations." *Sociology Quarterly*, 19:545–54.

Oakley, Ann. 1972. *Sex, Gender and Society.* London: Temple Smith.

O'Brien, Tim. 1979. *If I Die in a Combat Zone, Box Me Up and Ship Me Home.* New York: Delacorte.

Parent, Dale. 1988. "Shock Incarceration Programs." Paper presented at the American Correctional Association Winter Conference, Phoenix.

Pisciotta, Alexander W. 1983. "Scientific Reform: The New Penology at Elmira, 1876–1900." *Crime and Delinquency*, 29:613–30.

Rabinowitz, Stanley. 1982. "Inauguration for Adulthood: The Military System as an Effective Integrator for Adult Adaptation: An Israel Air Force Base Perspective." *Psychological Reports*, 51:1083–86.

Raspberry, William. 1987. "Boot Camp—In Prison: An Experiment Worth Watching." *Washington Post*, March 21: Section H, p. 21.

Raupp, Edward R. 1978. *Toward Positive Leadership for Initial Entry Training. A Report by the Task Force on Initial Entry Training Leadership.* Fort Monroe, VA: United States Army Training and Doctrine Command.

Rogers, Carl R. 1975. "Empathic: An Unappreciated Way of Being." *Journal of the Counseling Psychologist*, 5:2–10.

Ruddick, Sara. 1983. "Drafting Women: Pieces of a Puzzle." Pp. 214–43 in *Conscripts and Volunteers: Military Requirements, Social Justice and the All-Volunteer Force*, edited by R. K. Rullinwinder. Totowa, NJ: Rowman and Allenheld.

Rudoff, Alvin and T. C. Esselstyn. 1973. "Evaluating Work Furlough: A Follow-Up." *Federal Probation*, 37:48–53.

Rusche, Georg and Otto Kirchheimer. 1939. *Punishment and Social Structure.* New York: Columbia University Press.

Satir, Virginia. 1972. *Peoplemaking*. Palo Alto, CA: Science and Behavior Books.

Schwendinger, Julia R. and Herman Schwendinger. 1985. *Adolescent Subcultures and Delinquency*. New York: Praeger.

Sitomer, Curtis J. 1987. "Some Young U.S. Offenders Go to 'Boot Camp'—Others are Put in Adult Jails." *Christian Science Monitor*, October 27:1.

Sonkin, Daniel Jay, Del Martin and Leonard E. Aurbach Walker. 1985. *The Male Batterer: A Treatment Approach*. New York: Springer.

Sticht, Thomas G., William B. Armstrong, Daniel T. Hickey and John S. Caylor. 1987. *Cast-Off Youth Policy and Training Methods from the Military Experiences*. New York: Praeger.

Stiehm, Judith H. 1981. *Bring Me Men and Women: Mandated Change at the U.S. Air Force Academy*. Berkeley: University of California Press.

———. 1982. "The Protected, the Protector, the Defender." *Women's Studies International Forum*, 5:367–76.

———. 1989. *Arms and the Enlisted Woman*. Philadelphia: Temple University Press.

Sullivan, Mercer. 1983. "Youth Crime: New York's Two Varieties." *New York Affairs: Crime and Criminal Justice*. New York: New York University Press.

Taggart, Robert, III. 1972. *The Prison of Unemployment*. Baltimore: Johns Hopkins University Press.

Thornton, David, Len Curran, David Grayson and Vernon Holloway. 1984. *Tougher Regimes in Detention Centres: Report of an Evaluation by the Young Offender Psychology Unit*. London: Her Majesty's Stationery Office.

Thornton, William E. and Jennifer James. 1979. "Masculinity and Delinquency Revisited." *British Journal of Criminology*, 19:225–41.

Tolson, Andrew. 1977. *The Limits of Masculinity: Male Identity and the Liberated Woman*. New York: Harper & Row.

Walker, Lenore. 1983. "The Battered Woman Syndrome Study." Pp. 31–48 in *The Dark Side of Families: Current Family Violence Research*, edited by D. Finkelhor, R. J. Gelles, G. Hotaling and M. Straus. Beverly Hills: Sage.

Walter, Timothy L. and Carolyn M. Mills. 1980. "A Behavioral-Employment Intervention Program for Reducing Juvenile Delinquency." Pp. 185–206 in *Effective Correctional Treatment*, edited by R. R. Ross and P. Gendreau. Toronto: Butterworths.

Wamsley, Gary L. 1972. "Contrasting Institutions of Air Force Socialization: Happenstance or Bellwether?" *American Journal of Sociology*, 78:399–417.

Wilson, William Julius. 1987. *The Truly Disadvantaged: Inner City, the Underclass, and Public Policy*. Chicago: University of Chicago Press.

Yudkin, Marcia. 1982. "Reflections on Wolf's *Three Guineas*." *Women's Studies International Forum*, 5:263–69.

Yuval-Davis, Nira. 1985. "Front and Rear: The Sexual Division of Labor in the Israeli Army." *Feminist Studies*, 11:649–75.

15

Changes in Prison Culture

Geoffrey Hunt
Stephanie Riegel
Tomas Morales
Dan Waldorf

Since Clemmer (1958) published the *Prison Community* in 1940, sociologists and criminologists have sought to explain the culture of prisons. A key debate in this literature centers on the extent to which inmate culture is either a product of the prison environment or an extension of external subcultures. Those in the former camp, such as Sykes and Messinger (1977), Cloward (1977), and Goffman (1961), have argued that the inmate social system is formed "as a reaction to various 'pains of imprisonment' and deprivation inmates suffer in captivity" (Leger and Stratton 1977:93). These writers saw

From *Social Problems,* Vol. 40, No. 3, pp. 398–409, © 1993 by the Society for the Study of Social Problems. Reprinted by permission.

the prison as a total institution in which the individual, through a series of "status degradation ceremonies," gradually became socialized into prison life. Analysts such as Irwin and Cressey (1977) challenged this view of prison life, arguing that it tended to underestimate the importance of the culture that convicts brought with them from the outside. They identified two dominant subcultures within the prison—that of the thief and the convict—both of which had their origins in the outside world.

Our interview material did not clearly support one or the other of these opposing views and instead suggested that other dynamics of prison life were key to understanding inmates' experiences. Salient in inmate interviews was a greater degree of turmoil than was common to prison life in the past. The reasons for this turmoil were complex and included newly formed gangs, changes in prison population demographics, and new developments in prison policy, especially in relation to gangs. All these elements coalesced to create an increasingly unpredictable world in which prior loyalties, allegiances, and friendships were disrupted. Even some of the experienced prisoners from the "old school" were at a loss as to how to negotiate this new situation. Existing theories were not helpful in explaining our findings for the current dynamics could not be attributed solely to forces emanating from inside the prison or outside it.

The Sample

The sample was designed to include offenders who had been released from prison. Respondents lived in the Oakland and San Francisco area and, during 1991 and 1992, were located through contacts with ex-convict organizations, education programs, and respondents in a street gang study. Using a snowball sampling technique (Biernacki and Waldorf 1981), we eventually contacted 39 men, of whom 46 percent (18) identified themselves as gang members, and 38 percent (6) said they were members of street gangs prior to entering prison. The ethnic backgrounds of respondents were as follows: 16 Chicanos, 14 African-Americans, 5 whites, 2 Native Americans, 1 French Creole, and 1 Chilean. The youngest was 19 and the oldest 60.

The vast majority of respondents had long criminal histories and had served several prison sentences in many different California state prisons. However, within the interviews we concentrated on obtaining information about their last major prison term, which we stipulated had to have lasted for at least one year. Thirty-eight percent (15) of our sample had been convicted for drug related offenses, including selling, distribution, and possession. Robberies (21 percent) were the second major category, followed by burglaries (16 percent), and embezzlement (6 percent). Respondents were sent to a wide range of California prisons including Avenol, Solano, San Quentin, Tracy, Susanville, Folsom, Soledad, Corcoran, Vacaville, and Pelican Bay, and while there, they served a median of 19 months. We used a structured but open-ended interview schedule and in addition to asking questions about ethnicity, age, arrest history, and the different prisons where they served time, the bulk of our interviews concentrated on knowledge of prison gangs and their perceptions of changes in prison life.

Because the sample was relatively small, results can not be considered definitive. Nevertheless, they provide insight not only into contemporary prison life but also into the role of gangs. The available literature on gangs, with a few notable exceptions (see Moore 1978; Jacobs 1974, 1977), takes a correctional and institutional perspective and consequently has made little or no attempt to examine the prisoners' point of view.

The Established California Prison Gangs

According to various accounts (Camp and Camp 1985; Davidson 1974; Irwin 1980; Moore 1978; Porter 1982), the first California prison gang was the Mexican Mafia—a Chicano gang, believed to have originated in 1957 in the Dueul Vocational Institution prison. This Chicano group began to intimidate other Chicanos from the northern part of the state. The nonaligned, predominantly rural Chicanos organized themselves together for protection. They initially called themselves "Blooming Flower," but soon changed their name to La Nuestra Familia. Like the Mexican Mafia, La Nuestra Familia adopted a military style structure, with a general, captains, lieutenants, and soldiers. However, unlike the Mexican Mafia, La Nuestra Familia had a written constitution consisting of rules of discipline and conduct.

The Texas Syndicate, a third Chicano gang, followed the model of the Mexican Mafia and La Nuestra Familia and utilized a paramilitary system with a president at its head. Its members are mainly Mexican-American inmates, originally from Texas, who see themselves in opposition to the other Chicano groups, especially those from Los Angeles, who they perceive as being soft and too "Americanized."

Both black and white prisoners are also organized. The general view on the origins of the Black Guerilla Family (B.G.F.)—the leading black gang—is that it developed as a splinter group of the Black Family, an organization reportedly created by George Jackson. The authorities were particularly wary of this group, both because of its revolutionary language and reports that its members, unlike those of other gangs, regularly assaulted prison guards.

The Aryan Brotherhood—the only white gang identified in California prisons—originated in the late 1960s. It is said to be governed by a 3-man commission and a 9-man council who recruit from white supremacist and outlawed motorcycle groups. According to prison authorities, it is a "Nazi-oriented gang, anti-black [which] adheres to violence to gain prestige and compliance to their creed" (Camp and Camp 1985:105).[1]

The available sociological literature on older prison gangs is divided on the issue of their relationship to street gangs. On the one hand, Moore in discussing Chicano gangs argues that they were started by "state-raised youths and 'psychos'" (1978:114) inside the prisons, while Jacobson sees them as an extension of street gangs. Although Moore sees the gangs as initially prison inspired, she describes a strong symbiotic relationship between the street and the prison. In fact, she notes that once the gangs were established inside the prisons, they attempted to influence the street scene. "The Mafia attempted to use its prison-based organization to move into the narcotics market in East Los Angeles, and also, reputedly, into some legitimate pinto-serving community agencies" (1978:115).

Institutional Attempts to Control the Gangs

Prison authorities see gangs as highly undesirable and have argued that an increase in extortion, intimidation, violence, and drug trafficking can be directly attributed to their rise. In responding to prison gangs, the California Department of Corrections (CDC) introduced a number of strategies and policies, for example, using "confidential informants," segregating gang members in different buildings and prisons, intercepting gang communications, setting up task forces to monitor and track gang members, locking up gang leaders in high security prisons, and "locking down" entire institutions. These changes were perceived by our respondents who saw the CDC as increasingly tightening its control over the prison system and the gangs.

Prison Guards

In spite of the "official" view that gangs should be eradicated, many prison authorities hold a more pragmatic view and feel that the gangs have "had little negative impact on the regular running of prison operations" (Camp and Camp 1985:xii). Moreover, as Cummins (1991) has noted, there is often a considerable discrepancy between the official stance and what takes place within particular prisons. This point was emphasized by our respondents who portrayed guards' attitudes toward the gangs as complex and devious, and saw the guards as often accepting prison gangs and in some cases even encouraging them. In supporting this view, they gave three reasons why guards would allow gangs to develop or continue.

First, some noted guards' financial incentive to encourage gang behavior. They suggested that guards are keen to create "threats to security" which necessitate increased surveillance and, consequently, lead to overtime work.

> They have a financial interest in getting overtime. . . . Anything that was "security" meant that there were no restrictions in the budget. So if there are gangs, and there are associations. if there is some threat in that focus of security. they make more money (Case 17).

Others went even further and told us that some guards benefited from gangs' illegal activities.

> Well, you know the guards, aren't . . . you'd be surprised who the guards affiliated with. Guards have friends that's in there. They have their friends outside. you know. Guards'll bring drugs in. Sell 'em. Guards will bring knives in, weapons. food. The guards play a major role (Case 7).

Not only were guards involved in illegal activities, but the practice was often overlooked by other guards. For example, as one respondent philosophically replied in answer to our question: "Were individual guards involved in illegal gang activities?"

> Well, I think you have guards that are human beings that . . . don't really want to do more than they have to. So if they see a guard doing something a little shady, it's easy to turn a blind eye because of the hassle it would take to pursue it (Case 16).

Finally, in addition to these financial incentives, some believed that guards encouraged gang activities and conflict in order to control the prison inmates more effectively and "keep the peace out of prisons" (Case 32).

> They perpetuated the friction because, for instance, what they would do is . . . give false information to different groups. . . . Something to

> put the fear so that then the Latino would prepare himself for a con-
> flict. . . . And so everybody's on point and the next thing you know a
> fight would break out and the shit would come down. So it was to their
> interest to perpetuate division amongst the inmates so that they would
> be able to better control the institution. Because if you are spending
> your time fighting each other you have no time . . . to fight the estab-
> lishment (Case 34).

This divide and rule policy was emphasized by many of our respondents and was seen as a major contributory factor in prisoner conflicts.

Jacketing and the Use of Confidential Informants

According to our respondents, another prison administration
tactic was "jacketing"—officially noting in a prisoner's file that he was
a suspected gang member. Once identified as a gang member, a prisoner could be transferred to a high security prison or placed in a special housing unit. "Jacketing," which is similar to the "dirty jacket"
procedure outlined by Davidson (1974), was seen by our respondents
as a particularly arbitrary process and one in which the prisoner had
little or no recourse.

> Like I said, if you're a sympathizer you could be easily jacketed as a
> gang member. You hang around with 'em. You might not do nothing.
> But hang out with 'em. Drive iron with 'em. Go to lunch with 'em (Case
> 1).

Many respondents felt the process was particularly unfair because
it meant that a prisoner could be identified as gang member and "jack-
eted" purely on the basis of information from a confidential informant.
Confidential informants or "snitches" supplied intelligence information to prison authorities about inmate activities, especially
gang-related activities.

> Now let's say you and I are both inmates at San Quentin. And your cel-
> lie gets in a fight and gets stabbed. So all of a sudden, the Chicano who
> is a friend of your cellie says that he'll get the boys and deal with this.
> They talk about it but nothing happens. All of a sudden one of the
> snitches or rats, says I think something is cooking, and people are
> going to make a move to the administration. What will happen is that
> they [the administration] will gaffel up you and me and whoever else
> you associate with and put us all on a bus straight to Pelican Bay. They
> will say we have confidential reliable information that you guys are
> planning an assault on Billy Bob or his gang. . . . And you're wonder-
> ing, you've never received a disciplinary infraction. But by God now,
> information is in your central file that you are gang affiliated, that
> you're involved in gang violence (Case 16).

Our respondents distinguished between two types of snitching—dry and hard.

> Dry snitching is a guy who will have a conversation with a guard and the guard is just smart enough. He'll say you talk to Joe, don't ya? You say, oh, yeah, Joe's a pretty good ol' boy, I heard he's doing drugs but don't believe it. He might smoke a few joints on the yard, but nothing hard. He just dry snitched. He indirectly dropped a lug on Joe. And then you got the guy who gets himself in a jam and goes out and points out other inmates (Case 16).

Dry snitching could also refer to a prisoner supplying general information to guards without implicating anyone by name. This allowed the prisoner to develop a "juice card" or a form of credit with the guard.

> A "juice card" is that you have juice [credit] with a particular guard, a lieutenant, a sergeant or somebody that is part of staff. . . . Let's say that somebody is dry snitching. By dry snitching I mean that they might come up to their juice man that has a "juice card," let's just say it is a sergeant of the yard, and they might go up there and say, "Hey I hear that there is a rumble coming down. I can't tell you more than that but some shit is going to come down tonight." So they alert the sergeant right. The sergeant tells him, "I owe you one." Now the guy might come up to the sergeant and say, "Hey remember you owe me one, hey I got this 115 [infraction] squash it." "Okay I will squash it." That is the "juice card" (Case 34).

Many of our respondents felt there was a growing number of snitches (also see Stojkovic 1986). A key factor promoting this growth was the pressure exerted by the guards—a point denied by the prison authorities in Stojkovic's research.

Pressure could be applied in a number of ways. First, if for example a prisoner was in a high security unit, he often found himself unable to get out unless he "debriefed"; i.e., provided information on other gang members. Many respondents felt that this was an impossible situation because if they didn't snitch their chances of getting out were minimal. As one respondent remarked:

> They [the guards] wanted some information on other people. . . . So I was put between a rock and a hard place. So I decided I would rather do extra time, than ending up saying something I would later regret (Case 10).

Second, if the guards knew that a prisoner was an ex-gang member, they might threaten to send him to a particular prison, where he would be attacked by his own ex-gang.

> See there is a lot of guys in there that are drop outs from whatever gang they were in, and they are afraid to be sent to a joint where some

other tip might be. They even get threatened by staff that if they don't cooperate with them they will be sent to either Tracy, or Soledad and they are liable to get hit by their own ex-gang so they cooperate (Case 40).

However, it would be inaccurate to suggest respondents accused only the prison authorities, since many also pointed out other developments within the prison system, and especially within the prison population, to explain what they described as a deteriorating situation.

Prison Crowding, the New Gangs, and the "Pepsi Generation"

Since 1980, the California prison population has increased dramatically from 24,569 to 97,309 (California Department of Corrections 1991). The net effect of this expansion has been severe overcrowding in the prisons. In 1970, prison institutions and camps were slightly underutilized and the occupancy rate stood at 98 percent. By 1980, they were full, and in 1990, the rate had risen dramatically to 180 percent of capacity. Currently, the inmate population stands at 91,892, while bed capacity is only 51,013. In order to cope with this overcrowding, institutions have been obliged to use all available space, including gymnasiums and dayrooms.

Many respondents graphically described the problems created by this situation and complained about the deterioration in prison services. However, in talking about prison overcrowding, they tended to concentrate more on the changes in the characteristics of the inmates currently arriving. Specifically, they focused on the growth of new gangs, the immaturity of new inmates, and the problems they caused within the prison. Respondents felt this change in prison population characteristics had a major effect on day-to-day activities, and contributed to the fragmentary nature of prison life.

The New Gangs

According to our respondents, although all five of the older gangs still exist, their importance has diminished. The reasons for this appear to be twofold. First, many of the older gang members have either dropped out, gone undercover, or have been segregated from the rest of the prison population. Second, a new crop of gangs has taken center stage. In other words, prison authorities' efforts to contain the spread of gangs led, unintentionally, to a vacuum within the prison population within which new prison groupings developed.

Information on these new gangs is relatively limited in comparison with information on the older gangs. Thus it is difficult to be precise about their structure and composition. Moreover, a further complication is whether or not these groups fit current definitions of what constitutes a gang. For instance, if we adapt Klein and Maxson's (1989) definition of a street gang—community recognition as a group or collectivity, recognition by the group itself as a distinct group, and activities which consistently result in negative responses from law enforcement—then these new groupings constitute gangs if the prison is considered the community. However, if we compare them with the Mexican Mafia, La Nuestra Familia, or the Black Guerilla Family, which have developed hierarchies or clearly articulated constitutions, they constitute instead territorial alliances which demand loyalties and provide security and protection. Regardless of whether these groups fit traditional definitions, respondents made it clear they had a significant impact on the traditional prison loyalties and allegiances and contributed to conflicts amongst the prisoners.

Chicano and Latino gangs. Among Chicanos, the Nortenos and the Surenos are the most important groupings or gangs. These two groups are divided regionally between the North and South of California, with Fresno as the dividing line.[2] Although regional loyalties were also important for the Mexican Mafia and La Nuestra Familia, the regional separation between North and South was not as rigid as it is today for Surenos and Nortenos.

In addition to the Nortenos and the Surenos, two other groups were mentioned—the New Structure and the Border Brothers. Our respondents provided differing interpretations of the New Structure. For instance, some noted it was a new Chicano group made up of Nortenos which started in San Francisco, while others implied it was an offshoot of La Nuestra Familia. Opinions differed as to its precise relationship to La Nuestra Familia.

The Border Brothers are surrounded by less controversy. Their members are from Mexico, they speak only Spanish and, consequently, keep to themselves. Most of our respondents agreed this was a large group constantly increasing in size, and that most members had been arrested for trafficking heroin or cocaine.

Although there was little disagreement as to the Border Brothers' increasing importance, which was partly attributed to their not "claiming territory," there was, nevertheless, some dispute as to their impact on the North/South issue. Some respondents saw the Border Brothers as keeping strictly to themselves.

> The Border Brothers don't want to have anything to do with the Surenos-Nortenos—they keep out of that 'cause it's not our fighting and all of that is stupid. . . . Either you are a Chicano or you're not. There is no sense of being separated (Case 3).

Others predicted that in the future, the Border Brothers will become involved in the conflict and will align themselves with the Surenos against the Nortenos.

> It used to be Border Brothers over there and Sureno and Norteno, stay apart from each other. . . . But now what I see that's coming out is that the Border Brothers are starting to claim Trece now.[3] What I think is going to happen, to the best of my knowledge, is that the Surenos instead of them knockin' ass with the Nortenos, they're going to have the Border Brothers lock ass with the Nortenos due to the fact that they're South and all that. Maybe in a few years we will see if my prediction is true or not (Case 36).

Black gangs. The Crips, originally a street gang from South Central Los Angeles, is the largest of the new black gangs. It is basically a neighborhood group.

> I.: So the Crips is more a neighborhood thing than a racial thing?
>
> R.: Oh yeah! That's what it stems from. It stems from a neighborhood thing. There's one thing about the Crips collectively, their neighborhoods are important factors in their gang structures (Case 5).

The Bloods are the traditional rivals of the Crips. Although, like the Crips, they are a neighborhood group, they do not attribute the same importance to the neighborhood.

> They're structured geographically in the neighborhood, but it's not as important as it is for the Crips. Only in LA is it that important. Bloods from LA, it's important for them but they don't have as many neighborhoods as the Crips. But anywhere else in Southern California the neighborhoods are not that important. Only in LA (Case 5).

The 415s is a third black prison gang emerging recently. The group is made up of individuals living within the 415 San Francisco Bay area telephone code.[4] Although the group's visibility is high, especially in the Bay area, the organization appears to be loosely structured, so much so that one of our respondents suggested that the 415s were more an affiliation rather than a gang.

All of these gangs are said to be producing a significant impact on prison life. Whereas previously there were four or five major gangs, today there are nine or ten new groupings, each with its own network of alliances and loyalties. These crosscutting and often conflicting allegiances have a significant impact on prison life. They produce a confusing, disruptive situation for many prisoners and can even produce problems for existing friendships. As one Puerto Rican respondent noted, "When I first started going to the joints . . . it wasn't as bad to associate a guy from the North and the South. It wasn't that big of a deal" (Case 39). But as the fragmentation increased and dividing lines became more rigid, this type of friendship was much less acceptable. According to many of our respondents, another consequence of fragmentation was an increase in intraethnic conflict, especially amongst the black population.

> Back then there was no Crips, there was no Bloods, or 415s. It is a lot different now. The blacks hit the blacks. When the blacks at one time were like the B.G.F. where the blacks would stick together, now they are hitting each other, from the Crips, to the Bloods, to the 415, are pretty much all enemies (Case 39).

The picture provided by our respondents is one of an increasing splintering of prison groupings. Allegiances to particular groups, which had previously seemed relatively entrenched, are now questioned. Friendships developed over long prison terms are now disrupted, and where previously prisoners made choices about joining a gang, membership has now become more automatic, especially for Chicanos. Today, what counts is the region of the state where the prisoner comes from; if he comes South of Fresno, he is automatically a Sureno, if he is from North of Fresno, he becomes a Norteno.

Pepsi Generation

Respondents not only described the conflict arising from the new divisions within the prison population, but also attributed this conflict to new prison inmates. They emphasized that the new generation of prisoners differed from their generation—in their dress, attitudes, and behavior toward other prisoners and the prison authorities. Respondents described themselves as convicts who represented the "old school."

> In my point of view there is what is called the old school. . . . And the old school goes back to where there is traditions and customs, there is this whole thing of holding your mud, and there is something you don't violate. For instance you don't snitch, you are a convict in the sense that you go in and you know that you are there to do time. And there is two sides. There is the Department of Corrections and there is you as the convict (Case 34).

A convict, in this sense, was very different from the present day "inmate" who they described as not having:

a juvenile record or anything like that, and so that when they come in they have no sense of what it is to do time. . . . The inmate goes in there and he goes in not realizing that, so that they are doing everybody else's number or expect somebody else to do their number. Which means for instance, that if they can get out of something they will go ahead and give somebody up or they will go against the code. Say for instance, the food is real bad and the convict would say, look we have to do something about this so let's make up a protest about the food and present it to the warden. And the convict will go along with it because it is for the betterment of the convicts. The inmate will go and go against it because he wants to be a good inmate and, therefore, he is thinking about himself and not the whole population (Case 32).

The prisons were full of younger prisoners who were described disparagingly by our respondents as "boys trying to become men," and the "Pepsi Generation," defined as

the young shuck and jive energized generation. The CYA [California Youth Authority] mentality guys in a man's body and muscles can really go out and bang if they want. They are the youngsters that want to prove something—how tough and macho and strong they are. This is their whole attitude. Very extreme power trip and machismo. The youngsters want to prove something. How tough they are. And there is really very little remorse (Case 16).

According to our respondents, the "Pepsi Generation" went around wearing "their pants down below their ass" (Case 40) and showing little or no respect for the older inmates, many of whom had long histories of prison life which normally would have provided them with a high degree of status. Disrespect was exhibited even in such seemingly small things as the way that the younger prisoners approached the older inmates.

They'll come up and ask you where you are from. I had problems with that. They come with total disrespect. It seems like they send the smallest, youngest punk around and he comes and tries to jam you. You know, you've been around for a long time, you know, you've got your respect already established and you have no business with this bullshit. . . . And here you have some youngster coming in your face. talking about "Hey man, where you from?" (Case 2).

This view was graphically corroborated by a 38-year-old Familia member who described the young inmates in the following way:

They're actors. Put it this way, they're gangsters until their fuckin' wheels fall off. . . . I'm a gangster too. But there is a limitation to everything. See I can be a gangster with class and style and finesse and respect. Get respect and get it back. That is my motto, my principle in life. Do unto another as you would like do have done to you. These kids don't have respect for the old timers. They disrespect the old men now (Case 36).

The "younger generation" was not only criticized for its disrespect, but for its general behavior as well. They were seen as needlessly violent and erratic and not "TBYAS"—thinking before you act and speak.

I think they're more violent. They are more spontaneous. I think they are very spontaneous. They certainly don't use TBYAS. I think their motivation is shallower than it was years ago (Case 16).

Their behavior had the effect of making prison life, in general, more unpredictable, a feature many of our respondents disliked.

They have nothing but younger guys in prison now. And ah, it has just changed. I don't even consider it prison now anymore. I think it is just a punishment. It is just a place to go to do time. Which now since there are so many children and kids in prison it is hard to do time now. It is not like it used to be where you can wake up one morning and know what to expect. But now you wake up and you don't know what to expect, anything might happen (Case 12).

Inmate Culture Reassessed

Inmates' picture of prison life is of increasing uncertainty and unpredictability; more traditional groupings and loyalties are called into question as new groups come to the fore. Whereas previously, prisoners believed a clear dividing line existed between convicts and authorities, today they see this simple division disintegrating. This occurs because, in their attempt to control the spread of prison gangs, authorities introduced a series of measures which contained the gangs, but also unexpectedly created a vacuum within the organizational structure of the prison population—a vacuum soon filled by new groups. Group membership was taken from newer inmates, who, according to our respondents, had not been socialized into the convict culture. The dominance of these groups soon led to an environment where the rules and codes of behavior were no longer adhered to and even the more experienced prisoners felt like newcomers. Moreover, the ability of prisoners to remain nonaligned was hampered both by developments amongst the prisoners and by the actions of the authorities. For example, a Norteno arrested in the South and sentenced to a southern prison would find himself in a very difficult and potentially dangerous situation.

> You'll see some poor northern dude land in a southern pen, they ride on [harass] him. Five, six, seven, ten deep. You know, vice versa—some poor southern kid comes to a northern spot and these northern kids will do the same thing. They ride deep on them (Case 2).

Study respondents portrayed prison culture as changing, but the change elements they identified were both inside and outside the institution. The available theoretical approaches, which have tended to dichotomize the source of change, fail to capture the complexity and the interconnectedness of the current situation. Furthermore, the information we received produced no conclusive evidence to prove whether or not the street scene determined the structure of gangs inside the prison or vice versa. For example, in the case of the Crips and the Bloods, at first glance we have a development which supports the approaches of Jacobs (1974) and Irwin and Cressey (1977). The Crips and the Bloods originated in the neighborhoods of Los Angeles and transferred their conflicts into the prison environment. In fact, according to one respondent, once in prison, they bury their intragang conflicts in order to strengthen their identities as Crips and Bloods.

> Even when they are "out there" they may fight amongst themselves, just over their territory. . . . But when they get to prison they are wise enough to know. we gotta join collectively to fend off everyone else (Case 5).

However, although the Crips and Bloods fit neatly into Jacobs' perspective, when we consider the case of the 415s and the Nortenos and the Surenos, we find their origins fit more easily into Cloward's (1977) alternative perspective. According to two accounts, the 415s began in prison as a defense group against the threatening behavior of the Bloods and the Crips.

> It [the 415s] got started back in prison. In prison there is a lot of prison gangs . . . and they were put together a lot. They got LA—gangs like the Bloods and the Crips, and they are putting a lot of pressure on the people from the Bay area. And we all got together, we got together and organized our own group (Case G189).

Originally, the Nortenos and Surenos existed neither on the streets nor in the adult prisons but within the California Youth Authority institutions. Gradually this division spread to the adult prisons and soon became powerful enough to disrupt the traditional loyalties of more established gangs. Furthermore, in-prison conflicts soon spread to the outside and, according to information from our San Francisco study, Norteno/Sureno conflicts are beginning to have a significant impact on the streets.

Conclusion

Prisons today are in a turmoil. From both the Department of Corrections perspective and the interview material, it is clear that the prison system is under immense pressures. As the prison population expands and the Department of Corrections attempts to find more bed space, the problems within the prisons multiply. The impact of this situation on the inmates is clear from the interviews—they complain about the increased fragmentation and disorganization that they now experience. Life in prison is no longer organized but instead is viewed as both capricious and dangerous.

For many, returning to prison after spending time outside means being confronted by a world which they do not understand even though they have been in prison many times before. Where once they experienced an orderly culture, today they find a world which operates around arbitrary and ad hoc events, and decisions seem to arise not merely from the behavior of their fellow prisoners but also from prison authorities' official and unofficial decisions. Where before they understood the dominant prison divisions—prisoners versus guards and black versus white inmates—today they find new clefts and competing allegiances. The Chicanos are split not only between the Mexican Mafia and La Nuestra Familia but also North versus South. A relatively unified black population is divided into different warring camps of Crips, Bloods, and 415s.

The world portrayed by our respondents is an important corrective both to the criminal justice literature, which portrays prison life in very simplistic terms, and to those theoretical approaches which attempt to explain prison culture solely in terms of internal or external influences. Our interviews have shown that the linkages between street activities and prison activities are complex and are the result of developments in both arenas. Therefore, instead of attributing primacy to one set of factors as opposed to the other, it may be more useful and more accurate to see the culture and organization of prison and street life as inextricably intertwined, with lines of influence flowing in both directions.

Notes

[1] In addition to these five major groupings, other gangs, including the Vanguards and the Venceremos, are referred to in the literature. Today these groups seem to have disappeared altogether or may in some cases have been incorporated into other gangs. For a further discussion of California gangs, see Castenedo (1981), Conrad (1978), and a report by EMT Associates, Inc. (1985) to the California Department of Corrections. For information on prison gangs in other

parts of the United States, see Beaird (1986), Buentello (1984), Crist (1986), Fong (1990, 1991), Jacobs (1977), and Lane (1989).

[2]There was some disagreement as to the precise dividing line between North and South. Although Fresno was often cited, others said Bakersfield was the dividing line.

[3]The term Trece has a number of meanings especially amongst Chicanos in Los Angeles where it refers to "eme," or "m," the 13th letter in the Spanish alphabet. "Eme" is also used to describe the Mexican Mafia.

[4]It should be noted that during 1992, telephone area codes in the Bay area were changed to two codes—415 and 510. The gang's name refers to the period when one code covered the entire Bay area.

References

Beaird, Lester H. 1986. "Prison gangs: Texas." *Corrections Today* 48 July: 12, 18–22.

Biernacki, Patrick, and Dan Waldorf. 1981. "Snowball sampling: Problems and techniques of chain referral sampling." *Sociological Methods and Research* 10:141–63.

Buentello, Salvator. 1984. "The Texas Syndicate." Texas Department of Corrections. Unpublished report.

California Department of Corrections. 1991. *Historical Trends: Institution and Parole Population, 1970–1990*. Offender Information Services Branch. Data Analysis Unit. Sacramento.

Camp, George, M., and Camille, G. Camp. 1985. *Prison Gangs: Their Extent, Nature and Impact on Prisons*. U.S. Department of Justice, Office of Legal Policy, Federal Justice Research Program. Washington, DC.

Castenedo, Esteban P. (compiler). 1981. *Prison Gang Influences on Street Gangs*. Sacramento: California Department of Youth Authority.

Clemmer, Donald. 1958. *The Prison Community*. New York: Rinehart and Co.

Cloward, Richard. 1977. "Social control in the prison." In *The Sociology of Corrections*, ed. Robert G. Leger and John R. Stratton, 110–32. New York: John Wiley and Sons.

Conrad, John. 1978. "Who's in charge? Control of gang violence in California Prisons." In *Report on Colloquium on Correctional Facilities, 1977*, ed. Nora Harlow. Sacramento, CA: Department of Corrections.

Crist, Roger W. 1986. "Prison gangs: Arizona." *Corrections Today* 48 July: 13, 25–27.

Cummins, Eric. 1991. "History of gang development in California prisons." Unpublished paper.

Davidson, R. Theodore. 1974 (reissued 1983). *Chicano Prisoners: The Key to San Quentin*. Prospect Heights, IL: Waveland Press.

EMT Associates, Inc. 1985. *Comparative Assessment of Strategies to Manage Prison Gang Populations and Gang Related Violence*. Vol. 1–8. Sacramento: California Department of Corrections. Unpublished report.

Fong, Robert S. 1990. "The organizational structure of prison gangs: A Texas case study." *Federal Probation* 54:1.

Fong, Robert, and Salvator Buentello. 1991. "The detection of prison gang development: An empirical assessment." *Federal Probation* 55:1.

Goffman, Erving. 1961. *Asylums*. Garden City, NJ: Anchor.

Irwin. John. 1980. *Prisons in Turmoil*. Boston: Little, Brown and Company.

Irwin, John, and Donald Cressey. 1977. "Thieves, convicts, and the inmate culture." In *The Sociology of Corrections*, ed. Robert G. Leger and John R. Stratton, 133–47. New York: John Wiley and Sons.

Jacobs, James. 1974. "Street gangs behind bars." *Social Problems* 21:395–409.

———. 1977. *Stateville: The Penitentiary in Mass Society*. Chicago: University of Chicago Press.

Klein, Malcolm W., and Cheryl L. Maxson. 1989. "Street gang violence." In *Violent Crime, Violent Criminals*, ed. Neil Allen Weiner and Marvin E. Wolfgang. Newbury Park, CA: Sage.

Lane, Michael P. 1989. "Inmate gangs." *Corrections Today* July: 98–128.

Leger, Robert G., and John R. Stratton. 1977. *The Sociology of Corrections: A Book of Readings*. New York: John Wiley and Sons.

Moore, Joan W. 1978. *Homeboys: Gangs, Drugs, and Prison in the Barrios of Los Angeles*. Philadelphia: Temple University Press.

Porter, Bruce. 1982. "California prison gangs: The price of control." *Corrections Magazine* 8:6–19.

Stojkovic, Stan. 1986. "Social bases of power and control mechanisms among correctional administrators in a prison organization." *Journal of Criminal Justice* 14:157–66.

Sykes, Gresham M., and Sheldon L. Messinger. 1977. "The inmate social system." In *The Sociology of Corrections*, ed. Robert G. Leger and John R. Stratton, 97–109. New York: John Wiley and Sons.

16

The Prison-Industrial Complex

Steven R. Donziger, Editor

The Federal Government
The Department of Justice and the Artificial Case
for More Incarceration

Citizens who look to the government for leadership on crime issues may be disappointed. The federal government often puts out reports that make current policies appear successful or make popular policies appear necessary.

Exaggerating the Threat of Violence

The U.S. Department of Justice, for example, helps to foster the illusion that almost all Americans caught in the web of the criminal justice system are truly dangerous. A 1991 analysis of state prison inmates published by the Department made the following assertion: *94 percent of inmates had been convicted of a violent crime or had a previous sentence to probation or incarceration.*[1] This statistic has been cited by journalists, think tanks, and politicians at every level of government to justify the rapid expansion of the prison population.[2]

The claim is highly misleading. Consider the following claim: "94 percent of the people in America are more than nine feet tall or less than six feet tall." A reader not already aware of the scarcity of nine-foot people might think that America is full of them. The six-foot part of the disjunction does the work and the nine-foot part contributes little. A similar structure infects the government statement that 94 percent of inmates were convicted of a violent crime or had been convicted previously. The magic is in the word "or." It permits the government to consolidate two very different classifications into a single claim. The result is an exaggeration of the extent to which violent criminals populate our prisons.

In fact, government statistics demonstrate that fewer than half of the state prison inmates were convicted of violent crimes. In state prisons, *nearly three times as many offenders had never been convicted of a violent crime as had ever been convicted of one.* Had the government intended to accurately convey what the numbers disclosed, it could have said: *Most prisoners are not violent now and have not been violent in the past.*

The perception of the violent recidivist stalking the public provides a misguided view of the true repeat offender and plays into the "bait and switch" aspect of crime policy. People on probation or parole in any given year account for only 3 percent to 5 percent of all violent offenses known to police that occur each year.[3] A Justice Department study found that only 17.9 percent of state inmates are violent recidivists—that is, they are incarcerated for a violent offense and had committed a prior violent offense.[4] There is a huge difference between 94 percent and 17.9 percent.

The Artificial Case for More Incarceration

In 1992, at the end of the tenure of Attorney General William Barr, the Department of Justice published *The Case for More Incarceration*. The document was produced as part of a determined campaign by the Department of Justice to convince states and cities to build more prisons. It is worth looking at in detail because it is a classic example of how crime data can be misused.[5]

In support of its push for more prisons, the Department of Justice cited data from a 1987 government study that claimed the imprisonment of one inmate "saves" society $430,000 per year.[6] If this figure were true, society would be getting a 17–to–1 rate of return on its investment in prisons based on how much it costs to incarcerate one person for one year. This is a rate of return almost unheard of in the history of private business, much less government, and it invited scrutiny by a number of experts. It turns out that the study arrived at the $430,000 figure by *assuming* that each prisoner (if not incarcerated) would commit 187 street crimes *per year* at a "cost" to the victim of $2,300 per crime. This cost was estimated to result from the value of stolen property or the medical expenses associated with personal injury. Even assuming the cost is accurate, the claim that each inmate would commit 187 street crimes per year is regarded by almost all criminologists as a gross exaggeration. The researchers who came up with the original claim have since retracted it.[7]

Criminologists Franklin Zimring and Gordon Hawkins carefully analyzed the claim of $430,000 in cost savings.[8] They concluded that if the assumptions underlying the study were true, crime in the United States would have disappeared several years ago. Zimring and Hawkins worked the calculation like this: the study estimated there are about 42.5 million crimes reported each year in the United States. If each prisoner commits 187 crimes per year, you would only need to lock up a total of 230,000 additional criminals to wipe out all 42.5 million crimes! Prison populations increased by over 230,000 inmates between the time the Department of Justice collected the data and published the report, yet crime was as prevalent as ever. In fact, there are still between 30 and 40 million crimes reported each year with the prison population now at 1.5 million. Despite the fact that the government study was discredited, Attorney General Barr continued to use it to convince states to build more prisons.

Barr was so eager to pitch his plan for increased prison space that in 1992 the Justice Department flew dozens of state officials at taxpayer expense to a conference in Washington, D.C. After the conference, many participants expressed resentment at the attempt by the federal government to influence their crime policies. One account of the conference said, "A number of officials expressed anger about the format . . . saying the choice of speakers and topics reflected a tightly orchestrated attempt by the Justice Department to stifle dissent."[9] Chase Riveland, Secretary of Corrections for the state of Washington, said: "I would strongly dispute the Attorney General's contention that 94 percent of the people in our correctional systems are violent and/or recidivist. That's not true. In the state of Washington, the bulk of our people are not violent offenders."[10] The former Director of Corrections of Pennsylvania expressed similar sentiments. "The federal government does not have the same cost constraints as the states," said Joseph D. Lehman. "I think it's irresponsible for the Justice Department to put out this message here that we are going to solve the crime problem by building more prisons."[11]

The Hype Over the Threat of Random Murder

Another example of statistical maneuvering by the government is the claim that murder is so random that all Americans now have a "realistic" chance of being a victim of homicide. The murder rate has remained stable in the United States for the last twenty years, so in its latest Uniform Crime Report the FBI could not simply claim that the threat of homicide is increasing. The FBI concluded instead that "something has changed in the constitution of murder to bring about the unparalleled level of concern and fear confronting the Nation."[12] The FBI settled upon increased *randomness* in killing as the cause of alarm, and this is the claim that hit the headlines. *USA Today*, for example, ran a headline that said, "Random Killings Hit a High." The subtitle claimed, "All Have 'Realistic' Chance of Being Victim, Says FBI."[13]

Random killings by strangers are among the most frightening of crimes. Even insignificant fluctuations in the statistics can mean a deep personal tragedy for an innocent victim and his or her family. Yet despite the claim by the government, random murders are not increasing. The following table was created using the government's data starting with the first year the figures were tabulated.

Murder Victim/Offender Relationship					
	1976	1980	1985	1990	1993
Murder Rate	8.8	10.2	7.9	9.0	9.5
% by stranger	13.8%	13.3%	14.5%	14.0%	14.0%
% unknown to police	24.9%	35.8%	26.9%	35.0%	39.3%

Note: Rate is per 100,000.

Source: U.S. Department of Justice, Federal Bureau of Investigation. Data provided by the Criminal Justice Information Services Division.

The data reveal that the murder rate and the percentage of murders committed by strangers have been relatively stable in recent years. The increase is in the number of killings committed by assailants whose identity is unknown to authorities—a trend that most criminologists believe is related to the drug trade, where the killer is unknown to the police but is likely known to the victim. It is fair to claim that the vast majority of such drug-related murders are not *random* even though the assailant is *unknown* to the police.

With all that in mind, consider the report's conclusion: "Every American now has a realistic chance of murder victimization in view of the random nature the crime has assumed. This notion is somewhat supported by the fact that a majority of the Nation's murder victims are now killed by strangers or unknown persons." There is that magical "or" again. The FBI combines stranger murders, which are constant, with unknown murders, which are increasing, to support a claim that does not accurately represent reality.

The FBI claim that "every" American suddenly has a "realistic" chance of being murdered is puzzling. While the number of homicides is higher than one might hope, it does *not* present every American with a new "realistic" chance of being murdered. Occupation is also a factor. Convenience store clerks, for example, are much more likely to be murdered than accountants. Tragically, it is young minority males in the inner city who run a completely disproportionate risk of being killed by street crime. One might even make a case that unless you belong to this high-risk group or have a high-risk job, your odds of being murdered have actually *decreased* in recent years.

One indication that the Department of Justice is less than forthright is that it sometimes downplays its own research when it cuts against official government policy on crime. Release of a 1994 government study that indicated that federal prisons housed a substantial portion of nonviolent offenders for long terms was postponed for several weeks.[14] The study contained information that could have been used to shorten sentences for nonviolent drug offenders at a time when "get tough" crime issues were being hotly debated in Congress. Though much information on crime released by the government is useful, the Commission has a concern that a significant portion of it is subject to political influence.

In addition to being the leading story on network newscasts, crime is often the most common theme in political advertisements among both major political parties.[15] Many political ads play into the prevailing myths of a rising crime rate to justify promises to end parole and build more prison cells.

Special-Interest Groups

Many special-interest groups focus on crime. One group, the National Rifle Association (NRA), is a leading example of an organization that tries to convince the public to support prison expansion. Although known primarily for its vigorous opposition to gun control legislation, the NRA in recent years has entered the battle over crime policy with a flourish. Its agenda appears to be to divert public fear of violent crime away from support of gun control legislation and toward tougher law enforcement and prison expansion. The clout of the NRA is enormous: It counts 3.4 million members and a budget of approximately $140 million, and has the largest single political action committee in the nation.[16] It may have more influence over crime policy than any other private organization, so its claims are worth analyzing in detail.

On the eve of the vote on the 1994 federal crime bill, the NRA bought full-page advertisements in major newspapers urging Congress to increase its allocation for new prison construction from $13 billion to $21 billion and to eliminate crime prevention programs. The ads were part of a public relations initiative called *CrimeStrike*, whose stated purpose was to create a "citizen's movement" to "put real justice back in our criminal justice system" and to "keep violent criminals off our streets." The NRA bankrolled the first "three strikes" initiative in Washington, helped fund a similar, successful ballot initiative in California, and financed a successful campaign to convince the Texas legislature to spend $1 billion on new prisons.

The NRA's Case for More Prisons

The basis for much of the NRA claim that we need more prisons is a report produced by *CrimeStrike* in 1994 called "The Case for Building More Prisons." This paper misuses criminal justice data in a manner strikingly similar to "The Case for More Incarceration," published by the Department of Justice in 1992.

Selective Use of Data. To prove that "serious" victimization dropped from 1980 to 1991, the NRA chose to include in its measure the four violent crimes (murder, rape, robbery, and assault) and also the nonviolent offense of burglary. The inclusion of burglary makes no sense until one realizes that burglary is the crime that decreased the most in the 1980s. By mixing in the nonviolent crime of burglary, the NRA could make it look as if violent crime had dropped significantly when in fact it did not. Indeed, burglary alone accounts for 91 percent of the supposed decrease in violent crime documented in the NRA chart. If burglary were not included, one would find that the serious violent crime rate declined by only 4 percent from 1980 to 1991 despite a 150 percent increase in the number of inmates. If, for example, the NRA had elected to include auto theft instead of burglary in its chart, the crime rate would have *increased*.

Choice of Time Frame. The NRA uses 1980 as a starting point to measure changes in crime because data from that year skews the chart in favor of its desired conclusion. The reason is that 1980 was a peak year for high crime rates; thus, any comparison to a later year would tend to show that crime dropped. In reality, two distinct trends are evident from 1980 to 1991. From 1980 to 1986, incarceration rates rose by 65 percent and violent crime declined by 16 percent. From 1986 to 1991, incarceration increased by 51 percent, but violent crime also increased by 15 percent. The NRA's own data therefore show no clear relationship between incarceration and violent crime.

It is entirely proper for a special-interest group to publish material that advances its goals. When the facts underlying the conclusion are distorted so severely, however, the ethics become more problematic.

The Prison-Industrial Complex

If crime has decreased, one might ask why Americans are constantly warned of perils lurking around the corner. Part of the answer lies in the media attention devoted to firearms violence among young people. Another part of the answer lies in an unexplored corner of the American economic-political landscape. In this corner, fear of crime drives investment and crime control is a source of profit. We call this corner the "prison-industrial complex." Like the military-industrial complex that dominated defense policy during the Cold War, this crucible of private companies and government exercises a powerful influence on crime policy.

The government and private security companies now spend almost as much money on crime control each year as the Pentagon spends on national defense. In the last twenty years, spending on crime control has increased at over twice the rate of defense spending.[17] One hundred billion dollars of public money is spent on law enforcement every year. An additional $65 billion is spent on private security. There is nothing unusual or improper in a private business or individual making money from a government program. But there is an ethical difference when the source of private profit is the growing number of prisoners on the public dole—especially given the evident failure of crime policy to carry out its duties in the most cost-effective manner. From the use of "The Club" to reduce auto theft to home security devices sold by Radio Shack and Sears, crime has become big business, and it is growing rapidly.

Technology Can Improve Crime Fighting and Save Lives

There is no doubt that some efforts by private companies to improve crime-fighting technology are beneficial. Bulletproof vests have saved the lives of an estimated 1,500 law enforcement officers since being introduced in the early 1970s. Computer technology can speed up the filing of crime reports from police cars, saving thousands of work-hours and freeing up more police to patrol the streets. Equipment is being developed to force cars to stop, lessening the need for high-speed chases that cause injury and lawsuits. One company has developed a sticky foam that can freeze suspects who are about to attack or flee.

As laudable as these developments are, they still require caution and vigilance. As we have seen countless times in the area of national defense—a few years ago small bolts sold to the Pentagon cost taxpayers several hundred dollars each—the goals of private industry and the public interest can diverge. While the public is interested in safety, private industry is also concerned with profits. The continued growth of prisons is thus in the interests of the crime control industry, regardless of whether there is a need for more prisons as a matter of public safety.

Prisoners as Raw Material for the Prison Industry

Nils Christie, a Norwegian criminologist and the author of *Crime Control as Industry*, claims that companies that service the criminal justice system need sufficient quantities of raw materials to guarantee long-term growth. An economist looking at almost any industry might make the same simple statement. In the criminal justice field, Christie suggests a frightening scenario: that *the raw material is prisoners*, and industry will do what is necessary to guarantee a steady supply. For the supply of prisoners to grow, criminal justice policies must ensure a sufficient number of incarcerated Americans regardless of whether crime is rising or the incarceration is necessary.

Not all jails and prisons are operated by the government. Increasingly, states and counties are subcontracting the construction and operation of their correctional facilities to private companies, a trend we will examine shortly. In a 1994 article, the *Wall Street Journal* asserted that the private corrections industry uses the war against crime as a lucrative business market much the way the defense industry used the threat of Communism during the Cold War.[18] The article suggested that the prison-industrial complex, like the military-industrial complex, is based on an "iron triangle" between government bureaucracy, private industry, and politicians. The three entities create interlocking financial and political interests to push for a particular policy. In this case, that policy is the expansion of the criminal justice system.

The American prison-industrial complex involves some of the largest investment houses on Wall Street. Goldman Sachs and Co. and Smith Barney Shearson Inc. compete to underwrite jail and prison construction with private, tax-exempt bonds that do not require voter approval. Titans of the defense industry such as Westinghouse Electric and Alliant Techsystems, Inc., have created special divisions to retool their products for law enforcement. Publicly traded prison companies such as the Corrections Corporation of America and Wackenhut Corporation, as well as correctional officer unions, also exercise a powerful influence over criminal justice policy. Private companies are growing rapidly as the correctional population expands, and they are aggressively "exporting" their formula for private jails and prisons to other countries.

The Private Correctional Industry

With more than $250 million in annual revenues, the twenty-one companies that operate private jails and prisons occupy a central position in the prison-industrial complex.[19] They manage 88 prisons under contract with governments that incarcerate about 50,000 inmates. These businesses have experienced a phenomenal rate of growth, given that in 1984 only 2,500 inmates were in private prisons.[20] Though private facilities incarcerate a small portion of the overall correctional population, *the rate of growth of private facilities is currently more than four times the rate of growth of state facilities*.[21] And there is ample reason to believe that as the number of inmates increases—as well as the cost of maintaining them—states will increasingly turn to private companies as a way to save money.

Private Facilities Claim to Operate More Efficiently. The idea behind private jails and prisons is to remove the operation of a facility

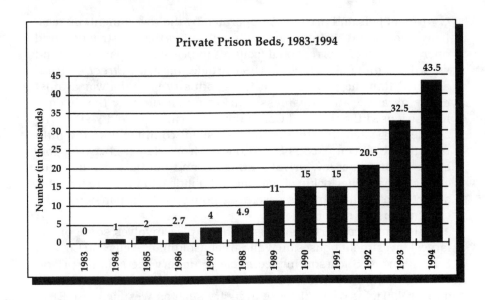

Private Prison Beds, 1983-1994

Source: Thomas, Charles W. (June 30, 1994), *Private Adult Correctional Facility Census*.

from government so it can be run cheaper and more efficiently by a private company.[22] The government pays the company a fixed amount for each day a prisoner is incarcerated, generally about $40. Partly because of lower salaries (private prisons tend to use non-union labor), private facilities claim to operate with a cost savings of 10 to 20 percent over state-run institutions.

Criticisms of Private Facilities. Detractors of private facilities argue that as a matter of public policy, control over an individual's life should not be contracted out to the lowest bidder. Because of the fixed sum paid for each prisoner, in order to maximize profits there is inherent pressure to provide a minimum of services. In so doing, programs such as drug treatment that are proven to lower recidivism might be scrapped solely because they are even slightly more costly. Privatization also raises questions about liability. To what extent, for example, should a private correctional officer with uncertain training be allowed to use force against a prisoner? If an inmate is injured, is it the private company or the government that is responsible? Finally, critics point out that the public usually has diminished control over the financing of private facilities.

The Corrections Corporation of America. Healthy profits await companies able to win contracts from state corrections agencies. The largest private prison company, the Corrections Corporation of

America (CCA), had profits in 1993 of $4 million on $100 million of revenue—a 57 percent increase from the previous year.[23] The founders and officers of CCA include people with major political influence among both Democrats and Republicans.[24] Among them are Doctor Crants, who gave $5,000 to the national Democratic party, and Thomas Beasley, former chair of the Tennessee Republican party. Also on the board is T. Don Hutto, former commissioner of corrections for Arkansas and Virginia. A prestigious law firm, Covington & Burling, represents the company's Washington interests.

Founded in 1983, the CCA controls 30 percent of the private corrections market and is traded on the New York Stock Exchange. Most of its contracts are in Texas, Tennessee, and Louisiana, but it recently launched marketing efforts in the Northeast. In two years, the company expects its profits to double as it increases the number of prison beds it controls from 13,000 to 25,000.[25] Its financial officer recently described the 1994 federal crime bill, which allocated $9.7 billion for prison construction, as "very favorable to us."[26]

The CCA has engaged in extensive marketing to increase the size of the private correctional market and to strengthen its position within that market. In its annual report, it describes itself as the "industry leader in promulgating the benefits of privatization of prisons and other correction and detention facilities . . . the Company from time to time retains registered lobbyists who assist the Company with promoting legislation to allow privatization of correctional facilities."[27] Ted Goins, an investment analyst at Branch, Cabell, & Co. in Richmond, listed CCA as a "theme stock" for the 1990s. In his report on the CCA, Goins cited the federal crime bill and constraints on government spending as reasons "we expect a dramatic increase in the number of prisoners being served by private companies." As a result, Goins gave CCA "a strong buy rating to our clients familiar with the risks of investing in smaller capitalized companies."[28]

Esmor Correctional Services. Esmor Correctional Services, Inc., a publicly traded company based in New York, illustrates the pitfalls of the private corrections industry. Six years ago in New York City, Esmor turned a small hotel near Kennedy Airport into a prison under contract with the federal Immigration and Naturalization Service (INS). The hotel was used to detain the overflow of illegal immigrants who arrived at the airport. Esmor parlayed that one contract into a chain of ten detention centers and boot camps in several states. By 1995, it had grown into the fifth-largest private corrections company in the country, with $36 million in annual revenue.

Esmor recently won a bidding war with other private corrections companies to manage a 300-bed detention center for illegal immigrants in Elizabeth, New Jersey. Esmor was awarded the contract for

$54 million, a full $20 million less than the next highest bid. Once awarded the contract, the company hired correctional staff with little or no experience, served a substandard diet to the inmates, and shackled detainees in leg irons when they met their lawyers. Despite repeated warnings from lawyers and staff that inmate frustration was rising, the company did virtually nothing to correct the problems. In the summer of 1995, the detention center exploded in violence. The uprising injured twenty detainees and caused damage in excess of $100,000.

According to staff at the facility, in order to keep costs in line with the low bid, the company cut corners and created the conditions for the disturbance. One correctional officer told a local newspaper he was placed on duty with no training and no prior experience in corrections or security. His wages were $8.60 per hour. Carl Frick, who served as the facility's first warden, said Esmor officials had instructed him to lie to INS officials about conditions at the facility. He said he was instructed to renegotiate a food service contract because $1.12 per day was considered too expensive for an inmate's meals. "They don't want to run a jail," said Frick, referring to the Esmor officials. "They want to run a motel as cheaply as possible. Money, money, money, that's all that was important to them. It was ridiculous." The local county prosecutor mocked Esmor as "privatization at its worst" and called for the closing of the detention center until the problems could be fixed.

What to Do with Private Prisons

Despite the problems with Esmor, it appears that some private corrections companies manage inmates better than some state-run facilities. A large number of state-run prisons are overcrowded and offer little opportunity for inmates to gain the skills needed to function on the outside. If private companies can operate facilities with sufficient control but also adequate care for the needs of inmates, then they should be allowed to make realistic bids on correctional projects. Their performance should be assessed by how well inmates do after release.

The trend toward using prisoners as a source of profit must be thought through carefully. Private companies have a built-in incentive to cut corners when providing drug treatment and other services to inmates that can lower the chance crime will be committed after release. Private companies also have a financial interest in supporting measures that will increase the need for construction of correctional facilities, regardless of whether those measures are needed. We should consider whether private companies should be allowed to lobby legislators to pass laws that will expand the inmate population. State and local governments should subject the performance of private facilities to a rigorous external review by an independent body.

Industries Benefit from Prison Expansion

In addition to private corrections companies, many other companies are positioned to profit from the billions of dollars flowing into local and state-run corrections systems. Private firms provide an untold number of goods and services to facilities, including food service, personnel management, architectural design, medical services, drug detection, vocational assessment, and transportation.[29] Companies also sell protective vests for correctional officers, closed-circuit television systems, fencing, flame-retardant bedding, clog-proof waste disposal systems, furniture, clothes, perimeter security systems, and a host of other products.[30] The American Jail Association holds an annual convention for companies to market their products. Last year, advertisements for the convention asked people to "Tap into the Sixty-Five Billion Local Jails Market." "The local jail market is very lucrative!" the flier said. "Jails are BIG BUSINESS!!"

Correctional Medical Services of St. Louis provides medical care to 150,000 inmates—three times as many as it served in 1987.[31] The fiscal outlook for Correctional Medical Services is promising because longer sentences create older inmates and thus more demand for medical services. Advertising for prison products and services in *Corrections Today*, the industry trade magazine, has tripled since 1980. Finally, the Census Bureau reports that the hiring and training of correctional officers is the "fastest-growing function . . . out of everything the government does."[32] More than 523,000 full-time employees worked in corrections in 1992—more than all the people employed by any Fortune 500 company except General Motors.[33]

Correctional Facilities as a Rural Growth Industry

Another side of the "iron triangle" of the prison-industrial complex is communities that look to prisons as a source of economic growth. Even though most offenders come from cities, since 1980, the bulk of new prison construction has taken place in economically depressed rural communities—so much so that demographers consider the punishment of crime to be a leading rural growth industry.[34] Rural areas house such a large portion of the prison population that *5 percent of the national increase in rural population from 1980 to 1990 is accounted for by prisoners*.[35] In rural counties acquiring a jail or

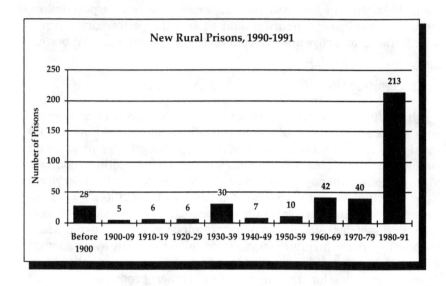

Source: Beale, Calvin L. (June 1993), "Prisons, Population, and Jobs in Nonmetro America," *Rural Development Perspectives*, vol. 8, no. 3, p. 16.

prison, the new inmate population amounted to nearly half of all population growth during the 1980s.

Correctional Facilities Considered a Bonanza for Economic Development. Many small towns compete to convince state officials that their community will be the best location for prison facilities that could last for as long as a century.[36] A typical prison might have several hundred staff members and a payroll of several million dollars. Free labor from prison work crews can alleviate the strains on small-town budgets; in Florida, for example, prisoners paint public buildings and clean roads and parks.[37] Economic benefits come not only from payroll, but also from construction, purchases from local vendors, and increased tax revenues from employees moving into the area. Also, jails and prisons are tax-exempt.

Low Community Opposition in Rural Areas. Opposition to the construction of new prisons is often lowest in rural areas that are in need of economic development. In 1984, twenty-three state correctional departments reported local opposition to prison construction; four years later, that number had dropped to five, and twenty-four departments reported only community support.[38] In Texas, fifty towns recently solicited a new prison from the Texas Department of Criminal Justice. Some towns "bombarded the board . . . with incentives that range from country club memberships for wardens to long-horn cattle for the prison grounds." A town in Illinois put together a rap song and bought television time as part of a public relations blitz for state legislators.[39] In Minnesota, the small town of Appleton (pop. 1,500) issued $28.5 million in bonds to build a new prison *before* it had a commitment that its cells would be needed.[40] Ernie Van Sant, chief of prison construction for the California Department of Corrections, suggested a reason why so many towns want prisons: "We are not an industrial developer. We don't use a lot of chemicals. We're somewhat recession-proof."[41] In areas where the industrial or agricultural base is in decline, prisons present a bright alternative.

Economic Benefits Are Often Not as High as Anticipated. Many local leaders have ended up disappointed with the economic impact of new prisons. A quarter of all California towns with a state prison have a median family income below the federal poverty line.[42] The prison complex in Susanville, a small town in northeastern California, recently doubled its capacity to 10,000 inmates. The subsequent influx of family members of the inmates has strained social services, diminished the quality of education by increasing class size, increased crime, and divided residents over the need for the prison. A study of the effects of a new prison in Washington state found that it changed the character of the town: Residents started locking their doors and social problems increased.[43] The private prison in Appleton, Minnesota, remained empty months after it opened because the state could not afford to send prisoners there. Nevertheless, the town still had to pay exorbitant sums to staff the vacant prison in the hope that other states would rent the cells to absorb their overflow of prisoners.

Signs of Corruption. A recent investigation by the *Los Angeles Times* revealed that the state of California has paid exorbitant sums to rural landowners for property where it builds prisons.[44] Sellers included major farming corporations, a timber company, a bank, and wealthy businesspeople. Many of the individuals who sold property for prison construction were also campaign donors. In one egregious case, a 5,000-acre farm was bought in 1990 for $374 per acre. Two weeks later, the owners asked the California Department of Corrections to buy the land as a site for a new prison. After the intervention of a local legislator who co-authored the "three strikes" legislation, the state paid $3,500 an acre for the farm—almost ten times the original purchase price. The state then spent another $3 million to clean up pesticides and other toxins from the land. It turned out that the owners of the farm had donated money to the political campaigns of the state legislator who intervened on their behalf.

The Rise of the Correctional Officers

A byproduct of the expansion of the prison-industrial complex is the increasing influence of unions of prison guards over criminal justice policy. As the number of inmates has grown, so has the number of guards needed to watch over them.[45] The doubling and tripling of correctional officers in most states has created enormous clout for the unions that represent them. In Illinois, for example, the union of prison guards pushed through legislation to ban the privatization of prisons and to stiffen sanctions against inmates found carrying weapons.[46] The Michigan Corrections Organization has opposed proposals to lower the rate of incarceration by making prisoners eligible for boot camps.[47] "It's becoming a dollar-driven corrections policy in the state," says Mel Grieshaber, the legislative coordinator for the union.[48]

Nowhere are prison guards more active and powerful than in California. The guards' union in California, the California Correctional Peace Officers Association, boasts that thirty-eight of forty-four bills it pushed in the state legislature under the last three governors were enacted.[49] The union has grown in a decade from 4,000 to 23,000 correctional officers, parole agents, and prison counselors. It has achieved an extraordinary pay and benefit plan under which the average salary for a correctional officer is $55,000 a year, far above the $43,000 paid to public school teachers and more than a tenured associate professor with a Ph.D. in the California state university system.

Collecting about $8 million a year in dues, the union has become the second-largest campaign donor in the state.[50] It spends about $1 million during each election cycle to support candidates for governor and the legislature who promote prison expansion. Its contributions are twice as large as those of the California Teachers Association, which has ten times as many members. In 1992, the union gave its largest contribution—over $80,000—to a relatively unknown candidate who ran against an outspoken critic of prison expansion who was chairperson of the Ways and Means Committee. The unknown candidate lost. The union donated the second-highest amount in support of the "three strikes and you're out" ballot initiative and spent more than $1 million on behalf of Governor Pete Wilson's last campaign. "We think we put Wilson over the top," said union president Don Novey.

Conclusion

There is nothing more viscerally disturbing than the fear of being the victim of a violent crime. Much of that fear has a legitimate basis in fact, for violent street crime is a real threat, particularly in the inner city. Yet fear of crime rather than crime itself drives much criminal justice policy in the United States. Fear of crime and crime are not the same thing. Policies based on fear are not the same as policies based on fact.

Particularly troubling is the part of our fear that does not stem from the threat of crime, but is instead created by the way crime data is presented. This often convinces us to spend tax dollars so that we *feel* like we are lowering the fear even though we are not lowering the crime. Also alarming is the fact that some entities—business and government among them—*profit financially or politically when fear is high*. The more fear can be inflamed, the more intense public passion about crime becomes and the easier it is to gain votes by proposing harsher sentences and more prisons. It is also easier for private companies to get new business, for retailers to expand the market for home security devices, and for unions of correctional officers to increase their salaries. And through it all, this fear can be used to get additional "raw material" to feed the growth of jails and prisons.

Notes

[1]U.S. Department of Justice, Bureau of Justice Statistics. *Survey of State Prison Inmates, 1991*. Washington, DC: U.S. Government Printing Office.

[2]See, e.g., Dilulio, John J. January 20, 1995. *Crime in America: Three Ways to Prevent It*. Congressional Testimony. Washington, DC: Brookings Institution.

[3]U.S. Department of Justice, Bureau of Justice Statistics. August 1995. *Probation and Parole Violators in State Prison, 1991*. Washington, DC: U.S. Government Printing Office: 10; U.S. Department of Justice, Federal Bureau of Investigation. August 30, 1992. *Crime in the United States—1991*. Washington, DC: U.S. Government Printing Office: 10.

[4]U.S. Department of Justice, Bureau of Justice Statistics. July 1987. Bulletin. *Recidivism of Felons on Probation, 1986–89*. Washington, DC: U.S. Government Printing Office: 6.

[5]Tonry, Michael. February 1993. General Barr's Last Stand. *Overcrowded Times*. Vol. 4, no. 1, pp. 2–3.

[6]U.S. Department of Justice, Bureau of Justice Statistics. July 1987. Bulletin. *Making Confinement Decisions*. Washington, DC: U.S. Government Printing Office.

[7]Greenwood, Peter, and Susan Turner. March 1987. *Selective Incapacitation Revisited*. Santa Monica, CA: Rand Corporation.

[8]Zimring, Franklin, and Gordon Hawkins. October 1988. The New Mathematics of Imprisonment. *Crime and Delinquency*. Vol. 34, no. 4, pp. 425–36.

[9]Fischer, Craig, ed. April 1, 1992. Washington Report: Justice Department Raises Eyebrows with Focus on Need for Prisons. *Criminal Justice Newsletter*. Vol. 23, no. 7. Washington, DC: Pace Publications.

[10]Ibid.

[11]Ibid.

[12]U.S. Department of Justice, Federal Bureau of Investigation. December 4, 1994. *Crime in the United States—1993*. Washington, DC: U.S. Government Printing Office: Section V.

[13]Davis, Robert, and Sam Vincent Meddis. December 5, 1994. Random Killings Hit a High. *USA Today*: 1A.

[14]U.S. Department of Justice. February 1994. *An Analysis of Nonviolent Drug Offenders with Minimal Criminal Histories*. Washington, DC: U.S. Government Printing Office.

[15]Kurtz, Howard. November 2. 1994. Ads Use Crimes' Pain for Candidates' Gain. *Washington Post*: A1; September 9, 1994. In 1994 Political Ads, Crime Is the Weapon of Choice. *Washington Post*: A1.

[16]Butterfield, Fox. June 26, 1995. Aggressive Strategy by N.R.A. Has Left Its Finances Reeling. *New York Times*: 1.

[17]U.S. Department of Justice, Bureau of Justice Statistics. September 1992. Bulletin. *Justice Expenditure and Employment, 1990*. Washington, DC: U.S. Government Printing Office: 4, Table 4; U.S. Department of Defense. March 1994. *National Defense Budget Estimates for FY 1995*. Washington, DC: Office of the Comptroller of the Department of Defense: 147, Table 7–1.

[18]Thomas, Paulette. May 12, 1994. Making Crime Pay: Triangle of Interests Creates Infrastructure to Fight Lawlessness. *Wall Street Journal*: A1.

[19]Ramirez, Anthony. August 14, 1994. Privatizing America's Prisons, Slowly. *New York Times*: sec. 3, p. 1.

[20]Thomas, Charles W. March 1, 1995. *Private Adult Correctional Facility Census*, 8th ed. Gainesville, FL: Private Corrections Project, University of Florida: vii.

[21]Ibid.

[22]See, e.g., Robbins, Ira P. April-May 1986. Privatization of Corrections: Defining the Issues. *Judicature*. Vol. 69, no. 6, pp. 325–31.

[23]Ramirez, Anthony. August 14, 1994. Privatizing America's Prisons, Slowly. *New York Times*: sec. 3, p. 1.

[24]Thomas, Paulette. May 12, 1994. Making Crime Pay: Triangle of Interests Creates Infrastructure to Fight Lawlessness. *Wall Street Journal*: A1.

[25]Ramirez, Anthony. August 14, 1994. Privatizing America's Prisons, Slowly. *New York Times*: sec. 3, p. 1.

[26]Thomas, Paulette. May 12, 1994. Making Crime Pay: Triangle of Interests Creates Infrastructure to Fight Lawlessness. *Wall Street Journal*: A1.

[27]Securities and Exchange Commission (SEC). *Annual Report of Form 10-K Under the Securities Exchange Act of 1934 for the Fiscal Year Ended December 31, 1993*: Corrections Corporation of America. Washington, DC: SEC: 11.

[28]Goins, Ted. 1994. *Institutional Research*. Richmond, VA: Branch Cabell.

[29]Lilly, J. Robert, and Paul Knepper. April 1993. The Corrections-Commercial Complex. *Crime and Delinquency*. Vol. 39, no. 2, p. 154; Robbins, Ira P. April-May 1986. Privatization of Corrections: Defining the Issues. *Judicature*. Vol. 69, no. 6, p. 326.

[30]Lilly, J. Robert, and Paul Knepper. April 1993. The Corrections-Commercial Complex. *Crime and Delinquency*. Vol. 39, no. 2, p. 155.

[31]Meddis, Sam Vincent, and Deborah Sharp. December 13, 1994. Prison Business Is a Blockbuster. *USA Today*: 10A.

[32]Ibid.

[33]Ibid.

[34]Beale, Calvin L. June 1993. Prisons, Population and Jobs in NonMetro America. *Rural Development Perspectives*. Vol. 8, no. 3, pp. 16–19.

[35]Ibid., p. 17.

[36]See, e.g., Welch, Randy. March 1991. Praying for Prisons. *State Legislatures*: 28–30; Lane, Laura. February 20, 1994. Prisons a Growing Industry. *Sunday Herald-Times* (Bloomington/Bedford, IN): A1, A10; Beale, Calvin L. June 1993. Prisons, Population and Jobs in NonMetro America. *Rural Development Perspectives*. Vol. 8, no. 3, pp. 16–19; LaGanga, Maria L. October 18, 1994. New Prisons No Panacea for Ills of Rural California. *Los Angeles Times*.

[37]Welch, Randy. March 1991. Praying for Prisons. *State Legislatures*: 29.

[38]LaGanga, Maria L. October 18, 1994. New Prisons No Panacea for Ills of Rural California. *Los Angeles Times*: A6.

[39]Welch, Randy. March 1991. Praying for Prisons. *State Legislatures*: 28.

[40]*New York Times* News Service. February 4, 1993. With Private Prison, Town Hopes Crime Will Pay. *Chicago Tribune*: 6.

[41]LaGanga, Maria L. October 18, 1994. New Prisons No Panacea for Ills of Rural California. *Los Angeles Times*: A6.

[42]Ibid.

[43]Carlson, Katherine A. January 1992. Doing Good and Looking Bad: A Case Study of Prison/Community Relations. *Crime and Delinquency*. Vol. 38, No. 1: 56–69.

[44]Morain, Dan. Firm Reaps Profit from Desolate Prison Site. *Los Angeles Times*.

[45]See, e.g., December 1991. The Growing Clout of Prison Guards. *Governing*: 37; Schiraldi, Vincent. October 1994. *The Undue Influence of California's Prison Guards' Union: California's Correctional-Industrial Complex*. San Francisco: Center on Juvenile and Criminal Justice; Domanick, Joe. September 2–8, 1994. Who's Guarding the Guards? *LA Weekly*: 20–26; Hurst, John. February 6, 1994. The Big House That Don Novey Built: Working the PR, Spreading Big Bucks, A Candy Union Boss Demands More Prisons and Top Pay for His Guards. *Los Angeles Times Magazine*: 16.

[46]December 1991. The Growing Clout of Prison Guards. *Governing*: 37.

[47]Ibid.

[48]Ibid.

[49]Foote, Caleb. June 1993. *The Prison Population Explosion: California's Rogue Elephant*. San Francisco: Center on Juvenile and Criminal Justice: 12.

[50]Alexander, Kim. July 1993. *Deep Pockets: 1991–92 Top Ten Contributors to California Legislative Campaigns*. Sacramento: California Common Cause; Foote, Caleb. June 1993. *The Prison Population Explosion: California's Rogue Elephant*. San Francisco: Center on Juvenile and Criminal Justice: 12.

17

"This Man Has Expired"
Witness to an Execution

Robert Johnson

The death penalty has made a comeback in recent years. In the late sixties and through most of the seventies, such a thing seemed impossible. There was a moratorium on executions in the U.S., backed by the authority of the Supreme Court. The hiatus lasted roughly a decade. Coming on the heels of a gradual but persistent decline in the use of the death penalty in the Western world, it appeared to some that executions would pass from the American scene [cf. *Commonweal*, January 15, 1988]. Nothing could have been further from the truth.

Beginning with the execution of Gary Gilmore in 1977, over 100 people have been put to death, most of them in the last few years. Some 2,200 prisoners are presently confined on death rows across

From Commonweal, Vol. 116, No. 1 (January 13), pp. 9–15, © Commonweal Foundation 1989. Reprinted by permission.

the nation. The majority of these prisoners have lived under sentence of death for years, in some cases a decade or more, and are running out of legal appeals. It is fair to say that the death penalty is alive and well in America, and that executions will be with us for the foreseeable future.

Gilmore's execution marked the resurrection of the modern death penalty and was big news. It was commemorated in a best-selling tome by Norman Mailer, *The Executioner's Song*. The title was deceptive. Like others who have examined the death penalty, Mailer told us a great deal about the condemned but very little about the executioners. Indeed, if we dwell on Mailer's account, the executioner's story is not only unsung; it is distorted.

Gilmore's execution was quite atypical. His was an instance of state-assisted suicide accompanied by an element of romance and played out against a backdrop of media fanfare. Unrepentant and unafraid, Gilmore refused to appeal his conviction. He dared the state of Utah to take his life, and the media repeated the challenge until it became a taunt that may well have goaded officials to action. A failed suicide pact with his lover staged only days before the execution, using drugs she delivered to him in a visit marked by unusual intimacy, added a hint of melodrama to the proceedings. Gilmore's final words, "Let's do it," seemed to invite the lethal hail of bullets from the firing squad. The nonchalant phrase, at once fatalistic and brazenly rebellious, became Gilmore's epitaph. It clinched his outlaw-hero image, and found its way onto tee shirts that confirmed his celebrity status.

Befitting a celebrity, Gilmore was treated with unusual leniency by prison officials during his confinement on death row. He was, for example, allowed to hold a party the night before his execution, during which he was free to eat, drink, and make merry with his guests until the early morning hours. This is not entirely unprecedented. Notorious English convicts of centuries past would throw farewell balls in prison on the eve of their executions. News accounts of such affairs sometimes included a commentary on the richness of the table and the quality of the dancing. For the record, Gilmore served Tang, Kool-Aid, cookies, and coffee, later supplemented by contraband pizza and an unidentified liquor. Periodically, he gobbled drugs obligingly provided by the prison pharmacy. He played a modest arrangement of rock music albums but refrained from dancing.

Gilmore's execution generally, like his parting fete, was decidedly out of step with the tenor of the modern death penalty. Most condemned prisoners fight to save their lives, not to have them taken. They do not see their fate in romantic terms; there are no farewell parties. Nor are they given medication to ease their anxiety or win their compliance. The subjects of typical executions remain anonymous to the public and even to their keepers. They are very much alone at the end.

In contrast to Mailer's account, the focus of the research I have conducted is on the executioners themselves as they carry out typical executions. In my experience executioners—not unlike Mailer himself—can be quite voluble, and sometimes quite moving, in expressing themselves. I shall draw upon their words to describe the death work they carry out in our name.

Death Work and Death Workers

Executioners are not a popular subject of social research, let alone conversation at the dinner table or cocktail party. We simply don't give the subject much thought. When we think of executioners at all, the imagery runs to individual men of disreputable, or at least questionable, character who work stealthily behind the scenes to carry out their grim labors. We picture hooded men hiding in the shadow of the gallows, or anonymous figures lurking out of sight behind electric chairs, gas chambers, firing blinds, or, more recently, hospital gurneys. We wonder who would do such grisly work and how they sleep at night.

This image of the executioner as a sinister and often solitary character is today misleading. To be sure, a few states hire free-lance executioners and traffic in macabre theatrics. Executioners may be picked up under cover of darkness and some may still wear black hoods. But today, executions are generally the work of a highly disciplined and efficient team of correctional officers.

Broadly speaking, the execution process as it is now practiced starts with the prisoner's confinement on death row, an oppressive prison-within-a-prison where the condemned are housed, sometimes for years, awaiting execution. Death work gains momentum when an execution date draws near and the prisoner is moved to the death house, a short walk from the death chamber. Finally, the process culminates in the death watch, a twenty-four-hour period that ends when the prisoner has been executed.

This final period, the death watch, is generally undertaken by correctional officers who work as a team and report directly to the prison warden. The warden or his representative, in turn, must by law preside over the execution. In many states, it is a member of the death watch or execution team, acting under the warden's authority, who in fact plays the formal role of executioner. Though this officer may technically work alone, his teammates view the execution as a shared responsibility. As one officer on the death watch told me in no uncertain terms: "We all take part in it; we all play 100 percent in it, too. That takes the load off this one individual [who pulls the switch]." The formal executioner concurred. "Everyone on the team can do it, and nobody will tell you I did it. I know my team." I found nothing in my research to dispute these claims.

The officers of these death watch teams are our modern executioners. As part of a larger study of the death work process, I studied one such group. This team, comprised of nine seasoned officers of varying ranks, had carried out five electrocutions at the time I began my research. I interviewed each officer on the team after the fifth execution, then served as an official witness at a sixth electrocution. Later, I served as a behind-the-scenes observer during their seventh execution. The results of this phase of my research form the substance of this essay.

The Death Watch Team

The death watch or execution team members refer to themselves, with evident pride, as simply "the team." This pride is shared by other correctional officials. The warden at the institution I was observing praised members of the team as solid citizens—in his words, country boys. These country boys, he assured me, could be counted on to do the job and do it well. As a fellow administrator put it, "an execution is something [that] needs to be done and good people, dedicated people who believe in the American system should do it. And there's a certain amount of feeling, probably one to another, that they're part of that—that when they have to hang tough, they can do it, and they can do it right. And that it's just the right thing to do."

The official view is that an execution is a job that has to be done, and done right. The death penalty is, after all, the law of the land. In this context, the phrase "done right" means that an execution should be a proper, professional, dignified undertaking. In the words of a prison administrator, "We had to be sure that we did it properly, professionally, and [that] we gave as much dignity to the person as we possibly could in the process. . . . If you've gotta do it, it might just as well be done the way it's supposed to be done—without any sensation."

In the language of the prison officials, "proper" refers to procedures that go off smoothly; "professional" means without personal feelings that intrude on the procedures in any way. The desire for executions that take place "without any sensation" no doubt refers to the absence of media sensationalism, particularly if there should be an embarrassing and undignified hitch in the procedures, for example, a prisoner who breaks down or becomes violent and must be forcibly placed in the electric chair as witnesses, some from the media, look on in horror. Still, I can't help but note that this may be a revealing slip of the tongue. For executions are indeed meant to go off without any human feeling, without any sensation. A profound absence of feeling would seem to capture the bureaucratic ideal embodied in the modern execution.

The view of executions held by the execution team members parallels that of correctional administrators but is somewhat more restrained. The officers of the team are closer to the killing and dying, and are less apt to wax abstract or eloquent in describing the process. Listen to one man's observations:

> It's a job. I don't take it personally. You know, I don't take it like I'm having a grudge against this person and this person has done something to me. I'm just carrying out a job, doing what I was asked to do. . . . This man has been sentenced to death in the courts. This is the law and he broke this law, and he has to suffer the consequences. And one of the consequences is to put him to death.

I found that few members of the execution team support the death penalty outright or without reservation. Having seen executions close up, many of them have lingering doubts about the justice or wisdom of this sanction. As one officer put it:

> I'm not sure the death penalty is the right way. I don't know if there is a right answer. So I look at it like this: if it's gotta be done, at least it can be done in a humane way, if there is such a word for it. . . . The only way it should be done, I feel, is the way we do it. It's done professionally; it's not no horseplaying. Everything is done by documentation. On time. By the book.

Arranging executions that occur "without any sensation" and that go "by the book" is no mean task, but it is a task that is undertaken in earnest by the execution team. The tone of the enterprise is set by the team leader, a man who takes a hard-boiled, no-nonsense approach to correctional work in general and death work in particular. "My style," he says, "is this: if it's a job to do, get it done. Do it and that's it." He seeks out kindred spirits, men who see killing condemned prisoners as a job—a dirty job one does reluctantly, perhaps, but above all a job one carries out dispassionately and in the line of duty.

To make sure that line of duty is a straight and accurate one, the death watch team has been carefully drilled by the team leader in the mechanics of execution. The process has been broken down into simple, discrete tasks and practiced repeatedly. The team leader describes the division of labor in the following exchange:

> The execution team is a nine-officer team and each one has certain things to do. When I would train you, maybe you'd buckle a belt, that might be all you'd have to do. . . . And you'd be expected to do one thing and that's all you'd be expected to do. And if everybody does what they were taught, or what they were trained to do, at the end the man would be put in the chair and everything would be complete. It's all come together now.
>
> So it's broken down into very small steps. . . .
>
> *Very small*, yes. Each person has one thing to do.
>
> I see. What's the purpose of breaking it down into such small steps?
>
> So people won't get confused. I've learned it's kind of a tense time. When you're executin' a person, killing a person—you call it killin', executin', whatever you want—the man dies anyway. I find the less you got on your mind, why, the better you'll carry it out. So it's just very simple things. And so far, you know, it's all come together, we haven't had any problems.

This division of labor allows each man on the execution team to become a specialist, a technician with a sense of pride in his work. Said one man,

> My assignment is the leg piece. Right leg. I roll his pants' leg up, place a piece [electrode] on his leg, strap his leg in. . . . I've got all the moves down pat. We train from different posts; I can do any of them. But that's my main post.

The implication is not that the officers are incapable of performing multiple or complex tasks, but simply that it is more efficient to focus each officer's efforts on one easy task.

An essential part of the training is practice. Practice is meant to produce a confident group, capable of fast and accurate performance under pressure. The rewards of practice are reaped in improved performance. Executions take place with increasing efficiency, and eventually occur with precision. "The first one was grisly," a team member confided to me. He explained that there was a certain amount of fumbling, which made the execution seem interminable. There were technical problems as well: The generator was set too high so the body was badly burned. But that is the past, the officer assured me. "The ones now, we know what we're doing. It's just like clockwork."

The Death Watch

The death-watch team is deployed during the last twenty-four hours before an execution. In the state under study, the death watch starts at 11 o'clock the night before the execution and ends at 11 o'clock the next night when the execution takes place. At least two officers would be with the prisoner at any given time during that period. Their objective is to keep the prisoner alive and "on schedule." That is, to move him through a series of critical and cumulatively demoralizing junctures that begin with his last meal and end with his last walk. When the time comes, they must deliver the prisoner up for execution as quickly and unobtrusively as possible.

Broadly speaking, the job of the death watch officer, as one man put it, "is to sit and keep the inmate calm for the last twenty-four hours—and get the man ready to go." Keeping a condemned prisoner calm means, in part, serving his immediate needs. It seems paradoxical to think of the death watch officers as providing services to the condemned, but the logistics of the job make service a central obligation of the officers. Here's how one officer made this point:

> Well, you can't help but be involved with many of the things that he's involved with. Because if he wants to make a call to his family, well, you'll have to dial the number. And you keep records of whatever calls he makes. If he wants a cigarette, well he's not allowed to keep matches so you light it for him. You've got to pour his coffee, too. So you're aware what he's doing. It's not like you can just ignore him. You've gotta just be with him whether he wants it or not, and cater to his needs.

Officers cater to the condemned because contented inmates are easier to keep under control. To a man, the officers say this is so. But one can never trust even a contented, condemned prisoner.

The death-watch officers see condemned prisoners as men with explosive personalities. "You don't know what, what a man's gonna do," noted one officer. "He's liable to snap, he's liable to pass out. We watch him all the time to prevent him from committing suicide. You've got to be ready—he's liable to do anything." The prisoner is never out of at least one officer's sight. Thus surveillance is constant, and control, for all intents and purposes, is total.

Relations between the officers and their charges during the death watch can be quite intense. Watching and being watched are central to this enterprise, and these are always engaging activities, particularly when the stakes are life and death. These relations are, nevertheless, utterly impersonal; there are no grudges but neither is there compassion or fellow-feeling. Officers are civil but cool; they keep an emotional distance from the men they are about to kill. To do otherwise, they maintain, would make it harder to execute condemned prisoners. The attitude of the officers is that the prisoners arrive as strangers and are easier to kill if they stay that way.

During the last five or six hours, two specific team officers are assigned to guard the prisoner. Unlike their more taciturn and aloof colleagues on earlier shifts, these officers make a conscious effort to talk with the prisoner. In one officer's words, "We just keep them right there and keep talking to them—about anything except the chair." The point of these conversations is not merely to pass time; it is to keep tabs on the prisoner's state of mind, and to steer him away from subjects that might depress, anger, or otherwise upset him. Sociability, in other words, quite explicitly serves as a source of social control. Relationships, such as they are, serve purely manipulative ends. This is impersonality at its worst, masquerading as concern for the strangers one hopes to execute with as little trouble as possible.

Generally speaking, as the execution moves closer, the mood becomes more somber and subdued. There is a last meal. Prisoners can order pretty much what they want, but most eat little or nothing at all. At this point, the prisoners may steadfastly maintain that their executions will be stayed. Such bravado is belied by their loss of appetite. "You can see them going down," said one officer. "Food is the last thing they got on their minds."

Next the prisoners must box their meager worldly goods. These are inventoried by the staff, recorded on a one-page checklist form, and marked for disposition to family or friends. Prisoners are visibly saddened, even moved to tears, by this procedure, which at once summarizes their lives and highlights the imminence of death. At this point, said one of the officers, "I really get into him; I watch him real close." The execution schedule, the officer pointed out, is "picking up momentum, and we don't want to lose control of the situation."

This momentum is not lost on the condemned prisoner. Critical milestones have been passed. The prisoner moves in a limbo existence devoid of food or possessions; he has seen the last of such things, unless he receives a stay of execution and rejoins the living. His identity is expropriated as well. The critical juncture in this regard is the shaving of the man's head (including facial hair) and right leg. Hair is shaved to facilitate the electrocution; it reduces physical resistance to electricity and minimizes singeing and burning. But the process has obvious psychological significance as well, adding greatly to the momentum of the execution.

The shaving procedure is quite public and intimidating. The condemned man is taken from his cell and seated in the middle of the tier. His hands and feet are cuffed, and he is dressed only in under-shorts. The entire death watch team is assembled around him. They stay at a discrete distance, but it is obvious that they are there to maintain control should he resist in any way or make any untoward move. As a rule, the man is overwhelmed. As one officer told me in blunt terms, "Come eight o'clock, we've got a dead man. Eight o'clock is when we shave the man. We take his identity; it goes with the hair." This taking of identity is indeed a collective process—the team makes a forceful "we," the prisoner their helpless object. The staff is confident that the prisoner's capacity to resist is now compromised. What is left of the man erodes gradually and, according to the officers, perceptibly over the remaining three hours before the execution.

After the prisoner has been shaved, he is then made to shower and don a fresh set of clothes for the execution. The clothes are unremark-able in appearance, except that velcro replaces buttons and zippers, to reduce the chance of burning the body. The main significance of the clothes is symbolic: they mark the prisoner as a man who is ready for execution. Now physically "prepped," to quote one team member, the prisoner is placed in an empty tomblike cell, the death cell. All that is left is the wait. During this fateful period, the prisoner is more like an object "without any sensation" than like a flesh-and-blood person on the threshold of death.

For condemned prisoners, like Gilmore, who come to accept and even to relish their impending deaths, a genuine calm seems to prevail. It is as if they can transcend the dehumanizing forces at work around them and go to their deaths in peace. For most condemned prisoners, however, numb resignation rather than peaceful acceptance is the norm. By the accounts of the death-watch officers, these more typical prisoners are beaten men. Listen to the officers' accounts:

> A lot of 'em die in their minds before they go to that chair. I've never known of one or heard of one putting up a fight. . . . By the time they walk to the chair, they've completely faced it. Such a reality most people can't understand. Cause they don't fight it. They don't seem to have anything to say. It's just something like "Get it over with." They may be numb, sort of in a trance.

> They go through stages. And, at this stage, they're real humble. Humblest bunch of people I ever seen. Most all of 'em is real, real weak. Most of the time you'd only need one or two people to carry out an execution, as weak and as humble as they are.

These men seem barely human and alive to their keepers. They wait meekly to be escorted to their deaths. The people who come for them are the warden and the remainder of the death watch team, flanked by high-ranking correctional officials. The warden reads the court order, known popularly as a death warrant. This is, as one officer said, "the real deal," and nobody misses its significance. The condemned prisoners then go to their deaths compliantly, captives of the inexorable, irresistible momentum of the situation. As one officer put it, "There's no struggle. . . . They just walk right on in there." So too, do the staff "just walk right on in there," following a routine they have come to know well. Both the condemned and the executioners, it would seem, find a relief of sorts in mindless mechanical conformity to the modern execution drill.

Witness to an Execution

As the team and administrators prepare to commence the good fight, as they might say, another group, the official witnesses, are also preparing themselves for their role in the execution. Numbering between six and twelve for any given execution, the official witnesses are disinterested citizens in good standing drawn from a cross-section of the state's population. If you will, they are every good or decent person, called upon to represent the community and use their good offices to testify to the propriety of the execution. I served as an official witness at the execution of an inmate.

At eight in the evening about the time the prisoner is shaved in preparation for the execution, the witnesses are assembled. Eleven in all, we included three newspaper and two television reporters, a state trooper, two police officers, a magistrate, a businessman, and myself. We were picked up in the parking lot behind the main office of the corrections department. There was nothing unusual or even memorable about any of this. Gothic touches were notable by their absence. It wasn't a dark and stormy night; no one emerged from the shadows to lead us to the prison gates.

Mundane considerations prevailed. The van sent for us was missing a few rows of seats so there wasn't enough room for all of us. Obliging prison officials volunteered their cars. Our rather ordinary cavalcade reached the prison but only after getting lost. Once within the prison's walls, we were sequestered for some two hours in a bare and almost shabby administrative conference room. A public information officer was assigned to accompany us and answer our questions. We grilled this official about the prisoner and the execution procedure he would undergo shortly, but little information was to be had. The man confessed ignorance on the most basic points. Disgruntled at this and increasingly anxious, we made small talk and drank coffee.

At 10:40 P.M., roughly two-and-a-half hours after we were assembled and only twenty minutes before the execution was scheduled to occur, the witnesses were taken to the basement of the prison's administrative building, frisked, then led down an alleyway that ran along the exterior of the building. We entered a neighboring cell block and were admitted to a vestibule adjoining the death chamber. Each of us signed a log, and was then led off to the witness area. To our left, around a corner some thirty feet away, the prisoner sat in the condemned cell. He couldn't see us, but I'm quite certain he could hear us. It occurred to me that our arrival was a fateful reminder for the prisoner. The next group would be led by the warden, and it would be coming for him.

We entered the witness area, a room within the death chamber, and took our seats. A picture window covering the front wall of the witness room offered a clear view of the electric chair, which was about twelve feet away from us and well illuminated. The chair, a large, high-back solid oak structure with imposing black straps, dominated the death chamber. Behind it, on the back wall, was an open panel full of coils and lights. Peeling paint hung from the ceiling and walls; water stains from persistent leaks were everywhere in evidence.

Two officers, one a hulking figure weighing some 400 pounds, stood alongside the electric chair. Each had his hands crossed at the lap and wore a forbidding, blank expression on his face. The witnesses gazed at them and the chair, most of us scribbling notes furiously. We did this, I suppose, as much to record the experience as to have a distraction from the growing tension. A correctional officer entered the witness room and announced that a trial run of the machinery would be undertaken. Seconds later, lights flashed on the control panel behind the chair indicating that the chair was in working order. A white curtain, opened for the test, separated the chair and the witness area. After the test, the curtain was drawn. More tests were performed behind the curtain. Afterwards, the curtain was reopened, and would be left open until the execution was over. Then it would be closed to allow the officers to remove the body.

A handful of high-level correctional officials were present in the death chamber, standing just outside the witness area. There were two regional administrators, the director of the Department of Corrections, and the prison warden. The prisoner's chaplain and lawyer were also present. Other than the chaplain's black religious garb, subdued grey pinstripes and bland correctional uniforms prevailed. All parties were quite solemn.

At 10:58 the prisoner entered the death chamber. He was, I knew from my research, a man with a checkered, tragic past. He had been grossly abused as a child, and went on to become grossly abusive of others. I was told he could not describe his life, from childhood on, without talking about confrontations in defense of a precarious sense of self—at home, in school, on the streets, in the prison yard. Belittled by life and choking with rage, he was hungry to be noticed. Paradoxically, he had found his moment in the spotlight, but it was a dim and unflattering light cast before a small and unappreciative audience. "He'd pose for cameras in the chair—for the attention," his counselor had told me earlier in the day. But the truth was that the prisoner wasn't smiling, and there were no cameras.

The prisoner walked quickly and silently toward the chair, an escort of officers in tow. His eyes were turned downward, his expression a bit glazed. Like many before him, the prisoner had threatened to stage a last stand. But that was lifetimes ago, on death row. In the death house, he joined the humble bunch and kept to the executioner's schedule. He appeared to have given up on life before he died in the chair.

En route to the chair, the prisoner stumbled slightly, as if the momentum of the event had overtaken him. Were he not held securely by two officers, one at each elbow, he might have fallen. Were the routine to be broken in this or indeed any other way, the officers believe, the prisoner might faint or panic or become violent, and have to be forcibly placed in the chair. Perhaps as a precaution, when the prisoner reached the chair he did not turn on his own but rather was turned, firmly but without malice, by the officers in his escort. These included the two men at his elbows, and four others who followed behind him. Once the prisoner was seated, again with help, the officers strapped him into the chair.

The execution team worked with machine precision. Like a disciplined swarm, they enveloped him. Arms, legs, stomach, chest, and head were secured in a matter of seconds. Electrodes were attached to the cap holding his head and to the strap holding his exposed right leg. A leather mask was placed over his face. The last officer mopped the prisoner's brow, then touched his hand in a gesture of farewell.

During the brief procession to the electric chair, the prisoner was attended by a chaplain. As the execution team worked feverishly to secure the condemned man's body, the chaplain, who appeared to be upset, leaned over him and placed his forehead in contact with the prisoner's, whispering urgently. The priest might have been praying, but I had the impression he was consoling the man, perhaps assuring him that a forgiving God awaited him in the next life. If he heard the chaplain, I doubt the man comprehended his message. He didn't seem comforted. Rather, he looked stricken and appeared to be in shock. Perhaps the priest's urgent ministrations betrayed his doubts that the prisoner could hold himself together. The chaplain then withdrew at the warden's request, allowing the officers to affix the death mask.

The strapped and masked figure sat before us, utterly alone, waiting to be killed. The cap and mask dominated his face. The cap was nothing more than a sponge encased in a leather shell with a metal piece at the top to accept an electrode. It looked decrepit and resembled a cheap, ill-fitting toupee. The mask, made entirely of leather, appeared soiled and worn. It had two parts. The bottom part covered the chin and mouth, the top the eyes and lower forehead. Only the nose was exposed. The effect of a rigidly restrained body, together with the bizarre cap and the protruding nose, was nothing short of grotesque. A faceless man breathed before us in a tragi-comic trance, waiting for a blast of electricity that would extinguish his life. Endless seconds passed. His last act was to swallow, nervously, pathetically, with his Adam's apple bobbing. I was struck by that simple movement then, and can't forget it even now. It told me, as nothing else did, that in the prisoner's restrained body, behind that mask, lurked a fellow human being who, at some level, however primitive, knew or sensed himself to be moments from death.

The condemned man sat perfectly still for what seemed an eternity but was in fact no more than thirty seconds. Finally the electricity hit him. His body stiffened spasmodically, though only briefly. A thin swirl of smoke trailed away from his head and then dissipated quickly. The body remained taut, with the right foot raised slightly at the heel, seemingly frozen there. A brief pause, then another minute of shock. When it was over, the body was flaccid and inert.

Three minutes passed while the officials let the body cool. (Immediately after the execution, I'm told, the body would be too hot to touch and would blister anyone who did.) All eyes were riveted to the chair; I felt trapped in my witness seat, at once transfixed and yet eager for release. I can't recall any clear thoughts from that moment. One of the death watch officers later volunteered that he shared this experience of staring blankly at the execution scene. Had the prisoner's mind been mercifully blank before the end? I hoped so.

An officer walked up to the body, opened the shirt at chest level, then continued on to get the physician from an adjoining room. The physician listened for a heartbeat. Hearing none, he turned to the warden and said, "This man has expired." The warden, speaking to the director, solemnly intoned: "Mr. Director, the court order has been fulfilled." The curtain was then drawn and the witnesses filed out.

The Morning After

As the team prepared the body for the morgue, the witnesses were led to the front door of the prison. On the way, we passed a number of cell blocks. We could hear the normal sounds of prison life, including the occasional catcall and lewd comment hurled at uninvited guests like ourselves. But no trouble came in the wake of the execution. Small protests were going on outside the walls, we were told, but we could not hear them. Soon the media would be gone; the protectors would disperse and head for their homes. The prisoners, already home, had been indifferent to the proceedings, as they always are unless the condemned prisoner had been a figure of some consequence in the convict community. Then there might be tension and maybe even a modest disturbance on a prison tier or two. But few convict luminaries are executed, and the dead man had not been one of them. Our escort officer offered a sad tribute to the prisoner: "The inmates, they didn't care about this guy."

I couldn't help but think they weren't alone in this. The executioners went home and set about their lives. Having taken life, they would savor a bit of life themselves. They showered, ate, made love, slept, then took a day or two off. For some, the prisoner's image would linger for that night. The men who strapped him in remembered what it was like to touch him; they showered as soon as they got home to wash off the feel and smell of death. One official sat up picturing how the prisoner looked at the end. (I had a few drinks myself that night with that same image for company.) There was some talk about delayed reactions to the stress of carrying out executions. Though such concerns seemed remote that evening, I learned later that problems would surface for some of the officers. But no one on the team, then or later, was haunted by the executed man's memory, nor would anyone grieve for him. "When I go home after one of these things," said one man, "I sleep like a rock." His may or may not be the sleep of the just, but one can only marvel at such a thing, and perhaps envy such a man.